What Do We Know about War?

What Do We Know about War?

Second Edition

Edited by
John A. Vasquez

ROWMAN & LITTLEFIELD PUBLISHERS, INC.
Lanham • Boulder • New York • Toronto • Plymouth, UK

Published by Rowman & Littlefield Publishers, Inc.
A wholly owned subsidiary of The Rowman & Littlefield Publishing Group, Inc.
4501 Forbes Boulevard, Suite 200, Lanham, Maryland 20706
www.rowman.com

10 Thornbury Road, Plymouth PL6 7PP, United Kingdom

British Library Cataloguing in Publication Information Available

Library of Congress Cataloging-in-Publication Data

What do we know about war ? / edited by John A. Vasquez. — 2nd ed.
    p. cm.
  Includes bibliographical references and index.
  ISBN 978-1-4422-1263-3 (hbk. : alk. paper) — ISBN 978-1-4422-1264-0 (pbk. :
alk. paper) — ISBN 978-1-4422-1265-7 (electronic)
  1. War. 2. War—Causes. 3. Peace. 4. Peace-building. I. Vasquez, John A., 1945–
U21.2.W477 2012
355.02—dc23

                                                                        2011044791

∞™ The paper used in this publication meets the minimum requirements of American National Standard for Information Sciences—Permanence of Paper for Printed Library Materials, ANSI/NISO Z39.48-1992.

Printed in the United States of America

To My Mother, Helen J. Vasquez

Contents

Preface

It seems that war is always with us. Yet, as Ecclesiastes reminds us, a time of war will eventually give way to a time of peace. The struggle of humanity has been to break this cycle so that the time of peace lasts. The foundation of this struggle has always rested on the shoulders of those who could provide answers to why war occurs and how it can be prevented. Studying war, for many scholars, has been a way to bring about peace, not a way to perfect the *ultima ratio regum* of coercion, as Louis XIV referred to his cannons of war. Even though knowledge does not guarantee a political solution to public problems, without knowledge there can be little reasonable expectation for the amelioration of perennial problems such as war.

This book reports on one approach to the study of peace and war: the use of the scientific method to identify those factors that promote the outbreak of interstate war and those factors that promote peace. Within contemporary society this has become an important and fairly widespread movement among international relations scholars, especially political scientists. This movement is one of the best hopes of humanity for solving the intellectual puzzle of war because it replaces the solitary efforts of past great thinkers, such as Thucydides and Freud, with a large number of researchers committed to using the best method of inquiry humanity has invented. Their approach permits a division of labor and the creation of a body of research findings that will provide a cumulation of knowledge. Having many minds work on the same problem in a sustained manner may have payoffs that have eluded previous efforts.

The second edition of this book, coming a decade after the first, serves as a report of what we know to date in terms of the research conducted by international relations scholars, most of whom are political scientists. All the chapters are new, and a number of new authors have been added.

Trying to summarize the findings on a particular subject is an ambitious goal, and to have any hope of achieving it, scholars would have to have sustained interaction and discussion. Fortunately, much of this discussion had already taken place before the contributors to this book were invited to meet for a three-day conference in October 2010 at the University of Illinois at Urbana-Champaign to see what we had learned as a community of peace researchers. Except for two political scientists and one geographer, all of the scholars had known each other for a number of years and had regularly seen each other at annual meetings, especially that of the Peace Science Society (International), which has provided an important forum for discussion and the exchange of research.

Many but not all of the scholars have either been associated with or used data from the Correlates of War project. Given that it has been a decade since the last edition and the book is still being used in the classroom, the time seemed ripe to reassess the question that J. David Singer started out with: What have we learned about the correlates of war? The October conference was organized around a set of factors that research in the field had identified as important in bringing about war or in bringing about peace. The majority of participants were asked to focus on a specific factor. Does this variable or factor increase or reduce the probability of interstate war? In light of existing research, can a pattern be documented? If there is disagreement about whether a pattern exists, what research designs can be constructed that would resolve the empirical disagreement? If there is a pattern, how do we explain it? Can alternate explanations be found in the literature? Which of these have been tested or supported by empirical evidence?

Several scholars were also invited to serve as discussants and to later write up their reflections on the lessons that could serve to help advance the scientific study of peace and war. At the conference, each of the papers was discussed and sometimes even debated. The chapters were then prepared in light of the conference and subsequent criticisms. The end result is a fairly detailed report of what has been learned about those factors that are most related to the onset of war and the creation of peace.

A number of organizations and individuals helped to make the conference and the book a reality. The conference was made possible by a Hewlett International Conference Grant from International Programs and Studies (IPS) at the University of Illinois. My thanks to Wolfgang Schlör, interim associate provost of IPS, for his support. Funding was also provided by the Department of Political Science, the Cline Center for Democracy, and ACDIS (the Program in Arms Control, Disarmament, and International Security); my thanks to William Bernhard, Pete Nardulli, and Colin Flint, the respective heads of each of these units. Lastly, the Thomas B. Mackie Research Fund provided essential support. This generous gift to the university not only made the conference possible, but also a host of research activities I have conducted since coming to the University of Illinois seven years ago. Two staff members helped with the logistics. Kathy Anderson-Conner of ACDIS was the main conference administrative co-coordinator and took overall responsibility for getting things done. Sheila Roberts of the Cline Center made all the travel arrangements. I am immensely grateful to both of them for making the conference run smoothly.

Special thanks go to Andy Owsiak, who was the academic co-coordinator for the conference. As the graduate student assistant for the conference, he did everything from constructing the web page to corresponding with the contributors. My thanks also to Gillian Gryz, who handled the logistics during the actual weekend of the conference and helped prepare the conference papers for publication. My gratitude also to Emily Barrett, who came in like the cavalry at the last minute to tie up all the loose strings so the manuscript, copyedited manuscript, and page proofs could get submitted in an orderly fashion. Each of these people eased my burden at busy times and did a professional job. Delinda Swanson once again expertly prepared the references, as she has done for a number of my books. Publishing the book with Rowman & Littlefield and working with Susan McEachern has been a distinct pleasure, from the time we discussed the idea of a second edition to the last detail. She, and the other members of the staff—Grace Baumgartner and Janice Braunstein—smoothed the way and made this process go much faster than it would have at any other press. My thanks also to the copy editor—Matt Evans—for an expertly done job. Let me also repeat the acknowledgment to Matthew Melko that I made in the first edition: a number of years ago he organized a panel entitled "What Do We Know about War?" The title and the search for answers have stuck with me.

The doctoral students at the University of Illinois (as well as my colleagues in international relations) provided an exceptional intellectual environment both during the conference and while I was working on the book. My thanks to them for their enthusiasm for the project and the help they provided. These and the many other students of peace science give us assurance that the future is bright. At the same time, the last decade has seen the passing of several peace researchers who have given much—J. David Singer, the founder and first director of the Correlates of War project; Stuart Bremer, his successor; and Paul Senese, my coauthor on *The Steps to War*. Their contributions still inform us.

Let me also express my appreciation to Marie Henehan, who has always provided emotional support (even during times, especially when I was preparing the first edition, that were very pressing for her) and has always been someone with whom I could share and test out ideas, including many of those in this book.

Lastly, I dedicate this book to my mother, Helen J. Vasquez. Born in the year the United States entered World War I, married shortly after Pearl Harbor, and keeping the peace in the family during the sixties, she, like millions of other Americans, was touched by war, even though she avoided its worst scourges. She was always supportive of me and instilled in me a sense of work that has been immensely useful in my academic life. More importantly, she provided a sense of love without which no life would be worth living. We were saddened to lose her in 2010, but we were glad that at ninety-two she still had all her wits about her.

John A. Vasquez, Block Island, RI

Introduction

John A. Vasquez

For most of history, intellectuals and scholars have pondered what causes war, owing in no small part to the horrors of war. Despite this long history of inquiry, it has been only relatively recently that a group of scholars has come together to study the factors related to the onset of war through the application of the scientific method and the use of data analysis to delineate patterns. In 1964, J. David Singer founded the Correlates of War project with the intention of collecting reproducible data that would serve as the foundation for creating a body of scientific knowledge on war.[1]

Since the mid-1960s, a very large number of scientific studies on war have been published by numerous scholars using Correlates of War data. Indeed, one of the things that separates the Correlates of War project from the early efforts of Lewis Richardson, Pitirim Sorokin, and Quincy Wright has been its ability to bring together a community of scholars to focus on researching the onset of war even when they have not been part of the project. The project itself has helped sustain a wider peace research community dedicated to the use of scientific analysis to study war and the conditions of peace. It is not an exaggeration to say that in the last forty-five years, more social scientists have been working on this set of related research questions than at any other time in history. What have they learned?

This book has been written to answer this question. Rather than producing a secondary study of that research, this book brings together those scholars who are actively engaged in research to answer the question themselves. The emphasis here is on international relations scholars. Many of the contributors are associated with the Correlates of War project, but a number of other scholars reflecting different theoretical approaches, projects, and research programs have been included. This book, however, is not just another compendium that reports the results of various projects; rather, it attempts to provide a systematic discussion of what we think we know about the onset of war after all of this research and what we need to do to confirm this knowledge and extend it.

Of course, the knowledge we have about war is not as definitive as knowledge produced in physics. Nonetheless, that does not mean that we know nothing or that everything is a matter of perspective. The word *knowledge* is used in this book to indicate that certain hypotheses have passed at least a modicum of rigorous tests using reproducible data—in other words, that the knowledge claims are based on some sort of rigorous examination of evidence and are not just based on speculation or intellectual argument. This does not mean that further inspection may not lead to different conclusions. Science is a process, not necessarily an end product. This is especially the case when one is working at the frontiers of knowledge in a young science, as are the contributors to this book. In a sense, this is a book about what we know *now*, what we have learned about war within international relations inquiry in the last forty-five years or so.

The book is divided into three parts. Part I examines what has been learned about factors that promote interstate war. A chapter is devoted to each of the factors that have been thought to be important in bringing about war. Each author reviews and/or presents research to determine the extent to which the factor in question is responsible for increasing the probability of war. Each author discusses the theoretical implications of the findings and lays out fruitful areas for further inquiry. Almost all of the research discussed in this section shares a common research design and perspective—each piece of research tries to identify what factors distinguish the comparatively few militarized disputes that go to war from the overwhelming number that do not.

In chapter 1, Paul R. Hensel looks at the role of territory as well as contiguity in the onset of both severe conflict (militarized interstate disputes, MIDs) and war. Using the issue data of the Issue Correlates of War (ICOW) project, he provides some original analyses profiling how territorial issues give rise to conflict and how they are managed to avoid war. He reviews findings on the war proneness of territorial issues and MIDs and also compares the role of territory with contiguity. While the latter is important, he provides evidence to show that it is not as potent a factor as territory for the onset of conflict and war when territorial issues are highly salient. For Hensel, one of the key factors that distinguishes disputes that go to war from those that do not is the issue at stake.

Chapters 2 and 3 focus on the role of alliances in bringing about war. In chapter 2, Choong-Nam Kang examines the existing Correlates of War research on alliances and provides an original empirical analysis to support the contention that alliances are generally associated with the occurrence of war.

Yet this relationship is not straightforward, as it seems to operate differently depending on the temporal domain being examined and the type of actors. Further, Kang evaluates the effects of alliances on dispute initiation and whether defensive alliances can deter conflict. Whereas Kang focuses on and utilizes the formal alliance data of the Correlates of War project, Brett Benson in chapter 3 focuses on the contributions of the ATOP (Alliance Treaty Obligations and Provisions) data of Leeds et al. (2000). He provides original data analyses that focus on whether certain types of alliances serve to deter conflict (i.e., militarized interstate disputes). He presents a new classification of alliances based on their compellent or deterrent characteristics. He then compares his classification against ATOP's and finds many fewer cases of successful deterrence. Part of the discrepancy with Leeds (2003) may result from her use of the dyad year, which Benson argues accentuates the impact of a few alliances.

Chapters 4 and 5 look at interstate rivalry. In chapter 4, Brandon Valeriano examines the origins of rivalries and the interactions that make states become rivals. Based on original data analyses, he presents evidence that alliances and arms races are key factors that lead to rivalry onset, in addition to having territorial disputes. His findings underscore how power politics behaviors (alliances, military buildups, and rivalry) reinforce one another, while at the same time he disentangles their effects. He also briefly looks at what factors come first—alliances or arms races—and finds that typically alliances come early in a relationship and arms races later.

In chapter 5, Diehl and Goertz review the research and findings on interstate rivalry and update their chapter from the first edition by using the new Klein et al. (2006) data. As before, they show that states that are rivals have a much higher probability of going to war than other types of states, which means that pairs of states that have recurring disputes are more likely to have a war. This conclusion confirms the general notion that violence encourages violence and that war is often the outcome of an interactive process. Diehl and Goertz also review the research and findings on interstate rivalry related to both its maintenance and its termination. They conclude by noting a number of potential avenues for future research, including the role of domestic politics and how rivalry interacts with other factors that influence conflict behavior.

In chapter 6, Susan G. Sample examines the role of arms races in bringing about war, with an emphasis on new challenges to the finding that military buildups and arms races are associated with the escalation of militarized disputes to war. In particular, she examines through original research the claim that mutual military buildups are a function of rivalry, which is the real factor bringing about war, that is, that the influence of arms races is in effect spurious. Using various measures, she is able to resolve a number of contentious questions in this debate and provide evidence that shows that mutual military buildups are a factor in bringing about war in both rivals and nonrivals so that they are in fact a step to war and not just a function of rivalry. Sample's chapter points to the kind of research that will become increasingly frequent in the future, namely, looking at how the various factors that promote war impact each other.

In chapter 7, Daniel Geller looks at the role of capability in bringing about and preventing war, with a focus on nuclear capability. In light of existing research, he evaluates the predictions of three schools of thought that relate nuclear weapons to conflict behavior: nuclear revolution; risk manipulation, escalation, and limited war; and nuclear irrelevance. After reviewing the evidence, the chapter concludes that while nuclear powers may often escalate their disputes short of war (for purposes of risk manipulation), war between nuclear powers is highly unlikely. Given this, conventional forces will retain importance regardless of how nuclear weapons proliferate.

Part II of the book examines the factors that promote peace, with an emphasis on the democratic peace and its critics. In chapter 8, Sara McLaughlin Mitchell reviews the findings on the democratic peace. She then goes on and examines the logic and evidence consistent with the normative explanation of the democratic peace. She points out the importance of norms and intergovernmental organizations (IGOs) in bringing about peace and how a Kantian system of democratic states can change the behavior of even nondemocratic states by changing their norms. This means that the system as a whole will become more peaceful as the number of democratic states increases. In chapter 9, Michael Mousseau presents an alternative to the democratic peace. He argues that the democratic peace is really a (social) market-capitalist peace. He presents the logic of this explanation and tests it with new data. He also distinguishes it from other versions of the capitalist peace which do not emphasize the importance of a culture of social contracts. In chapter 10, Douglas M. Gibler argues that the theory of the territorial peace can explain both the democratic peace as well as zones of peace among nondemocratic states. In addition and of equal importance, the territorial peace can explain the external factors that promoted the rise of democracy in the first place. Gibler argues that neighbors are at peace when they have stable borders; the reason joint democracies do not fight each other is that they have few, if any, serious territorial disputes. He then goes further and says the presence of external territorial MIDs increases centralization of the state and makes it difficult for it to become democratic. Conversely, once neighbors settle their borders, this creates a benign environment for the emergence of democracy.

Part III assesses what lessons and conclusions can be drawn from the attempt to identify correlates of war and peaceful eras. In chapter 11, Rasler and

Thompson set much of the previous work on both war and peace in a larger context. They argue that previous work has failed to fully incorporate the extent to which war itself impacts on a host of international processes and dynamics that the field has been trying to explain. They look at the impact war has had on state development and other historical processes (including economic processes). They then review the connection between state making and war in several regions, producing evidence consistent with some of the claims made by Gibler. Their study is important not only for the alternative framework that is presented but for the implications it poses for the democratic peace.

The next four chapters are shorter pieces that were invited to reflect on the various aspects of the scientific study of peace and war. In chapter 12, Peter Wallensteen reflects on the work of the Correlates of War in terms of how its future work may be affected by changes in the international system, the key actors who make war, and the different types of conflict that exist. He presents some data to buttress his concerns and concludes with a call for a program on the correlates of peace. In chapter 13, Zeev Maoz reviews some of the achievements of the scientific study of peace and war, how they were attained, and some of the positive lessons. However, for progress to continue, it is also important to see what was not done and the costs of that. Maoz looks at the limitations of normal science, some of the restrictions posed by the methods that have predominated, and the challenges that need to be addressed. He ends with some specific suggestions for dealing with complexity. In chapter 14, Jack S. Levy deals with one of the new concepts aimed specifically at dealing with complexity—the paths to war. He provides a trenchant critique of the concept and explores ways to make it more useful so that it can live up to its promise. In chapter 15, Colin Flint, a geographer, brings an outside perspective. He provides a number of insights that only someone not so close to the enterprise can. He also shows how some of this research can be connected to perspectives in geography and what lessons in that discipline might be useful to apply and what mistakes might be avoided, like spatial fetishism. In particular he focuses on network analysis, one of the areas that Maoz sees as promising. He also scrutinizes the effect of normal science research. He concludes by outlining some of the ways in which normal science limits the normative and policy goals that originally motivated much of peace science and how that might be corrected.

In chapter 16, Vasquez brings together the various analyses and reviews from the previous chapters to address the question What do we know about war? Each of the chapters is summarized, and the main factors associated with war or with peace are delineated, with the proper caveats. Each section concludes with a listing of the major topics and questions that need to be addressed to advance further the scientific study of peace and war.

The analyses presented in this book show that the early strategy J. David Singer took in the Correlates of War project of trying to identify and document patterns through empirical analysis has borne fruit. Such an investigation has been inductive, but not blindly inductive in the sense of being theory free (see his early theoretical statements, reprinted in Singer [1979]). Singer never said that research should be conducted without any guidance from theoretical analyses. What he has maintained in reaction to the data-free traditionalist-dominated fifties is that theory in the absence of systematic evidence is really speculation. Research and theory construction must go hand in hand. As findings become clearer, we begin to learn what is and is not related to the onset of war. Not everything is a correlate of war, and not all correlates are of equal theoretical significance.

The research reviewed in this volume has presented a road map of what we know to date. While we still have a long way to go, it is clear that we know a great deal more today than we did forty-five years ago. All of the factors analyzed in this book appear to play some role in the onset of war. States that dispute territorial issues have a higher probability of going to war than other states. Certain kinds of alliances increase the probability of war involvement. As disputes recur between the same parties, the probability that one will escalate to war increases substantially. Building up one's military in the context of ongoing militarized disputes makes it more likely that this dispute or one within a few years will escalate to war. We have also learned that norms can reduce the likelihood of militarized disputes and their escalation to war and that democratic states seem to be able to better manage their disputes with other democratic states so as to avoid war, at least in the post–World War II period. In addition, nuclear weapons have made it less likely that states with second-strike capability will fight a nuclear war and that states with an ongoing arms race will go to war. At the same time, symmetrical nuclear states are apt to become involved in more militarized disputes, and whether nuclear deterrence will always work in the future in every instance is open to question.

While other factors may promote or inhibit the onset of war, these appear to be among the major ones for which some systematic evidence exists. These research findings will enrich our attempts at explanation, which then will give rise to new research that will further refine our knowledge about war and about peace. Scientific knowledge is not so much an end as it is a process that produces usable bits of information along the way. We hope that this volume has produced some usable bits of information as we search for the "causes" of war.

NOTE

1. This is not to say that there were not several other attempts to study war, either through investigating crises that lead to war (e.g., the 1914 studies of Robert North [Holsti, North, and Brody 1968; Choucri and North 1975] and the later International Crisis Behavior project [Brecher and Wilkenfeld 1989, 1997]) or through analyzing the dynamics of international conflict (e.g., Rummel 1979; Guetzkow 1968).

Part I

FACTORS THAT BRING ABOUT WAR

Chapter One

Territory

Geography, Contentious Issues, and World Politics

Paul R. Hensel

Research on the sources of militarized conflict has typically emphasized characteristics of states or the interstate system, with little emphasis on the geographic context of relations between states. Vasquez (1998), for example, finds that realist variables such as capabilities and alliances accounted for most variables and hypotheses used in early quantitative research. The contents of this volume and such compilations as Midlarsky's (1989–2009) *Handbook of War Studies* volumes indicate a substantial broadening of the research agenda in recent decades, although a number of chapters continue to address capabilities or alliances, and many of the additional chapters address such nongeographic topics as democracy and norms. The present chapter considers the impact of geographic factors on militarized conflict.

This chapter begins with research treating geography as what Diehl (1991) terms a "facilitating condition for conflict," affecting the ease with which states are able to engage in conflict. It then focuses in more detail on the specific issues over which states contend, starting with Diehl's notion of territory or other geographic issues as a "source of conflict" and then moving on to consider the management of issues through peaceful means. For each body of research, I summarize the central theoretical arguments that have been suggested before reviewing the empirical evidence, supplemented by a series of original analyses. The chapter concludes by assessing the connection between geographic factors and armed conflict, and discussing possible directions for future research in this area.

GEOGRAPHY AS A FACILITATING
CONDITION FOR CONFLICT

Early research on geography and armed conflict generally followed Diehl's (1991) notion of geography as a facilitating condition for conflict. This approach suggests that even if territory and borders "do not *cause* wars, they at least create *structure of risks and opportunities* in which conflictual behavior is apparently more likely to occur" (Starr and Most 1978: 444). As Starr (2005: 389–91) notes, this approach is closely related to geographers' conceptions of "space," "location," and "distance," emphasizing how close actors are to each other. This suggests that geography matters to the extent that it influences force projection capabilities, threat perception, and interaction opportunities—each of which can affect the likelihood of armed conflict.

Theoretical Arguments

The most basic argument on proximity and conflict is that war can only occur between states that can reach each other militarily. Boulding's (1962) "loss of strength gradient" suggests that the military capabilities of a state are greatest within its borders and decline as the state tries to project these capabilities farther away. Bueno de Mesquita (1981: 83) similarly argues that "the greater the distance between a nation's seat of power and the place where its power must be brought to bear in a war, the smaller the proportion of its total capabilities that it can expect to use." Along these lines, Lemke (2002) attempts to identify pairs of states that can reach each other militarily, based on distance, the type of terrain between the states, and their technology levels.

The implication is that adversaries that cannot reach each other with sufficient military capability are unlikely to engage in militarized conflict, regardless of any other conditions that might be expected to influence conflict. As a result, many scholars limit their analyses of conflict patterns to "politically relevant dyads," which generally include contiguous states and dyads that include at least one major power (e.g., Lemke and Reed 2001; Benson 2005). Major powers are assumed to be able to project their military capabilities anywhere around the world, so many applications of the proximity approach explicitly limit the conflict-reducing effects of distance to the so-called minor powers.

A second argument is the interactions perspective (Vasquez 1993). From this perspective, states that are located near each other—particularly those that share a border—will tend to interact more than states located farther apart. For example, Bolivia typically interacts much more frequently with Brazil than it does with Botswana or Bangladesh. The interactions perspective suggests that this greater interaction produces a greater likelihood of conflict between states, because there are more interactions that have the potential to produce conflict.

A third argument based on proximity suggests that events closer to home are seen as more threatening than more distant events and are therefore more salient to policy makers. Starr and Most (1978), for example, argue that bordering states face greater uncertainty in their relations than more distant states, which can exacerbate the well-known security dilemma and lead to the outbreak of conflict. Similarly, Diehl (1985, 1991) suggests that proximity affects states' willingness for conflict, as well as their opportunity; events such as political instability or revolutions are thus more worrisome to policy makers when they occur in a neighboring state than when they occur farther away.

This is not to suggest that distant states never pose security threats, but such arguments imply that leaders will tend to pay closer attention to that which is near than that which is distant. The threat dimension of proximity is expected to compound the effects of proximity that derive from military reachability. Nearby states should thus be more likely than distant states to engage in conflict because of their overlapping interests and perceived security threats, as well as because of their ease in projecting sufficient military capabilities against each other.

Empirical Evidence

It should be noted that distinguishing empirically between the different theoretical effects of proximity is very difficult, and most analysts do not attempt to make this distinction. Nonetheless, the contention that proximity or contiguity is related to militarized conflict is intuitively appealing and appears to fit with a quick reading of recent history; world newspapers are full of conflicts between neighboring states. Systematic research on militarized conflict supports this preliminary impression.

One important pattern relating proximity to conflict concerns the frequency of armed conflict between nearby states. Table 1.1 examines the contiguity of participants in militarized conflict since 1816, focusing on the initial participants ("originators") in each conflict in order to avoid distorting the results by including large numbers of states that later joined ongoing conflicts like the world wars. Conflict is measured using version 3.10 of the Correlates of War (COW) project's Militarized Interstate Dispute (MID) data set, which includes interactions between nation-states involving the explicit threat, display, or use of militarized force (Ghosn, Palmer, and Bremer 2004); this table also reports results for disputes that escalate to the point of battle-related fatalities or to full-scale war, defined as sustained

Table 1.1.   Contiguity and Militarized Conflict (all dyads, 1816–2001)

Type of Contiguity	Conflicts Beginning between Contiguous Adversaries			
	1816–1945	*1946–1989*	*1990–2001*	*Total*
(A) COW Militarized Interstate Disputes				
Land	357 (44.2%)	661 (56.4%)	246 (70.3%)	1,264 (54.2%)
Sea	92 (11.4)	181 (15.4)	54 (15.4)	327 (14.0)
None	359 (44.4)	331 (28.2)	50 (14.3)	740 (31.8)
(B) Fatal MIDs				
Land	63 (58.3%)	190 (81.9%)	49 (86.0%)	302 (76.1%)
Sea	13 (12.0)	14 (6.0)	3 (5.3)	30 (7.6)
None	32 (29.6)	28 (12.1)	5 (8.8)	65 (16.4)
(C) War-Level MIDs				
Land	33 (60.0%)	20 (90.9%)	4 (80.0%)	57 (69.5%)
Sea	9 (16.4)	0 (0.0)	0 (0.0)	9 (11.0)
None	13 (23.6)	2 (9.1)	1 (20.0)	16 (19.5)

combat between regular armed forces that results in at least one thousand battle deaths. Contiguity is measured with version 3.10 of the COW Direct Contiguity data set (Stinnett et al., 2002), which is used to identify states that share a land or river border as well as those that are separated by no more than four hundred miles of open sea.

As table 1.1 indicates, over half of all militarized disputes between 1816 and 2001 began between adversaries that shared a land or river border, and another 14 percent began between adversaries that are contiguous by sea. These numbers are even stronger for more severe forms of conflict, with at least 80 percent of fatal disputes and wars beginning between states that share a land or sea border. Table 1.2 focuses on minor powers, which have fewer foreign policy interests farther from home that might lead them to armed conflict, as well as less ability to project their military power against more distant adversaries. The impact of contiguity is even greater for all three levels of conflict in the minor power context. Only around 18 percent of all militarized disputes, 5 percent of fatal disputes, and 5 percent of full-scale wars between minor powers begin between adversaries that do not share a land or sea border.

Importantly, these figures have not decreased over time, even as advances in communications and transportation have brought distant lands closer together. Both militarized disputes generally and fatal disputes have been more likely to involve contiguous adversaries in later historical eras, and interstate wars (despite a small number of cases in the post–Cold War era) remain around their average across the period of study. These results appear

Table 1.2. Contiguity and Militarized Conflict in Minor Power Dyads

Type of Contiguity	*Conflicts between Two Minor Powers Beginning between Contiguous Adversaries*			
	1816–1945	*1946–1989*	*1990–2001*	*Total*
(A) COW Militarized Interstate Disputes				
Land	199 (71.6%)	560 (71.3%)	207 (85.5%)	966 (74.0%)
Sea	16 (5.8)	73 (9.3)	18 (7.4)	107 (8.2)
None	63 (22.7)	152 (19.4)	17 (7.0)	232 (17.8)
(B) Fatal MIDs				
Land	41 (83.7%)	167 (92.3%)	46 (95.8%)	254 (91.4%)
Sea	4 (8.2)	4 (2.2)	1 (2.1)	9 (3.2)
None	4 (8.2)	10 (5.5)	1 (2.1)	15 (5.4)
(C) War-Level MIDs				
Land	17 (77.3%)	16 (100%)	4 (100%)	37 (88.1%)
Sea	3 (13.6)	0 (0.0)	0 (0.0)	3 (7.1)
None	2 (9.1)	0 (0.0)	0 (0.0)	2 (4.8)

to be driven by the independence of so many new states since World War II, many of which have unsettled questions with their new neighbors and lack the force projection capability to confront more distant adversaries. In any case, proximity is not becoming less relevant for conflict patterns over time. Contiguous states account for a clear majority of interstate conflict, and this pattern has remained strong over time.

This is consistent with the work of Bremer (1992), who reports that contiguity produces the strongest effect of seven explanations for war being compared, increasing the probability of war by over thirty-five times. Bremer concludes by recommending that contiguity should be included in almost all empirical studies of war, at least as a control variable. Focusing on conflict escalation rather than outbreak, Diehl (1985) finds that the probability of dispute escalation to war is much greater for dyads in which at least one of the states is contiguous to the site of the dispute. Similarly, Senese (1996, 2005) and Senese and Vasquez (2008) find that contiguous adversaries are more likely to become involved in armed conflict as well as to escalate their disputes to more serious levels.

Studies of war diffusion also report strong evidence that contiguity contributes to the spread of armed conflict. States bordering a belligerent in an ongoing war are more likely to join the war than are other states (e.g., Starr and Most 1978; Siverson and Starr 1991), and recent work investigates how civil wars can spread to involve neighboring states (e.g., Gleditsch, Salehyan, and Schultz 2008; Salehyan 2009). Beyond armed conflict, geographic proximity also affects the diffusion of such phenomena as democratization (e.g., Starr 1991; Gleditsch 2002a). Furthermore, these findings generally hold whether proximity is measured by the simple presence or absence of a land border or by incorporating such factors as terrain (e.g., Lemke 2002) or distance (e.g., Gleditsch and Ward 2001).

Evaluation

In short, proximity increases the risk of armed conflict. Contiguous states are more prone to dispute and war than more distant states, particularly for minor powers, and they are more likely to escalate their confrontations. Yet the strength of the empirical relationship is not matched by an equally strong understanding of why this relationship holds. For example, little effort has been made to distinguish between reachability, interactions, and threat perception as explanations for the impact of proximity. This may not be a major shortcoming if proximity is only considered a control variable, but it does limit the value of proximity as a primary theoretical influence on conflict behavior.

Another potential shortcoming is the relatively static nature of proximity in the relationship between states over time. Proximity between states is basically a constant; countries rarely gain or lose borders over time.[1] As a result, the proximity explanation faces difficulties in accounting for the outbreak of rare events such as conflict and war, since a constant independent variable cannot account for fluctuations in a dependent variable. Proximity may be a necessary condition for war, at least in the trivial sense that states must be able to reach each other before they can fight, but it does not seem to be a satisfactory cause of war by itself.

The proximity perspective also encounters difficulties in explaining why increased interactions should necessarily lead to greater conflict. A substantial literature by scholars such as Karl Deutsch suggests that greater levels of communication and transactions can contribute to cooperation and peace instead of war, and research based on gravity models (e.g., Deardorff 1998; Robst, Polachek, and Chang 2007) finds a strong connection between proximity and trade, investment, and other more cooperative outcomes. Starr and Thomas (2005) may have highlighted at least part of the answer by using geographic information systems (GIS) technology to measure the attributes of each border. At least for the 1981–1992 period covered by their study, borders with high ease of interaction and high salience are associated with a reduced risk of conflict, suggesting that much could be gained by reconceptualizing borders beyond simply dichotomizing between states that are contiguous and those that are not.

TERRITORIAL ISSUES AND CONFLICT

While the notion of geography as a facilitating condition for conflict accounted for most early research, more recent work has tended to focus on what Diehl (1991) describes as geography as a source of conflict. This approach emphasizes geography-related matters as the specific objects of contention between states. Most scholarly attention along these lines has focused on contention over territorial sovereignty (e.g., Vasquez 1993).

Hensel (2001a; Hensel, Mitchell, Sowers, and Thyne 2008) discusses the central tenets of a contentious issue-based approach to studying world politics, which begins with a disagreement between two or more states over some type of issue(s). States that disagree over an issue have many options that might be used to pursue their issue-related goals, ranging from the threat or use of force to bilateral negotiations with the adversary or turning to third-party mediation or arbitration to help settle the issue. Under such an approach, the nature of the issues at stake between two states should influence both their bargaining strategies and the consequences of the bargaining process. In particular, issues that are seen by decision makers as more "salient," or important, are expected to be more likely to lead to militarized conflict and more difficult to resolve to both sides' satisfaction. To many scholars of international relations, territorial issues are considered the most salient of all issues, accounting for the widespread focus on territory in research on issues.

Theoretical Arguments

Although many types of issues may be salient enough to lead to war, the territorial perspective suggests that territorial issues are especially salient and especially likely to lead to conflict and war (Vasquez 1993; Hensel 1996). Scholars have long argued that territory is "conspicuous among the causes of war" (Hill 1945: 3) and "perhaps the most important single cause of war between states in the last two or three centuries" (Luard 1970: 7). Territory is described as highly salient for three reasons: its tangible or physical attributes, its intangible or psychological value, and its effects on a state's reputation.

Perhaps the most obvious benefit of territory is the tangible elements that it contains (Goertz and Diehl 1992b; Hensel 1996). Many territories have been valued because they contain strategic minerals, oil, freshwater, or fertile agricultural land. Certain territories are considered valuable because they provide access to the sea or to major trade routes, particularly when they include deepwater ports, warm-water ports, or control over strategic waterways. Territory may be valued when it includes major population centers with their own industry and infrastructure. Another tangible benefit of territory is its contribution to a state's perceived power and security. Strategic territories such as the Golan Heights or the Sudetenland may allow for advance warning of an impending attack and may contribute to national defense, particularly to the extent that the territory contains defensible geographic features. Fearon (1995: 408) argues that territory with such strategic attributes can be an important source of war even for adversaries who would otherwise prefer a negotiated settlement, because the transfer of strategic territory can alter the two sides' relative bargaining positions. That is, control over the transferred territory may increase the gaining side's ability to win a future confrontation, which may make both sides reluctant to allow the peaceful transfer of such territory to an adversary.

Beyond its physical contents, territory can also be important to states for less tangible reasons (Hensel 1996; Newman 1999; Hassner 2003; Goddard 2006). Territory is argued to lie at the heart of national identity and cohesion, with the very existence and autonomy of a state being rooted in its territory (e.g., Murphy 1990: 531). Many territories are seen as important for their perceived historical connections with a state or its citizens, particularly to the extent that the territory in question was the scene of significant events for a culture or religion. A prominent example is the Serbian attachment to Kosovo, considered the historical center of Serbian culture and identity, long after Serbs ceased to be the ethnic majority within Kosovo. Similarly, Bowman (1946: 177) argued that there is a "profound psychological difference" between the transfer of territory and other types of interstate interactions, because of the strong personal feelings and group sentiments evoked by territory.

This intangible or psychological importance of territory may result in the creation of what Fearon (1995) terms "effectively indivisible issues." To Fearon, most disputed issues are divisible, in the sense that they can be divided between two antagonists—perhaps through side payments or linkages with other issues—in such a way as to make peaceful compromise preferable to war for both sides. Some issues, though, may become effectively indivisible because of mechanisms such as domestic politics. Fearon (1995: 390) mentions the example of territory: "Nineteenth- and twentieth-century leaders cannot divide up and trade territory in international negotiations as easily as could rulers in the seventeenth and eighteenth centuries, due in part to domestic political consequences of the rise of nationalism." Toft (2003) makes a similar point regarding ethnic conflict, arguing that the members of a nation can develop an attachment to territory that becomes indivisible from their conception of self and nation, essentially preventing compromise over what is considered a vital part of the national identity. In short, territory can have "a psychological importance for nations that is quite out of proportion to its intrinsic value, strategic or economic," and territorial issues are seen as arousing sentiments of pride and honor more rapidly and more intensely than any other type of issue (Luard 1970: 7).

Beyond its tangible and intangible value, territory can be important for reasons of reputation (Hensel 1996). That is, if a leader gives in to an adversary over territory, other adversaries might be encouraged to press their own demands on other issues. Schelling (1966: 118) makes a similar point about the importance of reputation in crisis behavior: "What is in dispute is usually not the issue of the moment, but everyone's expectations about how a participant will behave in the future. To yield may be to signal that one can be expected to yield." To Schelling (1966: 124), a country's reputation is one of the few things worth fighting for; even parts of the world that are not intrinsically worth the risk of war by themselves can be important because of the precedents that may be set for events in other parts of the world and at later times. Because of the high perceived salience of territory, states' actions over territorial issues may be more likely to produce reputational effects than actions over other types of issues. Walter (2003, 2006) notes a similar pattern for secessionist movements, with states that face multiple secessionist threats acting more coercively to avoid showing weakness against one adversary that would encourage other movements.

If territorial issues are more salient than other issues because of their tangible, intangible, or reputational importance, scholars have suggested, interaction over territory should be different from interaction over other issues. The literature on territorial disputes (e.g., Vasquez 1993; Hensel 1996; Vasquez and Henehan 2001) suggests that territorial issues should be more prone to militarized conflict behavior than most other issue types, and confrontations over territory should be more escalatory than confrontations over other issues.

Similarly, territorial issues are argued to be more difficult to resolve than most other types of issues. Bowman (1946: 178), for example, noted that any territorial solution—no matter how fair it may seem—carries with it the risk of future attempts to regain lost territory. Arguments may always be raised in the future over historical claims to the lost territory, especially in border zones of mixed ethnic or linguistic composition, and subsequent incidents may always be used to refocus attention on such claims. Bowman (1946: 180–81) further suggested that two or more states can often have irreconcilable claims to the same piece of territory, and that in some territorial disputes there may be no logical solution that both sides can find acceptable. Vasquez (1993) thus suggests that territorial issues can be very difficult to settle, and if two adversaries are unable to settle their territorial questions early in their relationship, the resulting dispute is likely to last for many years.

Empirical Evidence

Table 1.3 examines the frequency of territorial issues in modern armed conflicts, drawing from several prominent data sets. The first row of this table traces the prevalence of territorial issues in wars between 1648 and 1989, as compiled by Holsti (1991). Over three-fourths of all wars involved contention over territory, often along with other issues.[2] Turning to the MID data examined earlier, more than one-fourth of all militarized disputes between 1816 and 2001 have involved explicit contention over territorial issues, with the remainder involving such nonterritorial issues as the composition of governments or disagreements over specific policies. Territorial issues are even more prominent in more severe forms of conflict, with approximately half of all fatal disputes and full-scale wars involving territory.

Focusing on changing trends over time, table 1.3 reveals that the proportion of militarized disputes involving contention over territory has not changed meaningfully over time, declining from 30.2 percent of all disputes between 1816 and 1945 to 27.7 percent since 1945, then increasing to 31.4 percent since the end of the Cold War. Similarly, there do not appear to be any meaningful decreases in the prevalence of territorial issues in fatal disputes or wars. Territorial issues have thus remained prominent as a source of interstate conflict and war.

Turning to the impact of territorial issues on conflict behavior, scholars have found substantial differences in conflict behavior when territory is at stake. Militarized disputes involving territorial issues are much more likely

Table 1.3. Territorial Issues and Militarized Conflict

| Type of Conflict | Proportion of Conflicts Involving Territorial Issues | | | | |
	Pre-1816	1816–1945	1946–1989	1990–2001	Total
Holsti Interstate Wars (1648–1989)	48 / 57 (84.2%)	29 / 38 (76.3%)	22 / 30 (73.3%)	N/A	99 / 125 (79.2%)
COW Militarized Interstate Disputes (1816–2001)	N/A	244 / 808 (30.2%)	325 / 1,173 (27.7%)	110 / 350 (31.4%)	679 / 2,331 (29.1%)
Fatal MIDs (1816–2001)	N/A	53 / 108 (49.1%)	115 / 232 (49.6%)	26 / 57 (45.6%)	194 / 397 (48.9%)
War-Level MIDs (1816–2001)	N/A	29 / 55 (52.7%)	12 / 22 (54.6%)	3 / 5 (60.0%)	44 / 82 (53.7%)

than nonterritorial disputes to escalate to higher severity levels (e.g., Hensel 1996; Vasquez and Henehan 2001; Senese and Vasquez 2008). Confrontations over territory are also more likely to lead to recurrent conflict or rivalry than confrontations over other issues, and many territorial changes are followed by future conflict between the involved states (Diehl and Goertz 1988; Hensel 1996, 1999; Tir and Diehl 2002; Tir 2006). These results indicate that leaders appear to see territory as worth the risk of escalation in order to protect or advance their interests.

Focusing on militarized conflict within territorial claims, Huth (1996; Huth and Allee 2002) finds that the level of conflict over an ongoing territorial claim is increased by a number of claim characteristics associated with issue salience. In particular, militarized conflict appears to be more likely in the presence of ties to a bordering minority, the presence of shared ethnic or linguistic groups along the border, a stalemate in negotiations, or an attempt by the target state to change the status quo (among other factors). Similarly, Hensel (2001a) finds that claim salience increases the likelihood of militarized conflict, along with a longer history of militarized conflict over the territorial claim and an accumulation of unsuccessful attempts to settle it peacefully.

Another way to look at the impact of territorial claims is to see how relations between the claimants differ while their claim is ongoing, as compared to the period before or after the claim. For example, Simmons (2005) finds that an ongoing territorial claim greatly reduces bilateral trade between the claimants. Preliminary research by Hensel (2006) suggests that settling a dyad's last territorial claim greatly improves relations between the claimants, even reducing the risk of nonterritorial conflict between the former adversaries. Owsiak (2012) finds that states with a signed border agreement experience less armed conflict, echoing Gibler's (1996) findings on conflict between states that have signed an alliance that includes a territorial settlement component. Gibler (2007) and Gibler and Tir (2010) even see the settlement of territorial issues as contributing to democratization, producing a "territorial peace" that allows both democracy and peace to take root; this is consistent with an interesting finding by Hutchison and Gibler (2007) that facing an external territorial threat greatly reduces individual willingness to extend democratic freedoms within society.

The next tables offer further insight into the impact of territorial issues, while also considering the role of contiguity. It is common to think of territorial disputes as overlapping closely with borders, as many of the best-known territorial issues have been between such neighbors as France and Germany or India and Pakistan. Indeed, before systematic data collection had addressed the contentious issues involved in conflicts, evidence on the relationship between contiguity and conflict was seen as being consistent with the territorial explanation for war, even if not as definitive evidence of the specific issues involved (e.g., Vasquez 1993).

Table 1.4 examines the impact of contiguity and territorial issues on dispute severity for primary disputants, breaking down each dispute into pairs of participants (dyads) to obtain the clearest illustration of conflict patterns in multiparty disputes that may involve many different adversaries. This table reports the results of a logistic regression analysis of dispute escalation to fatalities or war, controlling for the impact of capability imbalance and dyadic democracy. It should be noted that the relationship between contiguity and territorial issues is far from perfect; adversaries that are contiguous by land contend over territorial issues in 38 percent of their militarized disputes, as do 22 percent of those that are contiguous by sea and around 15 percent of those that are noncontiguous, allowing for a useful comparison of the effects of territory and contiguity.

The results in table 1.4 indicate that both contiguity and territorial issues increase the risk of dispute escalation. Contention over territorial issues significantly increases escalation to either fatalities or war compared to disputes that only involve nonterritorial issues ($p < .001$). Contiguity by land significantly increases escalation to both fatalities ($p < .001$) and war ($p < .02$) compared to disputes between noncontiguous adversaries, although contiguity by sea does not have a statistically significant effect on escalation to either fatalities ($p < .87$) or war ($p < .15$). These results are consistent with those

Table 1.4.   Territorial Issues, Contiguity, and Dyadic Dispute Escalation

Variable	Model I: Escalate to Fatalities Est. (S.E.)	Model II: Escalate to War Est. (S.E.)
Territorial Issues		
Territorial Issue	0.82 (0.09)***	0.94 (0.18)***
Contiguity		
Contiguous by Land	0.95 (0.13)***	0.65 (0.28)**
Contiguous by Sea	0.03 (0.18)	0.49 (0.34)
Intercept	−1.74 (0.29)***	−4.22 (0.58)***
Capability Imbalance	−0.68 (0.31)**	0.11 (0.62)
Joint Democracy	−0.58 (0.19)***	−0.63 (0.42)
N	3,384	3,847
Likelihood Ratio χ^2	256.07	45.59
	$p < .001$ (5 d.f.)	$p < .001$ (5 d.f.)

*$p < .10$, **$p < .05$, ***$p < .01$

of Senese (2005) and Senese and Vasquez (2008), who find that contiguity increases the risk of armed conflict occurring, but that even after considering the impact of contiguity through selection models, territorial issues greatly increase the risk of escalation.

Table 1.5 examines the outbreak of armed conflict between states over on-going territorial claims, as measured by version 1.1 of the Issue Correlates of War (ICOW) territorial claims data set.[3] The earlier tables have examined the conflict behavior of all dyads in the interstate system that have been involved in militarized conflict over any issue, but they have been limited to armed conflicts that have already broken out. By starting with a set of cases that have territorial disagreements, table 1.5 allows us to examine whether contiguity affects the outbreak of conflict over territory, while considering the impact of other factors that have been found to be relevant by past research (Hensel 2001a; Hensel, Mitchell, Sowers, and Thyne 2008).

The first important result is that both the salience of the territory and the way that this issue has been managed recently have a significant impact on the likelihood that one of the claimants will threaten or use militarized force over the issue. The ICOW project measures salience with a twelve-point index of characteristics of the claimed territory that make it more valuable to one or both claimants, such as strategic location or the presence of valuable resources (Hensel, Mitchell, Sowers, and Thyne 2008). The more salient a claimed territory is according to this salience index, the more

Table 1.5. Influences on Armed Conflict over Territorial Claims

Variable	Est. (S.E.)
Territorial Issues	
Salience Index	0.13 (0.03)***
Recent MIDs	0.82 (0.07)***
Recent Failed Talks	0.22 (0.06)***
Contiguity to Territory	
Both Contiguous	0.40 (0.42)
One Contiguous	0.44 (0.41)
Intercept	−3.72 (0.60)***
Capability Imbalance	−1.80 (0.49)***
Joint Democracy	−0.65 (0.26)**
N	8,170
Likelihood Ratio χ^2	392.42
	$p < .001$ (7 d.f.)

*$p < .10$, **$p < .05$, ***$p < .01$

likely militarized conflict is ($p < .001$). Furthermore, conflict is more likely when the claim has seen more unsuccessful negotiations ($p < .001$) or more militarized conflict ($p < .001$) in recent years, using a weighting scheme that considers both the number and recency of such events in the past ten years (Hensel, Mitchell, Sowers, and Thyne 2008).

While these results are quite consistent with previous research on the management of territorial issues, contiguity seems to have little systematic impact. The model in table 1.5 includes variables indicating how many of the claimants are contiguous to the claimed territory by either land or open sea. While both variables have positive coefficients, indicating that they are associated with a higher risk of conflict, neither effect is statistically significant ($p < .35$ for one side, $p < .29$ for both). This result does not change if contiguity is measured by land only (excluding contiguity by sea), if it is measured separately for the challenger and target state in the claim, or if contiguity is measured between the two claimant states' homelands rather than between each claimant and the territory in question.

Evaluation

Territorial issues have been prominent among the many sources of armed conflict. Over one-fourth of all militarized disputes have involved territorial issues, as have roughly half or more of more serious conflicts. While states sharing land borders are most likely to fight over territorial issues, more distant states also do so often enough that there is far from a perfect overlap between contiguity and territorial issues in conflicts. When both contiguity and territory are considered in the same analysis, contention over territorial issues significantly increases the risk of dispute escalation, showing that territory has an independent effect on conflict behavior beyond reachability or other facilitating factors.

Analysis using territorial claims data indicates that characteristics of the territorial issue itself—the salience of the claimed territory, as well as recent patterns in the way that this issue has been managed—play a central role in the outbreak of armed conflict over the issue. In contrast, contiguity does not seem to play a systematic role. History is full of examples where neighboring states have fought repeated wars over territorial issues, but many neighbors are able to manage their territorial claims peacefully and avoid any form of armed conflict; and many more distant adversaries have engaged in conflict over their territorial issues. The most important distinction between territorial claim dyads and other types of adversaries thus appears to lie in their contention over territorial issues.

PEACEFUL MANAGEMENT OF TERRITORIAL ISSUES

While armed conflict has been the focus of most scholarly research on territorial and other contentious issues, this is not the only way that such issues are managed. The issues approach emphasizes the variety of ways that issues can be managed or settled. Militarized conflict is one option, but leaders may also choose to negotiate bilaterally with their adversaries, negotiate with nonbinding third-party assistance through such techniques as good offices or mediation, or even submit their claim to a binding third-party arbitral or adjudicated decision. A variety of research has considered the factors that influence choices between these different settlement techniques.

Theoretical Arguments

Hensel (2001a) and Hensel, Mitchell, Sowers, and Thyne (2008) emphasize the salience of the claimed territory as an influence on multiple types of settlement techniques. Not only are more salient territories expected to lead to more armed conflict, they suggest, but such territories should also lead the claimants to the greater use of peaceful techniques to try to achieve their goals. They also discuss recent issue management, with factors such as recent armed conflict or recent failed negotiations over the same issue increasing the likelihood of peaceful management techniques as the leaders and potentially interested third parties seek to prevent the issue from exploding into armed conflict. Other scholars have focused on specific attributes of the claimed territory (e.g., Huth 1996; Huth and Allee 2002) or on the characteristics of potential third parties (e.g., Hansen, Mitchell, and Nemeth 2008; Crescenzi et al. 2011; Gent and Shannon 2011) in trying to understand when different settlement techniques are more likely to be employed.

A number of recent studies have also made interesting arguments about how domestic politics might condition the choice of techniques. For example, Allee and Huth (2006) suggest that submission of a territorial claim to a legally binding third-party decision can be desirable as a way to provide domestic political cover if the concessions that might be needed to settle the claim bilaterally are seen as impossible in light of domestic politics. Simmons (1999, 2002) suggests that binding techniques are most likely to be used by leaders who are unable to secure domestic ratification of bilateral settlements. Turning to individual leaders, Chiozza and Choi (2003) suggest that the length of a leader's tenure in office and his or her experience with armed conflict while in office will affect decisions to pursue a peaceful settlement of an ongoing claim.

Empirical Evidence

The broadening of the research focus from armed conflict to issue management more generally began with the collection of data on territorial disagreements in world politics. Several recent studies have compiled information on the prevalence of territorial claims in the modern era. Huth and Allee (2002) identify 348 territorial claims that were active between 1919 and 1995. Focusing on a longer time period, the ICOW project (Hensel, Mitchell, Sowers, and Thyne 2008) finds competing claims to 122 distinct pieces of territory in the Western Hemisphere and Western Europe between 1816 and 2001, and preliminary ICOW research suggests that there will be between 450 and 500 distinct claimed territories by the time data collection is completed for the entire world. It seems clear, then, that territorial disagreements have been common in the modern interstate system.

The issues approach has made important contributions by emphasizing the variety of ways that issues can be managed. As it turns out, though, armed conflict is neither the most frequently used nor the most successful technique for managing issues, and a much more comprehensive picture of issue management emerges when the alternatives are considered. Table 1.6 examines the likelihood that a given territorial claim will experience armed conflict, both for all claims and for "highly salient" claims (those that have a score of at least eight out of twelve on the ICOW salience index).

Both for all territorial claims and for the most salient cases, just over half of the claims (55 percent) never produce even a single militarized dispute. It seems clear that contention over territory, by itself, is no guarantee of armed conflict; even the most salient territorial issues are slightly more likely to experience no armed conflict at all than to have one or more militarized disputes. Salience does seem to affect the prospects for the escalation of conflicts that do occur, though. While the likelihood of experiencing some form of armed conflict is nearly identical for both territorial claims in general and highly salient claims, more than two-thirds of the highly salient territories that experience conflict (twelve of seventeen, or 70.5 percent) experience at

Table 1.6. Frequency of Militarized Conflict over Territorial Claims

	Claims with at Least One Armed Conflict	
Level of Conflict	All Territorial Claims	Highly Salient Territorial Claims
No Armed Conflict	68 (55.7%)	21 (55.3%)
Only Nonfatal Conflict	31 (25.4)	5 (13.2)
1+ Fatal Conflicts	23 (18.9)	12 (31.6)
Total	122	38

Note: There is one observation per claimed territory; if that area has been the subject of more than one claim over the period of study, all of the claims are aggregated together.

Table 1.7. Peaceful and Militarized Management of Territorial Claims

	Settlement Attempts per Claim (% of all attempts)	
Settlement Technique	*All Territorial Claims*	*Highly Salient Territorial Claims*
Militarized Conflict	1.68 (17.0%)	3.11 (19.6%)
Bilateral Negotiations	5.92 (59.7)	7.97 (50.1)
Third-Party Activities	2.31 (23.3)	4.82 (30.3)
Total	9.91	15.90

Note: There is one observation per claimed territory; if that area has been the subject of more than one claim over the period of study, all of the claims are aggregated together.

least one fatal conflict, compared to less than half overall (twenty-three of fifty-four, or 42.6 percent).

Table 1.7 examines both militarized and peaceful techniques for the management of territorial claims. The average territorial claim has experienced 1.68 militarized conflicts, and the average highly salient claim has experienced nearly double this figure at 3.11 conflicts. These conflicts represent only a relatively small proportion of all attempts to manage the claims, though. Bilateral negotiations between the claimants are the most common technique, accounting for more than half of attempts to manage all claims (59.7 percent) or the most salient claims (50.1 percent). Third-party techniques such as good offices, mediation, or arbitration are also more common than conflict, accounting for 23.3 percent of settlement attempts overall and 30.3 percent of attempts to settle highly salient claims. Militarized conflict accounts for less than one-fifth of attempts to manage territorial claims, both for all claims (17.0 percent) and for highly salient claims (19.6 percent).

We now consider the effectiveness of these settlement techniques. Table 1.8 examines the likelihood that a given settlement attempt will end

Table 1.8. Ending of Territorial Claims

	Did Settlement Attempt End Most/All of Claim?		
Settlement Technique	*No*	*Yes (%)*	*Total*
Militarized Conflict	185	20 (9.8%)	205
Bilateral Negotiations	312	68 (17.9)	380
Third Party: Nonbinding	119	29 (19.6)	148
Third Party: Binding	9	30 (76.9)	39
Total	625	147 (19.0)	772

$\chi^2 = 96.58$ (3 d.f.)
$p < .001$

Notes: This table only includes settlement attempts that addressed the substance of the claim. Functional and procedural attempts are excluded because even if they had succeeded, they would not have ended the claim.

contention over most or all of the territorial claim as reported in the ICOW data set, focusing only on attempts to settle the substance of the claim. Almost half of the successful attempts—68 of 147, or 46.3 percent—involved bilateral negotiations between the claimants, but the success rates of the different techniques are very instructive. The greatest success comes from binding third-party arbitration or adjudication, with over three-fourths of such attempts (76.9 percent) ending most or all of the claim; this is consistent with Allee and Huth (2006) and Mitchell and Hensel (2007). There is little difference in success between bilateral negotiations (17.9 percent) and nonbinding third-party activities (19.6 percent), but armed conflict is much less successful than any of the peaceful techniques (9.8 percent). While conflict attracts most of the headlines, then, it is much less successful at ending a territorial claim than the various peaceful techniques. Furthermore, many claims that end militarily are soon followed by the outbreak of a new claim, as the side that lost the territory begins its own claim to recover the lost land (as with Syria's claim for the return of the Golan Heights or France's for the return of Alsace-Lorraine after these territories were lost).

Evaluation

These results suggest several important conclusions about attempts to manage or settle territorial claims. First, despite the emphasis on militarized conflict in existing research, militarized conflict accounts for only a small fraction of all efforts to settle territorial claims, and militarized techniques are much less successful at ending claims than are peaceful techniques. Bilateral negotiations account for more than half of all settlement attempts and nearly half of all successful claim endings, while third-party techniques outnumber armed conflict in frequency and (particularly for binding techniques) outperform military techniques in effectiveness.

Also, it seems clear that the salience of the territory affects the actions that are taken to resolve a given claim. Militarized conflict is more frequent in claims involving high-salience territory, with nearly double the average number of conflicts for the most salient claims. Yet more salient claims also experience an increase in peaceful settlement activities, with over one-third more bilateral negotiations and more than twice as many third-party activities for the most salient claims as well.

We should be careful not to overemphasize the militarized side of claim management, as even the most salient territories see frequent efforts to manage or settle the claim peacefully. The fact that so many peaceful attempts are made suggests that any given round of negotiations or mediation over a highly salient claim is unlikely to succeed—for example, see the numerous efforts to address the claims over Kashmir or the Golan Heights. But even leaders contending over highly salient issues are much more likely to try to pursue their claims through peaceful techniques than through armed conflict.

SUMMARY

Recent research has examined a number of possible explanations for a possible linkage between geography and conflict. There can be little doubt that geographic factors affect interstate conflict in systematic ways. The theoretical explanations discussed in this chapter, supported by a variety of empirical evidence, suggest a number of important conclusions about interstate conflict and implications for future research.

Contiguous adversaries are more conflict prone than more distant states, accounting for more than half of all armed conflict since 1816 and more than two-thirds of more serious forms of conflict. The impact of contiguity is even more prominent for minor powers, with more than three-fourths of all minor power conflicts being fought between neighbors. Contiguity also increases the risk that a given conflict will escalate to more severe levels, at least for contiguity by a direct land or river border; the impact of contiguity by sea is weaker.

Territorial issues seem to be especially likely to lead to armed conflict, accounting for over one-fourth of all armed conflict and at least half of the more serious forms of conflict. Contention over more salient territory increases the risk of armed conflict, and contention over territorial issues greatly increases the risk that conflict will escalate to higher severity levels. Furthermore, this escalatory impact of territorial issues seems to be above and beyond any effect of contiguity; even noncontiguous states are involved in a number of territorial disputes, and the conflictual impact of territory remains strong after controlling for contiguity.

Finally, it is important to consider the peaceful dimension of territorial claim management as well as the more prominent militarized dimension. Just under half of all territorial claims experience even a single armed conflict, and militarized threats or actions account for less than one-fifth of all efforts to manage or settle territorial claims. Militarized techniques are also less successful at ending territorial claims, with only one-tenth of such efforts ending most or all of the claim in question. In contrast, even the least successful peaceful technique—bilateral negotiations—is nearly twice as successful, and binding third-party techniques are nearly eight times as likely to end the claim.

In keeping with the theme of this volume, it seems safe to conclude that geography—in the form of both proximity and territorial issues—greatly

increases the risk of armed conflict. Many questions on this topic remain to
be answered, though. I now conclude with suggestions for future research.

Directions for Future Research

Mitigating Factors

While both contiguity and territorial issues greatly increase the risk of armed
conflict, neither factor can be considered sufficient for armed conflict. Despite the conflictual effects of contiguity, many neighbors have peaceful
relations where military force is not even considered. Furthermore, despite
the conflictual effects of territorial issues, many territorial claims (including
many with high salience) are managed peacefully with no resort to force.
Future research could benefit by greater insight into how each factor can be
mitigated through other actions or processes.

Liberal and institutional scholars suggest a number of factors that might
be relevant, ranging from joint democracy to the development of stronger
institutional and economic ties between countries. For example, since World
War II, Western Europe has shifted from one of the world's most conflictual
regions to one of the most peaceful. Some might explain this shift by the development and strengthening of liberal democracy and institutions such as the
European Union, which may have helped to mitigate the otherwise dangerous
effects of proximity. Along these lines, Brochmann and Hensel (2009, 2011)
find that jointly democratic dyads that share at least one river are less likely
than others to begin explicit river claims, and that stronger networks of shared
intergovernmental organization (IGO) memberships increase the likelihood
and effectiveness of negotiations over any claims that do begin. Similarly,
a number of studies discussed above suggest that ending territorial claims
improves relations between the former claimants; this might help to explain
why many neighbors ultimately find themselves at peace after long periods of
conflict. Future research should do more to investigate these and other factors
that might help to account for the lack of armed conflict between many pairs
of neighbors, as well as the lack of even a single conflict in more than half
of all territorial claims.

Better Conceptualization and Measurement of Borders and Issues

As discussed above, it could be argued that generally tangible stakes such
as territory might be more amenable to peaceful division and settlement
than more symbolic stakes such as prestige or ideology. Yet the intangible
importance of territory would seem to counter any potential advantages that
might be gained from the concrete territorial object of dispute, by infusing the

disputed territory with symbolic or transcendent qualities that make division more difficult (Vasquez 1993: 77–78) and potentially creating what Fearon (2005) termed "effectively indivisible issues." In a preliminary investigation, Hensel and Mitchell (2005) find that claims to territory with higher levels of intangible salience are significantly more conflict prone than other claims, although such claims also appear to be more amenable to peaceful agreement—which few would have expected. It may be that another factor is behind this apparently surprising result, or it may be that territorial issues in general have so much intangible salience (regardless of the details of any particular piece of territory) that a more appropriate comparison would be between territorial issues and other issue types. In any case, more research is needed before clear conclusions can be drawn.

More detail would also be desirable in the measurement of both borders and territorial issues. Efforts to measure the salience of territorial issues have, for the most part, been limited to dichotomous measures of whether or not a certain factor (e.g., valuable resources or a strategic location) is present in a claimed territory. Recent years have seen the availability of detailed information about terrain, resources, cities, infrastructure, and other features that might increase the salience of a particular piece of territory. Such information could be used with geographic information systems (GIS) software to produce much more detailed measures of territorial salience, whether measuring characteristics of borders (Starr 2002; Starr and Thomas 2005) or of claimed territories (Dzurek 2000). The needed information is generally not available in time-series form that could be used to study several centuries of territorial claims. Yet, at least for recent decades, much might be learned from such improved measures of salience, just as research on civil war has benefited from geocoding of terrain, resource endowments, and population characteristics.

Research treating geography as a facilitating condition for conflict might also benefit from expanding the focus beyond the simple distance between two actors. Several scholars have examined region-level effects, whereby the characteristics of an entire region might affect states in the region (e.g., Hensel and Diehl 1994; Enterline 1998; Gleditsch 2002a). Others have begun to use network analysis to gain a more detailed understanding of the complex relationships between actors than would be possible through dyadic analyses (e.g., Maoz et al. 2005; Hafner-Burton, Kahler, and Montgomery 2009). Each of these approaches offers potential benefits for understanding conflict behavior.

Origins of Contentious Issues

While much progress has been made in studying the management of contentious issues, less is known about the beginning of contention. It seems unlikely that such issues arise randomly, and as with many other phenomena in world politics, there may be important selection effects that relate the initial process of claim origin to subsequent processes of claim management or escalation. If so, studying the conditions under which different types of claims are most likely to arise may be essential to our ability to develop a clear understanding of their impact on conflict.

Huth (1996) compares a population of territorial claims with a random sample of uncontested borders to help understand the conditions under which claims are most likely to begin. He finds that a border is more likely to be subjected to an active territorial claim when the territory in question has a strategic location, high economic value, or shared ethnic or linguistic groups along the border and when a potential challenger state previously lost territory, and less likely when a prior border agreement has been signed to settle the border. Focusing on the emergence of river claims between states with shared rivers, Brochmann and Hensel (2009) find that lower levels of water availability, higher demands on water, longer rivers, and cross-border rivers all increase the likelihood of river claims, while joint democracy in the riparian states and greater relative capabilities by the downstream state decrease this likelihood.

While these initial efforts offer some useful insights, more remains to be learned. For territorial issues, for example, the legacies of colonial rule may have an important impact on both the origin and management of territorial claims over postcolonial borders (Hensel, Allison, and Khanani 2008). Colonial powers rarely considered the interests or desires of the indigenous peoples when acquiring or expanding their colonial possessions, with the result that colonial borders often separated preexisting political or economic units or combined units that did not wish to be together. Furthermore, borders between the possessions of a single colonial power may not have been clearly determined or marked, because the colonizer cared more about obtaining the resources from its possessions than about clearly delineating which of its possessions included the resource in question. There are thus many reasons to expect that former colonial borders could be challenged after independence, and there are many anecdotal stories that such actions or decisions during the colonial era led to bloody claims after independence.

Additional Contentious Issues

The broader issues approach that is associated with this territorial explanation could be tested more effectively by collecting data on nonterritorial issues, to help assess the extent to which territory is treated differently from other issues, as well as the extent to which different issue types show similarities. The ICOW project is collecting data on river and maritime issues as well as territorial issues, and preliminary results suggest that all three issue types show important similarities in management patterns (Hensel, Mitchell, Sowers, and Thyne 2008). For example, higher levels of issue salience greatly increase the likelihood of both armed conflict and peaceful settlement techniques regardless of the type of issue under contention, even if there are differences in the overall conflict propensity of the different issue types. Histories of recent armed conflict or failed negotiations over the issue also increase the likelihood of both conflict and peaceful techniques for each issue type.

Beyond these similarities, though, it would be instructive to examine some of the differences between issue types. Scholars have begun to examine both conflict and cooperation over international rivers (e.g., Dinar 2009; Tir and Ackerman 2009; Wolf 1998). Focusing explicitly on river issue management in a way that is directly comparable to the territorial analyses discussed in this chapter, Brochmann and Hensel (2009, 2011; Hensel, Mitchell, and Sowers 2006) have found important similarities to the management of territorial issues, while also finding that river-specific factors such as water scarcity and river treaties can have a powerful influence on negotiations over river claims. For example, (depending on the specific measure being used) water scarcity generally makes river claims more likely to begin, but also makes negotiations over such claims more likely to be attempted and to succeed. The existence of at least one relevant river treaty makes negotiations more likely, and closer ties between the claimant states make negotiations both more likely and more successful. Future research could benefit from greater consideration of both river and maritime issues as the data become available.

It would also be desirable to collect data on other types of issues. Hensel, Mitchell, Sowers, and Thyne (2008) suggest that territorial issues typically have high levels of both tangible and intangible salience, while river and maritime issues typically have high tangible but low intangible salience. Future work might be able to benefit by studying issues with higher intangible than tangible salience, such as identity issues (where the concern is the treatment of one's ethnoreligious kinsmen rather than annexation of the territory where they live), as well as issues with relatively low levels of both tangible and intangible salience for most members of society (such as questions affecting one or several individuals or a single firm or industry). Collecting data on such issues would allow a much more complete understanding of how issues are managed and how both tangible and intangible issue salience affects states' interactions.

Geography, Territorial Issues, and Intrastate Conflict

Finally, it may be worth broadening the focus of this body of research beyond the interstate dimension of conflict that is the focus of the present volume.

Geography and territorial issues are not exclusively interstate in nature, and the civil war literature has begun to examine the territorial dimensions of internal conflicts. For example, Walter (2003, 2006) explicitly draws from the territorial issues literature in interstate conflict in order to study government responses to internal challenges. A great deal of recent civil war literature has focused on resources such as diamonds or oil as objects of or contributors to the fighting; much of the literature on ethnic conflict or secession has a clear territorial dimension. Other work has emphasized terrain or other geographic factors as facilitating conditions that might help or hinder insurgency, as well as investigating international influences from neighboring countries. There is a great potential for learning across the interstate-intrastate conflict divide with respect to geography as both a facilitating condition for conflict and a source of conflict, and work along these lines should be encouraged.

NOTES

1. Change in proximity is possible—albeit rare—with the acquisition or loss of territory due to military conquest or the acquisition or loss of colonies. For example, Ecuador and Brazil initially shared a border in the nineteenth century, but several territorial changes left Peruvian and Colombian territory between their current borders.

2. This table focuses on the issues at stake for the initial participants in each conflict. The Holsti results are produced by combining Holsti's issue types of "territory," "strategic territory," "territory (boundary)," and "colonial competition." This table only considers full-scale interstate wars from Holsti's list, excluding internal conflicts and subwar disputes.

3. This version of the ICOW data set covers the period 1816–2001 and includes claims to territory in the Western Hemisphere and Western or Nordic Europe.

Chapter Two

Alliances

Path to Peace or Path to War?

Choong-Nam Kang

Do alliances promote peace? Or do they increase the probability of war? This is one of the core questions in the studies of international relations, and scholars have long investigated this puzzle to unveil the true relationship between alliances and war. Indeed, a good deal of scientific knowledge from theoretical work and empirical investigations has been accumulated in this field of study. In addition, scholars have also made extensive efforts to construct and update comprehensive data sets, including the Correlates of War (COW) Formal Alliances data (Singer and Small 1966; Small and Singer 1969; Gibler and Sarkees 2004) and the Alliance Treaty Obligations and Provisions project (Leeds et al. 2002), and these extensive data sets enable researchers to conduct more systematic and broader empirical investigations. All of these scholarly efforts have provided useful theoretical explanations and have discovered many important empirical findings, which improve our understanding of the impact of alliances. However, it also seems true that many parts of the puzzle still remain unanswered, and thus the question of the impact of alliances on war is still open to debate in many aspects.

So, what do we know about the relationship between alliances and war from previous scientific studies, and what research remains to be done to account for the relationship between alliances and war more accurately? In this chapter, I attempt to answer these questions. To this end, first I review the contending theoretical grounds and empirical findings provided by previous studies in regard to the effects of alliances on both the occurrence of war and the initiation of militarized disputes. After this review, I empirically reassess the impacts of alliances on dispute initiation with more specified empirical models in order to resolve the disagreements of previous studies and to answer the question of what makes the difference in previous findings. By doing so, this chapter enables us to assess what we

27

know about the effects of alliances on war occurrence and dispute initiation. Lastly, I conclude this chapter with some suggestions for future research to enhance our understanding of the effects of alliances on conflict, based on what we do not know about the effects of alliances on war.

CONTENDING THEORETICAL GROUNDS OF THE RELATIONSHIP BETWEEN ALLIANCES AND CONFLICT

Alliances are a form of military collaboration among member states. Thus states' concerns for security are a critical motive in and the purpose of forming alliances.[1] As a policy tool for states to manage national defense and security, the effects of alliances on international conflict have been one of the core queries in alliance studies. Mainly two contending explanations have been provided by various studies using diverse approaches: one group of researchers argues for a negative association between alliances and war, while the other group of scholars claims a positive effect of alliances on war.

Scholars who claim a negative impact of alliances on war develop their theoretical arguments from the intrinsic security function of alliances, and the balance of power theorists are among them. For the balance of power theorists, a balance of power or equality of power is an important condition for maintaining the stability of the international system by avoiding hegemony.[2] In the anarchic international system, alliances serve to achieve a balance of power by aggregating the power of member states in an alliance bloc against hegemons or threats (e.g., Waltz 1979: 126, 168; Walt 1987: 17–28). Hence, alliances are argued to prevent war by maintaining the balance and equilibrium of the system (e.g., Gulick 1955: 61–62). In a similar vein, alliances also can prevent war by reducing the level of uncertainty in the system, which can result in war due to miscalculation and misperceptions (Singer, Bremer, and Stuckey 1972: 23). Alliances, as a costly signal, also make the intervention of allied states more credible. If a target's allies are more likely to intervene, a potential challenger will be less likely to initiate an attack (Smith 1995; Leeds 2003).[3] Hence, alliances deter attacks and decrease the probability of war by lowering uncertainty.

While these scholars explain the negative impact of alliances on war through balancing or deterrence through power, other studies focus on a restraining function of alliances (Pressman 2008; see also Schroeder 1976). Pressman (2008) focuses on internal restraint of alliances. According to Pressman, a strong state forms an alliance with a weaker state to restrain a new ally from a course of action that the strong state does not support, including going to war with other states outside the alliance. However, with his case studies, Pressman concludes that this restraining effect is limited and effective only under certain conditions including when a strong state in an alliance successfully mobilizes its power resources.

In contrast to the realist literature and orthodoxy linking alliances to peace, other scholars maintain that alliances are more likely to result in war because alliances generate and aggravate the spiral effect of the security dilemma. Alliances increase the security of signatories but can make others outside the alliances insecure. In other words, forming alliances with one state leaves other states outside the alliance feeling vulnerable and thus makes them seek counteralliances (Kaplan 1957: 24). That is, although a state's initial purpose in forming alliances is to enhance its own security, alliances end up heightening the threat perceptions of opposing states and the level of hostility, which generates the spiral effect of the security dilemma. This intensified hostility aggravates the situation and makes war more likely. Therefore, alliances are thought to increase the probability of war rather than to preserve peace through power (Vasquez 1993).

EMPIRICAL FINDINGS ON THE EFFECTS OF ALLIANCES ON WAR

Alliance Effects on War between Signatories and Other States

Then, what does the empirical evidence say to us about the relationship between alliances and war? Although the two contending theoretical explanations sound plausible and have provided important theoretical and logical grounds for later studies, the findings of empirical investigations have provided more support for the positive relationship between alliances and war. Singer and Small (1966) is one of the first systematic empirical investigations supporting the positive relationship between alliances and war. Singer and Small's finding for the 1816–1945 period shows that states with higher alliance activities are engaged in war more often than others, and this relationship is stronger for mutual defense pacts. Singer and Small also find that states that have been in the system longer are likely to have more alliances and to get involved in more wars than newer states in the system. These empirical patterns suggest a positive association between alliances and war, although Singer and Small have not examined the relationship directly. Levy (1981) also reports in his seminal work that alliances are more often followed by war involving at least one allied state, rather than by peace. This positive association has occurred during the last five centuries except for the nineteenth century and is stronger for great power alliances. This finding supports the hypothesis that alliances are more positively associated with war even though the relationship is not consistent across the time periods and shows a negative association in the nineteenth century.

Gibler and Vasquez's study (1998; see also Gibler 2000) is another example supporting the positive relationship between alliances and war onset. Gibler and Vasquez see threat perceptions as the core source of the positive effect of alliances and maintain that alliances consisting of major powers or states that won their last wars should be more prone to war because those alliances are perceived as highly threatening by other states. Their empirical findings support this claim by demonstrating that alliances with those characteristics are more frequently followed by war within five years after the formation of such an alliance, both in the nineteenth and the twentieth centuries as well as the whole test period of 1495 to 1980. Gibler and Vasquez's findings provide direct support for the logic that alliances aggravate the threat perceptions of the opposing states and thus make war more likely. In the same logical vein, Gibler's other studies (1997b, 2000) provide additional support for this argument by showing the positive relationship between threat perceptions and the effect of alliances on conflict. His empirical finding demonstrates that a certain type of alliance, territorial settlement treaties, does not increase threat perceptions and removes a source of conflict, and thus these alliances actually decrease the probability of war.[4] Therefore, his finding suggests that the effect of alliances depends on whether alliances heighten threat perceptions.

Moul (1988) presents another interesting aspect of the relationship between alliances and war. Moul argues that predicting how other great powers would act is important for a "predatory" great power in determining whether to wage a war against a weaker state. In other words, when a "predatory" great power clears its back from a potential threat posed by another great power by forming a nonaggression pact with that great power, the "predatory" great power is more likely to wage a war against a weaker state. Moul finds that this is the case for the time period of 1815 to 1935. This finding reveals that alliances increase the probability of war between a signatory and a nonsignatory while constraining war between signatories.

Leeds (2005b) also shows an increasing impact of alliances on the expansion and escalation of disputes to war, with a focus on the role of alliances in the crisis bargaining process. According to Leeds, alliances add more parties to the negotiation process, and where more parties are involved, multilateral conflicts are more likely to escalate to war than in bilateral conflicts. Hence alliances are argued to indirectly increase the probability of war, and Leeds finds supportive evidence for this relationship.

Senese and Vasquez's series of work on the steps-to-war theory has investigated the relationship between alliance and war in a more direct and sophisticated way. The recent study of Senese and Vasquez (2008), in particular, provides very robust and convincing evidence for the effect of alliances. Senese and Vasquez (2008) maintain that not all alliances are relevant to a specific conflict involving a signatory, and thus, to unveil the true impact of alliances on war, researchers should consider only relevant alliances to a specific dispute. With this rationale, Senese and Vasquez develop a new concept, politically relevant alliances, defined based on allied states' capabilities and geographical regions. After determining the politically relevant alliances for a specific dispute, Senese and Vasquez comprehensively examine the differing effects of five different patterns of alliance ties of the dyads on the escalation of a militarized interstate dispute (MID) to war.[5]

The main empirical finding of Senese and Vasquez (2008) is that having outside alliances clearly increased the probability of war in the time period from 1816 to 2001. It is found that not only dyads where both states have outside alliances but also dyads where one side has outside alliances are more likely to go to war compared to when they have no alliance. This bellicose effect is greater when disputants confront issues with high stakes such as territorial issues. In addition, various interaction effects (either multiplicative or additive) between alliances and other risk factors, including arms races and rivalry, have also been found. Colaresi and Thompson (2005) find a similar type of positive interaction effect between external alliances and previous crises. Kang (2007) also finds that having outside alliances increases the probability of war much more for disputes between major powers and between states with strong capabilities. These interaction effects increase the probability of war dramatically.

Senese and Vasquez (2008) also report a pacifying effect of alliances on conflict between allies. Evidence shows that MIDs between allied states are much less likely to escalate to war compared to when there is no shared alliance in the dyad. However, the situation is quite different when states in the dyad (either one side or both sides) have other outside alliances besides the shared alliance. Senese and Vasquez find that even an MID between allied states is more likely to escalate to war if one state or both states in the dyad have any outside alliances. This finding suggests that the impact of outside alliances is much stronger and overwhelms the pacifying effect of alliances on conflict between allied states. This is clear supportive evidence for the increasing effect of alliances on the probability of war.

Another notable finding of Senese and Vasquez's investigations is that the war-prone effect of alliances is not consistent over time, as Levy (1981) has found. The tests with the whole period sample (1816–2001) and the subperiod sample of 1816 to 1945 show the clear positive effects of outside alliances on war, and the effects are greatest in the subperiod of 1816 to 1945. However, the test with the Cold War sample (1946–1989) shows a quite different result: dyads where both sides have outside alliances are less likely to go to war during the Cold War period. In addition, alliances decrease the probability of war between allies, and the decreasing effect is the same for dyads where allied states have outside alliances during the Cold War period.

This trend, however, is the case only for the Cold War period. Outside alliances turn out again to have an increasing effect on the probability of war in the post–Cold War period (1990–2001). In the post–Cold War period, "no alliance" is found to be the perfect indicator of peace, while one type of outside alliances (allied to each other and to outside alliances) shows a positive effect on the escalation to war. Therefore, the empirical findings from Senese and Vasquez's investigations suggest that alliances increase the likelihood of the outbreak of war with the exception of the Cold War period.

Then, why did alliances have a different effect during the Cold War, and what made alliances in the Cold War period different from those in other periods? Some factors could explain this discrepancy. This pacifying effect may be brought about by the combination of the fear of nuclear war and the tightened, polarized Cold War alliance structure. During the Cold War, both the United States and the Soviet Union had strong influence over the international system, and the two superpowers constrained their allies in order to prevent their allies' disputes from expanding to nuclear war (Senese and Vasquez 2008: ch. 7; Vasquez 2009: 379–81). Pressman's case studies (2008) on alliance restraint during the Cold War demonstrate this point well.[6] Hence, these factors, including the highly polarized international system, the strong influence of both superpowers over the system, and the great fear of nuclear war, could make alliances work differently. Considering other findings that having outside alliances increases the probability of war in the post–Cold War period where those factors are absent, this explanation sounds plausible.

Alliance Effects on War between Allies

While these findings demonstrate that alliances increase the probability of war between signatories and other states outside the alliances, other empirical studies provide evidence showing a preventive effect of alliances on war between allies. Although Bueno de Mesquita (1981) argues that allies are more likely to go to war than nonallied states, findings of later studies demonstrate a consistent negative impact of alliances on war between allies. For instance, Ray (1990), using a revised coding rule of interstate war and refined data of Bueno de Mesquita (1981), finds that MIDs between allies are less likely to escalate to war than MIDs between nonallied states, while allied states are more likely to become involved in MIDs. Bremer (1992) also shows that allies are less likely to go to war after controlling for contiguity. Maoz and

Russett (1993) confirm this negative relationship with their exhaustive dyadic analyses. Senese and Vasquez (2008), as illustrated above, provide another example of this effect and show a negative impact of alliances on war between allied states when they have no outside alliances. These findings consistently suggest two different impacts of alliances on war. Alliances decrease the probability of war between allied states while increasing the likelihood of war between member states and other states outside the alliances.

EMPIRICAL FINDINGS ON THE EFFECT OF ALLIANCES ON DISPUTE INITIATION

While the foregoing literature deals with the effects of alliances on war onset (i.e., whether alliances increase or decrease the probability of an MID escalating to war), other studies explore what effects alliances have on dispute initiation (i.e., whether alliances encourage a state to initiate a dispute or restrain a state from initiating a dispute in the first place). As a great deal of research in the study of international conflict has shown, the same factor can have a different effect on the dispute initiation stage and the war onset stage (e.g., Senese 2005). Previous studies have found that this is also the case for alliances. Indeed, researchers have found various differing results from contending theoretical veins.

Palmer and Morgan (2006; see also Morgan and Palmer 2003) provide clear findings for an increasing effect of alliances on dispute initiation. According to Palmer and Morgan, states pursue both maintenance-seeking and change-seeking policies as the capabilities of states increase. Since new alliances contribute to increasing states' available resources and capabilities, states having new alliances are more likely to initiate disputes (change seeking) and to reciprocate disputes (maintenance seeking). In addition, Palmer and Morgan maintain that the probability of dispute initiation should become higher when the capabilities of allies are greater because major power allies will contribute more to increasing a state's available resources than minor power allies. With respect to empirical evidence, Palmer and Morgan find that joining a new alliance clearly increases the probability of initiating an MID. The increasing effect is stronger for "strong" and "very strong" states than for states with "weak" and "average" power. Although they test only the effect of joining new alliances on dispute initiation, this is an important finding showing that alliances increase the probability of dispute initiation.

In contrast to Palmer and Morgan (2006), Krause (2004) argues for the restraining effect of alliances with major powers on the dispute initiation of minor states. Krause examines the combined effects of alliances and arms

transfers on the militarized dispute involvement of minor states. He finds
that when a minor state has a defense pact with a major power *and* receives
arms transfers from the major ally, the probability of dispute involvement of
minor states, as both an initiator and a target, is decreased for the time period
of 1950 to 1995. However, Krause does not find any statistically significant
effect of defense pacts alone on the dispute initiation of minor states, while
defense pacts are found to prevent a dispute initiated against the minor ally.
Thus, it seems to be hard to consider this finding as evidence showing a restraining effect of alliances on the dispute initiation of member states.

Compared to the preceding studies, Leeds (2003) takes quite a different
approach by focusing on provisions of alliances—what signatories promise
in their alliance agreement. Building on information theory (Morrow 1994;
Smith 1995; Fearon 1997), Leeds (2003) argues that the provisions of an alliance should be considered reliable and thus enable both signatories and other
states outside the alliance to anticipate the future behavior of the signatories
since signatories sink costs into alliances by pledging themselves to fulfill
commitments.[7] For instance, when a state has an alliance including provisions for military help, both signatories and an adversary can anticipate that
the allied states are more likely to fight alongside each other in a contingency
of militarized conflict. Hence, the provisions of an alliance affect the conflict
behavior of the states involved, and alliances should have the intended effect
that is shown in the alliance provisions.

Leeds (2003) finds supportive evidence for her argument. Offensive pacts
of a potential challenger encourage the challenger to initiate an MID, while
defensive pacts decrease the probability of dispute initiation against a state
with the defense pact. In addition, a relevant neutrality pact of a challenger
state also increases the probability of dispute initiation against a target by
reducing uncertainty. With this evidence, Leeds suggests that the effects of
alliances on conflict are different depending on what member states promise
rather than there being a certain intrinsic effect of alliances on conflict. In the
same vein, another recent study on defense pacts (Johnson and Leeds 2010)
finds that defense pacts have a muting effect on the initiation of disputes,
while no evidence is found that defense pacts increase the probability of
dispute initiation of allies. Hence, this study suggests defense pacts as a good
policy option since defense pacts lower the probability of militarized conflict.

In short, the previous findings are not consistent and clear so as to answer
the question of whether alliances increase the probability of dispute initiation or deter attacks against states with alliances. For instance, Palmer and
Morgan (2006) and Leeds (2003) provide inconsistent findings in regard to
the effect of alliances on dispute initiation. Then, why do the previous studies find differing evidence? What can explain these contradicting findings,

and how can we resolve the differences? Does it just result from different measurements or research designs? Or do other undiscovered factors create these differences? These questions should be answered theoretically and empirically in future research to unveil the true relationship between alliances and dispute initiation. As a first step, in this chapter, I empirically reexamine the findings of Leeds (2003), Johnson and Leeds (2010), and Palmer and Morgan (2006) by considering all of the factors that are not comprehensively considered in their studies.

REEXAMINATION OF PROVISIONS AND CAPABILITIES IN THE EFFECT OF ALLIANCES ON DISPUTE INITIATION

Although Palmer and Morgan (2006) find clear evidence for the positive effect of *new* alliances on dispute initiation, their findings are not enough to demonstrate whether alliances, as a whole, have such an impact, because they do not directly test the effect of enduring alliances in their study. This point should be reexamined. With respect to the findings of Leeds (2003) and Johnson and Leeds (2010), Leeds' theoretical model provides quite useful explanations and insights to investigate the effects of alliances on dispute initiation. However, Leeds' theoretical model and tests leave some important questions unanswered. For instance, Leeds' theoretical model does not consider some important differences in alliances such as allies' capabilities. If defense pacts prevent attacks by lowering the anticipated probability of military success for a potential initiator, defense pacts with major powers should have a greater muting effect on dispute initiation because the greater capability of a major power ally should greatly lower the expected probability of military success for an initiator. In this vein, the decreasing effect of defense pacts on dispute initiation could result mainly from defense pacts with major powers instead of defense pacts with minor states. If this is the case, the argument that a defense provision prevents attacks should be revised. Offense pacts are the same under this logic. This point should also be reexamined empirically.

To reexamine these previous contradictory findings, I use logit models with the specified alliance provisions and the capabilities of allied states. The sample is a politically relevant directed-dyad–year data set covering the time period of 1816 to 2001.[8] The sample includes only originators. The dependent variable is militarized interstate dispute (MID) initiation and is measured as whether the challenger of the dyad (state A) crosses the threshold of MID by threatening or displaying use of military force or by actually using military force against the target state of the dyad (state B). For this information, I rely on the Correlates of War (COW) project's Militarized Interstate Dispute data set (version 3.10) (Ghosn, Palmer, and Bremer 2004). For alliance variables, I make six mutually exclusive dummy variables based on different provisions, and the reference category of these dummy variables is "no alliance." I rely on the Alliance Treaty Obligations and Provisions (ATOP) project data set for all alliance information (Leeds et al. 2002; Leeds 2005a). In addition, I include other variables to control for the confounding effects of other potential influential factors on the dispute initiation. These variables include joint democracy, relative capability ratio between the challenger and the target of the dyad, contiguity, common interests measured with S score, and the number of previous MIDs that the dyad has experienced within the last three years.[9] I also employ the strategy suggested by Carter and Signorino (2010) to control for any potential temporal dependence of dispute initiation in the data.

Tables 2.1 and 2.2 show the results of the logit tests. Table 2.1 reports the effects of different provisions on dispute initiation. The findings are very similar to those of Leeds (2003) and Johnson and Leeds (2010). Offense pacts and neutrality pacts of challenger states increase the probability of dispute initiation. When challengers have offensive pacts or neutrality pacts with other states, they are more likely to initiate a militarized interstate dispute (MID) against a target state compared to when they have no alliance. On the

Table 2.1.   The Effects of Alliances on Dispute Initiation, 1816–2001

	Whole Sample (1816–2001)
Offense	.786*** (.159)
Defense	−110 (.131)
Neutrality	.437* (.214)
Nonaggression	.207 (.196)
Consult	.152 (.332)
Target's Defense Pacts	−.237* (.115)
Target's Other Alliances	−.196 (.164)
Joint Democracy	−1.163*** (.163)
Relative Capability Ratio	.308* (.144)
Contiguity	1.004*** (.121)
Common Interests (S)	−.470** (.156)
Number of Previous MIDs	8.911*** (.437)
Peace Years	−.077*** (.009)
Peace Years Square	.001*** (.000)
Peace Years Cube	.000*** (.000)
Constant	−4.660*** (.185)
N	163,616
Wald χ^2 (d.f.)	798.22 (15)***

Notes: Robust standard errors adjusted for clustering on the dyad are in parentheses.
    The reference category for all alliance variables in the model is "No Alliance."
***$p < .001$, **$p < .01$, *$p < .05$ (one-tailed).

other hand, when a target state has a defense pact with other states, the target state is less likely to be a victim of dispute initiation. However, defense pacts do not show any statistically significant effect on the dispute initiation of member states. In short, the results suggest that defense pacts mute dispute initiation against signatory states while not emboldening member states to initiate disputes. It is also found that only alliances with certain types of provisions increase the probability of dispute initiation. All results are the same as previous studies following Leeds' model (Leeds 2003, 2005b; Johnson and Leeds 2010). These findings provide more support to Leeds' claim (2003) than to other previous studies that argue for a positive impact of alliances on dispute initiation, since the results show that the effects of alliances are closely related to alliance provisions.

Table 2.2 demonstrates the effects of each alliance provision under different conditions, including time periods and the capabilities of states and allies. Overall, the results are quite different, not only from the findings in table 2.1 but also from the findings of previous studies including Leeds (2003) and Johnson and Leeds (2010). In these tests, I specify the conditions of alliances for the challenger and the target of the dyad based on provisions and the power status of allied states in order to examine whether the effects of alliances are related to the capabilities of allies. The results show that the effects of alliances depend not only on the alliance provisions but also on the allies involved, the capabilities of the allied states in particular. More specifically, offense pacts and neutrality pacts of challenger states increase the probability of dispute initiation. However, not all challenger states' offense and neutrality pacts have the same effects. Only offense pacts with major powers are found to have significant increasing effects. This suggests that states do not rely much on minor allies in initiating disputes even if minor allies promise offensive support. This may be due to states not being able to expect enough military support from minor allies.

The result for defense pacts is also interesting. Defense pacts sometimes show a decreasing effect on dispute initiation, but only with minor states do they have such an effect. It is quite surprising and different from the logic of the deterrence effect of alliances. As Leeds (2003) explains, the reason defense pacts prevent attacks is that a potential initiator expects an ally of its target to join and fight along with the target if they have a defense pact. Thus, the challenger would not initiate a dispute because the defense pact of the target decreases the chances for military success. According to this logic, a defense pact with major powers should have a greater preventive effect than defense pacts with minor states. However, the results demonstrate that only defense pacts with minor states have a decreasing effect on dispute initiation, while defense pacts with major powers do not show any statistically significant effect.

Table 2.2. The Effects of Alliances on Dispute Initiation (specified model), 1816–2001

	Model 1 Whole Sample	Model 2 1816–1945	Model 3 1946–1989	Model 4 1990–2001	Model 5 Minor Challengers (1816–2001)	Model 6 Major Challengers (1816–2001)
Offense w/Major	1.002*** (.178)	1.443*** (.239)	−.748* (.383)	—	2.175*** (.243)	.233 (.209)
Defense w/Major	−.051 (.145)	.171 (.232)	−.312 (.246)	.503 (.376)	−.079 (.179)	−.401* (.216)
Neutrality w/Major	.294 (.288)	.348 (.369)	.276 (.502)	†	−.395 (.499)	.055 (.332)
Nonaggression w/Major	.179 (.281)	†	.479 (.361)	.102 (.560)	.284 (.282)	†
Consult w/Major	.196 (.330)	.480 (.398)	.477 (.771)	†	.020 (.717)	−.210 (.351)
Offense w/Minor	−.139 (.273)	−.069 (.530)	−.024 (.347)	†	−1.254* (.640)	−.104 (.312)
Defense w/Minor	−.118 (.177)	.346 (.293)	−.048 (.293)	−.105 (.427)	.005 (.208)	−.676* (.314)
Neutrality w/Minor	.557* (.280)	.404 (.292)	1.012* (.603)	.398 (.439)	.764** (.286)	−2.047** (.664)
Nonaggression w/Minor	.234 (.259)	.291 (.612)	.270 (.377)	.271 (.542)	.248 (.282)	.540 (.629)
Consult w/Minor	.164 (1.017)	.444 (1.033)	†	†	†	−.417 (1.041)
Target's Defense w/Major	−.086 (.129)	.499** (.152)	−.249 (.269)	−.806* (.406)	.227 (.195)	−.372* (.204)
Target's Defense w/Minor	−.423* (.190)	−.320 (.338)	−.032 (.278)	−1.138** (.486)	.050 (.261)	−.741** (.275)
Target's Other Alliances	−.159 (.164)	−.072 (.242)	−1.769** (.585)	.427* (.229)	−.100 (.278)	−.135 (.196)
Joint Democracy	−1.187*** (.164)	−1.267*** (.359)	−.946*** (.260)	−1.273*** (.259)	−.935*** (.215)	−1.414*** (.257)
Relative Capability Ratio	.330* (.150)	.036 (.245)	.407* (.237)	1.130*** (.273)	1.141*** (.260)	−1.440*** (.330)
Contiguity	1.023*** (.120)	.636*** (.156)	1.587*** (.243)	2.252*** (.366)	.678** (.219)	1.053*** (.172)
Common Interests (S)	−.339* (.167)	.249 (.222)	−1.035*** (.252)	−1.708*** (.439)	−.209 (.247)	−.253 (.214)
Number of Previous MIDs	8.937*** (.437)	††	††	8.205*** (.669)	8.938*** (.542)	9.029*** (.760)
Peace Years	−.077*** (.009)	−.106*** (.014)	−.053 (.050)	−.165 (.254)	−.084*** (.011)	−.072*** (.013)
Peace Years Square	.001*** (.000)	.002*** (.000)	−.002 (.003)	−.004 (.057)	.001*** (.000)	.001*** (.000)
Peace Years Cube	.000*** (.000)	.000*** (.000)	.000 (.000)	.002 (.004)	.000*** (.000)	.000** (.000)
Constant	−4.805*** (.193)	−4.896*** (.237)	−4.941*** (.433)	−5.432*** (.588)	−5.245*** (.275)	−2.683*** (.352)
N	163,616	67,825	63,413	31,319	92,386	71,140
Wald χ^2 (d.f.)	843.91 (21)***	250.09 (19)***	228.10 (19)***	310.40 (16)***	654.19 (20)***	421.38 (20)***

Notes: Robust standard errors adjusted for clustering on the dyad are in parentheses. The reference category for all alliance variables in the model is "No Alliance."
† Perfect predictor of no MID initiation; †† perfect predictor of MID initiation
*** $p < .001$, ** $p < .01$, * $p < .05$ (one-tailed)

Further examinations of each time period provide more interesting findings with respect to the effect of defense pacts. Although defense pacts with minor states show a muting effect in the entire time period, this effect is not consistent across all time periods. Only for the post–Cold War period (1990–2001) do defense pacts with minor states show a decreasing effect on dispute initiation (model 4 in table 2.2). This is also the only period when potential target states' defense pacts with major powers have a decreasing effect on dispute initiation. Hence, defense pacts both with major powers and minor states have a muting effect on dispute initiation in the post–Cold War period.

However, this is the only period when defense pacts have a muting effect on dispute initiation. In the Cold War period, no statistically significant effect of defense pacts is found. More surprisingly, defense pacts with major powers of the target states show an increasing effect of dispute initiation in the period of 1816 to 1945 (model 2 in table 2.2). In other words, a state is more likely to initiate a dispute when its target has a defense pact with major powers compared to when the target has no alliance. These findings could be explained better by the threat perception argument (e.g., Vasquez 1993; Gibler and Vasquez 1998; Gibler 2000; Senese and Vasquez 2008) than the deterrence argument because defense pacts with major powers can heighten threat perceptions and thus invite dispute initiation as the steps-to-war model explains (Vasquez 1993). In short, although these findings should be theoretically explained in more depth, it seems to be clear that the muting effect of defense pacts found in some previous studies (e.g., Leeds 2003) is limited to the post–Cold War period and thus is hard to accept as a general effect of defense pacts.

With respect to temporal discrepancies, the effects of offense pacts show similar trends. The effects of offense pacts are in the opposite direction between the 1816–1945 period and the Cold War period. In the 1816–1945 period, offense pacts with major powers have a positive effect on dispute initiation, which is the same as in the entire time period, but it turns out to have a negative effect during the Cold War period. Neutrality pacts have the same effect as this trend. Neutrality pacts with minor states that are found to have a positive effect on dispute initiation show the same effect only in the Cold War period. This is another example of the temporal discrepancies of the effects.

Alliances affect states differently also depending on the capabilities of the states. The effects of alliances are clearly different between major powers and minor states. Target states' defense pacts (both with major powers and with minor states) have a muting effect, but only for major power challengers. Defense pacts with other major powers also constrain the major power challengers from initiating disputes. However, for minor challenger states, no defense pacts (either defense pacts of minor challengers or defense pacts of target states) show any statistically significant effects at the .05 level. This may be due to major powers being more worried about the possibility of expanding and escalating disputes resulting from a target's defense pacts, especially with other major powers. While no defense pact shows any significant effect (either emboldening or deterring) on dispute initiation by minor states, offense pacts increase the probability of dispute initiation, but only for minor challengers with major power alliances. For minor challengers, offense pacts with other minor states are found to have a negative effect on dispute initiation as opposed to Leeds' expectation (2003). These are clear examples showing that the effects of alliances also depend on who the benefactor and beneficiary of military support are.

Empirical findings from a reexamination of the previous contending findings seem to suggest some important points. More importantly, the muting effect of defense pacts that is found in previous studies (Leeds 2003; Johnson and Leeds 2010) is very limited. The effect is empirically true only for the post–Cold War period and for major power challengers. In other periods and for other states, defense pacts of target states do not show a significant muting effect on dispute initiation. Rather, defense pacts with major powers can heighten threat perceptions and thus increase the probability of dispute initiation against its member states for the time period of 1816 to 1945. Hence, these findings suggest that the deterrence effect argument should be reconsidered or at least applied to limited cases.

Another important point is that the effects of alliances depend not only on provisions but also on states—who the benefactor and beneficiary of military support are. This point suggests that information provided by alliance provisions can be interpreted differently by signatories and other states outside the alliances. Lastly, the effects of alliances on dispute initiation are very different from those in the war onset stage. Only a few types of alliances show significant effects on dispute initiation. In addition, the findings are still complicated and mixed across the time periods much more than in the war onset stage. These unclear findings point out the need for further study of the effect of alliances in this stage.

WHAT DO WE KNOW ABOUT THE RELATIONSHIP BETWEEN ALLIANCES AND CONFLICT?

A great deal of theoretical work and empirical findings has been accumulated in alliance scholarship, and the productive scholarly endeavor seems to lead us to a conclusion with respect to the alliance and war relationship. The most important conclusion we can make based on previous scientific studies, although it is still tentative, is that alliances increase the probability of war rather than prevent war. Despite the realist belief, a growing number of empirical findings and scientific studies have consistently confirmed this positive association between alliances and war. Although alliances may not be a cause of war, having outside alliances is found to be more likely to lead states to war rather than peace (e.g., Moul 1988; Gibler and Vasquez 1998; Leeds 2005b; Senese and Vasquez 2008). Studies suggest the increasing threat perceptions of alliances as the source of this unintended consequence of alliances (Gibler 1997b; Gibler and Vasquez 1998). Also, external alliances become more dangerous when states confront issues with high stakes such as territorial issues or when states have experienced disputes before (Colaresi and Thompson 2005; Senese and Vasquez 2008). In addition, studies with a focus on the role of alliances in crisis bargaining show that alliances increase the probability of escalation of multilateral conflicts that involve more parties resulting from alliances (Leeds 2005b).

However, this increasing effect of alliances does not hold for every time period, and a temporal discrepancy in the effects of alliances has been found (e.g., Sense and Vasquez 2008). In particular, Senese and Vasquez (2008) report that when both sides have outside alliances it increases the probability of war for the 1816–1945 period, but the same type of outside alliances decreases the probability of war for the Cold War period. Senese and Vasquez (2008; see also Vasquez 2009: 379–81) attempt to explain this discrepancy for the Cold War period by utilizing the polarized alliance structure in conjunction with the raised provocation threshold of war by nuclear weapons. The positive effect of outside alliances reappears in the post–Cold War period although it is not the same as in the 1816–1945 period. In short, the decreasing effect of alliances is limited to the Cold War period, and this anomaly can be explained theoretically.

In contrast to the bellicose effects of outside alliances on war between member states and others, alliances have also been shown to decrease the probability of war between member states (e.g., Ray 1990; Bremer 1992; Maoz and Russett 1993). However, this pacifying effect is also different depending on whether there is any outside alliance. This point suggests the importance of specifying the patterns of alliance ties in the dyad in exploring the effects of alliances (e.g., Senese and Vasquez 2008).

As we have seen, the relationship of alliances to war becomes clearer with the accumulated scientific findings. In contrast, the questions regarding the relationship between alliances and dispute initiation are still open. Some studies argue for the increasing effect of alliances on dispute initiation by allied states (e.g., Palmer and Morgan 2006), while others claim that the relationship is affected by the preventive effect of alliances on dispute initiation against allied states (e.g., Krause 2004). In addition, conditional effects of alliances depending on the alliance provisions are also claimed (e.g., Leeds 2003). Empirical findings for these contentions are mixed.

The results of reexamining the previous findings reveal quite interesting effects of alliances on dispute initiation. One major finding of this chapter regards the muting effect of defense pacts on dispute initiation. The muting effect of defense pacts is limited to the post–Cold War period and to disputes initiated by major powers. For other time periods, including the 1816–1989 period and the entire time period of 1816–2001, the muting effect does not exist. Hence, the argument that defense pacts are a good policy option for peace by decreasing dispute initiation would be misleading or at least a premature conclusion.

On the other hand, the encouraging effect of alliances on dispute initiation is also found to be limited to certain conditions. Only offense pacts with major powers show an encouraging effect on dispute initiation by signatory states. Also, only a few alliances are found to have significant effects on dispute initiation. This may be due to the fact that the role of alliances is smaller in states' decisions to initiate disputes than we expect, whereas once a dispute occurs, alliances increase the probability of war significantly. In addition, it should be noted that the findings demonstrate that not all alliances have the effects they are supposed to have according to their provisions. Instead, the effects of alliances on dispute initiation seem to depend more on who will do the supporting and who will receive the support.

Overall, the effects of alliances on dispute initiation are found to be quite different from their effects on war occurrence. While alliances generally increase the probability of war in certain periods, the effects of alliances are very limited in the dispute initiation stage. This difference requires future research to develop a theoretical explanation for why the role of alliances is different in the war occurrence stage and the dispute initiation stage. Scholarly efforts should be made to develop a comprehensive theory explaining the effects in both stages. Theoretical explanations for this point and pursuing empirical investigations will enable us to discover more robust findings.

Another important point provided by this chapter is the need for further studies of temporal discrepancies of the effects of alliances. As we have seen, not only in the war onset stage but also in the dispute initiation stage, temporal discrepancies have been found in the effects of alliances. Despite some attempts to explain temporal anomalies, little theoretical effort has been made to explain these anomalies or inconsistent effects across time periods. These temporal discrepancies should be theoretically explained in order to discover the true relationship between alliances and conflict. One possible answer could be related to the evolution of alliances. Alliances have evolved in many ways. Many large multilateral alliances have emerged since 1945. Alliances have also been more institutionalized, and many multilateral alliances have transformed into more multifunctional international organizations, especially after the Cold War. These changes could affect the functioning of alliances and states' perception of alliances. With these changes, the way states interact with each other through alliances could be changed, and these changes, if any, may affect the relationship of alliances to war. A new theory should be able to explain the different effects across time.

Lastly, it also should be noted that more scholarly efforts need to be made to solve the causality question between alliances and war. While previous alliance literature has improved our understanding of whether alliances increase the probability of war, it is also true that we still have many questions in the entire causal chain of conflict involving alliances that remain unanswered. One example is an endogeneity problem between alliances and conflict (e.g., King, Keohane, and Verba 1994: 198; Smith 1999). Although scholars have responded to this problem in many ways (e.g., Vasquez 1993: 164–65; Smith 1999; Signorino 1999; Senese and Vasquez 2008: 28–31; see also Benson's contribution to this volume), the previous literature has not yet provided a clear answer to this question. This should also be a task for future research in this field of study.

NOTES

1. Some studies of alliance formation maintain that security concerns are not the only purpose of alliances and the motives for states to form alliances vary (e.g., Altfeld 1984; Barnett and Levy 1991; Morrow 1991). Nevertheless, they do not deny that states' security concerns are an important motive in forming alliances.

2. See Levy and Thompson (2010b: ch. 2) for a useful discussion of the relationship between balance of power and the stability of the international system.

3. Smith (1995), however, maintains that the aggregate effect of alliances on war is ambiguous while the deterrence effect of defense pacts is predictable at the dispute initiation stage. That is, a defense pact of a target state decreases the probability of being attacked by a challenger, and this can decrease the probability of the outbreak of war. However, a defense pact also increases the probability that the target will resist an attack, and this can increase the probability of the escalation to war. Hence, Smith argues for focusing on the effect of alliances on states' behavior rather than on the incidence of war.

4. Although Gibler's (1997b) typology of alliances, territorial settlement treaties, is different from the definition of alliances in this study, his finding provides relevant evidence for the relationship between threat perceptions and the effects of alliances.

5. Senese and Vasquez (2008) categorize five different patterns of alliance ties of the dyad and make five mutually exclusive dummy variables. They are (1) allied

to each other, (2) only one side has an outside alliance, (3) both sides have outside alliances, (4) allied to each other and any outside alliances, and (5) no alliance. The category of "no alliance" is used as the reference category of the other alliance categories in their studies (Senese and Vasquez 2008).

6. The United States and South Korea during the Korean War can be a good example of this. According to Pressman (2008), the United States used the alliance to restrain South Korea from disrupting the armistice talks during the Korean War. See Pressman (2008: 29–33) for details.

7. See Leeds, Long, and Mitchell (2000) for a discussion and findings regarding the reliability of alliances.

8. Politically relevant dyads are defined as dyads in which the two states of a dyad are geographically contiguous on land or at least one of the states is a major power state. I generated this data set using the EUGene program (Bennett and Stam 2000).

9. The statistical model of this research is very similar to that of Leeds (2003) with very few exceptions (including the specified alliance variables, the added variable of the number of previous MIDs of the dyad, and the estimation technique).

Chapter Three

Alliances

ATOP Data and Deterrence

Brett V. Benson

The question of the deterrent effect of alliances has long been a subject of debate. Scholars have used various statistical approaches to show both that alliances deter (Siverson and Tennefoss 1984; Leeds 2003) and cause (Gibler and Vasquez 1998; Senese and Vasquez 2008) conflict. The issue was unresolved at the writing of the first edition of *What Do We Know about War?* (Gibler 2000; Maoz 2000). What have we learned since that time? Kang (this volume) thoroughly surveys extant research examining the connection between alliances and conflict, including studies that use both Correlates of War (COW) data and the Alliance Treaty Obligations and Provisions (ATOP) data. In this chapter, I focus on ATOP data. I discuss its contributions and some of its limitations. I then discuss some areas where the design of studies of alliances and conflict should be improved.

The goal of the ATOP project was to fill a gap in existing alliance data by providing detailed information regarding the content of formal alliances from 1816 to 1944 (Leeds et al. 2002). To the extent that researchers can now take a closer look at what particular features of an alliance agreement are more likely to correlate with measures of conflict, ATOP offers a promising platform from which to explore the relationship between alliances and conflict anew. One of the most significant contributions of the ATOP project over Correlates of War Annual Alliance Membership data (Singer and Small 1966; Small and Singer 1969) is a reclassification of alliances into categories more closely resembling the obligations contained in formal alliance agreements. The ATOP project defines alliances as "written agreements, signed by official representatives of at least two independent states, that include promises to aid a partner in the event of military conflict, to remain neutral in the event of conflict, to refrain from military conflict with one another, or to consult/cooperate in the event of international crises that create a potential for military conflict" (Leeds et al. 2002: 3). New categories include offensive pacts, defensive pacts, neutrality pacts, nonaggression pacts, and consultation pacts.

The promise of these data consists in the potential for testing recent theoretical developments in game theoretic research and institutionalist theory (Leeds et al. 2002: 3). Of particular relevance to the question of the deterrent effect of alliances are game theoretic studies showing that defensive types of alliances reduce the likelihood that an alliance member will be attacked (Morrow 1994; Smith 1995, 1998), but offensive types increase the likelihood that an alliance member will attack a targeted state (Smith 1995).

The logic of these two arguments is straightforward. Knowing that an alliance member is likely to fight with allied assistance, a prospective target of an offensive alliance is more likely to capitulate when attacked. Offensive alliance members will, therefore, be emboldened to attack the more acquiescent target. Benson (2011) challenges this argument on grounds that bargaining should make it possible to reach an agreement short of attack, especially for certain types of offensive alliances that specifically include demands targets can concede to so as to avoid being attacked.

Smith's (1995) argument for the effect of defensive alliances asserts that commitments from prospective defenders cause alliance protégés to be more willing to resist attacks by challengers. Consequently, prospective challengers are less likely to attack more resistant targets.

Leeds (2003) finds evidence for these predictions in the ATOP data. She tests the relationship between ATOP categories of offensive, defensive, and neutrality pacts and the initiation of militarized interstate disputes (MIDs) in directed dyads in the years 1816 to 1945. The analysis shows that offensive alliances increase the predicted probability of dispute initiation by .0040, defensive alliances decrease conflict by .0027, and neutrality pacts increase conflict by .0049. The primary contribution of Leeds' study using the novel ATOP categorization scheme is the conclusion that offensive alliances are dangerous and defensive alliances deter. Similar conclusions are reconfirmed in Johnson and Leeds (2010) using ATOP data extended through the year 2000.

Benson (2011) shows that ATOP classifications can be further refined. Findings using traditional categories depend on influential alliances, which consequently mask competing effects within existing categories. He therefore categorizes alliance agreements based on the promises of military support alliance members make. Alliance members agree to deliver some form of military support y once some condition x obtains. The content of the conditions x and the promised transfers of assistance y can vary. Agreements may condition intervention on some action in the history of conflict such as an attack by the adversary, or they may be broad enough to obligate alliance members to provide military assistance in any war involving a fellow signatory. Therefore, one dimension of Benson's typology of alliances is the level of specificity of the conditions in the promise to provide military assistance. If the promise stipulates some action that must be taken before alliance members are obligated to intervene, then the agreement is categorized as a conditional agreement. If signatories are obligated to assist in any war involving an ally, regardless of the actions that led to that war, then the agreement is classified as unconditional.

Conditions of agreements also pertain to the objective of the promise. Some agreements specify that alliance members are only obligated to defend allies' status quo holdings. The objective of this kind of promise is to deter an adversary from challenging the status quo. Other alliance commitments, however, obligate alliance members to assist a fellow signatory militarily even if that ally takes an action to revise the status quo and to benefit at the expense of an adversary. The objective of these promises includes compelling a change to the status quo. Therefore, alliance agreements can be classified as unconditional compellent, conditional compellent, unconditional deterrent, and conditional deterrent.

The terms of the military obligations contained in alliance agreements also vary. Alliance members may promise to assist with all possible means or to do whatever it takes to achieve the objective of the promise. Alternatively, they may specify a precise amount of support to be transferred. Yet, other agreements state that alliance members *may* intervene. Such alliances are called "probabilistic" agreements in Benson's typology.

In addition to dividing alliance agreements, Benson also disaggregates the conflict initiation variable to test more accurately expectations about alliances containing specific promises that activate only when particular types of hostilities have been initiated. Using the new alliance categories and a disaggregated conflict variable, Benson examines the relationship between these types of alliances and conflict between 1816 and 2000.

Benson's analysis finds that leaders rarely form compellent alliances, but when they do, they cause alliance members to initiate violent conflict unless they specify conditions in the alliance that targets can fulfill to avoid violence. That is, unconditional compellent agreements are positively associated with conflict initiation, whereas conditional compellent agreements are not. The reason conditional compellent alliances are not as dangerous as previously thought is because the specification of demands in some such alliances allows disputants to resolve differences through bargaining before military hostilities begin.

Benson also shows that deterrent alliances are not nearly as deterring as the literature using ATOP categories leads us to believe. Deterrence of violent initiations of conflict is limited to conditional deterrent alliances held by minor powers with major power allies. Many deterrent types of commitment exhibit no relationship with conflict initiation, and some deterrent alliances—unconditional deterrent types—are clearly associated with violent conflict. This competing effect among deterrent alliances gets overlooked when using the broad category of ATOP defensive alliance.

In this chapter, I summarize the issues of influence and categorization of alliance categories identified by Benson (2011). Then I address the problem of selection bias to probe the surprising finding that alliances do not appear to have the deterrent effect predicted by theory. In observational studies of alliances, a common problem is that leaders select into alliances for reasons that cause their occurrence in observational data to be distributed nonrandomly. Ideally, we would like to be able to "treat" a given dyad-year observation with an alliance and then compare the likelihood of conflict in the same dyad year with and without the treatment. Of course, this is not possible; in observational data those countries with and without alliances differ. If those differences are systematic, then observed correlations with conflict might result from factors causing states to select into or out of alliances, leading to biased estimation of the true treatment effect. Especially problematic is the strong likelihood that the factors causing states to select into or out of alliances are the same as those influencing leaders' conflict decisions, or even that anticipation of conflict itself affects leaders' decisions to enter an alliance. For example, the steps-to-war approach argues that alliances often form in the midst of or in anticipation of a crisis (Senese and Vasquez 2008).

I use matching methods to address potential problems of selection bias. This approach matches treated and nontreated observations on some relevant characteristics. The advantage of using data matched on observable characteristics is that it is possible to attribute differences in conflict behavior between treated and nontreated groups to the alliance and not to some observable confounding factor. I show that selection bias is dramatic in alliances designed to deter conflict initiation. After matching observations based on similarities in common determinants of conflict, I estimate the effect of conditional deterrent alliances on MID initiation. The deterrent effects, which are predicted by Smith (1995) but are nonexistent or underwhelming in the empirical models, are substantiated in the matched sample. Clearly, selection effects lead to biased estimates, and conditional deterrent alliances have the marginal effect of reducing MID initiation when some selection bias is eliminated.

In the next section, I review the issues of influential observations and categorization of alliance commitments. Then, in the following section, I address the matter of selection bias. In the final section, I provide some concluding thoughts about "what we know" about the relationship between alliances and conflict.

INFLUENTIAL OBSERVATIONS AND
CATEGORIZING ALLIANCE COMMITMENTS

A logistic estimation of MID initiation using standard control variables[1] and ATOP offensive and defensive alliance categories from 1816 to 2000 shows that ATOP offensive pacts are positively associated with conflict and defensive alliances are negatively associated. Model 1 in table 3.1 presents the results of the model, which appears in Benson (2011).[2] Note, however, that the finding on defensive alliances is *not* significant in this longer time period.[3] If we estimate the model on data prior to 1911 (model 2), we see that defensive alliances become significantly associated with conflict, but offensive alliances are not significant in this time period. Yet, when the ATOP data is cut so that the time period from 1910 to 2000 is analyzed (model 3), offensive alliances have a significant positive relationship with MID initiation, but defensive alliances are not significant.

The relationship between the ATOP categories and conflict appears to be sensitive to cuts in the temporal domain. Upon closer evaluation, World War II is an especially critical cut point for ATOP defensive alliances. Defensive alliances formed during World War II and after World War II have different effects on MID initiation than those formed prior to that time.

Why are the findings sensitive to cuts in the temporal domain? Benson (2011) and (Gibler and Wolford 2006) both show that the directed-dyad–year design leads to a handful of alliance agreements, particularly post–World War II alliances such as NATO, OAS, and the Warsaw Pact, comprising a disproportionate number of directed-dyad observations. This problem is not limited to the post-1945 period. According to Benson (2011), the 1856 offensive agreement signed by Austria, France, and Britain at the conclusion of the Crimean War, which targets every state in the system, results in 2,492 of the 8,648 observations of offensive alliances in the 1816–1944 ATOP data and 26 of the 178 initiations of conflict by states holding offensive agreements. Similarly, the Pact of Steel between Germany and Italy in 1939, which also targets all states in the system, results in 551 of the 8,648 observations of offensive alliances and 58 of the 178 observations of conflict initiation by a state holding an offensive agreement. Finally, the offensive agreement signed by Britain with Turkey and France in 1939 results in Britain having 339 observations, accounting for 22 of the 178 observations of conflict initiation by states holding an offensive agreement. These three agreements therefore comprise 3,382 of the 8,648 observations of offensive alliances in directed dyads prior to 1945, as well as 106 of the 178 observations of conflict initiation by states holding valid offensive commitments against the target of aggression prior to 1945.

Table 3.1. Logit Regression of the Initiation of Militarized Disputes, ATOP and Benson (2011) Data

	Model 1 1816–2000: ATOP Categories	Model 2 1816–1910: ATOP Categories	Model 3 1910–2000: ATOP Categories	Model 4 1816–2000: Benson (2011) Data
Joint Democracy	−0.683** (0.134)	0.496 (0.329)	−0.848** (0.146)	−0.661** (0.134)
Contiguity	1.490** (0.109)	0.853** (0.194)	1.755** (0.118)	1.487** (0.108)
Capabilities Ratio	0.960** (0.138)	1.424** (0.275)	0.857** (0.147)	1.014** (0.136)
S-score	−0.661** (0.123)	−0.457* (0.174)	−0.962** (0.136)	−0.764** (0.117)
Offensive Alliance	0.800** (0.102)	0.263 (0.195)	1.120** (0.113)	
Defensive Alliance	−0.073 (0.073)	−1.495** (0.223)	−0.082 (0.082)	
Unconditional Compellent				1.285** (0.122)
Conditional Compellent				0.316 (0.301)
Unconditional Deterrent				0.228* (0.109)
Conditional Deterrent				−0.184* (0.078)
Probabilistic Deterrent				−0.036 (0.101)
Constant	−3.759** (0.101)	−4.128** (0.189)	−3.570** (0.117)	−3.684** (0.098)
N	172,196	42,234	130,670	172,196

Notes: Standard errors in parentheses. Peaceyears suppressed.
*p < 0.05, **p < 0.01

The staggering influence of these agreements raises two problems for estimating the relationship between alliances and conflict. First, an agreement targeting every state in the system dramatically proliferates the number of directed-dyad–year observations associated with that alliance. If an agreement does not specify a target, it gets coded as targeting every state in the system. Consequently, minor coding errors can result in significant swings in statistical findings. Moreover, even if an alliance does not target a particular state, few agreements are truly designed to activate military obligations for every conceivable conflict arising between a signatory and any potential adversary for the life of the alliance. Suppose, for example, two prospective allies form a public alliance targeting another state, the identity of which is implicitly known to all relevant leaders. If signatories find it unnecessary to specify the targeted state in the alliance, then that alliance will be coded as targeting every state in the system, which can result in thousands of irrelevant dyad-year observations being flagged for having that alliance present. Consequently, the alliance gets credited for any conflict between a signatory and any other state while that alliance is in force, even if signatories agree that the alliance does not apply to those conflicts. Another possibility is that the alliance is associated with conflicts with the targeted state but there are no conflicts between signatories and other states miscoded as being targeted by the alliance. The statistical implication would be that the actual effect on conflict is washed away by thousands of nonconflict observations. The net effect of miscoding the targets of alliances in the directed-dyad–year design is a dramatic exaggeration of minor errors.

The second problem with influential observations is the severe consequence of disagreements in the appropriate categorization of an influential alliance. For example, compare the alliance signed at the conclusion of the Crimean War to the Pact of Steel. As Benson (2011) shows, both are coded as ATOP offensive, but only the Pact of Steel actually has an offensive objective. The post–Crimean War alliance is clearly a defensive agreement designed to enforce the terms of the Treaty of Paris. The commitment does not obligate signatories to support one another if a fellow member initiates revisionist conflict. Miscategorizing such an influential alliance results in a shift in an overwhelming number of observations from one alliance category to another.

Benson (2011) shows that the observed statistical relationship between ATOP categories and conflict is mostly driven by such influential alliances, particularly those during World War II. He uses a Cook's distance diagnostic test to measure the amount of influence a dyad exerts on the inferences from the model estimation. Cook's D (Cook 1977) is a test that combines information on residuals and leverage to measure the influence of each observation on the overall estimation of the coefficients. If the regression coefficients are sensitive to the elimination of the most influential observations (as determined by a recommended threshold), then those observations exert a disproportionate amount of influence on the fitted values, and the model or data should be reexamined to determine whether adjustments can be made to estimate a better fit of the data.

Benson (2011) finds that in Leeds' (2003) 1816–1944 sample, the finding for offensive alliances is especially sensitive to very few influential observations, a significant percentage of which occur during World War II. ATOP defensive alliances performed better in the Cook's D test. Outlying observations were not nearly so influential on the defensive alliance coefficient during the years 1816 to 1944. This is unsurprising given that model 2 demonstrates that defensive alliances perform best in the earlier half of the 1816–2000 data set. The reason is largely due to the fact that fewer defensive alliances were signed before World War II. Approximately 64 percent of defensive alliances were formed in the 61 years between 1939 and 2000, compared to 35 percent signed in the 124 years prior to 1939. After the onset of World War II, the structure of many deterrent types of alliance changed to allow preemptive defense, which alliances Benson (2011) classifies as unconditional deterrent. Prior to World War II, such alliances comprised 22 percent of all deterrent types of alliances and only 6 percent of the dyads in which targets held a deterrent alliance of any kind. After the start of World War II, the percentage of such alliances rose to account for 25 percent of the growing number of deterrent alliances. More significantly, unconditional deterrent agreements exploded from 860 dyad-year observations before 1939 to 11,982 afterward. Such alliances included several post–World War II Soviet alliances threatening to preempt Germany and Japan if either power threatened or challenged an alliance member. They also included 11 agreements signed during World War II that accounted for a sizeable 59 MIDs in 1,115 observations. These alliances, which contain different commitment mechanisms than other deterrent types of alliances, took on a more significant role in World War II and the Cold War period.

The influence of outlying observations naturally leads to the question of whether ATOP categories are too broad. Benson's (2011) new typology sorts alliances into finer categories according to the conditions triggering the alliance commitment. These include whether the agreement specifies an action by the adversary that will activate alliance members' military obligations and whether the alliance agreement is intended to deter or compel changes in the status quo. Table 3.2 reproduces Benson's classification of commitment conditions in alliance agreements. Another dimension in the typology sorts alliances according to whether alliance members promise to intervene with

Table 3.2. Conditions for Rendering Military Assistance by Alliance Category

		Conditions for Committing Assistance	
		None	Specific
Objective of Alliance	Compellence	Unconditional Compellent	Conditional Compellent
	Deterrence	Unconditional Deterrent	Conditional Deterrent

certainty or probabilistically once the conditions activating the alliance have been met. The categories of commitments in the typology include unconditional compellent, conditional compellent, conditional deterrent, unconditional deterrent, and probabilistic deterrent.

Unconditional compellent alliances are commitments between partners to assist one another regardless of the conditions giving rise to conflict. The classical example is the 1939 Pact of Steel between Germany and Italy. Conditional compellent alliances obligate partners to support one another in conflicts including those waged for the offensive purpose of changing the status quo in favor of one of the alliance members. Such agreements formalize specific demands targets can accede to in order to avoid being attacked by alliance members. An example is the 1832 agreement between the United Kingdom and France threatening offensive action unless the Netherlands made specific concessions. Few alliances were coded as only offensive in the ATOP data, and these were divided about evenly between unconditional and conditional compellent categories in Benson's (2011) typology.

On the deterrent side, unconditional deterrent alliances are commitments to assist alliance members militarily under the implied condition that alliance partners *not* force an offensive change in the status quo. Such alliances promise support for all defensive objectives including preemptive defense. Most of these alliances were coded as both ATOP offensive and defensive. However, twenty-two agreements having the same commitment mechanism were coded as only ATOP defensive. Spreading observations of the same type of commitment across different categories makes it difficult to isolate the effect of that type of commitment. Additionally, it can exaggerate, contradict, or wash away correlations of the actual category in which some of the observations are misplaced. Since such commitments are more likely than other deterrent types of commitments to be associated with conflict (Benson 2011), the implication for not isolating them in ATOP data is that their effect is watered down. This leads to the blanket conclusion that all types of alliances designed to deter conflict are functionally equivalent. When isolated in an independent category, however, unconditional deterrent alliances on the target side of the dyad are positively associated with conflict (model 4). In fact, such alliances held by major powers actually may *attract* violent initiations of conflict.

The category of conditional deterrent alliances obligates alliance partners to defend each other as long as fellow members do not force an offensive change in the status quo *and* a target of the alliance attacks an alliance partner. An example is the 1961 USSR–North Korea alliance, which commits each to defend the other in the event that one is attacked. This is the most prevalent type of deterrent alliance and most closely corresponds to the deterrent commitment analyzed by Smith (1995).

The final type of alliance in Benson's (2011) typology is the category classified as probabilistic deterrent. Such alliances create uncertainty about whether alliance members will provide assistance when war occurs. An example is the 1953 US alliance with the Republic of China, which is ambiguous with respect to the defense of some territories and allows the United States to escape its obligations should it decide, according to its "constitutional processes," not to intervene once conflict has broken out.

Benson (2011) estimates a model using these categories and compares the results and fitness of this model to other models designed to test alternative conceptions of alliances in international relations. The basic results of the typology, reproduced here in table 3.1, model 4, show that unconditional compellent alliances are positively associated with conflict, but conditional compellent alliances have no statistically significant relationship. Conditional deterrent alliances deter conflict, but this relationship is weaker than expected. Overall, such alliances are associated with an 18 percent decrease in the likelihood that a third party will initiate a conflict with an alliance member. Unconditional deterrent alliances can lead to conflict, and probabilistic deterrent alliances have no impact. Additional analysis in Benson's study shows that deterrence of *violent* conflict is limited to conditional deterrent alliances with a major power, and unconditional deterrent types are clearly associated with violent conflict when the holders of such commitments are major powers or revisionist.

Benson's (2011) approach to categorizing and analyzing alliances depicts a more nuanced explanation for how commitment mechanisms formalized in alliance agreements are related to conflict. Altogether, it disentangles some competing effects obscured by the ATOP categories and reveals that many alliances traditionally regarded as offensive may not be as dangerous as once thought. At least they do not cause alliance members to initiate militarized initiations of conflict (MIDs). On the other hand, the analysis paints a surprisingly grim picture of the deterrent effects of alliances. In the next section, I further investigate deterrent alliances, paying particular attention to the possibility that selection bias leads to the inference that alliances designed to deter fall short of their objective.

SELECTION BIAS AND MATCHING

This section addresses the problem of selection bias in estimating the effects of alliances on conflict. In particular, it is puzzling that Benson (2011) finds only weak deterrent effects for conditional deterrent alliances, which are the type of alliance commitment that Smith's (1995) model of alliances predicts will deter adversaries from initiating conflict against an alliance protégé. This gap between theory and the data leads us to ask why such alliance mechanisms do not appear to achieve their objective.

A possible explanation is that leaders systematically select into alliance agreements for reasons that bias the results. Statistical models of alliance and conflict treat alliance types as if they are randomly distributed exogenous variables. If leaders were, in fact, randomly assigned to defensive and offensive alliances, then our models would give us unbiased estimates of the causal relationship between these alliance categories and conflict. We might then be reasonably confident in inferences from our models.

However, unidentified but observable confounders might cause selection bias. Even more problematic for estimating a model of the effects of alliances is the possibility that the expectation of conflict itself likely affects leaders' decisions to join different types of alliances. In principle, instrumentation with a correlate of alliances will resolve such problems for causal inference, but most factors correlated with military alliances are also correlated with conflict. Consequently, my goal is not to eliminate endogeneity bias from the analysis. Instead, I will account for some selection effects related to factors that are also determinants of conflict.

Why might leaders select into different types of alliances? Leaders may form alliances that do not impose conditions on when alliance members may initiate when they anticipate that a common adversary is already likely to begin a conflict and the prospective alliance members wish to engage preemptively together. In this case, allies expect war to occur anyway, *regardless of an alliance agreement,* and the alliance serves as a coordination mechanism for allies intending to respond to their shared expectation. Similarly, leaders may also choose to join a compellent type of alliance if they believe a prospective ally is about to attack an adversary *even in the absence of the agreement* and they wish to be part of the victorious alliance.

Factors relating to conflict may also affect deterrent alliances. Prospective defenders may avoid defensive agreements when they anticipate that a conflict involving their prospective ally is imminent and they perceive the likelihood of losing as high. For example, leaders may choose to avoid binding themselves to the defense of another state when it is unclear who would win if that state and its adversary fought a war. On the other hand, if there is no uncertainty about how a state's assistance will impact the outcome of a war, then factors increasing the likelihood of conflict, such as contiguity, may cause leaders to form alliances to deter adversaries from taking hostile action. Consequently, some defensive agreements are signed when the states in question anticipate that future conflict is unlikely *even in the absence of the agreement,* or that conflict is likely but the chance of winning is high *only with an agreement.*

It is not clear what impact these selection effects have on the relationship between alliances and conflict. That factors related to conflict cause different alliances to be formed is a problem that has implications both for theoretical expectations and empirical testing. Regressions can only determine causality if the "treatment" of interest can be considered to be exogenous to the behavior of interest. Yet, in the case of alliances and conflict, determinants of conflict may be an assignment mechanism for selection into an alliance. Without some exogenous variation, the effect of alliances on conflict cannot be identified, and we cannot resolve whether alliances cause conflict or some other aspect affects both alliances and conflict participation (Signorino 1999; Smith 1999; Signorino and Yilmaz 2003). Ignoring endogeneity and selection problems by failing to account for strategic factors can lead to a misattribution of causality and identify a spurious empirical correlation between alliances and conflict even when alliances are disaggregated into offensive, defensive, and neutrality categories.

Below, I use matching methods to account for selection bias in the observational data. Matching was designed for situations of nonrandom treatment assignment in which a method cannot establish an experimental control.

In such instances, biased estimates are likely to result when comparing the treatment and nontreatment groups (Rubin 1979; Dehejia and Wahba 2002; Ho et al. 2007). It is likely that countries in different types of alliances bear systematic characteristics dissimilar to nonallied countries. Using a standard logistic method, we cannot rule out the possibility that any observed effect in the estimation results from the dissimilarities and not the alliance itself. Matching minimizes selection bias by limiting comparisons to observations manifesting similarities of all relevant observed characteristics except the presence or absence of the type of alliance being tested. This approach has been used in recent studies of international relations. Nielsen et al. (2011) use matching methods to estimate the effects of aid shocks on conflict, and Mattes and Vonnamhe (2010) use matching to analyze the relationship between nonaggression pacts and conflict.

I begin by estimating propensity scores measuring the estimated probability that a given country will hold the alliance type in question in a politically relevant dyad year. Propensity scores are estimated based upon observed characteristics affecting selection into the alliance. We might expect that some factors influencing states' decisions to form and remain in an alliance are the same factors that lead those states to become involved in conflict. Consequently, I match politically relevant observations on conventional determinants of conflict already used in alliance-conflict models (Leeds 2003; Benson 2011). Additionally, it has been observed that alliances exhibit different effects on conflict at different times (Benson 2011; Kang this volume), raising the possibility that temporal trends create systematic differences in allied and nonallied countries. Consequently, I also condition matching on a measure of time, in case patterns in alliance formation are contingent on temporal trends. Therefore, the variables I use for estimating propensity scores for different alliance categories are joint democracy, contiguity, s-scores, and capabilities ratio. The operationalization for these variables is the same as the control variables in models 1 through 4 in table 3.1. I also include a variable measuring consecutive five-year time intervals.

To estimate propensity scores, I analyze logistic models of leaders' selection into conditional deterrent alliances. The model estimates the likelihood that the matching variables are associated with the presence of a conditional deterrent alliance on the target side of a directed-dyad–year observation. Unsurprisingly, joint democracy and contiguity between the dyad initiator and target increase the likelihood that the target will hold a conditional deterrent alliance targeting the prospective initiator. Also, looking at the variable for five-year intervals, it appears that the propensity for conditional deterrent alliances to form increases over time. On the other hand, similarity of foreign policy preferences as measured by s-scores between the dyad

Brett V. Benson

initiator and target decreases the likelihood that the target will hold a conditional deterrent alliance.

I then create a matched data set consisting of a subset of observations matched according to similar propensity scores. I use caliper matching within a prespecified caliper range without replacement.[4] This approach balances the frequency of treated and untreated directed-dyad–year observations in the data. It also significantly reduces the sample size. The matched sample for offensive alliances includes 84,640 dyad-year observations instead of 172,161 in the unmatched sample.

Matching minimizes selection bias for conditional deterrent alliances. Figure 3.1 shows a comparison between the propensity of a conditional deterrent alliance in matched and unmatched data. In other words, it represents the estimated probability that a prospective initiator in a directed dyad year will hold a conditional deterrent alliance. The goal in matching is to achieve bal-

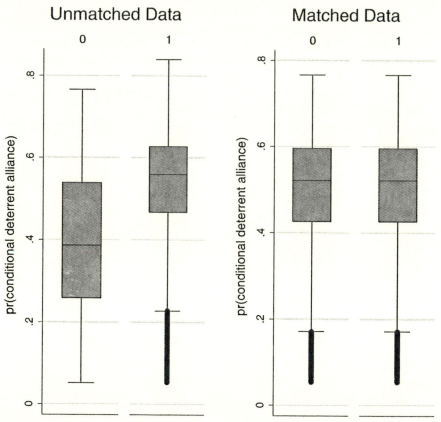

Figure 3.1. Propensity of Selection into Conditional Deterrent Alliance, Matched and Unmatched Data

ance between treated and untreated observations. As is clearly evident from the first panel in figure 3.1, conditional deterrent alliances are not balanced in unmatched data. This means that the probability of an observation being assigned to the treatment group (conditional deterrent alliance) is systematically different from its probability of being assigned to the control group (no conditional deterrent alliance). This confirms the nonrandom distribution and selection bias of conditional deterrent alliance agreements. After matching on common propensity scores, the propensity for the alliance type in question is significantly more balanced, suggesting that treated and untreated observations are similar on the observed characteristics driving selection (joint democracy, s-scores, capabilities ratio, contiguity, and time period) and only differ as to whether or not the relevant dyad state has the alliance in question.

With a balanced sample for each alliance type, it is now possible to estimate the effects of the treatment on the likelihood of an MID initiation in the dyad year. I analyze a logistic regression using the matched sample. Model 5 in table 3.3 presents the estimation of conditional deterrent alliances on matched data. It is immediately obvious that the coefficient on the treatment variable is greater than the same variable in the unmatched data (model 4 in table 3.1). Once the selection bias leading to the formation of a conditional deterrent alliance is accounted for, the likelihood of such alliances deterring an MID initiation increases. The predicted probability of a dyad initiator initiating an MID against a target holding a conditional deterrent alliance decreases from .0059 to .0044. This is a 26 percent decrease of the predicted probability of conflict (compared to an 18 percent decrease in the unmatched data). After accounting for selection effects, it appears that conditional deterrent alliances have a more substantial

Table 3.3. Logit Regression of the Initiation of Militarized Disputes, Matched Data

| | Model 5 Matched Data: Selection into Conditional Deterrent Alliance | |
	Logit	Marginal Effects
Joint Democracy	−0.768** (0.162)	−0.0036
Contiguity	1.493** (0.141)	0.0141
Capabilities Ratio	1.017** (0.180)	0.0060
S-score	−0.501** (0.161)	−0.0029
Conditional Deterrent	−0.256** (0.097)	−0.0015
Constant	−3.714** (0.123)	
Predicted Probability		0.0059
N	84,640	84,640

Notes: Standard errors in parentheses. Peaceyears suppressed.
**$p < 0.01$

deterrent impact on the likelihood that a prospective dyad initiator will initiate
conflict against a target holding such an alliance.

CONCLUSION

What do we know about the deterrent effects of alliances since the introduction of ATOP data? Foremost, the ATOP project is a major contribution in
providing previously unavailable detailed information about the content of
formal military alliances. The first cut at categorizing alliance types based
on this information found that offensive alliances are dangerous and defensive alliances deter. Ultimately, however, these findings do not hold because
influential outliers mask underlying competing effects within categories. Re-
categorization of alliance agreements according to the terms of the promises
contained in the agreements leads to a more nuanced explanation of the relationship. While some compellent alliances are associated with conflict, others
are not. In Benson (2011), unconditional compellent alliances are associated
with a 249 percent increase in the likelihood that holders of such alliances
will initiate conflict.

Additionally, not all deterrent alliances deter. In fact, major powers holding unconditional deterrent alliances may attract initiations of conflict, while
minor powers holding conditional deterrent alliances with major powers are
the most likely to experience the deterrence benefits of the alliance. Finding
that different types of deterrent alliances with major powers have different associations with conflict may reconcile inconsistent positions in the literature
that major power alliances both deter (Siverson and Tennefoss 1984) and lead
to crisis escalation (Senese and Vasquez 2008).

Even so, the deterrent effect of conditional deterrent alliances in Benson
(2011) is weak, with only an 18 percent decrease in the predicted probability of conflict. This finding is puzzling given that theory predicts that, all
else equal, commitments resembling conditional deterrent alliances should
deter conflicts against states holding such alliances. Selection effects that
cause systematic differences between states party to a conditional deterrent
alliance and those who are not members account for some of the distortion.
After matching treated and untreated observations based on factors related to
conflict, a clearer deterrent effect emerges. Conditional deterrent alliances are
more likely to deter challenges to those that hold them compared to the counterfactual in which the targeted state holds no alliance at all. Observations of
conditional deterrent alliances are not balanced in the unmatched data, leading to the conclusion that states often select into alliance because of factors

related to conflict. After accounting for this selection bias, the probability of deterrence increases by a nontrivial amount in the matched data.

A word of caution is in order about endogeneity bias. The matching analysis conducted here minimizes selection bias only for the observed factors included in the analysis. Even after carefully operationalizing alliance categories to map cleanly onto theory and then matching to account for selection bias based on observable variables that both lead to conflict and alliance formation, an unobservable confounding factor may still cause the observed correlations. Such a factor might include leaders' expectations about the likelihood of conflict. Indeed, it is entirely plausible that leaders who anticipate attacking or being attacked will be more likely to seek out and form unconditional compellent alliances. If so, estimates will be biased by endogeneity problems irresolvable by matching analysis. To specify a model to disentangle these relationships and give us confidence about causal inference, we need theoretical developments of alliance formation to guide empiricists as to how these factors interact. Additionally, it will be useful to identify valid instrumental variables for alliance formation unrelated to conflict.

Finally, research on alliances raises additional questions about the appropriateness of the directed-dyad–year design for studying these problems. Benson (2011) and Gibler and Wolford (2006) show how minor coding errors or disagreements can result in dramatic shifts in the numbers of observations associated with individual agreements, which leads to exaggerated effects in model estimation. In addition, strategic interactions involving alliances are not dyadic. A bilateral alliance targeting only one state involves a three-party strategic interaction. Multilateral alliances and those targeting more than one state involve even more players. Poast (2010) uses Monte Carlo simulations to show that using *dy*adic data to analyze *k*-adic interactions leads to inference problems. Yet, addressing the limitations of directed-dyad–year design by creating a triadic (or larger) design would result in massive data sets, create computational problems, and dramatically exacerbate the problems of exaggerated inferences discussed above. Poast suggests some possible approaches, including recommendations for minimizing computational limitations and coding variables in *k*-adic format. This is an area that requires more work and will benefit from improved theories of alliance formation to understand how *k*-adic tests of alliance formation and conflict should be designed.

In this chapter, I have discussed how the ATOP project and research using ATOP data have focused our attention on the importance of the content of alliances. I have also summarized existing work that improves categorization of alliances and reduces problems of influence. Recent attention to the content of alliances is a positive step forward, and additional research hurdles now demand attention. I have shown that even with improved measures of alliance content, selection bias nevertheless blurs inferences about the relationship between alliances and conflict. I have also highlighted some problems with the directed-dyad–year design, which have been identified by scholars. Further research dedicated to resolving selection and endogeneity bias as well as problems associated with matching the strategic interaction in alliance formation and conflict escalation to an appropriate data platform will move the study of alliances and conflict forward.

NOTES

1. Explanatory variables come from the EUGene package data sets (Bennett and Stam 2000). A dyad is jointly democratic if both members score greater than six on the Polity IV scale, and contiguous if they share a land or river border or are separated by fewer than twenty-five miles of water. These results are unaffected by different measures of contiguity. *S-scores* (Signorino and Ritter 1999), which measure the similarity of states' foreign policy positions based on their alliance portfolios, and *capabilities ratio* are also included as controls.

2. Models 1 through 3 use replication data of ATOP categories. Model 1 reproduces a model on the replication data extended through 2000 found in Benson (2011). Models 2 and 3 estimate new models based upon cuts in the temporal domain. Model 4 reproduces a model estimating the effects of Benson's (2011) typology.

3. A similar analysis of available replication data of Johnson and Leeds (2010) using the same logistic estimation method and controls as Leeds (2003) and Benson (2011) reveals that ATOP defensive agreements lose significance in the extended time period, and the coefficient gets very small.

4. I use a caliper value of 0.00001. Deterrence findings consistently result with varying caliper values. The predicted probability of deterrence increases with more restrictive (smaller) caliper values, which result in a smaller matched sample.

Chapter Four

Becoming Rivals

The Process of Rivalry Development

Brandon Valeriano

The recent understanding that the path to peace can be found through the elimination of persistent historical animosity in the form of rivalry (Vasquez 1993; Diehl and Goertz 2000; Thompson 2001) is an important step for the conflict studies field. Rivalries are a fundamental aspect of all conflictual interactions. The context of events is important. Ignoring rivalry and history has been a central flaw of the field of international relations. By understanding the historic and diplomatic factors behind the emergence of rivalry, the strategies employed by states to deal with potential threats, and the issues critical to long-standing enemies, we can attempt to find solutions to the scourge of institutional violence.

This chapter will explain the process through which states develop into rivals so that in the future we can predict and prevent rivalries from occurring in the first place. Intervention can only occur once the causes of the problem are understood. The goal here is to scientifically explain the process of becoming rivals.

Rivalry is simply a situation of long-standing, historical animosity between two entities with a high probability of serious conflict or crisis (see Diehl and Goertz herein). During rivalry, relative positions matter, and rivals will fight about anything and everything. A simple question needs to be answered about interstate rivalry: if states engaged in a rivalry can account for the majority of wars and disputes (Diehl and Goertz 2000; Thompson 2001) that have occurred since 1815, why have scholars failed to explain the beginnings of this important event? Research has uncovered little about why and how pairs of states become rivals.

The recent increase in the quantitative study of rivalry has largely identified who the rivals are (Diehl and Goertz 2000; Thompson 2001; Hewitt 2005), but not how such rivalries form and escalate. Questions about the development of rivalry are important if we are to understand the nature of conflictual interactions and seek to eliminate war from the system.

This chapter will proceed by briefly reviewing what a rivalry is and why the topic is so critical for studies of war and peace. I will then review findings in our discipline that seek to uncover how rivalries develop in the first place. The chapter will wrap up with a proposed theory to explain rivalry development and an empirical test of the theory.

WHAT IS RIVALRY?

The utilization of international rivalry as a concept has allowed the field of international politics to reconceptualize how the discipline studies conflict. In the past, the field concentrated on international war as the factor in need of explanation. If the rivalry situation accounts for over three-fourths of wars in the first place, the study of conflict and international politics should be orientated toward preventing and managing the most severe forms of rivalry before escalation to war takes place.

Rivalries are typically identified as some form of repeated, long-standing crisis or protracted conflict. Rivalries involve competition and struggle between two or more actors over some stake or issue that may change and vary from incident to incident. Some states are actually "addicted" to conflict with other states (Maoz 2004). The image of another state as an enemy endures in the relations between the states and in the minds of their elites and mass public.

Denying gains to a rival is a central theme in rivalry. Rivalry assumes a zero-sum game where one side seeks to ensure its own security through the destruction or immobilization of another state. Zizzo and Oswald (2001) performed an experiment in which their subjects could reduce other players' monetary payoffs, but only if they gave up some of their money first. They found that despite the assumption of self-interest, people put in this situation were willing to burn themselves rather than provide a gain for a rival. Two-thirds of the test subjects burned their opposing side even though it would be costly in terms of personal gains to do so. A similar dynamic works in rivalry situations. Rather than focusing on a narrow self-interest, states engaged in a rivalry are much more willing to go out of their way to deny a benefit to an enemy even if that means they harm their own security or personal well-being. Some rivals seek to wipe the other off the face of the earth, while most simply wish to deny any gains to their rival. Either way, rivalry produces a destructive relationship that only distracts the state from more pressing problems.

Rivalry simply means distrust, with some expectation of future violence. As Colaresi et al. (2007: 12) note, during a rivalry, each side exaggerates hostile actions and downplays the sincerity of cooperative actions. As a concept, rivalry is simply meant to denote a perpetual hostile relationship. It captures relationships characterized by selfishness, relative positions, mistrust, hostility, and animosity. Empirically, Diehl and Goertz (2000) define and operationalize rivalries as repeated conflicts with a certain degree of competitiveness and connection of issues. Competitiveness suggests that there is a consistent and conflictual relationship between the two parties with some expectation of future conflict. For rivalries to be observed, there must be some degree of serious competition. A connection of issues is also important for Diehl and Goertz (2000), since rivalry for them is not an isolated incident of conflict but should have linkages between disputes throughout the relationship.

In coding rivalries, a militarized interstate dispute (MID) is used to operationalize the competitiveness requirement.[1] Diehl and Goertz (2000: 44–46) operationalize an enduring rivalry as those pairs of states with six MIDs within a period of twenty years. Protorivalries are those dyads that have up to five MIDs but fail to reach the enduring rivalry requirement in a twenty-year period. Isolated conflicts, on the other hand, are those conflicts between dyads that involve one or two disputes and do not escalate to the proto- or enduring rivalry stage. The updated data set (Klein, Goertz, and Diehl 2006) covers the 1816–2001 period and does not consider isolated conflicts as rivals since these are not dyadic rivalries but short confrontations. Other changes include a more specific selection of who the rivals are. While the competitiveness rules have not changed drastically, now the Klein et al. (2006) data set eliminates those dyads in which there was no clear contact between the disputing parties as well as those dyads that were coded as fighting but actually left or entered the dispute before the other party did. They also eliminated disputes if the conflict had nothing to do with the overall rivalry context. The final data set includes 915 cases of isolated contact and 290 rivals. "Of the 290 cases of rivalry, 115 are enduring and 175 are proto-rivalries under the previous coding criteria" (Klein et al. 2006: 340).

Defining rivalry by the number of MIDs within a dyad may limit the ability of the operational definition to capture the true meaning of rivalry and to account for all cases. For that reason, William Thompson and a group of other scholars have developed an alternative method of coding rivalries. Thompson and coauthors believe that for a rivalry to be active, each side must regard the other as competitors, be the source of actual or latent threats, and recognize each other as enemies (Colaresi et al. 2008: 25). Using historical research, Thompson (2001) identifies a population of dyads (173 rivals from 1816 to

1999) that are strategic rivalries. The two differing methods of coding rivalry should not be in competition but should reinforce the idea that rivalry is an important empirical concept and should allow scholars to test their theories according to the data set that meets their needs.

WHAT DO WE KNOW ABOUT RIVALRY DEVELOPMENT?

The literature on interstate rivalry has only begun to identify factors leading a pair of states to initiate or develop into a rivalry. We therefore know little about how rivalries actually come about. Most factors that are said to account for the onset of rivalry are either events that induce the situation right away or events that accumulate to ultimately produce the outcome of rivalry.

Diehl and Goertz (2000) theorize that a political shock is a "virtual necessary" condition for the initiation and termination of a rivalry. A political shock is a traumatic event that occurs either in the international system (e.g., world wars, changes in power distribution, or periods of territory shifts) or at the internal-domestic level of politics (e.g., regime change or civil war). In an empirical analysis, Diehl and Goertz (2000) find a political shock to be associated with rivalry initiation 95 percent of the time (sixty out of sixty-three cases) for enduring rivalries. They theorize that a political shock allows a "window of opportunity" for rivalry initiation.

Colaresi (2001) looks at global war as a political shock that might bring about rivalry using a population of Thompson's (2001) strategic rivals. He finds that a war shock only leads to the termination of rivalry, not the initiation. It does seem clear that most rivalries begin at state birth (Colaresi et al. 2008: 84), which is a form of political shock.

Rivalries typically evolve or experience a trend of increasing conflict throughout their life. Hensel's (1999) escalating evolutionary approach to rivalries holds that rivalries are likely to advance and become "enduring" if the outcome of the first dispute is not resolved to both states' mutual satisfaction. Leng (1983, 2000) makes a similar point through many case study examinations. The evolutionary approach also holds that high levels of severe conflict (war) early in the life of a rivalry make confrontations in the future less likely yet still push the states to lock into rivalry early. In essence, choosing not to respond to a militarized dispute with the use of force diminishes the probability of future disputes (Hensel and Diehl 1994) and rivalry.

Dissatisfaction is likely to play a large role in rivalry relationships. Maoz and Mor (2002) find that dissatisfaction with the status quo and equality of capabilities are factors that influence the continuation of a rivalry. Rivalries will endure as long as neither side has the ability to demonstrably change the relationship and both sides are dissatisfied with the outcome of past disputes. Hensel's (1996) notion of evolutionary learning during a rivalry likely explains much of why dissatisfaction tends to fester. Suspicion, hostility, and grievances only grow through time, making it more likely that a rivalry will lock in and endure. Dissatisfaction also plays a part in the analysis conducted by Goertz, Jones, and Diehl (2005), which finds that stalemate outcomes early during a rivalry push the dyads to endure as enemies (see also Hensel 1996). These facts might lead us to conclude that how disputes are handled early in the life of a rivalry matters most.

One cannot forget the importance of domestic politics in the analysis of rivalry situations (Young and Levy 2011). Domestic factors such as leadership tenure (Colaresi 2001) and domestic instability (Mitchell and Prins 2004) can produce the outcome of rivalry. Leaders sometimes need external enemies to galvanize the population in support of their policies and will only choose to deescalate a rivalry if they are in a secure power position internally (Colaresi 2005). The unfortunate consequence of this tactic is that it likely makes rivalries endure and lock in. In fact, rivalries are almost impossible to terminate if both the public and leadership do not agree to end the hostile relationship. Leaders must play the ratification game on many levels (Putnam 1988) in order to achieve victory on policy initiatives. Domestic opinion can either force the continuation of a rivalry (Hensel 1998) or induce peace (Mor 1997).

Internal regime dynamics are also important factors in determining who might become rivals. Democracy reduces the likelihood of states entering into a rivalry in the first place (Hensel, Goertz, and Diehl 2000). There have only been two serious cases of rivalries beginning between two democracies, and only one of those cases (the United Kingdom versus the United States) contained two stable democracies for the entire duration of the conflict. Further research in the liberal paradigm looks at the impact of institutions on rivalries. Other scholars have found evidence that intergovernmental organizations (IGOs) reduce the duration of rivalries (Cornwell and Colaresi 2002; Prins and Daxecker 2008), but these two studies have not looked at the origins of rivalry and the impact on external institutions.

Stinnett and Diehl (2001: 21) argue that rather than having one cause, "[rivalries] emerge from the conjunction of a large number of small, individually weak factors." Stinnett and Diehl (2001) find that behavioral factors (linkages between disputes and dispute outcomes) and structural factors (political shocks and great power involvement) each have a small impact on rivalry initiation. Colaresi and Thompson (2002a) take a similar line and suggest two rivalry paths, one for positional rivalries (those concerned with global/strategic issues) and one for spatial rivalries (those concerned with territorial questions).

Contiguous rivals are likely to begin over spatial/territorial questions (Colaresi et al. 2008: 169, 180). Nondemocracy, militarization, and major power status increase the likelihood of positional rivals (Colaresi et al. 2008: 203), whose main source of disagreement seems to be based on geopolitical positioning rather than on specific locations and territories.

Colaresi et al. (2008: ch. 7) take a step back and ask if the factors that lead to war, as uncovered by Bremer (1992), lead to rivalry instead. Their analysis concludes by finding that dyads that are contiguous (being neighbors), are militarized, and contain a state that is either a regional or major power generally all contribute to the onset of rivalry.

Regarding war, there is a direct relationship between rivalry and war. This relationship may be a function of the number of disputes that rivalries engage in, yet this cannot be a tautological fact. Most wars only occur because of rivalry; rivalry leads to war. In fact, most wars occur near the beginning of the rivalry (Klein et al. 2006: 342). This suggests that the road to war and the outcomes of said wars may play a pivotal role in rivalry development.

Overall, we know relatively little about the onset of rivalries. Knowledge of the behavioral processes predating the onset of rivalry is particularly lacking. Why and when do states make choices that ultimately lead them down the rivalry path? States that are newly independent, lack the characteristics of democracies, or fail to engage in relevant international organizations are likely to become rivals, but these factors are largely processes that are outside the domain of foreign policy action and behavior. How do we explain the behavioral development of the process? To explain the process of rivalry onset, I develop a theory of power politics behavior on the road to conflict.

THE STEPS TO RIVALRY

The steps-to-rivalry model predicts that the development of rivalry will occur through a series of steps which combine to make a rivalry outcome probable. The model is not a deterministic process, but a process model whereby each action a state takes on the road to rivalry increases the probability of the event occurring. Events along the road to rivalry only make a rivalry outcome more probable, not automatic. The factors most likely to result in rivalry are power politics strategies such as the construction of alliances, participation in military buildups, and the use of escalating bargaining demands. When the application of these strategies is examined it is found that each factor actually leads to the onset of rivalry rather than deterrence and peace. Threatening actions, rather than preventing further conflict, actually make it more likely. This theory is counterintuitive to conventional wisdom in many ways, since the practices that I suggest bring about rivalry are typically seen as symptoms of rivalry, not causes.

The Model

This model considers the development of rivalry as a stepwise process. States that use realpolitik strategies in response to a potential enemy will increase the probability that the pair of states will eventually form an intense rivalry. Using these power politics strategies will make states lock into conflict that will escalate to the condition of dangerous rivalry and, quite likely, war.

The first step in the model is the existence of a contentious issue in dispute between two states. World politics is not about the distribution of influence in general, but about influence as it pertains to the decision-making calculus surrounding issues of importance to external state relationships. Early on, Diehl (1985) uncovered a connection between contiguity and major power rivalry. We now know that territorial issues are more critical than simple location dynamics (Senese 2005), yet early work on contiguity was crucial in highlighting the importance of territorial issues as steps toward rivalry (Huth 1996; Tir and Diehl 2002; Colaresi, Rasler, and Thompson 2007).

Territorial issues produce greater commitment by states in that the nature of the conflict becomes symbolic rather than divisible (Vasquez and Valeriano 2009). Issues are more difficult to resolve when they contain transcendent properties because solutions must deal with the abstract qualities of the issue under consideration. Territorial issues tend to generate realpolitik responses (Hensel 2000) due to the symbolic and abstract qualities of the territory under question. Rarely is a territorial dispute fought over a tract of land with a sure value; instead territorial disputes tend to be fought over desolate or inaccessible locations. While territory is concrete and divisible, in practice the disputes over territorial questions are never very simple to solve because of their transcendent properties.

Realpolitik actions aim to increase the security of one state, but usually they end up creating a decrease in the security of the potential rival. Perceiving a decrease in its own security, the opposing state employs its own realpolitik tactics in the context of pressing issues. The state seeks to "burn" or harm the enemy by denying them any sort of gain on pertinent issues. The situation develops into a conflict spiral and security dilemma, making the use of power politics tactics over salient issues the initial step on the road to rivalry.[2] Ethnic disputes handled in a similar fashion will also produce rivalry. The mechanism in operation is the choice of power politics strategies.

Alliances are the second step to rivalry. Alliances are written formal agreements between at least a pair of states that commit a state to either intervene in a conflict, agree to remain neutral in conflict, or consult the other state if conflict erupts (Gibler and Sarkees 2004). Traditionally alliances have been seen as factors that either add to power or deter aggression by opposing states. These two views have been challenged by history, which suggests either that alliances actually detract from power by being restraining factors (Schroeder 1994) or that they extend deterrence commitments to third parties, rendering direct deterrence irrelevant and illogical.

Alliances are the key trigger to the rivalry process. It seems that alliances are factors that lead to the onset of rivalry and also contribute to the onset of complex wars (Valeriano and Vasquez 2010). Alliances are meant to increase the security of one state but tend to decrease the security of both sides (Vasquez 1993). Instead of adding to the power of the state, demonstrating resolve, or deterring an aggressor state, alliances seem to lock states into a rivalry relationship by encouraging the development of similar strategies in the opposing side—either to catch up and achieve a balance of power or due to the psychological need of the leadership to demonstrate activity in the face of threats.

Alliances signal intent to another potential rival. Alliances increase insecurity and provoke military buildups as well as counteralliances rather than submission. The response to alliances formed by threats tends to be one of threat, reaction, and protection. There is a threat to a pressing issue at stake, and the other side responds; it chooses to escalate and not back down. When this happens, there are few options left to decision makers short of war, and one option is the formation and utilization of alliances to deter future escalation. Alliances do not deter future conflict but only encourage it.

The third step to rivalry is an arms race or mutual military buildup. These actions signify the rapid buildup and acceleration of two opposing state's military capabilities. Military buildups are a process by which two states compete to develop their capabilities to prevent attacks by another state. Two main elements make up the arms race relationship: interaction and acceleration (Richardson 1960; Sample 1998a, 1998b). An arms race signifies a competition between one state and another. A single state can have a military buildup, but this process is not mutual unless another state also competes and races. The other element fundamental to the arms race process is acceleration. The buildup of military capabilities must be significantly higher than in previous years to constitute a real threat to the other side. Without a significant buildup, how would the other side know that there is a strategic danger posed by its enemy?

The arms race process is relatively simple in that one state builds up its arms for either internal (domestic industry, internal threats, leadership turnover) or external (threats, force modernization, weapons advancements) reasons.

This buildup then compels a developing enemy to do the same, locking each side into rivalry. Counterintuitively, mutual military buildups decrease the security of both sides instead of providing further protection as most policy makers seem to believe. Building up an arsenal only increases the probability that the opposing side will build up its own arsenal in a similar manner. In this case, the security dilemma results whereby alliances and mutual military buildups create a context and provide the opportunity for the development of rivalry. A strategy of peace through strength sets in motion the security dilemma common in international politics (Herz 1950; Jervis 1979). Making an alliance or building up one's military may not always lead to war, but it will certainly be associated with rivalry relationships and development of the rivalry conflict spiral because of the psychological and strategic impact of such processes. When conducted in a climate of fear, threats, and aggressive posturing, arms races or alliances will lead to the development of rivalries.

The fourth step to rivalry is escalating bargaining demands. One constant truth in international interactions is that threats beget threats when demands are made in the context of repeated disputes. Threatening other international actors with violence and extreme demands only brings about the onset of international rivalry, not the resolution of the issue concerns. Under certain contexts, threats and provocations can be ignored as frivolous. What cannot be ignored is when the threats take on an escalating nature of increasing demands as time goes on. As threats escalate in terms of consequences, the probability of rivalry then increases.

Leng's (1983) early studies are important for uncovering this behavioral process critical to the onset of rivalry. The power politics style of international diplomacy focuses on utilizing power and resolve to spur concessions and achieve results. Unfortunately, demands escalate as successes are achieved in other arenas. Actors who participate in escalating threats are rejecting the prudential version of realism (Morgenthau 1948) in favor of a more offensive version of realist political theory (Mearsheimer 2001). Regrettably, the offensive version of realism fails to conform to reality and thus can lead a state to make bad decisions (Valeriano 2009). One such bad decision is the use of coercive bargaining tactics (Leng 1983) because they are assumed to be required responses when in fact they only set up the situation of rivalry.

Escalation is an unsuitable way to tackle a threat from an enemy. When an animal is threatened, cornered, and beaten, it tends to lash out rather than submit. Even in the face of overwhelming defeat, an opposing actor will lash out rather than be humiliated without responding. Vasquez and Valeriano (2010) demonstrate that escalating bargaining demands early in a rivalry are important correlates of some types of war. The remaining question is how escalating bargaining demands impact the process of rivalry development.

The prediction here is that when demands escalate early in a rivalry, the states will likely lock in as permanent rivals.

The fifth step to rivalry is rivalry linkages.[3] Very few scholars have investigated the impact of linkages between disputes. By linkages I do not mean how issues within a rivalry are linked, but how one dyadic rivalry is linked to another set of rivals or enemies. In short, how are rivalries connected, and how does this impact the development of a rivalry? Of course rivalry does not occur in isolation. When India fights Pakistan, every other state in the region is a witness. What is unclear is what impact the observation of these behaviors will have on relationships between developing enemies.

The view presented in this work follows the overarching power politics theme outlined in my steps-to-rivalry theory. When states utilize power and threats to spur favorable action in the opposing side, they are more likely to provoke an equal and escalatory reaction from the other side. The theory presented here suggests that movements to protect state security outside of a rivalry will escalate the rivalry of interest at the same time. Threats to another enemy will only provoke that enemy into responding and might also provoke other regional actors to join the developing fray.

The actions within one dyadic pairing will link up and impact the relationship of another pair of states. This type of interactive relationship is what I term a rivalry linkage.[4] Rivalries do not exist independent of other disputes between states. A dispute is linked to a rivalry if a party outside the dyad has a dispute with one member involved in a rivalry during the lifetime of that rivalry. The linkages between other disputes connect a rivalry to its ongoing threat environment in the region or the international community.

Major power status should also be included as a factor that can help predict who will become rivals. Major power states fit the profile of the type of state likely to engage in rivalry. They have expansive issue concerns, making it more likely that they will conflict with any state in the system over a foreign policy concern. Major power states have the economic ability to fund weapons purchases and increases, making military buildups more likely. Finally, major powers are typically sought after as alliance partners because of their power projection capabilities. Considering these three facts leads one to theorize that major powers will be more likely to engage in rivalry than minor powers.

HYPOTHESES

The hypotheses tested here treat rivalry as the dependent variable and seek to explain the process of rivalry development. This study will be concerned with factors that distinguish isolated conflicts from proto- and enduring rivalries.[5] Handling crises (or rivalries) with responses associated with power politics (alliance making and military buildups) will increase the probability that an isolated conflict between two states will become a protorivalry (three to five disputes) or an enduring rivalry (six or more disputes over twenty years). The use of power politics strategies leads a state on the path to a rivalry conflict spiral. Each state identifies the other as an enemy and attempts to deny benefits to that enemy. During the life of a rivalry, states send signals to each other. The formation of alliances and arms races are negative signals that may increase hostility between a dyad. From this logic, hypotheses 1.1 and 1.2 would be expected to be true.

H1.1. Pairs of states that form politically relevant alliances against each other are more likely to become involved in protorivalries and enduring rivalries.

H1.2. Pairs of states that participate in mutual military buildups are more likely to become involved in protorivalries and enduring rivalries.

Hypothesis 2 presents the additive probability hypothesis. In combination, the factors of politically relevant alliances, mutual military buildups, and territorial disputes are more likely to lead to dangerous (proto- or enduring) rivalries.

H2. Pairs of states that form politically relevant alliances against each other, participate in mutual military buildups, and have a significant number of territorial disputes are more likely to become involved in protorivalries and enduring rivalries.

In testing the additive models of rivalry development, this study will rely on multinomial logit modeling to determine the impact of each independent variable on the outcome. One independent variable in this study is politically relevant alliances, which are taken from the work of Senese and Vasquez (2008). Alliances are relevant only if they include a major power or a minor power target state from the same region as the dyad. The alliance must be formed at least three months prior to the dispute; only outside alliances were counted here (either both sides or one side had an alliance). No distinction was made between types of alliances or the purpose of the alliance. In the future it might be useful to further investigate the types of alliances that lead to rivalry, but first we must uncover the basic dynamics at work. Alliance information is taken from Correlates of War (COW) alliance version 3.0 (Gibler and Sarkees 2004). Mutual military buildups are taken from Sample's (2002) data, which includes both major and minor power mutual military buildups. Sample codes a mutual military buildup if both states exhibit an overall increase in military spending in the ten years prior to a dispute. This is in comparison to the military spending of the state over its entire history. Over a ten-year window, there must be a marked increase in expenditures during five years of the time under scrutiny.

The main dependent variable in this analysis is taken from Diehl and Goertz's (2000) coding of rivalry. Diehl and Goertz distinguish which pairs of states are the most dangerous rivals, enduring rivals: those which have had at least six disputes over a twenty-year period and who do not have any long-standing enmity directed toward the other. The next category is protorivalries, which includes pairs of states with three or more disputes within a twenty-year time period. Isolated conflicts represent the nonrivalry category because these dyads have only one or two militarized interstate disputes. While not examples of "peaceful" dyads, such isolated conflicts do represent nonrivalry interactions in that the disputes do not repeat and thus are a suitable reference category.

The unit of analysis is the historical rivalry dyad. Territory is clearly an important factor in the onset of war and is another variable used in this study. Per Vasquez and Leskiw (2001), a dyadic observation is coded as positive if 25 percent of the MIDs in a dyad are over territorial revisionist issues. According to our working definition of rivalry, rival dyads can and will fight over any issue relevant to their interactions, but territorial issues usually start the process. The control variables used in this study include contiguity and major powers. States that are contiguous are most likely to get into disputes (Bremer 1992). It is important to control for contiguity to ensure that findings on alliances are not spurious or driven by proximity rather than other factors. I also include status as a predictive variable, since major power states are more likely than any other type of state to become involved in conflict (Bremer 1992) and also rivalry (Colaresi et al. 2008).

DEVELOPING RIVALRY RELATIONSHIPS

Here the dependent variable is rivalry type. Predicted probabilities were calculated to suggest the substantive interpretations of each coefficient. Preliminary analysis (see Valeriano 2003) demonstrates that according to the base probability of the event, 51.6 enduring rivalries were expected to have positive alliance observations during this stage. The fact that 60 enduring rivalries display a positive observation for alliance formation shows that the relationship is strongly positive. Similar dynamics are at work for the protorivalry stage. For this category, 195 rivalries exhibit alliance behavior (out of a possible 223). The expected count was 182.6. These results give us confidence to proceed with a statistical examination of the topic.

Table 4.1 presents results of a multinomial logit test of hypothesis 1.1. The results support the proposition that states forming relevant alliances against each other are more likely to become involved in proto- and enduring rivalries but are less likely to be observed in isolated conflicts (hypothesis 1.1). For the enduring rivalry category, relevant alliances generate a coefficient of 1.556 and are statistically significant. Major power dyads generate a coefficient of 1.502 and are also statistically significant. For the protorivalry category, relevant alliances generate a coefficient of 0.511 and are statistically significant at .025. Major powers have a similar impact at 1.245, and the factor is statistically significant as well.

Predicted probabilities illustrate the statistics in a different way. If the values for relevant alliances and contiguity are set at one, the probabilities are .072 for enduring rivalry, .224 for protorivalry, and .702 for isolated conflicts.

Table 4.1. Relevant Alliances and Rivalry

Coefficient Estimates, Multinomial Logit Model for Rivalry Type						
	Outcome					
	Protorivalry			*Enduring Rivalry*		
Independent Variables	*Coefficient*	*S.E.*	*p > |z|*	*Coefficient*	*S.E.*	*p > |z|*
R. Alliance	0.511	.228	0.025	1.556	.594	0.009
Contiguity	0.262	.167	0.116	0.395	.273	0.149
Major Powers	1.245	.222	0.000	1.502	.321	0.000
Constant	−2.039	.227	0.000	−4.36	.579	0.000

Isolated conflict is reference category.
$N = 1166$
Prob. $> \chi^2 = 0.000$
Log likelihood = −769.631

	Predicted Probabilities for Rivalry Type		
	Isolated Conflict	*Protorivalry*	*Enduring Rivalry*
A) No Alliance + No Cont.	0.860	0.126	0.012
Alliance + Cont.	0.702	0.224	0.072
Difference	−0.158	0.098	0.060
B) No Alliance + No Cont. + No Major	0.875	0.113	0.011
Alliance + Cont. + Major Power	0.419	0.411	0.168
Difference	−0.456	0.298	0.157

If the values are set to zero, isolated conflict has a predicted probability of .860, having a negative difference of .158. While the highest predicted probability (.860) is found during the isolated conflict stage, it is important to note that this prediction is based on the absence of alliances and contiguity. When relevant alliances are observed, the probability decreases to .702. The direction of the relationship between isolated conflict and relevant alliances is negative or, simply, the lack of alliances during the isolated stage also corresponds to a lack of observed rivalries.

Protorivalry has a probability of occurring at .126, and enduring rivalry has a probability of .012 when relevant alliances are present. The probability for protorivalry almost doubles when the factors are present. The outcome increases close to six times for enduring rivalry (.072). The relationship is even stronger when the values are set to one for a relevant alliance, contiguity, and a major power dyad. For enduring rivalry, a positive observation results in a probability of .168, and a zero observation results in a value of .012.

A bivariate preliminary analysis (Valeriano 2003) once again demonstrates that there is a relationship between military buildups and rivalry. According to the enduring rivalry category, there should be 6.23 observations during this stage. In reality, there were 25 observations. Mutual military buildups occur more frequently than would be expected by chance. For the protorivalry category, there are 29 dyads that engage in mutual military buildups, while only 21 were expected.

Table 4.2 presents results for a multinomial logit test for hypothesis 1.2. The results support the proposition that states participating in mutual military buildups against each other are more likely to become involved in proto- and enduring rivalries. For the enduring rivalry category, military buildups generate a coefficient of 2.154, and this factor is statistically significant at .003. Major power dyads generate a coefficient of 1.125 that is statistically significant at .001. For the protorivalry category, military buildups generate a coefficient of 0.738 and are statistically significant at .003. Major power dyads have a similar impact at 1.08, and the factor is statistically significant at .001.

Predicted probabilities show that if the values for military buildup and contiguity are set at one, the probabilities are .242 for enduring rivalry, .288 for protorivalry, and .469 for isolated conflicts. If the values are set to zero, isolated conflict has a predicted probability of .765, creating a difference of −.296. Protorivalry has a probability of .194, with .040 for enduring rivalry. While the probabilities for the protorivalries do not increase much with military buildups, enduring rivalry moves from a probability of .040 to .242, representing an increase by a factor of six.

The relationship is even stronger when the values are set to one for a military buildup, contiguity, and a major power dyad. For enduring rivalry,

Table 4.2. Mutual Military Buildups and Rivalry Type

Coefficient Estimates, Multinomial Logit Model for Rivalry Type

	Outcome					
	Protorivalry			Enduring Rivalry		
Independent Variables	Coefficient	S.E.	$p > |z|$	Coefficient	S.E.	$p > |z|$
Military Buildups	0.738	.252	0.003	2.154	.304	0.003
Contiguity	0.145	.167	0.387	0.119	.283	0.672
Major Power	1.08	.224	0.001	1.125	.336	0.001
Constant	−1.49	.108	0.000	−3.709	.210	0.000

$N = 1,001$
Prob. $> \chi^2 = 0.000$
Log likelihood $= -695.924$

	Predicted Probabilities for Rivalry Type		
	Isolated Conflict	Protorivalry	Enduring Rivalry
A) No Buildup + No Cont.	0.765	0.194	0.040
Buildup + Cont.	0.469	0.288	0.242
Difference	−0.296	0.094	0.202
B) No Buildup + No Cont. + No Major	0.786	0.176	0.036
Buildup + Cont. + Major Power	0.249	0.401	0.349
Difference	−0.537	0.225	0.313

Note: Isolated conflict is reference category.

a positive observation results in a probability of .036, and a zero observation results in a value of .349. For protorivalry, if all values are set to zero, the probability is .176; if the values are set to one, the probability is .401.

Relevant alliances are the first and most important factor investigated. Those pairs of states that participate in relevant alliances (at least one outside alliance) are more likely to become involved in rivalry. This analysis shows that rivalry is more likely if states are involved in mutual military buildups. The probability of the occurrence of proto- and enduring rivalry increases when mutual military buildups are present. Accordingly, the probability of isolated conflict decreases when mutual military buildups are present. While mutual military buildups are consistent with the hypotheses presented here as probabilistic sufficient conditions of rivalry, they are not necessary conditions. Not all proto- or enduring rivals have experienced mutual military buildups.

It is clear that alliances are important for the development of rivalry. Prior to or during the first two disputes, it is likely that a proto- or enduring rivalry dyad used alliances to bolster their security. This usually results in the formation and development of rivalry itself rather than a decrease in tensions as policy makers typically hope. Any attempt to increase a state's security early in the process usually results in a perceived decrease in security for the opposing side. The power politics processes which these events trigger become the causal mechanism for the development of rivalry.

Extensive testing on the timing of events (Valeriano 2003) also reveals there is no consistent pattern like the one observed in the timing of mutual military buildups. In all likelihood, military buildups occur late in the life of a rivalry. There are forty-five cases of mutual military buildups during the early rivalry stage, and twenty-four of these led directly to war, thus ending the rivalry. Twenty-one of these cases did not lead to war, and these cases should be selected out for further qualitative investigation. One cannot assume that arms races will occur only during a rivalry relationship; rather, a significant number of mutual military buildups occur outside of rivalries.

THE COMPLETE ADDITIVE MODEL

Table 4.3 presents results for a multinomial logit test of what we call the complete additive steps-to-rivalry model. This table directly tests hypothesis 2. All the factors previously investigated are added into one model. Here we consider the combined effects of military buildups, alliances, territory disputes, contiguity, and major powers.

The results support the proposition that states that form politically relevant alliances, participate in military buildups, and fight territorial disputes are

Table 4.3.   Complete Rivalry Model

Coefficient Estimates, Multinomial Logit Model for Rivalry Type						
	Outcome					
	Protorivalry			*Enduring Rivalry*		
Independent Variables	Coefficient	S.E.	$p > |z|$	Coefficient	S.E.	$p > |z|$
Military Buildup	0.714	.258	0.006	2.105	.304	0.001
Alliance	0.496	.229	0.031	1.389	.591	0.019
25% Territory	0.454	.159	0.004	0.654	.274	0.018
Contiguity	0.223	.169	0.186	0.345	.280	0.218
Major Power	1.130	.220	0.000	1.150	.339	0.001
Constant	−2.220	.235	0.000	−4.789	.586	0.000

$N = 1,166$
Prob. $> \chi^2 = 0.000$
Log likelihood $= -739.569$

Notes: Isolated conflict is reference category. Robust standard errors.

more likely to become involved in proto- and enduring rivalries. For the enduring rivalry category, politically relevant alliances generate a coefficient of 1.389 and are statistically significant at .019. Military buildups produce a coefficient of 2.105 and are statistically significant at .001. The 25 percent territory variable produces a coefficient of 0.654 and is statistically significant at .018. Contiguity has a positive impact on the model but is not statistically significant at .218, much like the results in the other models. Major power dyads generate a coefficient of 1.15, and this coefficient is statistically significant.

For the protorivalry category, military buildups generate a coefficient of 0.714 and are statistically significant. Politically relevant alliances produce a coefficient of 0.496 and are statistically significant. The 25 percent territory variable also produces a positive coefficient of 0.454 and is statistically significant at .004.

Parts A and B of table 4.4 present the predicted probability results for military buildups and alliances if the values are set to one or zero for each observation. It is important to note that the steps-to-rivalry theory predicts the onset of protorivalry as well as or better than the onset of an enduring rivalry.

The relationship is even stronger when the values are set to one for politically relevant alliances, military buildup, and 25 percent territory. For enduring rivalry, a positive observation results in a probability of .2802, and a zero

Table 4.4. Predicted Probabilities for Complete Rivalry Model

	Isolated Conflict	*Protorivalry*	*Enduring Rivalry*
A) No Military Buildup	0.788	0.179	0.032
Military Buildup	0.555	0.259	0.185
Difference	−0.233	0.080	0.153
B) No Alliance	0.8495	0.137	0.013
Alliance	0.7531	0.199	0.047
Difference	−0.0964	0.062	0.034
C) Alliance, Mutual Military Buildup, 25% Territory			
No	0.8765	0.1143	0.0092
Yes	0.4259	0.2939	0.2802
Difference	−0.4506	0.1796	0.2710
D) Alliance, Mutual Military Buildup, 25% Territory, Major Power			
No	0.888	0.103	0.008
Yes	0.209	0.401	0.389
Difference	−0.679	0.298	0.381

observation results in a value of .0092. For protorivalry, if all values are set to zero, the probability is .1143; if the values are set to one, the probability is .2939. The final additive model shows a high probability for the combined factors of alliances, military buildups, 25 percent territory, and major powers. For enduring rivalry, the probability of rivalry occurring is .389 if the values for the factors are set to one (table 4.4, part D). For protorivalry, the probability is also close, at .401, for a rivalry to occur if the values for the factors are set to one.

It is clear that dyads that have territorial disputes (specifically more than 25 percent of the disputes are territorial in nature) are more likely to become rivals. While not every dispute in which a dyad fights has to be territorial to make the dyad dangerous, those dyads having a significant number of territorial disputes are likely to become rivals. Politically relevant alliances and mutual military buildups are all important conditions for rivalry development. Each event makes the outcome of rivalry more likely to occur. This theory is additive in that the factors of territorial disputes, major power involvement, mutual military buildups, and politically relevant alliances all combine to increase the probability of proto- and enduring rivalry occurrence.

From this study, a few typical paths to rivalry can be observed. The path with the highest probability of rivalry occurrence involves the use of politically relevant alliances, mutual military buildups, repeated territorial conflicts, and major power dyads.

Table 4.5 presents the rank-order probabilities of the occurrence of both enduring rivalry and protorivalry. There is a .013 probability of an enduring rivalry if the pair of states does not have an alliance. This probability

Table 4.5. Paths to Rivalry: Rank Order of Predicted Probabilities

Enduring Rivalry	
.389	Alliance, Military Buildup, Territory, and Major Powers
.280	Alliance, Military Buildup, and Territory
.239	Military Buildup and Territory
.185	Military Buildup
.066	Alliance and Territory
.047	Alliance
.013	No Alliance
Protorivalry	
.401	Alliance, Military Buildup, Territory, and Major Powers
.294	Military Buildup and Territory
.294	Alliance, Military Buildup, and Territory
.259	Military Buildup
.247	Alliance and Territory
.199	Alliance
.137	No Alliance

increases to .389 if they have a politically relevant alliance, a mutual military buildup, and territorial disputes, and are major powers. The base probability for protorivalry, if neither state has an outside alliance, is .137. This probability increases to .401 if the pair of states has an alliance, military buildup, territorial disputes, and is a major power.

CONCLUSION

The original query of this chapter was to determine what the field knows about the origins of rivalry. The use of traditional power politics is associated with severe manifestations of both war and rivalry. This analysis suggests that certain practices of power politics, namely alliances, are important conditions for setting in motion a pattern of recurring disputes that result in interstate rivalry, and then possibly warfare.

In this chapter, I have found that relevant alliances are key factors in the development of both proto- and enduring rivalry. The formation of alliances represents a significant step along the road to rivalry. When states use alliances in response to an initial dispute, they are likely to experience recurring conflict. I also find that mutual military buildups are probabilistic conditions for the development of rivalry. While mutual military buildups are not necessary conditions of rivalry, we do know that if a state participates in a mutual military buildup and it does not go to war during the first two disputes, the dyad is likely to become rivals.

It is also important to note that power politics foreign policy practices come into use early in the life of a rivalry. Dyads that are proto- or enduring rivals are likely to have formed politically relevant alliances early on. It remains for in-depth case studies to be undertaken to show the causal path between initial disputes, alliance formation, and escalation to the proto- and enduring rival stages.

This work has presented rivalry as a process, and these stages of rivalry development need to be taken into account in any analysis of the formation of rivals. One cannot look at enduring rivals alone but must also investigate the factors present in protorivals and isolated conflicts. The steps to rivalry are clear. Politically relevant alliances, mutual military buildups, territorial disputes, and major power dyads are more likely to become rivals if these factors are present. Added to previous findings regarding rivalry development (shocks, lack of democracy, born fighting, and escalating bargaining demands), we now have a start to the narrative story of rivalry origins.

I have argued that power politics strategies are dangerous precedents in international interactions. States that use power politics practices are likely to become dangerous rivals. While policy advice up to this point is premature, states should avoid threatening actions because it is likely that those actions will lead to security dilemmas and rivalry. Those states involved in rivalry are the most likely dyads to become involved in war. To avoid war, one must avoid rivalry in the first place.

NOTES

A special thanks to Armel Yver for editorial assistance and also to those who have commented on this project along its various stages.

1. A militarized interstate dispute is a threat, display, or use of force (Ghosn, Palmer, and Bremer 2004) condoned by government actors. Past efforts to code and categorize MIDs (Jones, Bremer, and Singer 1996) have had a large impact on the study of rivalry as a field. Without the existence of the MID data set, scholars would be hard pressed to identify who fights so often in the system.

2. Multiple issues are likely to make rivalries endure and persist (Dreyer 2010), but it is unclear if the number of issues at stake has an impact on the development of a rivalry.

3. Unfortunately, due to space limitations, data analysis for the hypotheses regarding escalatory tactics and rivalry linkages remains unexplored in this volume. Consult Valeriano (2003) for a full analysis.

4. Diehl and Goertz (2000) also investigate rivalry linkages, but they study how rivals are linked to other parties through alliances or mutual engagement in the same dispute, not how some disputes will influence new disputes.

5. A key reason the Diehl and Goertz (2000) data was used is because it contains variance on the dependent variable utilized here.

Chapter Five

The Rivalry Process

How Rivalries Are Sustained and Terminated

Paul F. Diehl and Gary Goertz

Rivalries, the protracted and militarized competitions between the same pair of states (e.g., India-Pakistan), are not root causes of war in the traditional sense, as might be alliances, arms races, or other factors. Rather, they are the context in which the majority of international conflict, and certainly its most dangerous elements, occur. Indeed, according to one study (Diehl and Goertz 2000), rivalries account for approximately three-fourths of militarized disputes; that is, when states engage in a military confrontation, it is likely not the first or the last time the states will clash over the same or related issues. Such confrontations are also more likely to escalate to war, as over 80 percent of wars take place within rivalry contexts. Rivalries are also the arenas in which other significant international interactions occur, most notably a disproportionate number of violent territorial changes such as Soviet acquisition of the Kuril Islands from Japan after World War II. Rivalries are also enormously expensive in terms of the defense and other resources needed to sustain them, as well as the opportunity costs (e.g., trade, development) occasioned by continuing patterns of hostility; indeed, rivalries are the context for most arms races (Rider, Findley, and Diehl 2011).

The empirical importance of rivalry has led it to assume a role as a standard variable in war studies, along with geographic contiguity and democracy. For example, Senese and Vasquez (2008) consider rivalries (recurring disputes) as one of the key components, along with alliances, arms races, and territorial disputes, in their steps-to-war model. Thompson and his colleagues (e.g., Colaresi, Rasler, and Thompson 2007) understand rivalry to be the key background condition under which a series of key conflict processes play out. One cannot understand, for example, the repeated wars between Israel and her neighbors without reference to the decades-long rivalries involving those states.

Incorporating rivalries into scholarly analyses is a gateway to assessing the prospects for war and detailing how those processes play out. To deal with the problem of war, forestalling or preventing the formation of rivalries is the most desirable solution. In chapter 4 of this volume, Valeriano outlines the conditions and processes associated with rivalry formation. Yet, failing at stopping their onset, what keeps rivalries going, and how can they be brought to an end? As rivalries continue, so too do the deleterious effects of war risk and resource diversion. In this chapter, we examine rivalry processes that lead to their maintenance, as well as those that promote termination. In many ways, these concerns are opposite sides of the same coin: factors that keep rivalries going are those that also inhibit their conclusion, and vice versa.

DEFINING RIVALRY

Rivalries are fundamentally about conflicting preferences or goals over some tangible or intangible good(s). Yet rivalries are distinguished from other conflicts in that they share a series of characteristics and can be differentiated from each other by variations along those dimensions: spatial consistency, duration, militarization, and linkage (see Klein, Goertz, and Diehl 2006; Diehl and Goertz 2000). The first dimension, spatial consistency, revolves around the character and number of actors. Actors in rivalries consist of states, and rivalries are dyadic (the rivalry idea can, however, be extended to nonstate actors and civil conflict; see DeRouen and Bercovitch 2008). Rivalries consist of the same pair of states competing with each other, and the expectation of a future conflict relationship is one that is specific as to whom the opponent will be; for example, India and Pakistan each regard the other as its primary enemy, and this has been true since independence (and is likely to remain so for the extended future). These two aspects of spatial consistency have gone virtually unchallenged and largely unaddressed in the literature.

A second dimension of rivalries is their duration. Historically, scholars focused on enduring rivalries (those lasting a generation or more) because of their importance in understanding international conflict. We and others (Colaresi et al. 2008) have always held that the concept of rivalry itself not be limited to "enduring" rivalries.[1] For a variety of methodological and theoretical reasons, it is crucial to allow for short-term rivalries (e.g., as a control group, to prevent selection bias).[2]

As a third dimension, we see rivalry relationships as forming a particular subset of international relations. We do not focus on relations in general, but militarized and conflictual ones in particular. When states are engaged in a rivalry, they have conflicting goals over the disposition of scarce goods.

Conflicting goals characterize many state relationships, but a rivalry is one in which the military component of foreign policy is an important element; much of foreign policy is conceived of and conducted in military terms, as it was between the United States and the Soviet Union during the Cold War. This dimension has been the one that has provoked much debate in discussions of rivalries. Thompson (2001; Colaresi et al. 2008) does not explicitly require overt military actions to qualify as a rivalry. Instead his conceptualization is based largely on perception, rather than action; states must regard each other as enemies. In a related fashion, there must be actual or latent threats that pose some possibility of becoming militarized, but these do not have to be manifest with any frequency.

Finally, the conflicts within rivalries are *linked*; that is, they are related over space and time. Events in a rivalry are not independent of one another but rather are interconnected by several elements (including the unresolved issues over which states dispute). There are two conceptual linkages between disputes. The first is the "pull of the past." Rivals have a joint history, and events in the rivalry (particularly past military confrontations) exercise an influence on present and future behaviors. This has been most evident in the Israeli-Syrian rivalry, as the seizure of the Golan Heights in the 1967 war is still the centerpiece of that competition. The second linkage element is in the form of expectations of future conflict. Rivals expect that mutual disputes, crises, and war are likely to continue into the future. These expectations condition current foreign policy choices, which then have downstream consequences for the dynamics of rivalries and their potential for peaceful resolution.

Some scholars have defined rivalries as only those conflicts occurring between states of equal capability. Vasquez (1996: 533) has most clearly stated this position, going so far as to argue that "relative equality is a prerequisite of rivalries." Thompson does not take a direct position that a measure of power symmetry should be included in the concept of rivalry. Nevertheless, he does state that "other things being equal, symmetrical capabilities should be expected to make rivalry more likely and more enduring" (2001: 573). Empirically, among those defined below, a significant number of rivalries occur between states that have disparate capabilities. Parity or preponderance does affect the dynamics of a rivalry (Klein et al. 2006), but this suggests that capability belongs as an independent variable explaining rivalry behavior rather than as a component of its definition.

Save for some disagreements on the militarized competition dimension and capability symmetry, there is general consensus on the conceptual components of rivalry. Operationally, there are a variety of ways to identify rivalry cases. Thompson and his colleagues (1995, 2001; Colaresi et al. 2008) use historical evaluation based largely on perception. Other approaches, including our own, rely in large part on conflict occurrence, whether this is by reference to militarized disputes (Diehl and Goertz 2000; Klein et al. 2006) or higher-level "crises" (Hewitt 2005). One might also add criteria related to the issues in disputes to the conflict occurrence component (Mitchell and Thies 2011). A straight comparison of these approaches produces different lists of cases. Nevertheless, empirically there has been remarkable consistency in results when using different definitions to address similar questions and in robustness checks on findings.

For our purposes in detailing patterns, we adopt the Klein et al. (2006) definition that rivalries generally consist of a sequence of at least three militarized interstate disputes (MIDs) between the same pair of states in temporal proximity to one another but occurring over an extended period of time (usually over ten years) so as not to be merely fleeting competitions (for exact specifications and exceptions, see Klein et al. 2006). A total of 290 cases meet this definition, with approximately 40 percent qualifying as "enduring" under previous conceptualizations.

As this chapter is concerned with rivalry maintenance and termination, we must be concerned with defining how we know that a rivalry is continuing, or symmetrically that it has ended. A rivalry is generally said to continue when there are unresolved issues between the rivals, there are still significant prospects for war, and a mutual enemy perception continues. Operationally, we have traditionally used the occurrence of MIDs as evidence that a rivalry is continuing; along with other scholars, we have more recently given consideration to other factors such as peace agreements and other interactions between the rivals. Yet, fundamentally, the effective definition for rivalry continuation (once it starts) is the absence of rivalry termination, and therefore it is the definition of the latter that is critical in this chapter.

Determining the termination date of rivalries is not as easy as it first might appear. Analysts might initially be drawn to evidence that the key issues in contention have been resolved (Bennett 1997). Peace agreements, international court decisions, and other events might suggest that the rivalry competition is over, but there are numerous instances in which states continued militarized clashes over the same, purportedly resolved issues (and in a short period of time) despite apparent signals of conflict resolution. For example, Argentina and Chile continued to dispute the Beagle Channel islands for many years, despite a treaty and then an international arbitration award that purportedly resolved the disagreement. Perceptual criteria that states no longer regard each other as enemies are very difficult to measure. Accordingly, we have usually relied on behavioral manifestations that rivalries have terminated, specifically the absence of MIDs for an extended period of time (conventionally ten to fifteen years). As with assessing cures for cancer, determining rivalry termination is post hoc, but it does prevent "false alarms" in calling a rivalry ended prematurely. The specific year or month in which a rivalry can be said to have ended, therefore, is not well specified in many of these treatments, and the end of the last MID is often used as a surrogate for more precise determinations.[3] Some efforts (Klein, Goertz, and Diehl 2008), incomplete at this writing, seek to establish more precise estimates of rivalry termination.

EMPIRICAL PATTERNS

Our intention is not to describe all aspects of rivalries (that is done elsewhere—see Diehl and Goertz 2000; Klein et al. 2006; Colaresi et al. 2008), but we focus primarily on those aspects that relate to their maintenance and termination. This sets the stage for the following sections that explore what we know about the factors that account for these patterns. We begin, however, with a general overview of rivalries and their relationship to international conflict in general, and war in particular. Table 5.1 provides the distribution of disputes for each category of conflict.[4]

Only about a third of militarized disputes are of the isolated variety. Almost 50 percent of militarized disputes occur within the context of enduring rivalries; thus, only a small percentage of all conflictual dyads (12.6 percent), and an even smaller percentage of all possible dyads, account for a majority of international disputes. The results are even more dramatic with respect to the most intense of enduring rivalries. Almost 30 percent of all disputes are generated by 3.9 percent of the rivalries, or forty-seven pairs of states.[5] Militarized disputes are used to define rivalries, and therefore one might expect greater dispute propensity in that context; yet, even given that dispute frequency is used to define rivalries, it is stunning that more than twice as many disputes as expected occur in enduring rivalries than in isolation.[6] The

Table 5.1. Rivalry Context and the Frequency of Interstate Conflict, 1816–2001

Rivalry Type	Number of Rivalries	Dispute Frequency	Probability of War (N with War)
Isolated Conflict	881 (72.7%)	1,217 (31.8%)	0.13 (118)
Proto-	178 (14.7%)	654 (17.1%)	0.26 (46)
Enduring	152 (12.6%)	1,960 (51.2%)	0.36 (54)
6–13 Disputes	105 (8.7%)	862 (22.5%)	0.23 (24)
>13 Disputes	47 (3.9%)	1,098 (28.7%)	0.64 (30)
All	1,211 (100%)	3,831 (100%)	0.18 (218)

Source: Klein, Goertz, and Diehl 2006.

vast majority of disputes (more than two-thirds) take place in some rivalry context, be it proto- or enduring.

In table 5.1, we also determine if at least one war occurs at some point in the rivalry. As indicated in the third column, the propensity for war grows dramatically as one moves from isolated conflict to the most severe enduring rivalries (almost five times as great in severe enduring rivalries than in isolated conflict). In the most protracted enduring rivalries, the chances are better than 64 percent that the two states will go to war at some point in their competition. These findings show that not only is the propensity of a single dispute ending in war greater, but so is the chance of war sometime in the relationship as the rivalry becomes longer and more serious.

Moving to patterns in maintenance and termination, one immediately notices that rivalries last a relatively long time. This is perhaps not surprising in that much of this research began as a study of *enduring* rivalries, which by definition include a long temporal component. Still, even when temporal elements were dropped from the operational criteria, rivalries are far from fleeting phenomena. Rivalries last on average for twenty-eight years and range from competitions that are less than ten years long to those that have lasted over 140 years (e.g., Japan-Russia/USSR). Even these numbers underestimate rivalry duration, given that many of the rivalries were still ongoing as of 2001 (the last data point), and therefore the data are "censored."[7] Alternative and more restrictive rivalry lists also find rivalries to be long lasting; Thompson's (2001; Colaresi et al. 2008: 38–50) rivalries have a mean duration of forty-eight years.

Most initial disputes between two states do not lead to long-standing rivalry competitions. Thus, in some sense, repeated conflict is far from the norm in international relations. Yet the long duration of those interactions that do produce rivalries suggests that there are forces promoting their maintenance, and these are not easily dislodged such that termination is accomplished.

A second concern deals with patterns of militarized disputes within the rivalries, and such disputes offer one of the bases (their frequency and temporal proximity) for defining rivalry. Save for a few exceptions,[8] all rivalries have at least three militarized disputes, by definition. Some rivalries have far more; the rivalry with the greatest number of disputes is the US-Russia/USSR competition, with fifty-nine disputes as of the last available data (2001). Thus, rivalries are built upon many different conflict incidents, and during their existence, violent interactions are often the norm.

Such interactions also occur frequently, with often little pause for conflict-free periods. The lapsed time from the end of one dispute to the beginning of the subsequent dispute in the average rivalry is very short. The mean "waiting" time for disputes in rivalries is 2.7 years with a median of 1.15 (Goertz,

Jones, and Diehl 2005). About 65 percent of the disputes in a rivalry take place within two years of each other, and 80 percent occur within three years. For example, in the US-Soviet rivalry, the Bay of Pigs dispute was followed in rapid succession by the Berlin Wall crisis and then the Cuban missile crisis, with several lesser confrontations sprinkled in between. There are also numerous disputes that start prior to the termination of the previous dispute. That is, some rivalries are so intense that the rivals clash simultaneously on different issues or in different locations. Such patterns indicate that rivalries are fueled repeatedly by military confrontations, and the successful resolution of a given dispute is not necessarily enough to facilitate the end of a competition that might involve simultaneous clashes.

Finally, we look to the periodicity of war within rivalries. Early analysis suggested no secular pattern in severity (escalatory or deescalatory) in rivalries (Diehl and Goertz 2000). Yet the vast majority of wars take place at or near the beginning of a rivalry. Nearly 50 percent occur by the third dispute, and about 90 percent happen by the sixth dispute. Equally apparent, wars do not occur later in the rivalry. Less than 10 percent of all the wars occur after the eleventh dispute. Indeed, if one tracks the occurrence of the *first* war in a rivalry, the probability is dramatically greater at the outset of a rivalry (e.g., India-Pakistan) than in its latter stages. This is suggestive that wars are not the driving force behind rivalry termination. Yet neither are they necessary for rivalry maintenance, as the likelihood of a dispute escalating to war remains relatively low, and largely unchanged, across the life of a rivalry. Looking at disputes as the unit of analysis, rather than wars, the likelihood that a dispute will escalate to war is approximately 10 percent in the first two phases of rivalry (the first six disputes in the rivalry sequence). That number drops, but not precipitously, to 6 percent for the disputes thereafter.

RIVALRY MAINTENANCE

We consider here what we know about the factors that keep rivalries going, most often indicated by the recurrence of militarized disputes over time.[9] Gartzke and Simon (1999) challenged the whole idea of rivalry maintenance, that there is any sort of dependency between conflicts involving the same pair of states. The rivalry process should be understood simply as the repetition of the same conditions producing the same outcomes over time. This suggests that rivalry events are independent of one another, and therefore rivalries themselves are epiphenomenal. This study has been widely discredited, as a variety of studies (Hensel 1994; Crescenzi and Enterline 2001; Colaresi and Thompson 2002b; Colaresi et al. 2008) have found very significant correlations between "rivalry variables" and the current dispute. These studies typically use some factors associated with previous disputes (or crises) to examine the dispute linkage question. In all cases, these variables are among the most influential of the model. Similarly, conflict studies that use the Beck, Katz, and Tucker (1998) "peace-years spline" also implicitly test hypotheses about dispute linkage; these spline variables are the elapsed time since the previous dispute. Again, almost without exception, these variables are statistically and substantively significant. Finally, common sense tells us in a number of cases that some prior events affect future confrontations, such as the 1974 Turkish invasion of Cyprus and its subsequent impact on Turkey's rivalries with Greece and Cyprus respectively, or the influence of the 1967 war on subsequent Arab-Israeli interactions.

Theoretical Formulations

Two major theoretical approaches to rivalries are the punctuated equilibrium (Diehl and Goertz 2000) and evolutionary (Hensel 1999; see also Maoz and Mor 2002) models. The former tends to emphasize structural influences (e.g., issues) in rivalries and consistency/stability in interactions from the onset of the rivalry. The latter gives greater weight to the initial interactions in rivalry, and such behavioral influences set the stage for future rivalry dynamics, including the greater likelihood of war over time. Most of the differences in the two formulations concern rivalry formation in the early stages and in the patterns of escalation. Once rivalries are established, however, there is consensus between the two approaches that rivalries are stable and not easily resolved, although this is more developed theoretically in the punctuated equilibrium explanation.

Each model postulates that rivalries go through several stages, and the processes that occur differ substantially according to the life cycle of the rivalry. During the initial phase, the rivals either resolve the disputes relatively quickly or patterns of hostility "lock in," with the consequence that the rivalry becomes enduring. Following the lock-in phase is one of "stasis," in which hostile interactions persist between the rivals with some regularity or consistency. In the period of stasis, rivalries experience a "basic rivalry level" or BRL (Diehl and Goertz 2000), an average level of hostile or cooperative interaction around which their relations vary. Periods of conflict and détente are seen as essentially "random" variations around this basic level; there is no secular trend toward more conflictual or more peaceful relations. Diehl and Goertz (2000) find that approximately 75 percent of rivalries exhibit flat or largely unchanging BRL patterns after lock-in.

Domestic Processes

There are several mechanisms by which the rivalry process is thought to be reinforced, most notably those associated with domestic processes. Elements of bureaucracy, public opinion, and democracy are cited as critical. One approach relies on an organizational policy model of decision making. When faced with a rivalry, governments devise policies to deal with it; these include alliance formation and arms acquisition, and such policies involve long-term commitments that are not easily reversed in the short term. McGinnis and Williams (2001) argue that bureaucratic policies harden over time in a rivalry, making rivalry behavior (such as arms races) hard to dislodge.

Bureaucratic inertia is reinforced by belief systems of the mass public and the leadership. Public opinion is a factor that supports continuation of the rivalry, as it constrains decision makers and makes it difficult for leaders to change course when the rival is viewed in enemy terms by the populace (McGinnis and Williams 2001). Similarly, Leng (2000) indicates that the belief systems of leaders are critical in crisis behavior, and these systems are largely defined by prior disputes and crises; the Arab-Israeli and India-Pakistan rivalries are illustrative. The views of the leadership and public are structured by the previous hostile interactions between rivals and indeed make future hostile interactions more likely, thereby perpetuating the cycle. Bureaucratic actions also reflect these views and represent brakes on dramatic policy changes away from rivalry hostility.

Consistent with some of these elements are the psychological underpinnings of rivalries that promote their maintenance (Thies 2001). States (and therefore the leadership) are said to become socialized into the rivalry and assume the behavioral attributes that are associated with the role of rival, including hostility. Presumably, the speed of this socialization process and the degree to which it reinforces behavior would be enhanced by the frequent and serious conflict that defines the initial stages of rivalry. Thus, in a constructivist conception, states acquire role identities as rivalries, and these can be reinforcing over time. A "culture" of rivalry and a set of interaction norms are created that are conducive to the development of rivalries and sustaining them.

A third domestic influence on the maintenance of rivalries revolves around several domestic political considerations beyond those associated with public opinion and bureaucratic policy. Ganguly and Thompson (2011) identify a set of domestic political processes that can impact rivalries, several of which can perpetuate rivalries. Most notable is rivalry outbidding. Colaresi (2005) contends that domestic players within rival states compete over the rivalry as an issue space, similar to other domestic political issues.

Rivalry outbidding occurs when competing domestic political groups agree on the primary external enemies of a state but try to outdo each other by advocating tougher policies against those enemies. The net benefit from such actions is greater support from the public, including electoral support. For example, accusations about "who lost China" among American political figures were common in the early part of the Sino-American rivalry. The effect on rivalries is to strengthen hard-line elements within society, reinforce hostility, and make it more difficult to make or accept conciliatory gestures. This is particularly important when rivalries are centered on territory (Goddard 2006; see Tir and Diehl 2002 for how common this is).

Related domestic processes include diversion and threat inflation (Ganguly and Thompson 2011). These refer to exaggeration of a rival's threat by elements within the government decision-making apparatus in order to facilitate particular domestic policies (e.g., increased military spending, domestic repression of opposition groups) or to facilitate some foreign policy initiative (e.g., arms sales to a given regime). A side effect is that hostility levels might increase between said state and its rival as a result of the policies undertaken. Diversionary action involves the use of military force by a state in order to direct domestic audiences away from internal problems. Although there is considerable debate on whether this effect occurs generally, there is stronger evidence that it is more common in the rivalry context (Mitchell and Prins 2004). Thus, domestic incentives might lead states to attack rivals and thereby prolong and deepen the rivalry; rivals are attractive targets for diversionary action because the costs of building an enemy image have already been paid, and the payoffs in terms of a rally-round-the-flag or similar effect are likely to be greater when the target is a rival versus another state. Thus, domestic political incentives produce actions that have the effect of making rivalries more entrenched.

Failures of Coercion and Conflict Management

Beyond the reinforcing effects of domestic processes on rivalry maintenance, the failure to resolve disputed issues (and the coercive strategies used by both rivals) also contributes to the continuation of rivalries (Goertz et al. 2005). Of course, the more issues involved in a rivalry (e.g., the more they "accumulate"), the more difficult it will be to find satisfactory solutions to all of them (Dreyer 2010). Rivalries fundamentally are about different preferences over some stakes, and rivalries can be expected to continue if neither side can prevail over the other. The failure of coercive strategies contributes in several ways to rivalry maintenance. Most obviously, the issue(s) in dispute are left unresolved. One or both sides in a conflict may try again to gain satisfaction through the use of military force. Indeed, it is not uncommon for the same rival to press its claims repeatedly. For example, Pakistan is always the revisionist state, and most frequently the side that initiates military force, in the forty or so disputes it has had with India over the status of Kashmir. Yet Pakistan is *never* successful in disputes with India, and the overwhelming majority end in stalemates. Thus, when coercion fails and the outcome leaves at least one side dissatisfied, there is a basis for rivalry continuation (Maoz and Mor 2002).

Even the status quo state in a rivalry may desire rivalry continuation. Usually it will prefer rivalry to conceding to its opponent. It must, however, be capable enough to resist the claims of its rival and not back down. Nevertheless, even weaker rivals can resist the demands of stronger enemies; Cuba has successfully resisted US efforts at regime change on that island for more than five decades. The stakes involved or the salience of the rivalry issues also must be significant enough to justify the costs and risks of the rivalry. Indeed, dissatisfaction with the outcomes of past confrontations leads states to adopt more coercive bargaining strategies in the future (see Leng 2000).

States would clearly prefer to end a rivalry by winning and thereby eliminate future challenges from an opponent. Yet coercion, which frequently produces stalemate outcomes to confrontations, often does not produce the desired result, and increased hostility toward an opponent and the other effects noted above are the likely consequences. In policy models, it is significant failure that typically prompts a reevaluation of policy. Stalemates indicate a fundamentally unchanged state of affairs.

Maoz (1984), Hensel (1994), and Grieco (2001) argue that stalemate outcomes increase the likelihood of future conflicts between the same pair of states. It is not merely single instances of indecisive outcomes that prompt rivalry maintenance, but a series of them, especially at the outset of the rivalry. It may take several instances of failure at coercion (and the lack of compromise outcomes) to signal to decision makers that the rivalry is unlikely to be resolved (Goertz et al. 2005). With that recognition, decision makers begin to plan for the long haul (longer-term defense decisions) in the expectation that the rivalry will continue. Such policies have the paradoxical effect of contributing to rivalry maintenance themselves.

Decisive outcomes that signal the success of coercion (victories by one side or the other) might undermine rivalry maintenance. Yet, some victories can have the effect of strengthening some rivalries, such as the effect of the first Persian Gulf war on the US-Iraq rivalry. The loser in the confrontation may be willing to fight again in order to recoup its losses. In some scenarios, winners may even seek greater gains, emboldened by their initial successes. For example, a state may gain territory from an opponent but still press further demands in the future (see Tir 2003 for a discussion of the logic underlying this process with respect to territorial disputes). Still, decisive outcomes are generally confined to the most severe confrontations (i.e., wars), and even these are increasingly rare over time.

The failure of coercion has downstream consequences; it is often much harder to resort to another option for ending the rivalry: negotiation and compromise. This produces another factor in rivalry maintenance—the failure of conflict management. Conflict management may be present early in the rivalry such that states reach accommodation before many confrontations take place. Early in a rivalry, conflict-generating policies as well as conflict management ones can be implemented. Depending on how the issues in dispute are handled, conflict management at the early stage can become conflict resolution (that is, the rivalry ends in the nascent stage). In contrast, failure at mediation, negotiation, and the like may sour participants (and third parties) on future diplomatic initiatives and reinforce the perception that the rivalry requires long-term commitments of resources and coercive policies, thereby contributing to its maintenance. Furthermore, in the rivalry context, real concessions may be viewed as insincere or even hostile (Colaresi and Thompson 2002a). Rivals might be reluctant to even make such peace overtures. For example, neither Turkish nor Greek leaders could make wholesale concessions on Aegean Sea claims without incurring the wrath of their populaces. Democratic states are generally more inclined than others to seek negotiation and compromise, but even those states are reluctant to do so in the context of an enduring rivalry (Huth and Allee 2002). Indeed, even risking future defeat in a war may be more desirable for a leader than granting concessions (see Colaresi 2004b for the muted political effects of losing a war during rivalry).

The punctuated equilibrium model suggests that rivalries lock in early and have extended periods of stasis. Implicit in our description of the rivalry maintenance process, flowing from the failures of coercion and conflict management, are two elements. First, rivalry maintenance is influenced less by single events and more by the entire history of the rivalry to date. As conflict events are related over time, there is no reason to think that the most recent dispute is the only one affecting the likelihood of rivalry maintenance. Second, the punctuated equilibrium model indicates that rivalries harden over time, and therefore the influence of various rivalry maintenance factors should dissipate over the life of the rivalry. Once a rivalry is well established and policies have been locked in for rivalry competition, mitigating factors (e.g., victory in a war, democracy) should be less important than had they occurred in earlier phases of the rivalry.

Empirical Findings

Although there are numerous ideas about how rivalry might be maintained, there have not been a commensurate number of studies that test those ideas empirically. Most commonly, there have been empirical studies of rivalry dynamics and escalation, and one can only infer that some of those effects also lead to the perpetuation of rivalries. As we suggest above, however, escalation to war in rivalries is not necessarily associated with rivalry maintenance or termination.

Particularly lacking have been tests of domestic-based approaches to rivalry maintenance. Colaresi (2005) contends that higher information concentration in the elite is evidence of outbidding. Combined with high expected costs, this should lead to the escalation of rivalries. He tests this proposition through the use of three case studies: the Ethiopian-Somali rivalry, the Israeli-Egyptian rivalry, and the Sino-American rivalry. The empirical analysis demonstrates that outbidding is occurring even if not directly tied to rivalry maintenance. Thies (2008) finds some evidence for role theory and the "culture of anarchy" referenced above, at least as it applies to a series of Latin American rivalries. This is suggestive more of how such factors permit rivalries to develop rather than necessarily maintain them, although one might again infer such an effect.

To our knowledge, only one empirical study (Goertz et al. 2005) has directly tested the ideas of rivalry maintenance, and this focused on the logic associated with the failure of coercion. The empirical results of their study are reproduced in table 5.2. Goertz and his colleagues indicate that stalemates

Table 5.2. Influence on Rivalry Maintenance

Variable	Model 1	Model 2
Stalemate	0.32**	0.36**
Victory	0.04	0.16
Dispute Severity	0.004*	0.003**
Rivalry Severity	−0.005*	−0.003**
Dispute Territory	−0.012	0.19
Rivalry Territory	0.73*	0.51**
Rivalry Duration	−0.004***	−0.006**
Rivalry Order	0.06*	0.06*
Democracy	−0.80*	−0.88*
Stalemate × Waiting	0.10**	0.09
Economic Capabilities		0.004
Military Capabilities		−0.04
Log Waiting	−0.80*	−0.72*
Constant	−2.55*	−2.45*
Wald χ^2	1,548.85*	1,341.75*
Pseudo R^2	0.28	0.27
N	15,258	11,297

Source: Goertz et al. (2005).
Notes: Method of analysis: logit with duration dependency parameter. Dependent variable: reoccurrence of dispute or not.
*$p \leq .001$, **$p \leq .05$, ***$p \leq .10$

are one sign of the failure of coercive or realist strategies; it makes intuitive sense, and this is confirmed empirically, that a stalemate in one conflict is often followed by another dispute. Yet there was no difference between compromise and victory in terms of the reduction in the risk for the occurrence of a future dispute.

Previous work had suggested that characteristics of the most recent dispute in a rivalry conditions whether another conflict will arise. Goertz et al. (2005), however, find that it is the history of the rivalry that matters in perpetuating future conflict. In their results, there is no relationship between whether the current dispute is about territory and future disputes. Considering how important territory is in the complete history of the rivalry, however, produces a massive impact on the occurrence of future disputes and therefore the continuation of the rivalry. Hence, rivalry maintenance is much more a question of whether the rivalry as a whole is about territory rather than whether the last dispute happened to be about territory. This historical effect might be mirrored by the impact of multiple issues in a rivalry, as accumulated rivalry issues also increase the likelihood of dispute occurrence (Dreyer 2010); note that the US-Soviet rivalry entailed a variety of disputed concerns on several continents.

A history of high-severity confrontations had a negative impact on rivalry maintenance even as the severity of the most recent dispute increased the hazard of a dispute reoccurring. In many rivalries, a loss in war incites a state to continue the conflict, rather than signaling that its realist strategies are costly and ineffective. For example, repeated defeats in wars (1948, 1956, 1967) only emboldened Arab states to continue their rivalry with Israel. In contrast, the weariness effect only appears when the average severity of disputes in the rivalry is considered.

Other rivalry contextual variables were significant influences on rivalry maintenance as well. The greater the number of previous disputes, the more likely is the occurrence of another dispute. Instead of conflict weariness, well-institutionalized rivalries (as suggested by the punctuated equilibrium approach) produce disputes in faster succession than shorter-term ones (of course, this is somewhat mitigated if those conflicts are severe). This is consistent with earlier notions that rivalries "lock in" and that hostility has a reinforcing effect. Yet, as a rivalry ages in terms of calendar time, the time until the next dispute actually increases. Well-established rivalries, well ingrained in society and government policy through generations, need less reinforcement to maintain themselves than those less established. Neither economic nor military superiority had an effect on the continuation of rivalries.

In summary, there are strong effects on rivalry maintenance from one aspect of the previous dispute (stalemate outcomes), but more importantly from the longer-term rivalry history. With a few exceptions, this is largely consistent with the punctuated equilibrium model: rivalry history as a whole has a greater impact than what happened recently in the rivalry.

Both the punctuated equilibrium and evolutionary models of rivalry suggest that there are changing patterns in the standard life cycle of a rivalry (Hensel 1999; Diehl and Goertz 2000). Some factors might have stronger effects in the initial stage of rivalry (dispute phases 1 and 2), when rivalries develop and lock in, than in later stages. Once again, Goertz et al. (2005) are the first to assess the likelihood of changing effects on rivalry over its life cycle.

In the developmental stage of rivalry (see also chapter 4 by Valeriano), it takes over a year before the impact of stalemate outcomes are felt in the rivalry relationship, and then they generate additional disputes. Democracy has a significant impact early on in rivalries. Even when higher levels of democracy do not head off militarized confrontations, they are able to mitigate long-term effects and effectively end some rivalries (see more on this in the next section). Severity is negatively associated with rivalry maintenance, suggesting that very severe confrontations at the outset of rivalries may delay the next conflict or even end the competitions. Yet we know that this is far from guaranteed; for example, the US-China and the Arab-Israeli rivalries each began with significant wars and still experienced frequent and extended disputes over a long period of time. Severity is very closely correlated with victory (i.e., one side is much more likely to prevail in a severe conflict, while low-severity conflicts overwhelmingly end in stalemate). Thus, democratic conflict management and realpolitik (severity) lead to a reduced risk of dispute reoccurrence. Territory also has a very strong impact on the evolution of rivalries at this early phase, consistent with the many arguments that territory is central to the development of enduring rivalries (Stinnett and Diehl 2001; Tir and Diehl 2002).

We note the above findings on rivalry development to contrast them with those below on the processes that facilitate the maintenance of rivalries after they are established. In the second phase of rivalry development, the severity of the rivalry no longer matters in influencing future disputes (low-level disputes between Ecuador and Peru, for example, do not lessen the likelihood of rivalry continuation). Rivalries have locked in, and the impact of previous disputes has dissipated. Several influences, however, retain some explanatory value. Democracy still has a pacifying effect. In contrast, territory continues to exacerbate the conflict, suggesting that the underlying issues of the rivalry remain important determinants of rivalry maintenance.

In the most advanced stage of rivalries (the most enduring ones), few of the early influences on rivalry maintenance remain relevant. The outcomes of recent disputes matter little, as almost 80 percent of disputes in this rivalry

phase now end in stalemate. Even wars do not necessarily serve to end a rivalry; high-severity conflicts between Japan and China in the 1930s did little
to prevent future confrontations. The democracy variable is also no longer
important; there are very few long-term rivalries between democracies, and
its effects are felt earlier in the competition rather than later. Consistent with
arguments about the importance of territory, however, rivalries over territory
have a much higher risk of producing future disputes and maintaining the
rivalry (Vasquez and Leskiw 2001; Tir and Diehl 2002; Goertz et al. 2005).
Thus, the history of territorial conflict, even from the early stages of the
rivalry, has a strong and lingering effect in promoting rivalry maintenance
despite many subsequent disputes and the significant passage of time.

RIVALRY TERMINATION

The termination of rivalries differs significantly from processes described
in the extensive literature about the termination of war. Wars take place at
various junctures of rivalries: at the beginning, middle, and ending phases.
Accordingly, understanding how a particular war ends offers few or no clues
to the end of a rivalry, which may persist for decades after war termination
(Bennett 1996). Cioffi-Revilla (1998) and Bennett (1998) show that rivalries
are more likely to end the longer they persist. Although the hazard rate for
rivalries may be increasing, their conflict level shows little sign of abating,
and the precise time point of rivalry termination largely cannot be predicted
by the hazard rate.

To some extent, rivalries do not terminate when the conditions for their
maintenance are in place. Accordingly, some research has noted that removing the source of disputatious behavior leads to the end of a rivalry.
Gibler (1997a) demonstrates that rivalries can end with the signing of an
alliance that is in effect a territorial settlement treaty. This finding is largely
consistent with research discussed above that suggests a strong territorial
component to the origins and maintenance of enduring rivalries. Yet the
absence of maintenance conditions does not necessarily provide an explanation for the ending of rivalries. There need to be specific factors that
facilitate rivalry termination.

Theoretical Formulations

There are a number of theoretical ideas about how rivalries end, and most
focus on the emergence of some significant change that facilitates the termination conditions. Change might be found domestically in one or both of the

rival states or in the external security environment. Most prominently, these are reflected in the punctuated equilibrium model (Diehl and Goertz 2000), which begins with the expectation that once established, rivalry processes are difficult to alter. If rivalries are the result of well-entrenched causes, then the end of a particular rivalry should be associated with some dramatic change that disrupts established patterns of behavior. Diehl and Goertz (2000) argue that political shocks are virtual necessary conditions for the end of rivalries. These can occur at the system level, with world wars and major shifts in the power distribution among those shocks most cited. Shocks might also occur within either of the rival states, with civil wars and regime change thought to open the possibilities for rivalry termination. In both cases, shocks can transform the preferences that states have for ending the rivalries. Most notably, shocks can lead to the rise of new alliances, sometimes with old enemies, in order to meet emerging threats. Domestic-level shocks can make ending rivalries a necessity for dealing with internal problems or can substantially change the policy preferences of the regime, such that the bargaining spaces and opportunities for ending rivalries are expanded.

Domestic-Level Changes

Cox (2010) sees domestic policy failure as the instigator of the rivalry termination process. His central argument is rooted in the idea that failures in policy prompt changes in preferences, which in turn expand the bargaining space in which rivals can agree to end their competitions. The first component in his model is domestic realignment that comes from a regime change or a new government within existing regime structures. Such changes stem from policy failures on the national level; problems stemming from national economic policy are a recurring theme, although Cox provides neither a list of possible failures nor a specification of what scope of failure is necessary to trigger the hypothesized effects. In his conception, simple regime change is not necessarily conducive to rivalry termination. The direction of the regime change is as critical as the domestic realignment itself. If one hawkish leader replaces another, then there is likely to be little impact on the rivalry. There must be a movement toward leadership that is "moderate" or "dovish," leaders who are more willing to make concessions and reach compromise with an enemy.

Preference change can come about in the absence of major domestic failures, and regime change in the direction of democracy should also be associated with rivalry termination. This theoretical logic is consistent with that of the "democratic peace," namely that democratic states are more likely to settle their disputes peacefully (Dixon 1994) and without resort to the military actions that sustain rivalries. Thus, when regime change in one or both rivals

—

leads to a democratic dyad, the expectation is that a rivalry will end thereafter. This was part of the logic that motivated the United States to invade Iraq and quickly establish a democratic regime there.

Cox (2010) argues that domestic realignment that leads to rivalry termination is less likely to produce changes in rivalry dynamics unless it is accompanied by foreign policy failure; domestic policy failure alone is not sufficient to alter rivalry dynamics, and foreign policy failures might not lead to changes in government if the domestic economy is healthy. Indeed Japan (and other states as well) has experienced a number of economic recessions over the past two centuries, and this has not often led to the end of its rivalries with other countries (see Klein et al. 2006). The combined domestic and foreign failures are said to produce a greater willingness to accept rivalry concessions, thereby opening up the bargaining space with a rival and making some kind of accommodation possible. This is consistent with the Diehl and Goertz (2000) argument that domestic shocks represent only necessary conditions for rivalry termination.

Changes in the External Environment

What drives foreign policy failure or at least the reassessment of foreign policy preferences? There seems to be some consensus around the importance of multiple, simultaneous rivals. Kupchan (2010) identifies these as creators of a "strategic predicament" that prompts a state to make a conciliatory gesture to one of its competitors. Bennett (1996) suggests that states might need to end one competition in order to concentrate on a new enemy. His analysis of rivalry termination also indicates that some rivalries end when the rivals begin to have common external security threats; in effect, the advent of new rivalries with negative links to extant rivalries causes the latter to end. For example, the rapprochement between the United States and China in the late 1960s was said to be driven by a mutual need to focus on the Soviet Union as a primary threat. Cox (2010) emphasizes the resource pressures that stem from multiple rivalries. He argues that resource strains emanating from multiple rivalries produce domestic policy failures as the government spends more on external rather than domestic needs.

Models of how rivalries end that depend largely on changes in one state run into the problem that rivalry termination is a joint decision (except for imposed military victories and total capitulations, outcomes that are relatively rare). Where does the second rival come in when the conditions for rivalry settlement arise in the first rival? Cox provides two answers, almost as an addendum to the basic argument. The first is that the preference change of the first rival might lead its set of acceptable resolutions to be enlarged such that its bargaining space of acceptable solutions now overlaps with that of its rival; unfortunately, this is difficult to observe prior to any agreement. Second, the other rival might also experience similar and simultaneous domestic and foreign policy failures, thereby making it more receptive to its opponent's peace overtures.

Empirical Findings

Empirically, we know that rivalries do not merely fade away but tend to end abruptly. This is consistent with the necessity of dramatic political shocks for the end of a stable process. Indeed, over 90 percent of the rivalries had their last dispute during or in the ten-year period after a political shock (Diehl and Goertz 2000). Most notable were dramatic changes in the power distribution in the international system, consistent with Colaresi's (2001) results showing that power deconcentration in the system was associated with the end of rivalries. At the system level, world wars and substantial territorial changes were not strongly associated with rivalry termination (Diehl and Goertz 2000).

Findings have been more robust at the state level with respect to shocks. Cox (2010) tested his model with comparative case studies of paired rivalries that differ with respect to whether they terminated or not (Israel's rivalries with Egypt and Syria, and Peru's rivalries with Chile and Ecuador, respectively), and the results largely confirmed his expectations about the importance of domestic and foreign policy failures prompting rivalry termination. Yet self-declared measurement problems and the likelihood of many false positives (economic downturns and foreign policy failures are common) raise concerns about the robustness of his results.

Stronger and clearer findings are present regarding the effect of regime change, especially when joint democracy has been the result. Few rivalries ever occur between two democracies (Conrad and Souva 2011), as disputes are settled before they become militarized, or they do not involve repeated conflict in the event that a violent confrontation does occur. What happens, though, when a rivalry begins under one dyadic regime configuration and a joint democratic dyad occurs later in the competition? Hensel, Goertz, and Diehl (2000; see also Prins and Daxecker 2008) examined such "regime change" rivalries, and there is strong confirmation that rivalries are more likely to end when both states become democratic (e.g., the lasting peace between Argentina and Chile following their democratic transitions in the 1980s). Nevertheless, this is not necessarily an immediate effect, as disputatious behavior might continue in the absence of full consolidation (e.g., Pakistan in the India-Pakistan rivalry) or even increase in the short run until the joint democracy effects are felt. Broader liberal processes, extensions of the democratic peace logic into the Kantian triad, might contribute to the end of rivalries as well, with common membership in international governmental organizations having such an effect and possibly increasing economic interdependence, although evidence on the latter is not as strong (Cornwell and Colaresi 2002; Prins and Daxecker 2008).

In his study of twenty enemy relationships that evolved into friendships, Kupchan (2010) inductively sees the end of rivalries as a process involving a series of steps. The aforementioned "strategic predicament" prompting a conciliatory gesture is the first stage ("unilateral accommodation"). The second stage involves reciprocal and positive responses ("reciprocal restraint") to such overtures by the other rival, often leaving the most difficult issues for later negotiation. Diplomacy takes over, and there are a series of gestures and actions over a period of years that reinforce the march toward peaceful relations. Any disputes are resolved peacefully, without jeopardizing overall relations. The process shifts from diplomats to the general public in a third stage. In a process that seemingly mirrors neofunctionalism, cooperation extends to all sorts of political, economic, and social realms ("societal integration"). The fourth and final phase ("generation of new narratives and identities") involves an attitudinal transformation in the rival states in which peoples come to identify themselves as friends rather than enemies. Kupchan argues that domestic political processes can derail the process, and somewhat surprisingly, economic interdependence had little effect in promoting rivalry termination. He also notes that democracy is not necessary for this transformation to occur.

Finally, there is also a plethora of empirical studies that seek to explain the end of the Cold War (e.g., Deudney and Ikenberry 1991–1992). Unfortunately, there are several problems with this literature if we are interested in insights on rivalry termination. First, much of the literature is concerned with explaining the collapse of the Soviet Union. The end of the superpower rivalry is then treated as one of many consequences of that collapse. Yet it is not clear whether there is a point being made about domestic political changes and the end of rivalries or whether the end of rivalries is somehow slightly different than the implosion of one of the rivals. Second, it is not clear (whatever the focus) that such studies can or are designed to be generalizable to rivalries other than the US-Soviet one.

Despite these limitations, Lebow (1994) has attempted to use the Cold War case to develop a set of conditions that he believes accounts for the thawing of US-Soviet relations under Gorbachev and the winding down of rivalries in general (Lebow 1997). For accommodation to occur, he argues that the presence of the following three conditions for one of the rivals is critical: (1) a leader committed to domestic reforms, where foreign cooperation is necessary for those reforms; (2) that rivalry and confrontation have failed in the past to achieve a rival's goals and are likely to fail in the future; and

(3) the belief that conciliatory gestures will be reciprocated. Thus, Lebow sees the end of rivalries as beginning from domestic political considerations and nurtured by diplomacy, not unlike a combination of the processes outlined by Cox (2010) and Kupchan (2010).

Bennett (1998) attempted to synthesize many of his and other findings on enduring rivalry termination through empirical testing of a large number of cases. He concludes that domestic political factors and issue salience seem to be most associated with rivalry termination. He finds distinctly mixed results on security concerns (the emergence of multiple rivalries) as a driving force behind the end of rivalries. He also gets mixed results on the impact of political shocks on rivalry termination. Yet his analysis of political shocks does not properly test the contention that shocks operate only as a necessary condition for rivalry termination (his analysis treats them as necessary *and* sufficient). Furthermore, his analysis assumes that political shocks have an immediate and single-year effect on rivalry behavior, a conception at odds with our contention that major political changes are likely to reverberate through the system over the course of several years, rather than having an effect only at a fixed point.

Overall, it appears that removing territorial disputes from a relationship helps promote rivalry termination, but then one is left with understanding what conditions lead to such settlements. Major changes in the relationship, especially political shocks, prompt the preference and opportunity changes needed. The clearest findings are that regime changes to joint democracy are effective. Various other factors, such as the rise of other external threats, economic interdependence, and the like, have as yet obtained only mixed support in limited studies.

CONCLUSION

The study of interstate rivalries has come a long way since its inception, when the primary concern was with defining a sample of cases and then using that list of rivalries to analyze a series of standard propositions about international conflict (e.g., deterrence). We now know a lot more about rivalries themselves—how they begin, what keeps them going, and how they end. In the course of this, we also have a greater understanding of the contexts and conditions under which states make decisions for war.

Although scholars have made great strides in rivalry research, there are still a number of lines of inquiry that hold promise to deepen our understanding and fill in gaps in our knowledge. We would like briefly to highlight several of these. First, some of the most promising lines of research about rivalry maintenance and termination concern the domestic political influences of those processes. New research has identified regime type, specifically democracy, as an important factor, consistent with the democratic peace research tradition. Yet there needs to be greater attention to electoral and selectorate incentives for rivalry maintenance and how domestic economic conditions influence various rivalry decisions. Other domestic shocks, such as the occurrence of natural disasters (Akcinaroglu, DiCicco, and Radziszewski 2011), might also shift domestic orientations toward a rival. There seem to be potentially compelling reasons for such influences to both prolong and shorten rivalries depending on their character and timing.

Second, even though rivalry is increasingly used as an explanatory factor in models of war, there is yet not enough attention to how it interacts with other factors. What is the interactive effect of rivalries with alliances, arms races, and other traditional conflict variables? The "steps-to-war" model (Senese and Vasquez 2008) posits a simple additive effect, but there might be good reasons that rivalry has joint effects with those factors. For example, is there a recursive and reinforcing relationship between alliance formation and rivalry maintenance? Are rivalries prerequisites for the emergence of factors such as arms races (Rider et al. 2011)? Do ending arms races, managing territorial claims, and/or dismantling alliances have an appreciable effect on rivalry maintenance and termination? Such synergistic and sequential relationships are as yet unexplored but are critical in further integrating rivalry into models of international conflict.

Third, for a subset of rivalries, their conclusions turn out to be a temporary lull before hostilities resume, albeit decades later in some instances; these might be referred to as "interrupted rivalries." Why does the end of some rivalries lead to extended periods of peace, without further hostilities (e.g., France-Germany after World War II), whereas others resume after they were apparently settled (e.g., Greece-Turkey)? We know little about interrupted rivalries and whether their reappearance can be accounted for by the same factors as those thought to be associated with rivalry initiation. Yet treating the beginnings of interrupted rivalries as unrelated to past interactions is a curious approach given that rivalry scholars have criticized others for not taking into account "history" in analyzing the dynamics of rivalries.

Fourth, most rivalry analyses do not take into account how rivalries are related to one another (a limited exception is found in Diehl and Goertz 2000). That is, just as individual disputes are related to one another, contemporaneous rivalries might influence each other's dynamics and state decision making; an example is the web of individual rivalries that make up the Arab-Israeli conflict. Network analysis (for an application to international relations, see Maoz 2010) seems ideally suited to account for how rivalries intersect with one another. Such interconnections impact war decisions, including the spread of war (Vasquez et al. 2011).

Finally, the end of rivalries leads to a concern with what kinds of relationships follow that termination. For example, the France-Germany and the Egypt-Israel rivalries were both particularly severe and extended over broad periods of time. The militarized aspects of their relationships have effectively ended, yet the state of relations in these two dyads is notably different. France and Germany are now in a condition of "positive peace." They have institutionalized a large number of cooperative ventures, most notably through their membership in the European Union and joint military exercises. Conversely, Israel and Egypt are in a condition of "negative peace." The two have not engaged in a militarized dispute since 1989, yet the relationship is "cool." In 2000, Egypt withdrew its ambassador in protest of the Israeli response to the renewed Intifada, and an expected, at least by Israel, strong commercial relationship between the two has never materialized. Klein et al. (2008) have begun to collect data on the kinds of relationships that exist in nonrivalry periods, but there are as yet no theoretical formulations or empirical analyses on what accounts for the range of postrivalry relationships.

Appendix: Enduring Rivalries, 1816–2001

State A	State B	Rivalry Period
United States	Canada	1974–1997
United States	Haiti	1869–1915
United States	Mexico	1836–1893, 1911–1920
United States	Ecuador	1952–1981
United States	Peru	1955–1992
United States	United Kingdom	1837–1861
United States	Spain	1816–1825, 1850–1898
United States	Yugoslavia	1992–2000
United States	Iran	1979–1997
United States	Russia/Soviet Union	1946–2000
United States	Libya	1973–1996
United States	Egypt	1956–1968
United States	Cuba	1959–1996
United States	Iraq	1987–2001
United States	China	1949–2001
United States	North Korea	1950–2000
Canada	Yugoslavia	1998–2000
Trinidad and Tobago	Venezuela	1996–1999
Belize	Guatemala	1993–2001
Honduras	El Salvador	1969–1993

(continued)

Paul F. Diehl and Gary Goertz

State A	State B	Rivalry Period
Honduras	Nicaragua	1907–1929, 1957–2001
Nicaragua	Costa Rica	1977–1998
Colombia	Venezuela	1982–2000
Colombia	Peru	1899–1934
Venezuela	Guyana	1966–1999
Ecuador	Peru	1891–1955
Bolivia	Paraguay	1886–1938
Guyana	Suriname	1976–2000
Ecuador	Peru	1977–1998
Peru	Chile	1852–1921
Brazil	United Kingdom	1838–1863
Chile	Argentina	1873–1909, 1952–1984
United Kingdom	Germany	1887–1921
United Kingdom	Italy	1927–1943
United Kingdom	Yugoslavia	1992–2000
United Kingdom	China	1950–1968
United Kingdom	Taiwan	1949–1955
United Kingdom	Japan	1932–1945
United Kingdom	Russia/Soviet Union	1876–1923, 1939–1999
United Kingdom	Turkey/Ottoman Empire	1827–1934
United Kingdom	Iraq	1958–2001
Netherlands	Yugoslavia	1992–2000
Netherlands	Indonesia	1951–1962
Belgium	Germany	1914–1940
Belgium	Yugoslavia	1992–2000
France	Germany/Prussia	1830–1940
France	Turkey/Ottoman Empire	1880–1938
France	Italy	1925–1940
France	Yugoslavia	1992–2000
France	Libya	1978–1987
France	Iraq	1990–1999
France	China	1870–1927
Spain	Yugoslavia	1992–2000
Spain	Morocco	1957–1980
Portugal	Yugoslavia	1998–2000
Germany	Italy	1914–1943
Germany	Yugoslavia	1992–2000
Poland	Yugoslavia	1999–2000
Hungary	Yugoslavia	1991–2000
Czech Republic	Yugoslavia	1999–2000
Italy	Turkey/Ottoman Empire	1880–1924
Italy	Yugoslavia	1923–1956, 1992–2000
Italy	Ethiopia	1923–1943
Albania	Yugoslavia	1992–2001
Croatia	Yugoslavia	1992–2000
Croatia	Bosnia and Herzegovina	1992–1996
Yugoslavia	Greece	1992–2000

State A	State B	Rivalry Period
Yugoslavia	Bulgaria	1913–1952
Yugoslavia	Norway	1998–2000
Yugoslavia	Denmark	1998–2000
Yugoslavia	Iceland	1998–2000
Yugoslavia	Turkey	1992–2000
Greece	Turkey/Ottoman Empire	1866–1925, 1958–2001
Greece	Bulgaria	1913–1952
Greece	Iraq	1982–1999
Cyprus	Turkey	1965–2001
Russia/Soviet Union	Norway	1956–2001
Russia	Georgia	1992–2001
Russia/Soviet Union	Iran	1908–1987
Russia/Soviet Union	Turkey/Ottoman Empire	1817–1829, 1876–1921, 1993–2000
Russia/Soviet Union	Afghanistan	1980–2001
Russia/Soviet Union	China	1862–1994
Russia/Soviet Union	Israel	1956–1974
Russia/Soviet Union	Japan	1861–2001
Armenia	Azerbaijan	1992–2001
Ghana	Togo	1961–1994
Cameroon	Nigeria	1981–1998
Chad	Libya	1976–1994
Congo (Brazzaville)	Democratic Republic of the Congo (Zaire)	1963–1997
Democratic Republic of the Congo (Zaire)	Uganda	1977–2001
Democratic Republic of the Congo (Zaire)	Zambia	1971–1994
Uganda	Kenya	1965–1997
Uganda	Rwanda	1991–2001
Uganda	Sudan	1968–2001
Tanzania	Burundi	1995–2000
Somalia	Ethiopia	1960–1985
Ethiopia	Sudan	1967–1997
Eritrea	Yemen	1995–1999
Zambia	Zimbabwe	1965–1979
Zambia	South Africa	1968–1987
Zimbabwe	Botswana	1969–1979
Morocco	Algeria	1962–1984
Libya	Sudan	1972–1984
Libya	Egypt	1975–1985
Sudan	Egypt	1991–1996
Iran	Iraq	1934–1999
Iran	Turkey	1981–2001
Iran	Saudi Arabia	1984–1988

(*continued*)

State A	State B	Rivalry Period
Iran	Afghanistan	1979–1999
Turkey	Iraq	1958–2001
Turkey	Syria	1955–1998
Iraq	Kuwait	1961–2001
Iraq	Israel	1948–1998
Iraq	Saudi Arabia	1961–2001
Egypt	Israel	1948–1989
Egypt	Jordan	1948–1962
Egypt	Saudi Arabia	1962–1967
Syria	Israel	1948–2001
Syria	Jordan	1949–1982
Jordan	Israel	1948–1973
Lebanon	Israel	1948–2001
Israel	Saudi Arabia	1957–1981
Afghanistan	Pakistan	1949–2001
Afghanistan	Tajikistan	1993–2001
Afghanistan	Uzbekistan	1993–2001
China	Taiwan	1949–2001
China	North Korea	1993–1997
China	South Korea	1950–1994
China	Japan	1873–1958, 1978–1999
China	India	1950–1987
China	South Vietnam	1956–1974
China	(North) Vietnam	1975–1998
China	Philippines	1950–2001
North Korea	South Korea	1949–2001
North Korea	Japan	1994–2001
South Korea	Japan	1953–1999
India	Pakistan	1947–2001
India	Bangladesh	1976–2001
Thailand	Laos	1960–1988
Thailand	Cambodia	1953–1998
Thailand	(North) Vietnam	1961–1995
Cambodia	South Vietnam	1956–1967

Source: Klein, Goertz, and Diehl (2006).

NOTES

The authors would like to thank Thorin Wright and Andrew Owsiak for their assistance, and John Vasquez, Peter Wallensteen, Zeev Maoz, and Jack Levy for their comments and suggestions.

1. Nevertheless, the criteria used by Thompson and his colleagues (Colaresi et al. 2008) include no *minimum* duration requirement.

2. In earlier conceptions, these were designated as "protorivalries" (Diehl and Goertz 2000).

3. The Thompson list (Colaresi et al. 2008) does provide precise dates for when rivalries have ended.

4. Using the criteria in Diehl and Goertz (2000), enduring rivalries are defined as those rivalries with at least six militarized disputes between the same pair of states and lasting at least twenty years. Isolated rivalries are one- and two-dispute rivalries. Protorivalries consist of those remaining rivalries not satisfying the definitional requirements of the other two categories. Given the application of these old coding rules to the newer rivalry data (Klein et al. 2006), the number of rivalries here is different than for the analyses below. That is, one cannot equate the 290 rivalry cases noted earlier and in subsequent analysis with any rivalry category, proto- or enduring, in the appendix (above).

5. Because rivalries are dyadic, multilateral disputes are divided into a series of dyadic disputes. The result is often that there are many more isolated conflicts than would otherwise be the case.

6. The expected percentage of disputes for each rivalry category is calculated by reference to the minimum number of disputes necessary for each rivalry category and the actual number of rivalries in each category. Note that this number might underestimate the "true" value, as the data end in 2001 and some cases currently coded as isolated conflicts or protorivalries might have matured into enduring rivalries in the last decade.

7. "Censored" means that at the time of the last data point (2001), the rivalry has not ended and we don't have the necessary information to tell if and when the rivalry might have ended after that point.

8. Most notably, cases of extended wars are coded as rivalries. Even though they might involve only one or two militarized disputes, they last sufficiently long (in some cases a decade) and at high levels of severity so as to meet the conceptual criteria for rivalry.

9. We do not review all the factors that influence the dynamics of rivalries or their escalation to war, except as they promote the continuation of rivalries. For a different focus on dynamics and escalation, see Colaresi et al. (2007).

Chapter Six

Arms Races

A Cause or a Symptom?

Susan G. Sample

Do arms races change the probability of war, or are they simply a symptom of conflict that is often mistaken for a cause? When the first empirical studies on the role of arms races were being conducted, the Cold War was ongoing, and the debate over the impact of arms buildups in causing or preventing war was politically bound to that conflict. Drawing on the apparently opposing lessons of the world wars, those of every political stripe made impassioned arguments about the threats to civilization itself inherent in the wrong policy choice. The consequences of choosing the wrong arms policy, arming when one should not, or not arming when one should, seemed catastrophic from any perspective.

Those who focused on the essentially unintended catastrophe of World War I argued that a comparable arms race in the nuclear era could result in annihilation of the human race, and they proposed substantial arms control negotiations, if not total nuclear disarmament, to avoid this nightmare. Those who believed that Hitler could have been stopped if Britain and France had clearly signaled their willingness and ability to counter German aggression in the early 1930s argued that only a clear demonstration of Western power, including maintaining a strong arsenal, would deter the Soviet Union from seizing available opportunities to be equally aggressive. For Americans and their allies making this argument, arms buildups signaled to the Soviet Union that aggressive actions would cost more than they were worth and thus helped maintain the "long peace" of the Cold War.

The high stakes then created fertile, and highly contested, ground for empirical research. Given the passion behind these arguments, and the high stakes, it is almost surprising just how much of this debate was held in the context of elegant theory but relatively little empirical evidence. Primarily drawing on examples culled from history, the world wars being the most obvious example, systematic evidence of the impact of arms buildups was in short supply for a good long time.

The political contest, however, did reflect the primary theoretical conflict that animated the first empirical studies, once they seriously began. Essentially, was there a relationship between arms buildups and war that was independent of measures for the distribution of power in the system? Theoretically, this question set up a contest between deterrence theory, on the one hand, and what has been termed the "hostile spiral" argument, on the other. Deterrence theory implied that while one might see a relationship between arms buildups and war, it would not be the "arms race" per se that was helping to cause the war. Rather, rapid arms buildups could have an impact on the distribution of power between states in a way that would increase the likelihood of war. While this is the position of deterrence theory, it was only sporadically argued in the empirical literature, a great deal of which was taken up with methodological questions and attempts to demonstrate that the first findings of a correlation must have been wrong, rather than suggesting that from the perspective of deterrence theory, they were simply irrelevant. In contrast to deterrence theory, the spiral of hostility argument held that arms races themselves dangerously altered the dynamics between states. This position typically assumed a more psychologically based framework, where arms buildups contributed to each party's belief in the other's aggressive intent, whether true or not, increasing the likelihood that states would consider violent conflict nearly inevitable, thus increasing its real occurrence.

I will begin this chapter with a review of this empirical literature and its theoretical underpinnings. In the past decade, however, the theoretical ground has shifted enormously under studies on the role of arms races in war. The basic question of whether arms buildups are related to peace or escalation of conflict has largely been settled in favor of the latter; while the circumstances of the Cold War merit special attention, arms buildups are typically related to escalation of conflict to war, even once one accounts for shifts in the distribution of capabilities between states. The premises of deterrence do not seem to be empirically accurate through most of the last two hundred years. At this point, the question is still whether arms races contribute to war or not, but the foundations of the debate have changed: is there a real and independent impact on the likelihood of war, presumably embedded in a more complex process such as that suggested by the steps-to-war thesis? Or, instead, are arms races simply symptoms of a larger phenomenon, like interstate rivalry, exercising no actual causal force of their own, but simply reflecting the conflictual nature of the relationship between some states?

Notably, both of these questions embed arms races into larger processes. While early studies focused on one variable at a time to attempt to discern its impact, we largely understand the multicausal nature of war at this point, and ultimately the challenge is one of understanding complex, dynamic interrelationships leading to war (Vasquez 1993, 2009; Colaresi, Rasler, and Thompson 2007). Nonetheless, it is important to discern which conditions realistically fit into those processes, and given the continued theoretical disagreement over their role, we address here the question of whether arms races are really worthy of continued consideration within these frameworks. By addressing several of the predicted incompatibilities of different theoretical arguments regarding arms races, this study attempts to provide an answer to that question.

THEORETICAL AND EMPIRICAL BACKGROUND

While arguments about the peaceful or dangerous impact of arms buildups trace back to the Latin, systematic empirical tests of the relationship between arms buildups and war really only emerged at the end of the 1970s. In a much-noted study, Wallace (1979) found that dyadic disputes between states were vastly more likely to escalate to war in the presence of an ongoing arms race than in its absence. The strength of his findings and their political implications led to almost immediate response, and the study was quickly challenged on multiple grounds, some methodological and some more theoretical.

Although there is no doubt that the methodological concerns were important ones, the resolution of the whole question unfortunately became bogged down in them. At issue in the studies was the empirical question of whether or not there was any relationship to be found between arms buildups and war. Most criticism of Wallace's study appeared to assume that the relationship he found was at least overstated if not completely an artifact of his methods. There were many questions about how to properly structure a test of the relationship and how to measure the key variable, as well as questions about what sample of disputes would be appropriate given the fact that disputes occurring during the world wars, in particular, could hardly be considered independent events. Ultimately, some of the issues that arose are more easily resolvable than others in testing the relationship between arms buildups and war.

Theoretically, the debate between Wallace and his critics reflected the two arguments that were then prevalent regarding the impact of arms buildups: the deterrence framework and the hostile spiral framework. The theoretical underpinnings of deterrence are rationality and the primacy of the material balance of capabilities between contestants in the international system. If a state has sufficient military capability, however achieved, to make the costs of aggressive behavior greater than the likely benefit, then escalation is unlikely.[1] Deterrence gets messy in practice when states misread or miscalculate willingness or ability to inflict those costs, but in theory, arms buildups should only be relevant to the likelihood of escalation when they alter the material capabilities of states in a substantial way. The assumptions of this framework help explain why most of Wallace's early critics assumed that methodological quirks had led to his findings and that resolution of those problems would eliminate the association between arms buildups and war.

In this context, Weede's (1980) response to Wallace more directly addressed the theoretical foundations of Wallace's work. Weede had several important critiques. Among them, he noted that the relationship between escalation and war seemed to be at least in part related to historical time period, suggesting that some historical periods lacked escalation no matter what Wallace's arms race index suggested. Weede (1980) also made a preliminary case for deterrence theory and the dubious relevance of Wallace's findings even if the correlation proved to be valid: he pointed out that those who argued in favor of deterrence were not concerned so much with an out-of-control arms race as with the status quo power (the United States in this case) losing the arms race (p. 286–87), thus allowing an opportunistic foe (the Soviet Union) to behave aggressively with impunity. Wallace's response was to code disputes based on whether the revisionist or status quo power was "winning" the arms race at the time of the dispute. In one test, Wallace (1980) found some relationship between the revisionist state advancing and escalation to war, but his later research (1982) did not find such a relationship, and he continued to find support for his earlier conclusion that arms races themselves were an independent factor contributing to escalation. From our perspective, however, the debate does suggest the importance of considering both distribution of power and arms races per se in our analyses to determine their independent effects.

Weede's more theoretical critique made it clear that the primary point of contention for deterrence theorists was that those who feared an arms race were ignoring the real issue: what happened to the balance of military capabilities when states were engaged in an arms race. It was shifts there that would actually determine the likelihood of war, not simply an arms race. Whether there was an "arms race," then, was not really even an interesting question from this perspective since the arms race was likely to simply be a symptom of ongoing political conflict (Kydd 2000), or an indication that the dissatisfied state in a pair was attempted to shift the distribution of capabilities in its direction (Werner and Kugler 1996). Thus, the legitimate focus of inquiry should be on the distribution of capabilities that arms policies created and whether that allowed potentially aggressive states opposing the status quo to challenge it (Weede 1980). Arms races themselves were not important.

A positive correlation, then, between arms races and war would be considered spurious by deterrence theory, but in actuality, there should not be a relationship at all once one has considered the balance of capabilities between states. To the extent that states use arms buildups as bargaining signals during ongoing political conflicts or rivalries, it is still essentially the balance of capabilities that determines the likelihood of conflict for deterrence theory itself. For the most part, variations in some predictions in the literature can be resolved by making the distinction as to whether one would expect a positive, but spurious, association in a bivariate context, or whether one would expect no relationship after controlling for distribution of capabilities. It is important to note that the empirical studies around the effects of arms buildups were strictly bivariate until the late 1990s, so much of the conversation was in that context.

In contrast to deterrence theory, the theoretical argument that arms buildups are inherently dangerous has generally been termed the "hostile spiral" thesis (Kydd 2000). In this argument, arms races are said to increase the probability of war through a psychological process of increasing threat perception. Because of the security dilemma, states must concern themselves with the arms buildups of foes and potential foes. This basic assumption of anarchy is then coupled with arguments derived from cognitive psychology regarding how individuals process information: seeing themselves at the center of others' planning, assuming that their messages are clearly understood by others, and so forth can lead to a situation where an ongoing military buildup, particularly in the context of a militarized dispute, is likely to be seen as evidence of direct and imminent threat to the security of the state, precipitating a hostile spiral when disputes occur in the context of military buildups. Countries feel progressively more threatened and respond in a progressively more threatening way (or their responses are perceived as more threatening). This argument assumes that war is not always a deliberate and rational choice but can happen though accident or misinterpretation. This theoretical framework is thus not concerned exclusively, or even primarily, with the distribution of material capabilities, but rather the interplay between the material threat of the arms buildup and a psychological dynamic in the minds of individuals in leadership positions that makes escalation seem more and more necessary, and consequently, more and more probable (Sample 1997).

A number of the methodological problems left over from the debates regarding Wallace's study were resolved by Sample (1997). Controlling for different samples of dispute dyads and different measures of mutual military buildups, she demonstrated that the relationship between arms buildups and dispute escalation among major states, while not as strong as Wallace's finding, was certainly positive and significant in bivariate tests. Further tests

(Sample 2000) demonstrated that this relationship continued to be significant in multivariate studies that controlled specifically for several variables related to the distribution of capabilities.

Subsequent testing, however, suggested that while military buildups were associated positively with escalation under some circumstances, they were not so under all circumstances. Moving beyond the original major state focus to consider disputes between minor states and disputes between major and minor states demonstrated that disputes between minor states, like those between major states, were significantly more likely to escalate in the context of an ongoing military buildup, but disputes between a major and minor state were not. Furthermore, breaking the whole Correlates of War period and using the escalation of a particular militarized dispute to war as the dependent variable revealed that the results were also dependent on historical era: the positive relationship disappeared after World War II (Sample 2002; Senese and Vasquez 2008). While patterns of escalation for both minor state disputes and mixed disputes existed in changed form after World War II, in neither case did it include a significant relationship between arms buildups and war (Sample 2002).

These findings both resolved many of the contemporary questions around the impact of arms buildups and created fertile new ground for theoretical, and ultimately empirical, questioning. There has been a fundamental shift of the theoretical ground under the arms-race–war question. The very complexity of the results indicating that the impact of arms races varies depending on the status configuration of the states involved and the time period considered suggests that to the extent arms buildups truly have an impact on the likelihood of war, it is not a simple one, and it is likely to be embedded in larger processes. Thus, the primary questions at this juncture are just what those processes are, what do they have to say about the role of arms buildups, and how can we create empirical tests to reasonably adjudicate between very differing theoretical claims? The two dominant theoretical frameworks for much of the conflict literature, the steps-to-war theory and the rivalry literature, have had essentially contradicting arguments regarding the role of arms buildups in war.

Within the steps-to-war thesis, arms races are considered to lead to a step increase in the probability of war. One of the primary paths to war begins with states contesting over territory, an issue demonstrated to be more conflict prone than virtually any other in the modern era (Vasquez 1993; Hensel 2000). States are not obligated to respond to the existence of a territorial dispute by escalating the conflictual aspects of the relationship, but they may very well do so. The coming of hard-liners to power and choices to form alliances and build up arms increase the probability that war will occur between the states. The steps-to-war argument suggests that the development of rivalry is one of the outcomes of a step process of policy choices, and if a rivalry develops, that too, as with each of the other steps, contributes to the likelihood of war occurring between the states. The theoretical premise of steps to war is that these are *steps*, that each one of them independently alters the dynamics of the relationship, increasing the probability of war (Senese and Vasquez 2008). Some of them, like the coming of hard-liners to power and policy choices to make alliances or build arms, are clearly not determined. They may or may not happen, though the pervasiveness of a realpolitik policy-making culture in international relations certainly encourages them. In the absence of one of the steps, however, the risk of war is simply lower. Arms races, then, like rivalry itself, independently increase the probability of war, making the relationship a causal one, and assessing *how* arms buildups affect subsequent decision making is a valid line of questioning if we wish to understand fully the causes of war.

In contrast, representing the basic assumption embedded in much of the rivalry research, Diehl and Crescenzi (1998) argue that arms races are simply an artifact of the rivalry relationship. Like war itself, they are likely caused by the fact of the rivalry, and thus any relationship between war and arms races is spurious. Diehl (1998) makes the argument that while some studies have treated rivalry as a "background condition" for examining such things as arms buildups, it is important to shift to the dynamics of rivalry as the primary focus of our inquiries because it is rivalry that fundamentally determines the probability of conflict: once a rivalry emerges, the rivalry itself shapes the interaction between the states and the policy choices they make. The political relationship between rivals is prone to a high likelihood of violent conflict and coincidentally leads them to engage in related policies, like building up arms. Within this framework, the relationship between arms races and war is illusory, a result of the rivalry between the countries, and is thus completely spurious. If this argument is true, then examinations of arms races as independent factors in the probability of war are misdirected. Arms races are not particularly worthy of continued study since they are a mere symptom of larger processes, not a causal variable.[2]

The basic premise that rivalries take on a force of their own and can explain other policy choices is quite powerful. One of the great contributions of this literature is also a reemphasis on historical relationships between states. However, if one does not automatically accept the assumption that it is pointless to do so, this framework also creates a number of challenges to empirically testing the independent impact of arms buildups. One of the difficulties comes in untangling the threads of rivalry from other theoretical arguments about arms buildups and deterrence. In literature during and about the Cold War, in particular, the different theoretical arguments tend to be blurred or interwoven in ways that make empirical analysis challenging. This blurring happens primarily when authors are making arguments about arms buildups and deterrence in the context of rivalry. Kydd (2000) argues, "The deterrence model indicates that arms races, because they are symptoms of international bargaining, will continue while there are outstanding political differences that are being negotiated" (p. 231). This is an argument that owes at least as much, if not more, to rivalry theory as it does deterrence theory. He also cites Paul Kennedy's defense of deterrence during the Cold War, saying that "arms races are a product of the same conflict that causes war, but do not themselves cause war" (cited in Kydd 2000: 231). Again, this is an argument about rivalry, not primarily about the distribution of capabilities and states' reading of it.

While the assertion that any statistical relationship between arms races and war is spurious is shared between deterrence theorists and much of the rivalry literature to date, it is worth noting that there are distinctive theoretical rationales behind the two claims and that these are relevant to empirical testing of the claims. For deterrence theory, arms buildups might or might not be particularly rapid, and they might or might not lead to shifts in the distribution of capabilities, but it is the latter that genuinely explains the likelihood of war between the involved states, not the simple fact that states are building their arms up at an unusual rate, or the fact that the states define each other as enemies. The implications of rivalry tend to get transferred to arguments about deterrence or arms buildups in ways that may not be appropriate if one considered those things separately from the rivalry. While the point of the rivalry literature is to *not* consider those things separately, in order to determine if that is indeed a valid approach in the first instance, one must do so.

The empirical literature on arms buildups untangles these threads to some extent already, even if inadvertently. Specifically, a distinction has been made between arms races, on the one hand, and mutual military buildups, on the other. Originally, most theoretical arguments were made about arms races themselves, situations in which two states are directly responding to each other's policies in an interactive fashion and arming at an unusually high rate (Huntington 1958; Wallace 1979). The hostile spiral model certainly assumes interaction, as do arguments about deterrence. In the current debates, the steps-to-war thesis argues that once states have begun a conflict over territory, they may very well enter an arms race—the assumption is clearly that they are responding to each other and the arms buildup is essentially related to the political conflict between them, not a coincidental buildup (Senese and Vasquez 2008). And the rivalry literature implies that genuine arms races are only likely to be seen in the event of a rivalry (Diehl and Crescenzi 1998; Gibler, Rider, and Hutchison 2005; Colaresi, Rasler, and Thompson 2007).

The major part of the empirical literature, however, including most tests of the steps-to-war thesis, has not used measures of arms races, but rather measures of mutual military buildups. Originally this was done for convenience: determining if a buildup is actually an arms race requires delving into the history of the relationship between the states and their decision making to determine if they were interacting. In contrast, measuring mutual buildups could be done with the data available, and thus it was a convenient proxy for the concept. A mutual military buildup was said to occur when each state was engaging in unusually rapid growth of the military, but the measure does not concern itself with the question of whether two states were actually interacting. As it turns out, this distinction can help us move forward in our empirical study of the impact of arming because it is not theoretically bound to rivalry.

Ultimately, then, the empirical question facing us is whether military buildups are simply an outcome of rivalry and are spuriously linked to war through that rivalry, or whether arms races have a real and independent impact on war causation. This information would let us know whether focus on the causes and effects of arms buildups is worthy of our attention, and it would also help us adjudicate some of the differences between the steps-to-war thesis and the rivalry literature. In truth, while the underlying theories are different, there is a great deal of empirical overlap in their explanations of war. Because of the commonalities, such as territorial conflict playing an important role in the emergence of rivalry (Hensel 2001b; Goertz, Jones, and Diehl 2005) and rivalry being a step on the road to war in the steps-to-war thesis (Senese and Vasquez 2008), it is important to find those distinguishing hypotheses that ultimately would allow us to determine which of the larger processes is really the best place to focus our intellectual energy. Determining whether arms buildups have an independent impact on the likelihood of war, since it is clearly a place where the theories differ, is a good start.

While this chapter includes new findings, at least three studies have made clear and noteworthy contributions already to the resolution of this question. Gibler, Rider, and Hutchison (2005) chose to accept some of the basic assumptions of the rivalry literature and then test the question of the independent impact of arms races within that framework. Specifically, wanting to take both deterrence theory and the arguments of rivalry seriously, they accepted the claim that arms races should only be seen within rivalries and then carefully examined disputes only within rivalries to determine if those characterized by ongoing arms races were then more likely to escalate. Unlike previous studies that used mutual military buildups, they did examine the historical record to determine that military buildups were, in fact, arms races. If arms races had no independent impact, there should have been no statistical relationship once one controlled for rivalry by removing nonrivalrous disputes from the analysis altogether. They found that disputes occurring in the context of ongoing rivalries were more likely to escalate when an arms race was present. They also found that arms races could be linked to dispute occurrence in the first place. If the arms-race–war relationship were simply spurious, this should not be so.

Likewise, Senese and Vasquez (2008), in their tests of the steps-to-war thesis, examine the impact of arms races while controlling for rivalry as a variable in tests using disputes as the unit of analysis (they also test their theory using rivalries as the unit of analysis). As an indicator of rivalry, they use both a measure of repeated disputes and Diehl and Goertz's (2000) enduring rivalry classification, which seem to have separate and positive impacts on the likelihood of war in their tests. They find that arms races have an independent effect, even when controlling for rivalry, though not under all historical circumstances. Colaresi, Rasler, and Thompson (2007) also test the steps-to-war thesis as an example of a truly multivariate theory of war causation. Using international crisis data rather than MID data, and using dyad years rather than disputes, they find that arms buildups have a significant impact on the likelihood of war for rivals, particularly after several disputes have already occurred between states.

Taken together, these findings suggest that arms buildups might indeed have an independent impact on war causation but that the consequences of rivalry and the way arms buildups are bound to it are profoundly important to understanding how wars come about. This chapter provides a new test of these relationships in an attempt to tease out some of the dynamics seen here.

METHODOLOGY

Do arms buildups have an independent impact on the probability of war? I would hypothesize that they do, even once we consider the impact of rivalry on interstate relationships. In the tests conducted here, I examine the impact of rivalry in two different ways, both by considering the results of the model when different measures of rivalry are used, and by examining patterns of escalation in cases both inside and outside of rivalry. The results indicate that the independent impact of arms buildups on war is indeed significant, and that it is conditional primarily, as previous research has suggested, on historical time period.

The dependent variable in this study is whether the specific dyadic MIDs escalated to war or whether another MID between the two states did so within five years.[3] I have begun with Maoz's dyadic MID data set (version 2.0) (Maoz 2005). Following Sample (2002), I further removed most disputes occurring during a major war, while allowing for staggered entry of major participants (such as the United States entering World Wars I and II well after the wars began).

The measure for arms buildups used here is a measure of mutual military buildups. As previously discussed, a mutual military buildup is defined as occurring when both countries in the dyadic dispute are involved in unusual buildups prior to the dispute (Sample 1997). I have updated the mutual militarized buildup data set created by Sample (1997) from the previous 1993 end date to 2001. The measure is based originally on one created by Horn (1987) and looks at the military expenditures of the ten years preceding the dispute. To be engaging in an unusual buildup, a country's expenditure growth rate over that ten years, accounting for inflation after the beginning of the twentieth century, must be higher than the average growth rate for that century, and it needs to be higher still for the five years immediately before the dispute. This attempts to ensure both that the military expenditure growth rates are unusual for that state and that they are accelerating prior to the dispute.

Using military buildups stands in clear contrast to the choice of Gibler, Rider, and Hutchison (2005) to specifically measure arms races themselves and evaluate their impact. My rationale for using the measure has to do with attacking the hypothesis from another quarter; by using military buildups, rather than arms races, I am able to both evaluate their impact on disputes occurring under conditions of rivalry and those occurring *outside* of rivalry. While we have appropriately focused a great deal of attention on what is happening *inside* of rivalries, the impact of arms buildups on nonrivalrous disputes might still tell us something important about the real role of arms buildups in conflict. Since the purpose of this chapter, then, is to determine if "arms races" are related to war and under what circumstances, by examining their role under different circumstances, we will hopefully have a more complete picture of the role of arms buildups, and perhaps a more nuanced picture of how rivalries work as well.

Multiple measures of rivalry exist, and while they all purport to tap into the same essential concept of states involved in a relationship in which competition is ongoing and expected into the indefinite future, they are not as highly correlated with each other as one might expect (Colaresi, Rasler, and Thompson 2007). Given this, I test the models using three different measures of rivalry. First, I employ the Alliance Treaty Obligations and Provisions data

(Leeds et al. 2000, 2002) to devise a new measure for rivalry. The ATOP data has considerable information about the treaties, including those in which particular states were named as specific threats to the signatories. Using this, I code a particular dyadic dispute as occurring within a rivalry if at least one party is signatory to a treaty in which the other is named as a specific threat.

This is a very conservative measure of rivalry, designed so in part because of the low level of correlation between other measures. There is virtually no doubt that the states involved are rivals, though there will be those commonly thought of as rivals not included. It requires not only that elites have determined that the other state is a principal security threat, but that they have also already made at least one policy around the fact: they have concluded a treaty with another state saying so. Because this treaty is a type of alliance, it means that this model is not ideal for fully testing the steps-to-war model or a multivariate model in which one of the questions is the impact of alliances, but that is not my primary goal here.

In addition to using the ATOP specific threat indicator, I use Thompson's (2001) rivalry measure and the Diehl and Goertz (2000) measure. Thompson defines rivalries through analysis of the historical record of elite perception. If the elites in two countries perceived the other country as an enemy, they are considered rivals, whether or not they have engaged in specific militarized conflict with one another. Diehl and Goertz define an enduring rival by the occurrence of at least six MIDs in a span of twenty years. There is value in both approaches—the validity of a careful reading of the historical record in the former, and clear and easily replicable operational rules in the latter—and the measures have the expected strengths and weaknesses of these approaches. They are the most widely used measures in the literature, and using them here, and in comparison with a third measure chosen for its essential conservatism, should give us some confidence in the robustness of the findings regarding arms buildups, while potentially allowing us to tease out some of the more complex linkages between arming and rivalry.

In these tests, as in previous research, I have controlled for several variables related to the distributions of power as well as a measure of the defense burdens of the states (following Sample 2002). Given the importance of the distribution of power to theoretical arguments about the impact of arms buildups, these are critical controls. I have included variables that estimate whether a power transition has occurred between the two states in the last decade, whether one has rapidly approached the other in power, or whether the states are equal in power or not. Each of these is based in its own right on substantial theoretical literatures suggesting their relative importance, and in each event, they could easily be correlated with arms buildups, thus giving the impression that it is the arms buildup, and not the power distribution, which is related to escalation.

Each dyad is coded as having experienced a power transition if one's Composite Index of National Capabilities (CINC) score passed the other in the decade preceding the dispute in question using the Correlates of War National Material Capabilities data version 3.02 (Singer, Bremer, and Stuckey 1972; Singer 1987). The theoretical argument connecting power transitions and war builds on the notion that when one state passes the other in power, it finds itself in a position to prosecute any outstanding conflicts with the other, conflicts that it had little hope of resolving in its favor when it was significantly weaker (Organski 1958).

Additionally, I measure whether the states are essentially equal in power or not. I determined that two states were at parity if the CINC score of the smaller one was at least 80 percent of that of the larger. The variable is measured dichotomously, equal or not. Within the literature going back several decades, there is substantial controversy over the role of power balances in encouraging or discouraging conflict. Classical balance of power theory stands in direct opposition to the power preponderance theory embedded in Organski's (1958) power transition theory. Given either theoretical case, it would seem that arms buildups that affected whether states were at parity or not would seem to have an impact on the probability of war if it is indeed the distribution of power that determines outcomes, making this a relevant control for the study.

The final variable related specifically to the distribution of power is the rapid approach. A rapid approach takes place when the gap in power, measured by CINC scores, closes by at least 40 percent in the preceding decade. Whether or not an actual transition has occurred, a rapid approach toward parity may convince one or both states in a dispute that it is necessary to escalate the conflict either to defend their current position or to alter the status quo. While a mutual military buildup may change the power balance between states, these are theoretically and empirically distinct variables (Wayman 1996).

The defense burden, a measure of the level of militarization, is included here as well. The defense burden is a measure of the proportion of a country's resources dedicated to military power in a given year. I code the variables dichotomously: one if at least one state in the dispute has a high defense burden, and zero otherwise. A high defense burden, in this instance, is determined by whether the country is spending more than a standard deviation above what would be predicted for that country given spending patterns among countries at the time (see Sample 1998b for details). This variable is intended to control for the possibility that arms buildups of whatever kind might be related to escalation because one or both states is spending more on its military than it can really afford. This could be related to escalation as states, particularly minor ones without deep pockets, could choose to prosecute disputes now rather than risk the underlying dispute reemerging later when they cannot afford the conflict. A country may be spending a significant portion of its resources on the military, but doing so consistently over a period of time and thus not exhibiting the signs of a mutual military buildup.

Evidence from previous studies suggests that it is important to know whether disputes are taking place when one or both parties have nuclear weapons (Sample 1998b, 2000; Senese and Vasquez 2008). The literature suggests both that mutual military buildups can increase the risk of escalation and that nuclear weapons possession may decrease it. There is a substantially decreased probability of dispute escalation after World War II, and to the extent that this is a result of nuclear weapons possession, the variable is vital to considerations of the impact of military buildups. I have included two variables here related to nuclear weapons possession: one for symmetrical nuclear dyads (both parties have nuclear weapons) and one for asymmetric dyads where only one country of the two has nuclear weapons. Both should show a reduced likelihood of escalation. Countries are coded as having nuclear weapons if they are declared nuclear powers at the time, since presumably known nuclear status would be critical to the deterrent effect. This means that India and Pakistan enter the data as declared nuclear states beginning in 1998, and virtually all disputes occurring after World War II between two major states are in the presence of nuclear weapons held by at least one party, if not both.

While it is not specifically a control variable, the issue under contention in the dispute is included in the model because a vast literature suggests the importance of territorial disputes in war causation. I have chosen to code this dichotomously, and disputes are either coded as territorial or not. Finally, the model also includes dummy variables to discern potential differences between escalation patterns of major states, minor states, and mixed dyads given evidence that major states seem more likely to escalate in general historically and previous findings that the structure of the dispute matters for its probability of escalation (Bremer 1992; Sample 2002; Wright 1962).

In order to answer the fundamental question of whether mutual military buildups do have an independent impact on dispute escalation, I take this model and evaluate it in two different ways. First, I estimate the model including all of the independent variables and separately using each of the measures of rivalry. Controlling for rivalry, are mutual military buildups still significantly related to dispute escalation? If arms buildups do in fact have an impact on war causation independent of rivalry, we should see a significant statistical relationship here.

After discussing the results of these models, I divide the data by those cases that occur in the context of rivalry from those that do not. Everything we know about rivalry suggests that the probability of dispute escalation must be much higher among those that are rivals, and I expect to find that. However, by examining disputes inside of rivalry separately from those outside of rivalry, we can evaluate more than simply that. Absolute probability of escalation aside, what do the dynamics of the disputes look like? Do we see similar patterns of escalation between countries inside and outside rivalry, just at different levels of probability? Or do disputes in the context of rivalry look different in other ways? Ultimately, do the answers to these questions tell us something important about the role of military buildups in war and the processes leading to war generally?

FINDINGS

The findings here demonstrate the complexity of the relationships in multicausal processes. In table 6.1, I examine three separate models, each employing a different indicator of rivalry, and controlling for rivalry by including it as a variable in the model. It is clear that mutual military buildups are strongly and significantly related to dispute escalation to war, and this is robust across measures of rivalry. As in earlier studies (Sample 2002; Senese and Vasquez 2008), the post–World War II era shows different patterns of escalation than those from the beginning of the Correlates of War period through World War II. In light of that, the data was tested in three ways: the entire Correlates of War period, 1816–2001; 1816–1944; and 1945–2001.

Before discussing the impact of mutual military buildups in the data, it is worth attending to the impacts of the different measures of rivalry. As demonstrated in table 6.1, each of the measures of rivalry is highly significant in the whole COW period. The Thompson (2001) measure is strongly related to an increased chance of escalation in both major periods—1816–1944 and 1944–2001—whereas each of the other measures fails to achieve significance in one period or the other. This finding is further evidence that while the measures intend to tap into a similar conflict process, the actual operationalizations can lead to somewhat different findings, a further justification for comparison of findings across different measures of rivalry.

As to the impact of arming, when controlling for the fact that the states involved are rivals, mutual military buildups remain significantly and positively related to dispute escalation. Over the whole COW period, states engaging in disputes characterized by mutual military buildups are at least 250 percent more likely to escalate to war within five years than when disputes occur without mutual military buildups.[4] Since rivalry itself is controlled for here, this clearly

Table 6.1. Estimations with Rivalry in the Model

Variable	B	S.E.	Wald	Sig.	Exp(B)
Mutual Military Buildup					
All Years	1.31	.21	37.80	.000	3.70
1816–1944	1.43	.29	24.17	.000	4.18
1945–2001	.86	.37	5.38	.020	2.35
Specific Threat					
All Years	1.00	.19	26.93	.000	2.72
1816–1944	1.00	.24	17.03	.000	2.71
1945–2001	.52	.39	1.81	.178	1.68
Defense Burden					
All Years	.16	.14	1.37	.241	1.17
1816–1944	.62	.19	10.51	.001	1.85
1945–2001	−.44	.22	3.99	.046	.64
Symmetric Nuclear					
All Years	−4.10	1.03	15.97	.000	.02
1816–1944	—				
1945–2001	−3.14	1.15	7.44	.006	.04
Asymmetric Nuclear					
All Years	−1.62	.22	55.45	.000	.20
1816–1944	—				
1945–2001	−1.02	.36	8.16	.004	.36
Territory					
All Years	1.08	.13	66.83	.000	2.95
1816–1944	.66	.20	10.93	.001	1.94
1945–2001	1.44	.19	60.42	.000	4.24
Rapid Approach					
All Years	−.78	.29	7.53	.006	.46
1816–1944	−1.07	.39	7.66	.006	.34
1945–2001	−.53	.47	1.26	.262	.59
Transition					
All Years	.92	.31	8.96	.003	2.50
1816–1944	1.29	.44	8.83	.003	3.65
1945–2001	.59	.52	1.28	.259	1.80
Equality					
All Years	.53	.22	5.92	.015	1.70
1816–1944	.85	.29	8.35	.004	2.34
1945–2001	.11	.36	.09	.766	1.11
Minor States					
All Years	−1.78	.21	70.24	.000	.17
1816–1944	−1.03	.29	13.14	.000	.36
1945–2001	−1.07	.58	3.41	.065	.34
Mixed States					
All Years	−.50	.21	5.61	.018	.60
1816–1944	−.40	.24	2.75	.098	.67
1945–2001	−.23	.55	.17	.680	.80

Variable	B	S.E.	Wald	Sig.	Exp(B)
Constant					
All Years	−1.10	.21	27.13	.000	.33
1816–1944	−1.25	.25	25.29	.000	.29
1945–2001	−1.86	.59	9.85	.002	.16

	Model Log-Likelihood	Model χ^2	Significance		Pseudo R^2
1816–2001	1,730.57	N = 2,582	377.01	d.f. = 11 <.001	.24
1816–1944	776.06	N = 756	137.53	d.f. = 9 <.001	.237
1945–2001	910.06	N = 1,826	102.72	d.f. = 11 <.000	.128

contradicts the notion that mutual military buildups are simply spuriously related to war because of their connection to rivalry. This finding also agrees with that of Gibler, Rider, and Hutchison (2005), as well as that of Senese and Vasquez (2008) and Colaresi, Rasler, and Thompson (2007), who use different measures of rivalry. Thus, the finding would seem to be robust.

The other findings in table 6.1 show both commonalities with earlier findings using simple escalation of dispute as the dependent variable rather than escalation of a dispute between the two states within five years, but there are also some very interesting differences. Over the whole Correlates of War period, we not surprisingly find that disputes over territory are far more prone to escalation than others. Disputes between minor states are significantly less prone to escalation over the whole Correlates of War period, as are those between one minor and one major state, although the latter is only true using the ATOP specific threat and the Diehl and Goertz (2000) rivalry measure. In contrast to earlier findings using escalation of a particular dispute as the dependent variable, the variables related to the distribution of power are also significant, suggesting that in contrast to many theoretical arguments, both arms race dynamics and the distribution of power may be relevant in understanding war.

It is clear that the world changes a great deal after World War II, whether as a result of nuclear weapons or otherwise. Over the whole period, nuclear weapons possession by one or both parties has a significant dampening effect on the probability of escalation, which suggests that much of the analogical debate over the impact of arms policies during the Cold War was simply wrong. Both nuclear variables are highly significant, with a clearly stronger relationship for symmetrical nuclear dyads than asymmetrical ones.[5] The overall patterns of escalation that exist, however, are substantially different between 1816–1944 and 1945–2001, though critical commonalities exist.

First and foremost, the relationship between mutual military buildups and escalation is significant in both periods when looking at both the ATOP model and the Thompson (2001) model, though its impact is somewhat reduced in the latter period. Arms buildups are not significantly related to escalation after World War II when using the Diehl and Goertz (2000) operationalization of rivalry, which might in part account for their earlier questioning of the relevance of the variable. Interestingly, after World War II, the relationships between the power variables and escalation disappear. Whatever impact power parity, power transitions, and rapid approaches toward parity had on the process of escalation through World War II, it seems to be gone in the postwar era. The impact of having a high defense burden is significant both before World War II and after, but it changes direction: after the war, a high defense burden is associated with a lower probability of escalation. Territory remains highly significant.

Taken altogether, these findings looking at the whole period and at the historical eras divided suggest that mutual military buildups do have a significant independent impact on dispute escalation, even when one considers the role of rivalry. Clearly, states involved in a rivalry are much more likely to escalate their disputes, but mutual military buildups (apparently even when they are not precisely arms races) contribute significantly to escalation separately from the way arms buildups are interwoven with rivalry relationships.

An examination of the predicted probabilities of disputes demonstrates the effect of the variables and of adding each variable to the situation. Table 6.2 contains the predicted probabilities of escalation using the ATOP specific

Table 6.2. Predicted Probabilities for Dispute Escalation

	Minor Disputes	Mixed Disputes	Major Disputes
No Nukes, All Variables at Zero	.05323	.16721	.24945
No Nukes, Mutual Military Buildup at One, All Others at Zero	.17227	.42635	.55162
No Nukes, Specific Threat at One, All Others at Zero	.13277	.35348	.47507
No Nukes, Specific Threat, Mutual Military Buildup, All Others at Zero	.36172	.66929	.77011
No Nukes, Specific Threat, Territorial Dispute, Mutual Military Buildup, High Defense Burden, Others at Zero	.66203	.87493	.92050
No Nukes, Specific Threat, Territorial Dispute, Mutual Military Buildup, High Defense Burden, Transition, Equality, and Rapid Approach	.89295[a]	—[b]	.92995[b]

[a]This calculation is without the states experiencing a rapid approach toward power in the preceding decade. Since that has a conflict-dampening effect, this predicted probability is likely overstated marginally. It is, however, illustrative.

[b]This calculation is without both states being at power parity, or equality. No case existed with that configuration. Given the impact of power parity on likelihood of escalation, this probability is likely understated marginally.

threat measure as an indicator of rivalry. While each of the measures of rivalry results in somewhat different results, these probabilities are sufficient to demonstrate the major findings.

Two major states engaging in a dispute, neither of which has nuclear weapons, and with all variables set to zero, have a .249 chance of escalating a dispute to war over the next five years. When the dispute includes a mutual military buildup, the probability of escalating that or another dispute within five years increases to .552. With no military buildup, but with a specific threat designation, the probability of escalation is .475. Put both together, with all other variables set at zero, and the probability of escalation increases to .770. With all variables set at one, the probability that two major states will escalate this or another dispute to war within five years increases to .921. The comparative figures for mixed pairs of states and minor states are lower but reflect the same patterns, with arms buildups clearly creating substantial increases in the probability of escalation both independently and in conjunction with the other variables.

At this point, I divide the data in a different way; rather than using the different indicators of rivalry as variables in the model, I divide the data on that basis and then examine the relationships between the other variables and escalation given whether or not the dispute is taking place in the context of rivalry or not. This division is a second method for controlling for the impact of rivalry on the relationship. It is the one chosen by Gibler, Rider, and Hutchison (2005), though they examined only disputes occurring within rivalry and did not look at those outside rivalry.

Given the emphasis placed on the conflictual nature of rivalry in the literature, the choice to primarily examine relationships within rivalry is understandable. However, a full comparison of the escalation processes inside *and* outside of rivalries might help illuminate the dynamics of some of the core relationships. Given the fact that patterns of escalation seem to change by more than just degree under different historical and structural circumstances (Sample 2002), it would seem prudent to ask just how the whole process within rivalry compares to the whole process outside of rivalry.

Table 6.3 shows the findings for all disputes in which the involved states are *not* rivals. These disputes, on the whole, should be less likely to escalate than disputes in which the participants are rivals, in keeping both with the statistical findings above and the theoretical foundations of the rivalry literature. And this is the case, though the distinctions are not quite as dramatic as one might expect. In any case, the patterns we see in nonrivalrous dyads can be important to our overall understanding of war causation just as disputes between minor states may tell us something important about war causation, even though they have a relatively lower probability of escalation than major state dyads.

Table 6.3.   Estimations for Disputes Outside of Rivalry

Variable	B	S.E.	Wald	Sig.	Exp(B)
Mutual Military Buildup					
All Years	1.46	.23	39.46	.000	4.29
1816–1944	1.72	.33	26.98	.000	5.59
1945–2001	.91	.39	5.52	.019	2.47
Defense Burden					
All Years	.02	.15	.01	.917	1.02
1816–1944	.40	.22	3.46	.063	1.50
1945–2001	−.48	.23	4.19	.041	.62
Symmetric Nuclear					
All Years	−3.99	1.03	15.02	.000	.02
1816–1944	—				
1945–2001	−2.96	1.15	6.59	.010	.05
Asymmetric Nuclear					
All Years	−1.47	.23	42.79	.000	.23
1816–1944	—				
1945–2001	−.89	.37	5.92	.015	.41
Territory					
All Years	1.06	.14	57.81	.000	2.89
1816–1944	.52	.22	5.69	.017	1.69
1945–2001	1.49	.19	60.63	.000	4.42
Rapid Approach					
All Years	−.81	.32	6.39	.012	.45
1816–1944	−1.03	.45	5.17	.023	.36
1945–2001	−.66	.50	1.73	.189	.52
Transition					
All Years	.87	.33	7.05	.008	2.39
1816–1944	1.08	.48	5.15	.023	2.95
1945–2001	.75	.52	2.03	.154	2.11
Equality					
All Years	.54	.24	5.33	.021	1.72
1816–1944	1.03	.33	9.48	.002	2.80
1945–2001	.03	.37	.01	.930	1.03
Minor States					
All Years	−1.92	.24	63.02	.000	.15
1816–1944	−1.25	.34	13.94	.000	.29
1945–2001	−1.02	.59	3.01	.083	.36
Mixed States					
All Years	−.67	.24	7.64	.006	.51
1816–1944	−.64	.28	5.21	.022	.53
1945–2001	−.20	.55	.14	.713	.82

Variable	B	S.E.	Wald	Sig.	Exp(B)
Constant					
All Years	−.94	.24	15.67	.000	.39
1816–1944	−.98	.28	12.36	.000	.38
1945–2001	−1.94	.60	10.51	.001	.14

	Model Log-Likelihood	Model χ^2		Significance		Pseudo R^2
1816–2001	1,532.095	N = 2,386	260.98	d.f. = 10	<.001	.196
1816–1944	636.185	N = 643	87.53	d.f. = 8	<.001	.188
1945–2001	857.19	N = 1,743	97.9	d.f. = 10	<.001	.139

In examining the findings reported in table 6.3, we see that the relationships are much as previously predicted. Among states that are not rivals, disputes are significantly more likely to escalate when the countries involved are part of an ongoing arms buildup. Over the whole COW period, these disputes are more than three times as likely to escalate within five years as disputes not occurring in the context of a buildup.[6] Territorial disputes are far more likely to lead to escalation within a five-year window as well. We see differences on the power variables related to measures of rivalry: all remain significant when using the ATOP variable, but only power transitions are significantly related over the whole period for the Diehl and Goertz (2000) measure, and the rapid approach, using the same measure, is only significant through World War II. None are significant using the Thompson (2001) indicator of rivalry. Overall, these findings demonstrate substantial consistency with the steps-to-war thesis.

When we look at the predicted probabilities of escalation in table 6.4 (again using the ATOP measure as illustrative, despite some differences across measures), we see that the overall probabilities of escalation are certainly smaller

Table 6.4. Predicted Probabilities for Dispute Escalation Outside of Rivalry

	Minor Disputes	Mixed Disputes	Major Disputes
No Nukes, All Variables at Zero	.05412	.16675	.28063
No Nukes, Mutual Military Buildup, All Others at Zero	.19701	.46182	.62586
No Nukes, Territorial Dispute, Mutual Military Buildup, High Defense Burden, Others at Zero	.41869[a]	.71584	.83982[b]

[a]Without the high defense burden, this predicted probability is .41482. For nonrivalrous dyads, the defense burden only has a marginal effect.
[b]This calculation includes a recent power transition and rapid approach, which should affect the probability of escalation in opposing directions. Other predicted probabilities for the cases including the power variables are not here because the case configurations do not exist.

than in the first model, but they are far from negligible. Two major states that are not officially rivals have a .28 chance of having a given dispute or another between them escalating within five years in the absence of nuclear weapons possession and with all other variables set to zero. The probability of the specific dispute escalating under these circumstances is .08. If the dispute is over territory, the probability of escalation within five years increases to .53; add a mutual military buildup and a high defense burden, and the probability jumps to nearly .84.[7] Mixed pairs of states in the same circumstances have a nearly .72 chance of escalating to war within five years.

Several things are clear about these findings controlling for rivalry by looking at only cases outside of rivalry. First, under the right circumstances, these states can have a relatively high probability of their disputes erupting into war, making nonrivals perhaps more interesting than we have heretofore considered them to be. Further, the patterns of escalation suggest support for a step increase in the probability of war as each of these variables is added to the mix. There is a pattern of escalation among these disputes that conforms in important ways with the steps-to-war thesis.

Finally, we can say with some confidence that the relationship between military buildups and war is not an artifact of rivalry. Outside of rivalry, it is clear that mutual military buildups have a significant and positive impact on escalation. This finding means that all of our theorizing and attempts to understand just how states interpret the military buildups of others and how this contributes to the likelihood of escalation are not irrelevant to understanding war causation. This is true even when the measure of an arms buildup is a mutual military buildup, not an arms race. In theory, actual arms races should have a much greater impact on the likelihood of escalation as they bind up a negative, interacting relationship with the arming process. However, in this case, because it was necessary to examine the relationship outside of rivalry, an arms race measure per se would not be appropriate, since it would make it impossible to distinguish the separate impacts of the negative relationship and the arms buildups. By using the measure of a mutual military buildup, we are able to do that.

In the final model, I examine all of these relationships only in cases of rivalry. Table 6.5 indicates the results of this set of tests, again examining the relationships over all of the years of the Correlates of War period, and then dividing it at the end of World War II.

Mutual military buildups among rivals are highly significant and positively related to escalation both over the whole of the Correlates of War period and before the end of World War II using both the subset of Thompson (2001) rivals and the Diehl and Goertz (2000) rivals. The variable is not significant using the ATOP measure; this is likely the result of the inherent conservatism

Table 6.5. Estimations for Disputes within Rivalry

Variable	B	S.E.	Wald	Sig.	Exp(B)
Mutual Military Buildup					
All Years	.63	.52	1.45	.228	1.87
1816–1944	.61	.62	.97	.325	1.83
1945–2001	.40	1.27	.10	.755	1.49
Defense Burden					
All Years	1.04	.37	7.77	.005	2.82
1816–1944	1.458	.494	8.721	.003	4.296
1945–2001	−.71	.93	.59	.443	.491
Symmetric Nuclear					
All Years	−21.94	13,844.24	.000	.999	.000
1816–1944	—				
1945–2001[a]					
Asymmetric Nuclear					
All Years	−3.67	1.08	11.46	.001	.026
1816–1944	—				
1945–2001	−3.85	1.79	4.65	.031	.021
Territory					
All Years	1.18	.46	6.65	.010	3.25
1816–1944	1.58	.62	6.55	.011	4.84
1945–2001	.71	.92	.60	.439	2.04
Rapid Approach					
All Years	−.94	.73	1.68	.195	.39
1816–1944	−1.07	.78	1.86	.173	.34
1945–2001	1.41	17,261.91	.000	1.000	4.08
Transition					
All Years	1.36	1.13	1.47	.23	3.91
1816–1944	1.54	1.36	1.29	.26	4.69
1945–2001	−22.96	43,742.98	.000	1.000	.000
Equality					
All Years	.74	.64	1.32	.25	2.09
1816–1944	.53	.68	.61	.44	1.70
1945–2001	1.00	17,261.90	.000	1.000	2.73
Minor States					
All Years	−1.23	.47	6.92	.009	.29
1816–1944	−.68	.60	1.31	.25	.51
1945–2001	19.63	15,319.90	.000	.999	3.36E8
Mixed States					
All Years	.32	.48	.45	.50	1.38
1816–1944	.42	.52	.65	.42	1.52
1945–2001	21.69	15,319.90	.000	.999	2.62E9

(continued)

Table 6.5. (*continued*)

Variable	B	S.E.	Wald	Sig.	Exp(B)
Constant					
All Years	−.81	.43	3.63	.057	.45
1816–1944	−.97	.47	4.35	.037	.38
1945–2001	−21.33	15,319.90	.000	.999	.000

	Model Log-Likelihood	Model χ^2		Significance		Pseudo R^2
1816–2001	181.562	N = 196	72.729	d.f. = 10	<.001	.427
1816–1944	125.916	N = 113	30.302	d.f. = 8	<.001	.314
1945–2001	44.856	N = 83	12.12	d.f. = 8	.146	.274

[a]When dividing the data set in this way, redundancies were created in the model, and the symmetric nuclear dyads variable was dropped in the calculation. Running the model dropping minor and mixed status and running it again simply using a nuclear variable that conflated asymmetric and symmetric dyads did not lead to substantively different results for any of the variables.

of the measure—rivalries in which a treaty has designated the other as a threat are probably particularly intense, and they clearly also represent an additional step to war in the very making of the treaty, so the relationship may be confounded here by questions of *timing* of steps, making statistical distinction difficult. Nonetheless, the findings using both the Thompson rivalry designation and the Diehl and Goertz measure are unequivocal. Military buildups are a clear and independent step toward war between rivals.

Within rivalry, territorial disputes are positively related to dispute escalation within a five-year window, and we see a reversal of the direction of the relationship between a high defense burden and war. A high defense burden is associated with an increased probability of war through World War II, but that relationship is reversed after World War II, when a high defense burden reduces the likelihood of war between states. Further, within rivalries, both power transitions and rapid approaches are significantly related to escalation through World War II, though not after, using both the Thompson (2001) rivalry designation and the Diehl and Goertz (2000) measure.[8]

Table 6.6 indicates the predicted probabilities of escalation within rivalry (using the ATOP measure simply for consistency) for illustrative purposes. Over the whole Correlates of War period, it is clear that military buildups, while not reaching conventional levels of significance with this measure of rivalry, still substantially increase the probability of a pair of states escalating a dispute to war within five years. Major states in a territorial dispute have a .59 chance of escalating a dispute to war within that time frame; a high defense burden increases the chance of war to .80, and a military buildup increases it to .88. An ongoing military buildup substantially increases the probability of escalation for minor and mixed rivals as well.

Table 6.6. Predicted Probabilities for Dispute Escalation inside Rivalry

	Minor Disputes	Mixed Disputes	Major Disputes
No Nukes, All Variables at Zero	.11530	.38095	.30819
No Nukes, Territorial Dispute, All Others at Zero	.29737	.66648	.59127
No Nukes, Territorial Dispute, High Defense Burden, All Others at Zero	.54365	.84905	.80284
No Nukes, Territorial Dispute, High Defense Burden, Mutual Military Buildup, All Others at Zero	.69015	.91317	.88390
No Nukes, Territorial Dispute, High Defense Burden, Mutual Military Buildup, Transition, Equality, and Rapid Approach	.94794[a]	—[b]	.92062[c]

[a]This calculation includes everything but a rapid approach. Given its negative impact on the likelihood of escalation, this probability is likely overstated marginally. These differences would account for the higher probability of escalation reported here for minor dyads than major ones. Despite their obvious shortcomings, I have included these predicted probabilities for illustrative purposes.
[b]No cases existed between mixed dyads with the relevant configuration of power variables.
[c]This calculation is without both states being at power parity or equality. No case existed with that configuration. Given the impact of power parity on likelihood of escalation, this probability is likely understated marginally.

DISCUSSION

What do we learn about the role of arms buildups in war causation from all of this, and what do we learn about war causation itself? As discussed, the theoretical arguments made about the role of arms races have shifted in the last decade. While earlier debates were animated by questions about arms buildups themselves in light of the debates around deterrence theory and policy, the current debates center around the role of arms buildups as embedded within other complex conflict processes.

The steps-to-war thesis contends that arms races, as one step on the realist road to war, have an independent impact on the likelihood that two states will go to war. If states do not take this step, the theory argues, the resulting probability of war is simply lower. War is the result of a series of choices and circumstances that independently and collectively increase the chance of war. Much of the rivalry literature to date, in contrast, has argued that arms races have no independent causal relationship with war. Rather, they emerge as symptoms of an ongoing rivalry, so that there may be a statistical relationship between arming and war when the dynamics of the rivalry are not taken into account, but the relationship largely disappears when they are.

Building on work in extant studies, I have examined the role of arms buildups while controlling for rivalry in different ways, first by taking rivalry itself as a control variable, and then by dividing the data into disputes within rivalry and disputes outside of rivalry. Doing this demonstrates that, examined through different lenses, mutual military buildups consistently have a substantial independent impact on the likelihood of war, at least through the end of World War II. Further, by using three different measures of rivalry and comparing the findings, we can have a better idea of what results are emerging because of the different measures of rivalry and where we are clearly finding consistency across the measures. The models in table 6.1 show remarkable consistency across conflict patterns, and while dividing the disputes by rivalry measure into rival and nonrival disputes shows that the operationalizations of rivalry themselves affect findings in some ways, it is evident that the relationship between arms buildups and war is a robust one.

Previous research has suggested that arms races would likely only be seen within rivalries and would be conflict producing only in such cases. We see here that arms buildups within rivals are indeed significantly related to dispute escalation. However, while it may conceptually be the case that a true arms race would only exist between rivals, empirically it is very clear that an ongoing mutual military buildup increases the likelihood of disputes escalating between nonrivals, and does so substantially.

Earlier theoretical arguments about the way arms buildups affect threat perception and increase hostility would seem appropriate here. Nonrival states find themselves, for whatever reason, in a militarized dispute in which the other party is rapidly arming. While they might not previously have concerned themselves with this military buildup, suddenly it seems central to their relationship and directly intended to threaten them. In a world in which states assume that realpolitik prescriptions should deter, the fact that the dispute occurs in spite of a country's own buildup seems to be further evidence that the intent of the other is threatening. The military buildup, then, has an impact on the perceived threat perception, thus exacerbating the conflict and increasing the threat of war. This finding and argument blend into the steps-to-war thesis quite cleanly, even while the test in this chapter is not explicitly a test of that theory.

While arms buildups have an independent impact on the likelihood of war, it is likely well that we consider their role within larger, multicausal processes, and the findings here suggest several questions. First, it is still worth considering exactly *how* military buildups affect the dynamic between states: Is the spiral model the best explanation? How much of this is psychological processes of threat perception, and how exactly does this relate to real material threat, particularly given the findings here that support the notion that the distribution of real capabilities and changes in it may also be important in predicting war? Additionally, since we know that arms buildups clearly increase the probability of escalation outside of rivalry, furthering the extant literature on whether such arms buildups have an impact on the likelihood of rivalry onset itself is important (see Valeriano, this volume). If they increase the probability of disputes between two states escalating to war within five years, what impact do they have on the relationship between the states generally?

And finally, what implications do these findings have for our attempt to adjudicate between the differing formulations of arms buildups within the steps-to-war thesis and the rivalry research? Demonstrating that nonrivals have fairly high probabilities of war under particular circumstances—circumstances that would seem to be precisely those predicted by the steps-to-war thesis—indicates that we would not want to focus on rivals to the exclusion of other relationships in the system or other dynamic processes. There is a great deal of complex interaction in the theoretical arguments of the two, but one area where they have differed is the prediction of the impact of arms buildups. Clearly, arms buildups are not spuriously associated with war. They are not simply an artifact of rivalry that has no independent impact on war; they are a step toward war.

NOTES

1. It has been argued (Fearon 1994a) that the dyadic dispute is a problematic unit of analysis in this case because general deterrence has already failed if a militarized dispute is occurring, possibly biasing the findings at phase of escalation. However, several studies (Sample 2000; Gibler, Rider, and Hutchison 2005; Colaresi, Rasler, and Thompson 2007) have found relationships between arming and the occurrence of disputes in the first place, suggesting that the impact of arms at the two stages is probably not different.

2. While I focus on the arguments made by Diehl and Crescenzi (1998) that are reflected in earlier and later work in the same vein, there is diversity in rivalry studies. While Diehl and Crescenzi (1998) argued that arms races were likely simply spurious to rivalry, and thus, for instance, arms buildups are not considered to have a potential influence on war or the maintenance of rivalry (Goertz, Jones, and Diehl 2005), Colaresi, Rasler, and Thompson (2007) make an argument for multicausal processes including the impact of arms buildups.

3. Historically and statistically, dyadic disputes are not precisely independent events. However, their use here is justified in two ways: first, it makes these findings easily comparable to the vast literature using them. Second, and significantly, Senese and Vasquez (2008), in testing the steps-to-war model, do so using different units of analysis partially for this reason, and they get essentially consistent results in their findings across different units of analysis. This would seem to indicate that the potential consequences for our findings and conclusions of using dyadic disputes are not fatal to valid analysis in any way.

4. Using the ATOP measure, Exp(B) = 3.70, so $(3.70 - 1) \times 100 = 270\%$; using the Thompson (2001) measure, Exp(B) = 3.59; using the Diehl and Goertz (2000), it is 3.48.

5. The variable for symmetrical nuclear dyads is not always significant in these models because of the overall lack of variation in the dependent variable.

6. ATOP measure, Exp(B) = 4.29; Thompson (2001) measure, Exp(B) = 5.62; Diehl and Goertz (2000) measure, Exp(B) = 3.84.

7. This last predicted probability is actually the predicted probability of a dispute between major states when no one has nuclear weapons, the dispute is over territory, at least one has a high defense burden, they are in the midst of a mutual military buildup, and there has been a rapid approach toward parity and a power transition in the previous decade. There simply are no cases in the data without the latter two variables on which to base a predicted probability; because they are not significant using this measure of rivalry, and they would seem to have opposite impacts here, I am assuming that their impact is small, and essentially they wash each other out anyway, thus making this predicted probability imperfect but a good illustrative estimate.

8. It is curious that the ATOP measure finds these variables only significant outside of rivalry, and the other measures find them significant inside rivalry only. Clearly, the distribution of power in which the conflict process takes place is important, and the rivalry measures are tapping into something different here, but what exactly that is must be left to future research.

Chapter Seven

Nuclear Weapons and War

Daniel S. Geller

The balance of conventional military capabilities is intrinsic to understanding patterns of war among nations.[1] However, cumulative knowledge relating to the effects of nuclear weapons possession on conflict interaction is largely absent. The present chapter seeks to provide a framework for analyzing the results of quantitative empirical research on this question and to identify any extant strong and consistent patterns in the interactions of states that can be associated with the possession of nuclear weapons.

Since 1945 a vast, sophisticated, and contradictory literature has developed on the implications of nuclear weaponry for patterns of international conflict. This theoretical and empirical work has principally focused on the effects of these weapons for the interaction of nuclear-armed states, although a small number of studies have explored the impact of a state's possession of nuclear weapons on the behavior of nonnuclear opponents.

Given the destructive capacity of these weapons, most of this work has concentrated on the requirements for successful deterrence. In categorizing the studies, Zagare and Kilgour (2000), for example, note that "classical deterrence theory" derives from the realist paradigm of international politics, and they subdivide this theory into two complementary strands: structural (or neorealist) deterrence theory and decision-theoretic deterrence theory. In contrast, Jervis (1979, 1984, 1988), among others, chooses to classify work on nuclear deterrence into three schools of thought: nuclear revolution theory; risk manipulation, escalation, and limited war; and nuclear irrelevance. The essence of these divisions involves a debate about what the possession of nuclear weapons does for a state that controls them. Does the possession of these weapons affect the behavior of nuclear and nonnuclear opponents in disputes over contested values? Do the weapons impart political influence and hold military utility, or are they useless as tools for deterrence, compellence, or war?

Nuclear strategy has principally concerned itself with the efficacy of nuclear weapons as a deterrent. One school of thought—nuclear revolution theory—characterized by the works of Brodie (1946, 1959, 1978), Waltz (1981, 1990, 2003), and Jervis (1984, 1988, 1989a), holds that the incredibly rapid and destructive effects of nuclear weapons creates a strong disincentive for nuclear-armed states to engage each other in disputes which might escalate to the level of war. The "nuclear revolution" means that nuclear weapons can deter aggression at all levels of violence and makes confrontations and crises between nuclear-armed states rare events. The maintenance of a nuclear second-strike capability is all that is required for a successful military deterrent force.

A second school of thought—risk manipulation, escalation, and limited war—emphasizes the problem of "risk" in confrontations between states in possession of nuclear weapons. The issue here is that in disputes between nuclear-armed states the use of nuclear weapons carries such enormous costs for both sides that any threat to use the weapons lacks inherent credibility. While allowing that a nuclear second-strike capability can deter a full-scale nuclear strike by an opponent, these analysts argue that states will manipulate the risk of dispute escalation and war for the purposes of deterrence and compellence (e.g., Schelling 1960, 1966; Kahn 1962, 1965; Gray 1979). In this view, crises and brinkmanship tactics become surrogates for war in confrontations between nations in possession of nuclear weapons (Snyder and Diesing 1977). Associated with this thesis is the concept of the "stability-instability paradox" (Snyder 1965) whereby nuclear-armed states are secure in the deterrence of general nuclear war but are free to exploit military asymmetries (including strategic and tactical nuclear asymmetries as well as conventional military advantages) at lower levels of violence (e.g., Kissinger 1957).

Yet another perspective holds nuclear weapons to be "irrelevant" as special instruments of either statecraft or war (Mueller 1988, 1989).[2] In this argument, nuclear weapons are not substantially different in their deterrent effect from conventional military forces, and, in John Mueller's view, developed nations will not engage each other in either conventional or nuclear wars—having already witnessed the devastation that can be produced with both types of weaponry. A related argument holds that the possession of nuclear weapons provides little or no coercive advantage in confrontations with either nuclear-armed or nonnuclear states. A number of quantitative empirical studies of deterrence failures and successes (in both direct- and extended-deterrence cases) have produced results supportive of this thesis. Additionally, a notable formal mathematical study of deterrence by Zagare and Kilgour (2000) demonstrates that raising the costs of war above a certain threshold has no effect on deterrence stability. In this work, Zagare and Kilgour also maintain that while nuclear weapons may increase the costs associated with a deterrent threat, they simultaneously decrease the credibility of the threat—and hence the stability of deterrence. These contrary effects serve to minimize the impact of nuclear weapons on deterrence. In short, nuclear and nonnuclear crises should exhibit the same patterns of escalation.

Over the past thirty years, empirical studies have attempted to generate evidence relating to these theories. The following sections discuss some of these works.

NUCLEAR WEAPONS AND PATTERNS
OF INTERNATIONAL CONFLICT

The Nuclear Revolution

Theory

The term "nuclear revolution" was coined by Robert Jervis (e.g., 1989a: ch. 1), although the initial recognition of the alterations in patterns of international politics likely to be wrought by nuclear weapons should be credited to Bernard Brodie (1946). As Jervis has noted:

> The changes nuclear weapons have produced in world politics constitute a true revolution in the relationships between force and foreign policy. The fact that neither [the United States nor the Soviet Union] can protect itself without the other's cooperation drastically alters the way in which force can be used or threatened. . . . The result is to render much of our prenuclear logic inadequate. As Bernard Brodie has stressed, the first question to ask about a war is what the political goal is that justifies the military cost. When the cost is likely to be very high, only the most valuable goals are worth pursuing by military means. . . . What prospective . . . goals could possibly justify the risk of total destruction? (Jervis 1989a: 13, 24)

Moreover, for Jervis (1989b), that this destruction was essentially unavoidable under any plausible strategy constituted the essence of the nuclear revolution. Jervis (1989a: 23–25) went on to enumerate changes in international politics directly attributable to the presence of nuclear weaponry, including the absence of war among the great powers, the declining frequency of great power crises, and the tenuous link between the conventional or nuclear balance among great powers and the political outcomes of their disputes.[3]

Kenneth Waltz (e.g., 1981, 1983, 1990, 2003) has been exceptionally prominent in developing and forwarding the thesis that nuclear weapons are a force for peace and that nuclear proliferation will lead to declining frequencies of war. Waltz argues that nuclear weapons are simply more effective in dissuading states from engaging in war than are conventional weapons:

> In a conventional world, states going to war can at once believe that they may win and that, should they lose, the price of defeat will be bearable (Waltz 1990: 743). A little reasoning leads to the conclusions that to fight nuclear wars is all but impossible and that to launch an offensive that might prompt nuclear retaliation is obvious folly. To reach these conclusions, complicated calculations are not required, only a little common sense (Waltz in Sagan and Waltz 1995: 113). The likelihood of war decreases as deterrent and defensive capabilities increase. Nuclear weapons make wars hard to start. These statements hold for small as for big nuclear powers. Because they do, the gradual spread of nuclear weapons is more to be welcomed than feared. (Waltz in Sagan and Waltz 1995: 45)

Given this logic, evidence consistent with an absence of war or the use of force short of war between nuclear-armed states and few (or a declining frequency of) crises between nuclear powers would be supportive of the nuclear revolution thesis.

Empirical Evidence

A number of quantitative empirical studies have produced evidence relevant to the nuclear revolution thesis. In an early study of the effects of nuclear weapons possession, Bueno de Mesquita and Riker (1982) present both a formal mathematical model and an empirical test of deterrence success. The model assumes the possibility of nuclear war (i.e., the use of nuclear weapons) when nuclear asymmetry exists (only one side possesses nuclear weapons) but assumes the absence of nuclear war among nuclear-armed states. The model indicates a rising probability of nuclear war resulting from nuclear proliferation to the midpoint of the international system where half of the states possess nuclear weapons, at which point any further proliferation results in a declining probability of nuclear war. When all nations possess nuclear weapons, the probability of nuclear war is zero. The supporting empirical analysis uses early Correlates of War (COW) project Militarized Interstate Dispute (MID) data for the years 1945 through 1976 for four classes of dyads: nuclear/nuclear, nuclear/nonnuclear with a nuclear ally, nuclear/nonnuclear, and nonnuclear/nonnuclear. The analysis examines the distribution of threats, interventions, and wars across the four dyad classes and indicates that the presence of a symmetric nuclear threat constrains conflict by reducing its likelihood of escalation to the level of war. The two classes of nuclear/nuclear and nuclear/nonnuclear with a nuclear ally have the highest probabilities of employing only threats and the lowest probabilities of engaging in interventions and wars. This evidence is consistent with the predictions of the nuclear revolution thesis.[4]

Rauchhaus (2009) provides a multivariate analysis of factors associated with both militarized interstate disputes and wars for all dyads between 1885 and 2000 (MID database). The data set used in his study contains 611,310 dyad years, and tests were performed on time sections from 1885–1944 and 1945–2000. He reports that in symmetric nuclear dyads (both states possess nuclear weapons) the odds of war drop precipitously. Rauchhaus concludes that Waltz and other nuclear revolution theorists find support for their thesis in the patterns uncovered by his study.

Asal and Beardsley (2007) examine the relationship between the severity of violence in international crises and the number of states involved in the crises that possess nuclear weapons. Using data from the International Crisis Behavior (ICB) project for the years 1918 through 2000, their results indicate that crises in which nuclear actors are involved are more likely to end without violence and that as the number of nuclear-armed states engaged in crises increases, the probability of war decreases. This evidence is interpreted as supportive of the nuclear revolution thesis: the presence of nuclear weapon states in international crises has a violence-dampening effect given the potential consequences of escalation and the use of nuclear force.

In a second study, Beardsley and Asal (2009a) hypothesize that nuclear weapons act as shields against aggressive behavior directed toward their possessors. Specifically, it is postulated that nuclear states will be constrained in engaging in aggressive actions toward other nuclear-armed powers. Data is drawn from the ICB project for the years 1945 through 2000 using directed dyads as the unit of analysis. The results indicate that nuclear opponents of other nuclear-armed powers are limited in their use of violent force. However, Beardsley and Asal (2009a: 251) also note that the "restraining effect of nuclear weapons on violent aggression does not appear to affect the propensity for actors to engage each other in general crises, in contrast with the expectations of . . . the 'nuclear revolution' model."

Evaluation

The nuclear revolution thesis maintains that there should be a general absence of war or the use of force short of war among nuclear-armed states. In addition, there is the expectation of few, or a diminishing number of, crises in nuclear dyads, as the fear of escalation will exert a powerful constraint on aggressive behavior.

Bueno de Mesquita and Riker (1982) present compelling evidence that nuclear asymmetry as well as the absence of nuclear weapons on both sides of a conflict is more likely to be associated with war. In their data, between

1945 and 1976 there were seventeen cases of war between nonnuclear states, two cases of war in asymmetric nuclear dyads, and zero cases of war in either nuclear dyads or nuclear/nonnuclear dyads where the nonnuclear party had a nuclear-armed ally. Rauchhaus' (2009) study also presents evidence that symmetric nuclear dyads are unlikely to engage in war. The article by Asal and Beardsley (2007) reports results consistent with those of Bueno de Mesquita and Riker (1982). Specifically, crises ending in war are not uncommon for confrontations engaging nonnuclear states and for confrontations in which only one state possesses nuclear weapons. However, as the number of nuclear participants increases beyond one, the probability of full-scale war diminishes. Similarly, Beardsley and Asal (2009a) show findings consistent with the nuclear revolution thesis: symmetric nuclear dyads engage in few crises where violence is the "preeminent" form of interaction. However, they also note that there appears to be no constraining effect produced by nuclear weapons on the occurrence of crises that exhibit lower levels of hostility in symmetric nuclear dyads.

Since the advent of nuclear weapons in 1945, there has been one war between nuclear-armed powers: the Kargil War of 1999 involving India and Pakistan (Geller 2005: 101). This conflict remained at the conventional level and surpassed the threshold of one thousand battle deaths set by the Correlates of War project for classification as a war (Singer and Small 1972; Small and Singer 1982). However, Paul (2005: 13) argues that despite the conventional military asymmetry between India and Pakistan (in India's favor) that existed at the time of the Kargil War, the development of Pakistani nuclear weapons actually permitted Pakistan to launch a conventional invasion of the disputed territory of Kashmir. As Paul explains, only in a long war could India mobilize its material superiority, but as a result of the development of Pakistani nuclear weapons, a long war becomes "inconceivable" without incurring the risk of nuclear escalation. Hence, Pakistan's leaders were emboldened to initiate a conventional war behind the shield of their nuclear deterrent despite their conventional military inferiority. This sole case of conventional war between nuclear-armed states—and its facilitation by the threat of unacceptable escalation provided by nuclear weapons—stands in stark contradiction to the predictions of nuclear revolution theory.[5]

These collective results provide only partial support for the nuclear revolution thesis. As the theory suggests, war between nuclear-armed states should be nonexistent or a very rare event. This prediction, to date (with one notable exception), has been upheld. However, Beardsley and Asal (2009a) report that symmetric nuclear dyads engage in an unexpectedly large number of crises—in contradiction to the predictions of nuclear revolution theory. This is an empirical question that will receive additional examination in the following section.

Risk Manipulation, Escalation, and Limited War

Theory

A second school of thought—risk manipulation, escalation, and limited war—finds its archetypal expression in the seminal work of Henry Kissinger (1957). According to this thesis (and counter to that of nuclear revolution theory), the possession of a nuclear second-strike capability may prevent a nuclear attack by an opponent on one's home territory, but not much else. Kissinger argued that the United States (and its NATO allies) required the ability to conduct successful combat operations at levels of violence below that of general nuclear war if the protection of Europe against Soviet aggression was to be a viable political goal. Some years later, Snyder (1965) discussed this as what was later termed the "stability-instability paradox." The essence of the paradox was that stability at the level of general nuclear war permitted the exploitation of military asymmetries at lower levels of violence—including strategic counterforce and tactical nuclear wars as well as conventional forms of combat. This thesis that strategic nuclear weapons possessed little political or military utility other than deterring a nuclear attack on one's home territory led to a number of works devoted to the analysis of tactics for coercive bargaining and limited war by Thomas Schelling (1960, 1966), Herman Kahn (1960, 1962, 1965), and others.[6]

As Snyder and Diesing (1977: 450) maintain, the primary effect of the possession of nuclear weapons on the behavior of nuclear adversaries is the creation of new constraints on the ultimate range of their coercive tactics—a result of the extraordinary increase in the interval between the value of the interests at stake in a conflict and the potential costs of war. They note that before the advent of nuclear weapons, this interval was comparatively small and states could more readily accept the risk of war in a coercive bargaining crisis or engage in war in order to avoid the loss of a contested value. In contradistinction, given even small numbers of nuclear weapons in the stockpiles of states, it is far more difficult to conceive of an issue worth incurring the high risk of nuclear war, much less the cost of actually fighting one.[7]

It is held that a direct result of the constraints created by the presence of nuclear weapons has been the attempt by nuclear powers to control, in a more finely calibrated manner, the threat and application of force in disputes with other nuclear-armed states. These developments find theoretical and empirical expression in the concept of "escalation," which is defined as the sequential expansion of the scope or intensity of conflict (Osgood and Tucker 1967: 127, 188).[8] In most standard formulations, escalation is conceived as a generally "controllable and reversible process"[9] which a rational decision maker can employ in conflict situations as an instrument of state policy (Osgood and Tucker 1967: 188). Decision makers estimate the relative bargaining power of the rivals and engage in increasingly coercive tactics that are designed to undermine the opponent's resolve. Controlled escalation occurs when each side is capable of inflicting major or unacceptable damage on the other but avoids this while attempting to influence the opponent with measured increases in the conflict level that incorporate the threat of possible continued expansion.

The measured application of force and the ability to control escalation in nuclear disputes are seen—by these strategic theorists—as indispensable for securing political values while minimizing risk and cost (Osgood and Tucker 1967: 137; Russett 1988: 284). A preeminent theorist in this school, Herman Kahn (1965: 3), described escalation as "an increase in the level of conflict . . . [often assuming the form of] a competition in risk-taking or . . . resolve." As this theory developed, conflict analysts elaborated the risks involved in the process and incorporated the manipulation of these risks as a possible tactic in one's strategy.[10]

Clearly, nuclear weapons have not altered the values at stake in interstate disputes (and the desire to avoid political loss) but rather have increased the rapid and immediate costs of war. As a result, in a severe conflict between nuclear powers, the decision maker's dilemma is to construct a strategy to secure political interests through coercive actions that raise the possibility of war without pushing the risk to an intolerable level. Some analysts argue that the solution to this problem has entailed an increase in the "threshold of provocation," providing greater area of coercive maneuver in the threat, display, and limited use of force (Osgood and Tucker 1967: 144–45; Snyder and Diesing 1977: 451; Lebow 1981: 277). Hostile interaction between nuclear powers under this higher provocation threshold can range from verbal threats and warnings, to military deployments and displays, to the use of force in limited wars.

It is frequently stated that the principal exemplar of this new form of competition is the local crisis. Obviously, crises have an extensive history in international politics, but the argument is made that the nuclear age has produced an expansion of steps on the escalation ladder and has intensified the maneuvering of nuclear rivals for dominant position in conflicts below the level of all-out war. For example, Snyder and Diesing (1977: 455–56) note that the expanded range of crisis tactics in the nuclear era can be linked to a new conception of crises as *surrogates* for war, rather than merely dangerous incidents that might lead to war. . . . [S]ince war is no longer a plausible option between nuclear powers, they have turned to threats of force and the demonstrative use of force short of war as a means of getting their way. The winner of the encounter is the one who can appear the most resolved to take risks and stand up to risks.

Given this logic, conflicts between nuclear powers should reveal different escalatory patterns than conflicts between states where only one side possesses nuclear arms or conflicts where neither side possesses nuclear arms. Specifically, disputes between nuclear powers should evidence a greater tendency to escalate—short of war—than nonnuclear disputes or disputes in which only one side possesses a nuclear capability.

Empirical Evidence

Kugler (1984) presents an empirical test of classical nuclear deterrence theory; the study examines whether nuclear weapons are salient in preventing the initiation or escalation of war to extreme levels. The analysis focuses on crisis interactions involving the United States, the Soviet Union, and China (PRC). The cases used in the analysis constitute fourteen extreme crises where nuclear nations were involved and where nuclear weapons "played a central role" (Kugler 1984: 477). The results indicate that crises of extreme intensity diminish as the threat of nuclear devastation becomes mutual. In other words, as the capacity of actors to destroy each other with nuclear weapons increases, there is a tendency to decrease the intensity of conflict, and to settle those crises that reach extreme proportions by compromise (Kugler 1984: 482). This suggests that deterrence of war by the symmetric possession of nuclear weapons operates in the conflict dynamics of great power crises.

As Siverson and Miller (1993: 86–87) note, the earliest systematic statistical work on the effect of nuclear weapons possession in the escalation of conflict is by Geller (1990). This study employs the Correlates of War (COW) Militarized Interstate Dispute (MID) data covering 393 MIDs between 1946 and 1976 and uses the MID five-level dispute hostility index in coding the dependent variable. The results indicate that dispute escalation probabilities are significantly affected by the distribution of nuclear capabilities. Comparing the escalatory behavior of nuclear dyads with the escalatory behavior of nonnuclear dyads in militarized disputes, it is reported that symmetric nuclear disputes indicate a far greater tendency to escalate—short of war—than do disputes for nonnuclear pairs: disputes in which both parties possess nuclear weapons have approximately a seven times greater probability of escalating

(.238) than do disputes in which neither party possesses nuclear arms (.032). The conclusion indicates that the presence of nuclear weapons impacts the crisis behavior of states, with disputes between nuclear states more likely to escalate, short of war, than disputes between nonnuclear nations.

Huth, Gelpi, and Bennett (1993) analyze ninety-seven cases of great power deterrence encounters from 1816 to 1984 as a means of testing the explanatory power of two competing theoretical approaches to dispute escalation. Dispute escalation is defined as the failure of the deterrent policies of the defender. Deterrence failure occurs when the confrontation ends in either the large-scale use of force or defender capitulation to the challenger's demands. For the post-1945 period, the findings indicate that for nuclear dyads the possession of a nuclear second-strike capability by the defender substantially reduces the likelihood of the confrontation ending either in war or in capitulation by the defender. However, the possession of nuclear weapons in great power dyads does not deter the challenger from initiating militarized disputes.

Asal and Beardsley (2007) examine the relationship between the severity of violence in crises and the number of states involved in the confrontations that possess nuclear weapons. Using data from the International Crisis Behavior project, the study includes 434 international crises extending from 1918 through 2001. The results indicate that symmetric nuclear dyads engage in an unexpectedly large number of crises—and that "crises involving nuclear actors are more likely to end without violence. . . . [A]s the number of nuclear actors increases, the likelihood of war continues to fall" (Asal and Beardsley 2007: 140). The authors also note that their results indicate there may be competing effects within nuclear dyads: specifically, that both sides will avoid war but engage in subwar levels of escalatory behavior (Asal and Beardsley 2007: 150n6).

Rauchhaus (2009) also attempts to test the effects of nuclear weapons possession on conflict behavior. The data are generated using the EUGene (version 3.203) statistical package for dyad years from 1885 through 2000 and for a subset period from 1946 through 2000. The findings indicate that in militarized disputes, symmetric nuclear dyads have a lower probability of war than do dyads where only one nation possesses nuclear arms. Moreover, in dyads where there are nuclear weapons available on both sides (nuclear pairs), the findings indicate that disputes are associated with higher probabilities of crises and the use of force (below the level of war). The author suggests that these results support the implications of Snyder's (1965) stability-instability paradox. The results are also supportive of the Snyder and Diesing (1977) contention that crises have become surrogates for war between nuclear-armed states where the manipulation of risk through coercive tactics is employed to secure political objectives.

Evaluation

Evidence consistent with the risk manipulation, escalation, and limited war thesis would include the presence of severe crises between nuclear powers that exhibited escalatory behavior short of unconstrained war but inclusive of the use of force. The limited conventional war of 1999 between India and Pakistan, initiated and carried out by Pakistan under the umbrella of its nuclear deterrent, is an extreme example of precisely this type of conflict interaction. It captures the logic of Snyder's (1965) stability-instability paradox and incorporates, as well, Schelling's (1960, 1966) and Kahn's (1960, 1962, 1965) descriptions of the use of limited war (with the risk of greater violence to follow) as a means of persuading an adversary to relinquish a contested value. In addition, Beardsley and Asal (2009a) report that symmetric nuclear dyads engage in an unexpectedly large number of crises—a finding that is consistent with the Snyder and Diesing (1977) contention that crises have become surrogates for war among nuclear-armed states. Similarly, Huth, Bennett, and Gelpi (1992) note that in great power dyads, the possession of nuclear weapons by the defender does not deter dispute initiation by a nuclear-armed challenger, and that an outcome of either war or capitulation by the defender is unlikely. In findings not inconsistent with those of Huth et al. (1992), Kugler (1984) reports that (between 1946 and 1981) as the capacity of nuclear actors to destroy each other increases, there is a tendency to decrease the intensity of the conflict. Lastly, both Geller (1990) and Rauchhaus (2009), in large-scale quantitative empirical analyses of escalation patterns in nuclear, nonnuclear, and mixed (asymmetric) dyads, report that symmetric nuclear dyads are substantially more likely to escalate dispute hostility levels—short of war—than are nonnuclear pairs of states. In Geller's study, the findings indicate that disputes in which both parties possessed nuclear weapons had approximately a seven times greater probability of escalation (.238) than did disputes in which neither party possessed nuclear arms (.032).

These cumulative findings are strongly supportive of the risk manipulation, escalation, and limited war thesis on the effects of symmetric nuclear weapons possession. Moreover, the case of the 1999 limited conventional war between India and Pakistan reflects both the logic of this school of thought as well as the patterns of escalation described in the large-scale quantitative studies of militarized disputes between nuclear-armed states.

Nuclear Irrelevance

Theory

The views of John Mueller are most commonly associated with the thesis of "nuclear irrelevance." Mueller (1988, 1989) made the highly controversial argument that nuclear weapons neither defined the stability of the post–World War II US-Soviet relationship nor prevented a war between the superpowers; he also maintains that the weapons did not determine alliance patterns or induce caution in US-Soviet crisis behavior. His contention is that the postwar world would have developed in the same manner even if nuclear weapons did not exist.

Mueller's logic allows that a nuclear war would be catastrophic, but that nuclear weapons simply reinforced a military reality that had been made all too clear by World War II: even conventional war between great powers is too destructive to serve any conceivable political purpose. Moreover, the satisfaction with the status quo shared by the United States and the Soviet Union removed any desire for territorial conquest that might have led to conflict, as each superpower held dominance in its respective sphere of influence. Similarly, provocative crisis behavior was restrained by the fear of escalation—and although the presence of nuclear weapons may have embellished such caution, the mere possibility of fighting another conventional war such as World War II would have induced fear and restraint on the part of decision makers. In short, nuclear weapons may have enhanced Cold War stability, but their absence would not have produced a different world. Mueller closes his argument with the extrapolation that war among developed nations is obsolescent. It may simply be that in the developed world, a conviction has grown that war among postindustrial states "would be intolerably costly, unwise, futile, and debased" (Mueller 1988: 78). In this sense, nuclear weapons lack deterrent value among developed states because—absent the incentive for war—there is nothing to deter.

In a related thesis, Vasquez (1991) holds that it is unlikely—given what is known about the complex conjunction of multiple factors in the steps to war—that any single factor, such as the availability of nuclear weapons, causes or prevents wars. He makes the nuanced argument, in discussing the long postwar peace between the United States and the Soviet Union, that

> There is little evidence to support the claim that nuclear deterrence has prevented nuclear war or that it could do so in the future, if severely tested. . . . Nuclear war may have been prevented not because of deterrence, but because those factors pushing the U.S. and the USSR toward war have not been sufficiently great to override the risks and costs of total war. (Vasquez 1991: 207, 214)

Of principal significance to Vasquez is the absence of a direct territorial dispute between the superpowers. Other factors that Vasquez believes contributed to the long peace include satisfaction with the status quo, the experience of the two world wars, the establishment of rules and norms of interaction between the superpowers, procedures for crisis management, and effective arms control regimes.[11]

A second area of application for the nuclear irrelevancy thesis involves asymmetric dyads. Little has been written about the effects of nuclear weapons on the patterns of serious disputes where this technology is possessed by only one side. However, what has been written suggests that in these types of conflicts nuclear weaponry may lack both military and psychological salience. For example, Osgood and Tucker (1967: 158) and Blainey (1973: 201) argue that tactical nuclear weapons are largely devoid of military significance in either Third World conflicts or insurgencies where suitable targets for the weapons are absent. An additional disincentive to the use of nuclear weapons against a nonnuclear opponent is that it might be expected to increase the pressures for nuclear proliferation and to incite international criticism and denunciation of the nuclear state (Huth 1988a: 428). It also has been suggested that a sense of fairness or proportionality contributes a moral aspect to the practical military and political inhibitions on using nuclear weapons against a nonnuclear opponent and that the set of these concerns has undermined the efficacy of nuclear power as a deterrent in asymmetric conflicts (Huth and Russett 1988: 38).

Moreover, Waltz (1967: 222) and Osgood and Tucker (1967: 162–63) caution against exaggerating the differences due to nuclear weapons between contemporary and historical major-power–minor-power (asymmetric) conflicts. Long before the advent of nuclear weapons, minor powers frequently defied or withstood great power pressure as a result of circumstances of geography, alliance, or an intensity of interests which the major power could not match.

In a similar argument, Jervis (1984: 132) examines the logic of escalation in a losing cause (presumably a tactic relating directly to disputes between nuclear and nonnuclear states) and suggests that a threat to fight a war which almost certainly would be lost may not be without credibility—indeed, there may be compelling reasons for actually engaging in such a conflict. Specifically, if the cost of winning the war is higher to the major power than is the value at stake in the dispute, then the confrontation assumes the game structure of "chicken." Hence, even if war is more damaging to the minor power than to the major power, the stronger may still prefer capitulation or a compromise solution to the confrontation rather than engaging in the fight. In sum, Jervis (1984: 135) argues that "the ability to tolerate and raise the level of risk is not closely tied to military superiority. . . . The links between military power—both local and global—and states' behavior in crises are thus tenuous."

The third area of application for the nuclear irrelevancy thesis involves policies of extended deterrence. The efficacy of nuclear weapons for the purposes of extended deterrence was an issue of immense importance throughout the Cold War. In fact, the positions on whether American strategic nuclear weapons were sufficient to deter a Soviet–Warsaw Pact invasion of Western Europe or whether substantial conventional and tactical nuclear weapons were necessary for successful deterrence constituted a continuing debate for decades. Nuclear revolution theory contended that the US strategic nuclear arsenal (with its ability to destroy the Soviet Union) was sufficient to induce caution and restraint on the part of the Soviet leadership. However, the strategists who formulated the stability-instability paradox argued that US strategic nuclear weapons would deter a direct nuclear strike on the United States itself, but little else. According to this logic, for the successful extended deterrence of an attack on Europe, the United States and NATO required effective combat forces that could fight at the level of conventional war and even war with tactical nuclear weapons. Escalation dominance was required to sustain extended deterrence. Of course, extended deterrence policies existed long before the development of nuclear weapons and applied to any situation where a powerful defender attempted to deter an attack against an ally by threat of military response. The issue at hand is the effectiveness of a strategic nuclear threat in sustaining a successful extended deterrence policy. The nuclear irrelevancy position is that such weapons lack extended deterrence significance.

In sum, the nuclear irrelevance thesis suggests that nuclear weapons have little salience in the interaction patterns of nuclear-armed dyads. Evidence consistent with this position would indicate that for symmetric dyads the possession of nuclear weapons or the nuclear balance does not affect crisis escalation, crisis outcomes, or dispute initiation patterns. In addition, if a set of practical, political, and ethical constraints has weakened the military advantage of possessing nuclear weapons in a serious dispute with a non-nuclear state, then the monopolization of nuclear capability will not confer a bargaining edge to the nuclear-armed state in an asymmetric crisis. The nuclear irrelevance school would also find support in findings indicating the absence of substantive effects resulting from possession of nuclear weapons in extended deterrence situations.

Empirical Evidence

In evaluating the empirical evidence regarding the nuclear irrelevance thesis, it is useful analytically to separate the studies into distinct categories: (1) findings involving the effects of nuclear weapons in nuclear-armed dyads, (2) findings involving the interaction patterns of nuclear-armed states against nonnuclear opponents, and (3) findings bearing on extended deterrence situations.

Nuclear Dyads   The examination of evidence relating to nuclear revolution theory upheld the prediction that, as the theory suggests, war between nuclear-armed states should be nonexistent or a very rare event (e.g., Bueno de Mesquita and Riker 1982; Rauchhaus 2009; Asal and Beardsley 2007). The success of this prediction (with the exception of the 1999 Kargil War) serves as the principal finding in support of the nuclear revolution thesis. However, this finding holds negative implications for the validity of the nuclear irrelevancy thesis. In other findings counter to the patterns hypothesized by the nuclear irrelevancy thesis, Geller (1990) reports results which indicate that the distribution of nuclear capabilities affects the patterns of escalation in militarized interstate disputes, and that symmetric nuclear dyads show substantially higher dispute escalation probabilities, short of war, than do nonnuclear dyads. Rauchhaus' (2009) findings mirror Geller's. Similarly, Beardsley and Asal (2009a) also note that the crisis behavior of symmetric nuclear dyads differs from that of asymmetric dyads. However, other evidence relating to crisis interaction patterns or crisis outcomes which indicates that nuclear weapons were inconsequential in the disputes serves to support the contention that nuclear forces are irrelevant in symmetric dyads.

Blechman and Kaplan (1978) provide an empirical analysis of 215 incidents between 1946 and 1975 in which the United States used its armed forces for political objectives. Their findings indicate that the strategic nuclear weapons balance between the United States and the Soviet Union did not influence the outcome of competitive incidents involving the two states (Blechman and Kaplan 1978: 127–29). Instead, the authors maintain that the local balance of conventional military power was more important in determining the outcomes of the confrontations (Blechman and Kaplan 1978: 527).

Kugler (1984) presents an empirical test of nuclear deterrence theory by examining whether nuclear weapons are efficacious in preventing the initiation or escalation of crises to the level of war. The case set is fourteen extreme crises between 1946 and 1981 involving the United States, the Soviet Union, and China. Of the fourteen crises, five involved nuclear-armed dyads (a nuclear power on each side). Kugler (1984: 501) concludes that "nuclear nations do not have an obvious and direct advantage over other nuclear . . . nations in extreme crises. Rather, conventional [military] capabilities are the best predictor of outcome of extreme crises regardless of their severity."

Huth, Bennett, and Gelpi (1992) examine militarized dispute initiation patterns among great power rivalries between 1816 and 1975 as a means of testing a set of explanatory variables drawn from multiple levels of analysis. The principal focus of the study is to investigate the relationship between the structure of the international system and the initiation of great power disputes. However, the analysis does include a variable coded for the possession of nuclear weapons by the challenger's rival. The findings indicate that the presence of (a defender's) nuclear weapons does not deter challengers from initiating militarized disputes among great powers (Huth, Bennett, and Gelpi 1992: 478, 513).

Gartzke and Jo (2009) examine the effects of nuclear weapons possession on patterns of militarized dispute initiation using a sophisticated multivariate model and data drawn from the COW MID database for directed dyads over the years 1946 through 2001. Their findings indicate that nuclear weapons possession has little effect on dispute behavior. The authors note that "instead, countries with security problems, greater interest in international affairs, or significant military capabilities are simultaneously more likely to fight and proliferate" (Gartzke and Jo 2009: 221). The relationship between nuclear weapons and MID initiation is rejected statistically; this finding applies to both symmetric (nuclear) and asymmetric (nuclear/nonnuclear) dyads.

Asymmetric Dyads   The nuclear irrelevancy school also maintains that the possession of nuclear weapons confers no bargaining advantage on the nuclear-armed power engaged in a confrontation with a nonnuclear state. Evidence pertaining to this prediction is discussed below.

In a seminal study examining the effects of nuclear weapons on conflict interaction patterns, Organski and Kugler (1980: 163–64) identify fourteen deterrence cases that occurred between 1945 and 1979 in which nuclear weapons could have been used. Seven of these cases involved a nuclear power in confrontation with a nonnuclear state (or a state with an "ineffective nuclear force"). Their findings indicate that in only one case out of the seven did the nuclear-armed state win: "Nonnuclear powers defied, attacked, and defeated nuclear powers and got away with it" (Organski and Kugler 1980: 176). In the six cases in which the nuclear power lost to a nonnuclear state, the winner was estimated to have conventional military superiority at the site of the confrontation (Organski and Kugler 1980: 177).

Kugler (1984) isolates fourteen cases of extreme crisis that occurred between 1946 and 1981 in which nuclear weapons were available to at least one party in the dispute. Of these fourteen cases, nine involved confrontations in which only one state had access to nuclear arms. In all nine cases, the outcomes of the crises favored the nonnuclear challenger (Kugler 1984: 479). Once again, the balance of conventional military capabilities—not nuclear weaponry—provided the best predictor of crisis outcome (Kugler 1984: 501).

Geller (1990) examines conflict escalation patterns in 393 serious interstate disputes (MIDs) between 1946 and 1976 among nations with both symmetric and asymmetric types of weapons technology. The findings indicate that for asymmetric dyads (with only one state in possession of nuclear arms), the availability of nuclear force has no evident inhibitory effect on the escalation propensities of nonnuclear opponents. In fact, the findings show that in this class of confrontation, both nonnuclear dispute initiators and targets act more aggressively than do their nuclear-armed opponents. The summation suggests that in confrontations between nuclear and nonnuclear states, war is a distinct possibility, with aggressive escalation by the nonnuclear power probable.

In two studies published in 1994 and 1995, Paul employs the case study method to examine the dynamics of asymmetric war initiation by weaker powers. Paul (1994) analyzes six cases of war initiation by weaker states against stronger states: three of these cases (China-US 1950, Egypt-Israel 1973, and Argentina–Great Britain 1982) involve nonnuclear nations initiating wars against nuclear-armed opponents. Paul (1994: 173) concludes that nuclear weapons appear to have limited utility in averting war in asymmetric dyads. He notes that, with either nuclear or conventional weapons, a significant military advantage may be insufficient to deter a weaker state that is highly motivated to change the status quo. In a more focused study, Paul (1995) discusses the possible reasons underlying the nonuse of nuclear weapons by nuclear-armed states against nonnuclear opponents. Here he analyzes two cases (Argentina–Great Britain in the Falklands War of 1982 and Egypt-Israel in the Middle East War of 1973) in which nonnuclear states initiated wars against nuclear opponents. Paul argues that in both cases nuclear retaliation by the targets was deemed highly improbable by the nonnuclear war initiators due to a combination of limited war goals and taboos (unwritten and uncodified prohibitory norms) against the use of nuclear weapons.

Rauchhaus (2009) attempts to test the effects of nuclear weapons possession on conflict behavior for asymmetric as well as for symmetric dyads using data generated by the EUGene (version 3.203) statistical program for dyad years from 1885 through 2000. The findings indicate that for asymmetric (nuclear/nonnuclear) dyads (in comparison to symmetric dyads) there is a higher probability of war. Asymmetric dyads are also more likely to be involved in militarized disputes that reach the level of the use of force (Rauchhaus 2009: 269–70). In short, the study produces results in opposition to the view that conflict between nuclear and nonnuclear states will be limited. As Rauchhaus (2009: 271) concludes, "Nuclear asymmetry is generally associated with a higher chance of crises, uses of force, fatalities, and war."

A study by Beardsley and Asal (2009b) produces findings that stand in counterpoint to the main body of analyses on conflict in asymmetric dyads. This work examines the question of whether the possession of nuclear weapons affects the probability of prevailing in a crisis. The data are drawn from the International Crisis Behavior project for directed dyads covering the years between 1945 and 2002. The findings indicate that the possession of nuclear weapons provides bargaining leverage against nonnuclear opponents in crises: nuclear actors are more likely to prevail when facing a nonnuclear state (Beardsley and Asal 2009b: 278, 289).

Extended Deterrence   The logic of the nuclear irrelevancy thesis suggests that nuclear weapons should be of little salience in extended deterrence situations. Evidence relevant to this prediction is discussed below.

Huth defines deterrence as a policy that seeks to convince an adversary through threat of military retaliation that the costs of using military force outweigh any expected benefits. "Extended deterrence" is then defined by Huth (1988a: 424) as a confrontation between a "defender" and a "potential attacker" in which the defender threatens the use of military force against the potential attacker's use of force against an ally (protégé) of the defender. There have been a large number of studies produced on the issue of the efficacy of extended nuclear deterrence—the majority of which report a body of consistent or complementary findings.

As noted in Harvey and James (1992), Bruce Russett's (1963) analysis of seventeen crises that occurred between 1935 and 1961 appears to be the first aggregate study of the factors associated with extended deterrence success and failure. Nine crisis cases involved defenders with a nuclear capability, and six of the nine cases resulted in successful extended deterrence. However, Russett draws no conclusions as to the independent effect of nuclear weapons on those outcomes. He does note that military equality on either the local (conventional) or strategic (nuclear) level appears to be a necessary condition for extended deterrence success.

Two studies published by Weede (1981, 1983) also deal with the effectiveness of extended nuclear deterrence. Weede examines 299 dyads between 1962 and 1980 for evidence relating to patterns of extended deterrence success or failure. His findings are supportive of the position that nuclear weapons assist in producing extended deterrence success.

Huth and Russett (1984) increased the size of Russett's (1963) sample set from seventeen to fifty-four historical cases of extended deterrence from 1900 through 1980. The findings indicate that the effect of nuclear weapons on extended deterrence success or failure is marginal. Of much greater import are the combined local conventional military capabilities of the defender and protégé; hence conventional, rather than nuclear, combat power is associated with the probability of extended deterrence success.

In two related studies, Huth (1988a, 1988b) examines fifty-eight historical cases of extended deterrence and reports findings similar to those found in Huth and Russett (1984). Specifically, the possession of nuclear weapons by the defender did not have a statistically significant effect on deterrence outcomes when the target itself was a nonnuclear power. In addition, the ability of the defender to deny the potential attacker a quick and decisive conventional military victory on the battlefield is correlated with extended deterrence success.

Huth and Russett (1988) present an analysis of Huth's (1988b) fifty-eight historical cases of extended deterrence success and failure. In this database, there were sixteen cases of extended deterrence crises where defenders possessed nuclear weapons. The findings indicate that a defender's nuclear capability was essentially irrelevant to extended deterrence outcomes; existing and locally superior conventional military forces were of much greater importance to deterrence success.

In an unusual work, Carlson (1998) combines a formal mathematical model with an empirical test of escalation in extended deterrence crises. Using Huth's (1988b) data extending from 1885 to 1983, the analysis examines the fifty-eight cases of extended deterrence crises. Measures include the estimated cost tolerance of both attackers and defenders. The findings indicate that low cost tolerance attackers are less likely to escalate a crisis to higher levels of hostility when the defender possesses nuclear weapons.

Evaluation

The empirical evidence regarding the nuclear irrelevance thesis has been divided analytically into three distinct categories: (1) findings involving the effect of nuclear weapons in nuclear dyads, (2) findings involving the interaction patterns of nuclear-armed states against nonnuclear opponents, and (3) findings relating to extended deterrence situations.

Regarding category 1—the effect of nuclear weapons on conflict patterns in nuclear dyads—the results are mixed. According to the logic of the nuclear irrelevancy thesis, nuclear-armed dyads should show identical conflict patterns to nonnuclear dyads. However, Bueno de Mesquita and Riker (1982), Rauchhaus (2009), and Asal and Beardsley (2007) all note that empirical probabilities of war are far lower for nuclear dyads than for nonnuclear dyads. Moreover, Geller (1990) reports results indicating that the distribution of nuclear capabilities affects escalation patterns in militarized interstate disputes, and that symmetric nuclear dyads show substantially higher dispute escalation probabilities—short of war—than do nonnuclear dyads. Rauchhaus' (2009) findings are identical to Geller's. Similarly, Beardsley and Asal (2009a) note that the crisis behavior of symmetric nuclear dyads differs from that of asymmetric dyads. In sum, contrary to the predictions of the nuclear irrelevancy school, these findings suggest that patterns of war and crisis escalation differ among symmetric nuclear dyads, asymmetric dyads, and nonnuclear dyads.

Nevertheless, there is a body of evidence for nuclear dyads which supports the nuclear irrelevancy thesis; these findings focus on the effects of the nuclear balance on crisis outcomes and the effect of nuclear weapons on patterns of dispute initiation. Both Blechman and Kaplan (1978; 215 incidents from 1946 to 1975) and Kugler (1984; five extreme crises between 1946 and 1981) report that the balance of nuclear forces in nuclear dyads was less significant in influencing the outcome of confrontations than was the local balance of conventional military capabilities. With regard to dispute initiation, Huth, Bennett, and Gelpi (1992) report a lack of salience regarding the availability of nuclear weapons for great powers and the initiation patterns of their militarized disputes. Gartzke and Jo (2009) similarly note that nuclear weapons show no statistically significant relationship to the initiation of militarized interstate disputes in either symmetric or asymmetric dyads. In sum, the findings of this subset of studies are consistent with the thrust of the nuclear irrelevance thesis regarding both the effects of the nuclear balance on crisis outcomes and the effects of the availability of nuclear weapons on dispute initiation patterns.

Category 2—focusing on the interaction patterns of nuclear-armed states against nonnuclear opponents—provides a second set of cumulative findings. Organski and Kugler (1980), Kugler (1984), Geller (1990), and Rauchhaus (2009) all conclude that the possession of nuclear weapons provides little leverage in the conflict patterns or outcomes of disputes in asymmetric dyads. Organski and Kugler (1980) note that in six cases out of seven, nonnuclear states achieved their objectives in confrontations with nuclear-armed states. Kugler (1984) reports that in nine crises between nuclear and nonnuclear states, the outcomes in every case favored the nonnuclear party. In both studies, conventional military capabilities at the site of the confrontation provided the best predictor of crisis outcome.

Geller's analysis indicates that in thirty-four asymmetric disputes with a nuclear initiator, the nonnuclear target matched or escalated the initiators' hostility level in twenty-four cases (71 percent); in fifty-six asymmetric disputes with a nonnuclear initiator, the nuclear target deescalated the crisis by failing to match or exceed the nonnuclear initiator's hostility level in thirty-five cases (63 percent). Overall, thirty-five of the total of ninety cases (39 percent) of asymmetric disputes reached the level in which force was used. These findings show that in this class of dyad, nonnuclear dispute initiators as well as targets act more aggressively than do their nuclear-armed opponents. The conclusion suggests that in confrontations between nuclear and nonnuclear states, the use of force, including war, is a distinct possibility, with aggressive escalation by the nonnuclear state probable. In such cases of asymmetric distribution of nuclear forces, the conventional military balance may well be the determinative factor in the outcome of the dispute.

The findings of Rauchhaus (2009) reinforce those discussed above: there is a higher probability of war in asymmetric dyads than in symmetric nuclear dyads, and asymmetric dyads are more likely than symmetric nuclear dyads to experience militarized disputes that engage the use of force. As Rauchhaus concludes, nuclear asymmetry is associated with higher probabilities of crises, use of force, and war than are symmetric nuclear dyads.

These results are consistent with the predictions of the nuclear irrelevance thesis regarding conflict patterns in asymmetric dyads: the possession of nuclear weapons confers no advantage to nuclear-armed states in disputes with nonnuclear opponents. Paul's (1994, 1995) case studies of instances of war initiation by nonnuclear states against nuclear-armed adversaries offer additional evidence in conformity to this pattern.

Category 3—extended deterrence crises—also provides a pattern of results. Studies by Huth and Russett (1984, 1988) and Huth (1988a, 1988b) report the essential irrelevance of a defender's possession of nuclear weapons to extended deterrence success. These studies indicate that existing and locally superior conventional military force is the factor most frequently associated with the majority of successful extended deterrence outcomes. Russett (1963) notes the ambiguous effects of nuclear capability in situations of extended deterrence and concludes that military equality on either the conventional or nuclear level appears to be minimally requisite for extended deterrence success. However, Weede (1981, 1983) reports evidence contrary to the general set of findings, specifically that nuclear weapons assist in producing successful outcomes in extended deterrence situations.

In sum, the cumulative findings in all three areas are consistent with some of the predictions of the nuclear irrelevance school and inconsistent with others. For symmetric nuclear dyads, a substantial set of findings indicate that patterns of war and crisis escalation differ between symmetric nuclear dyads, asymmetric dyads, and nonnuclear dyads. Counter to the logic of the nuclear irrelevancy thesis, nuclear weapons affect the nature of conflict interaction between nuclear-armed states. At the same time, there is a subset of findings consistent with the logic of nuclear irrelevancy for nuclear dyads: the nuclear balance does not affect the outcome of crises (the balance of local conventional military forces is more important), nor does the symmetric possession of nuclear weapons distinguish initiation patterns of militarized disputes from initiation patterns in asymmetric or nonnuclear disputes. Also supportive of the irrelevancy thesis are findings indicating that for asymmetric dyads, the possession of nuclear arms provides scant advantage in crises and confrontations with nonnuclear states. Escalation by the nonnuclear adversary and its use of force—including war—are outcomes with surprisingly high probabilities. Lastly, in extended deterrence situations, the cumulative findings indicate the essential irrelevance of nuclear weapons possession and point instead toward the salience of the local balance of conventional military forces in determining crisis outcomes.

CONCLUSION

This chapter has reviewed the three principal schools of thought regarding the effects of nuclear weapons possession on patterns of international conflict: (1) nuclear revolution theory; (2) risk manipulation, escalation, and limited war; and (3) nuclear irrelevance. Quantitative empirical works that produced findings relevant to evaluating the predictions of these schools were then collated by category and their results compared to the predictions.

For nuclear revolution theory, the findings offer limited, but not insignificant, support. For example, as predicted, wars among nuclear-armed states have been rare events. To date, with the exception of India and Pakistan in 1999, no militarized dispute between nuclear powers has reached the level of war (based on the coding rules of the Correlates of War project). As Waltz and Jervis have predicted, wars occur among nuclear-armed states at a far lower proportional frequency than in asymmetric or nonnuclear dyads. However, the prediction of nuclear revolution theory that there will be few crises among nuclear-armed powers has not been supported by the quantitative empirical evidence. Similarly, the prediction that those crises which do develop among nuclear powers will be settled rapidly and without serious escalation has not found empirical support.

For the risk manipulation, escalation, and limited war school, the evidence has proved more uniformly favorable. The prediction by Snyder and Diesing (1977) that crises among nuclear-armed states will be used as surrogates for war—with associated tactics (including the limited use of force) designed to increase risk and intimidate through dangerous escalatory behaviors—has been largely supported. Comparisons of crisis escalation probabilities between symmetric nuclear dyads, asymmetric dyads, and nonnuclear dyads clearly show higher escalation probabilities for nuclear dyads than for the other two classes, with disputes for nuclear dyads approximately seven times more likely to escalate—short of war—than disputes for nonnuclear dyads. Moreover, the case of the 1999 war between India and Pakistan conforms to the logic of Snyder's stability-instability paradox whereby limited war is fought between nuclear powers under the protective umbrellas of their nuclear deterrents.

The nuclear irrelevance school, like nuclear revolution theory, finds mixed support in the extant empirical evidence. The nuclear irrelevancy thesis can be categorized according to predictions involving (1) the effects of nuclear weapons in nuclear dyads, (2) the effects of nuclear weapons possession in asymmetric dyads, and (3) the effects of nuclear weapons in extended deterrence situations. Counter to the logic of this school, cumulative empirical evidence indicates that nuclear weapons do make a difference in certain types of conflict interaction. Patterns of war and crisis escalation differ between symmetric nuclear dyads, asymmetric dyads, and nonnuclear dyads, with nuclear dyads less likely to fight wars and more likely to exhibit crisis escalation patterns short of war than nonnuclear dyads.

Supportive of the contentions of the nuclear irrelevancy school are findings indicating that the nuclear balance does not affect the outcome of crises (the balance of local conventional military forces is more important), nor does the symmetric possession of nuclear weapons distinguish dispute initiation patterns in those dyads from initiation patterns in asymmetric or nonnuclear dyads. In asymmetric dyads, the possession of nuclear arms provides no discernable advantage in crises and confrontations. Escalation by the nonnuclear adversary and its use of force against its nuclear-armed opponent—including war—are distinct outcomes with surprisingly high probabilities. Lastly, in extended deterrence situations, the cumulative findings indicate the essential irrelevance of nuclear weapons possession and point instead toward the salience of the local balance of conventional military forces in determining outcomes.

Three conclusions may be drawn from the patterns discussed above.

1. Wars among nuclear-armed states are improbable. If confrontations do escalate to the level of violence, such violence will likely remain conventional. Hence, the spread of nuclear weapons increasingly supports the maintenance of the status quo.
2. Crises among nuclear powers have a higher probability of escalating—short of war—than do crises for asymmetric or nonnuclear dyads. Hence, nuclear powers engage in dangerous tactics involving the manipulation of risk as a means of securing policy objectives.
3. For nuclear dyads, the nuclear balance does not appear determinative of crisis outcomes; more important to outcomes is the local conventional military balance. In asymmetric dyads the possession of nuclear weapons does not impede aggressive behavior by a nonnuclear adversary. Hence, an advantage in nuclear weaponry does not translate into bargaining leverage in confrontations between nuclear-armed states or between nuclear states and their nonnuclear adversaries.

It is evident that the effects of nuclear weapons possession on patterns of international conflict are complex. Moreover, the patterns themselves may be subject to change as a result of events. For example, the future use of nuclear weapons in a war between nuclear-armed states or the use of such weapons in a war against a nonnuclear state might lead to different expectations of outcomes and thereby alter the subsequent strategic calculations and policy choices of decision makers. Unmistakably, nuclear weapons have raised the prompt and potential long-term costs of war. Empirical analysis has indicated in what way these weapons have affected the patterns of international conflict in the past. How these weapons may ultimately affect the future conflict patterns of states remains to be determined.

NOTES

I wish to thank John Vasquez, Jack Levy, and Peter Wallensteen for their expert commentaries on an earlier version of this chapter.

1. See Geller (2000b), "Material Capabilities: Power and International Conflict," in *What Do We Know about War?*, 1st ed., ed. John A. Vasquez.
2. As Mueller (1988: 55–56) notes, "nuclear weapons neither define a fundamental stability nor threaten severely to disturb it. . . . [W]hile nuclear weapons may have substantially influenced political rhetoric, public discourse, and defense budgets and planning, it is not at all clear that they have had a significant impact on the history of world affairs since World War II."
3. Others attributing to nuclear weapons causal significance for the "long peace" between the United States and the Soviet Union include the Harvard Nuclear Study Group (1983), Tucker (1985), Quester (1986), and Gaddis (1991). However, Levy (1989: 289–95), while noting the stability in the superpower relationship produced by nuclear weapons, cautions about pressures for preemptive war that may develop between nuclear-armed states.
4. Intriligator and Brito (1981) present a similar formal mathematical analysis of the effects of nuclear proliferation on the probability of nuclear war—but in this case without associated empirical data. The mathematical model demonstrates that the effects of nuclear proliferation on the probability of nuclear war depend on the number of existing nuclear weapon states and that proliferation may reduce rather than increase the probability of nuclear war. Once two or more states achieve a secure second-strike capability, the addition of new nuclear states decreases the incentive to initiate a nuclear war. However, Intriligator and Brito note that while the probability of a *calculated* nuclear attack may decrease as a result of proliferation, there may be an increase in the probability of accidental or irrational nuclear war as these weapons spread throughout the system.
5. For a different interpretation of the 1999 Kargil War—by Waltz—see Sagan and Waltz (2003: 109–24). Also see Basrur (2007–8) and Diehl, Goertz, and Saeedi

(2005) for analyses suggesting, like Waltz, that caution was imposed in the conduct of the Kargil War by nuclear weapons. For a sophisticated model of the effects of various levels of nuclear war between India and Pakistan, see Batcher (2004).

6. Major works, many using formal mathematical models, that explore the factors associated with deterrence, brinkmanship and the manipulation of risk, crisis stability, threat credibility, and the consequences of nuclear proliferation include those by Ellsberg ([1959] 1968, 1960), Brams and Kilgour (1985), Powell (1987, 1988), Kugler (1987), Nalebuff (1988), Langlois (1991), Wagner (1991), Brito and Intriligator (1996), Zagare and Kilgour (2000), Danilovic (2002), Morgan (1977, 2003), and Zagare (2007).

7. For example, see Bundy and Blight (1987/88: 30–92). Mueller (1988, 1989) presents an argument that, among developed countries, major war (nuclear or conventional) is no longer a realistic foreign policy option due to its massive destructive effects. But Mueller (1988: 56) also contends that nuclear weapons have not fundamentally affected the crisis behavior of major powers. For a response to this argument, see Jervis (1988).

8. Escalation theory is a subset of the more general body of theory on strategic interaction in international politics (e.g., Singer 1963).

9. Strategic theorists fully recognize, however, that escalation of conflict can occur irrespective of the desires of the participants due to factors of miscalculation or momentum. This possibility—and an appreciation of it—forms a key element in the work of some theorists in this school (e.g., Schelling 1966: ch. 3).

10. Other early works with sections on escalation that touch on the subject of risk are Kahn (1962: ch. 6), Snyder (1961: 252–58), Schelling (1966: 99–116, 166–68), Schelling (1960: appendix A), and Halperin (1963: chs. 1–2, 4). The issue of "costly signals" with regard to the credibility of threats and commitments are elaborations on the themes of these early studies on escalation (e.g., Fearon 1994a, 1994b, 1997; Schultz 1998). For example, Fearon (1997: 82) discusses the relative merits of the "tie-hands" and "sink-cost" signaling strategies. Fearon demonstrates (using formal methods) that costly signals are more successful if they involve a tie-hands strategy (create costs that would be paid ex post if they fail to uphold the commitment) rather than if a sink-cost strategy is pursued (which is only costly to the actor ex ante). The tie-hands strategy is connected to ex post domestic audience costs. The model also indicates that decision makers will not bluff with either type of costly signal; they will not incur or create costs and then fail to carry out the threat.

11. In a more recent work, Vasquez (Senese and Vasquez 2008) allows that nuclear weapons have raised the provocation threshold for total war: "What would have provoked a war between major states in the pre-nuclear era no longer does so" (Senese and Vasquez 2008: 62). Nevertheless, Vasquez (2009) continues to maintain that a proper evaluation of the effects of nuclear weapons on war is within the context of the "steps-to-war" model. For an alternative explanation of war based on a process of complex conjunctive causation, see Geller and Singer (1998) and Geller (2000a, 2004, 2005).

Part II

FACTORS THAT PROMOTE PEACE

Chapter Eight

Norms and the Democratic Peace

Sara McLaughlin Mitchell

Any analysis of what we know about interstate warfare would be incomplete without a discussion of the democratic peace. The democratic peace refers to the absence of interstate wars between democratic states, the reduced chances for democratic states to engage in militarized disputes among themselves, and the unlikely escalation of democratic militarized disputes to high levels of violence. The democratic peace literature is so broad and influential it has been the subject of multiple literature reviews (Russett 1993; Ray 1995, 2000; Chan 1997; Rosato 2003). These reviews typically focus on empirical findings in the democratic peace literature at the monadic, dyadic, and systemic levels of analysis[1] and on challenges to those findings, such as intervention by democratic states abroad (Hermann and Kegley 1996), conflict initiation by democratizing regimes (Mansfield and Snyder 1995), the rarity of democracy and conflict (Spiro 1994), and questions about reverse causality (Thompson 1996). Reviews of the democratic peace literature also highlight major theoretical explanations for the democratic peace, including realist, normative, structural, institutional, rationalist, feminist, and constructivist explanations.

While the normative approach to the democratic peace was viewed favorably in early empirical studies (Maoz and Russett 1993; Russett 1993), it faded into the background in the past twenty years as the bargaining model of war gained a strong foothold in the interstate conflict literature (Fearon 1995; Powell 2002; Reiter 2003). This turn toward the rationalist approach to the study of interstate war emphasized domestic institutions, audience costs, and commitment problems as the key to understanding conflict processes. Normative factors, such as peaceful norms for dispute resolution and respect for the rule of law, received less attention in the interstate war literature, especially in dyadic interstate conflict studies. However, systemic analyses of the democratic peace kept the normative approach alive in the intellectual conversation (Huntley 1996; McLaughlin 1997; Crescenzi and Enterline 1999; James, Solberg, and Wolfson 1999; Mitchell, Gates, and Hegre 1999; Harrison 2002, 2004, 2010; Mitchell, Kadera, and Crescenzi 2008; Crescenzi et al. 2011). The publication of Alexander Wendt's book (1999), *Social Theory of International Politics*, reinvigorated the normative approach as well, as Wendt focused on the emergence of a Kantian culture of anarchy at the systemic level.

When we consider the growth of democratic states in the international system over the past two centuries, we would be hard pressed to believe this has not altered interactions in global politics. Democratic states have increased from 19 percent of all states in 1900 to around 57 percent in 2009.[2] The absence of war between democratic countries paints an optimistic view of future peaceful international relations as the trend toward greater democratization in the world continues. "Democracies constitute for the first time in history a majority of the states in the international system. Therefore, the norms governing *their* relations have a better chance now than earlier to become the dominant mode of interaction in world politics" (Chan 1997: 59).

The notion that domestic characteristics of states have the potential to alter the rules and norms of interaction in the system is an idea that challenges neorealist perspectives that treat states as like units, motivated by the pursuit of power and security concerns (Waltz 1979). However, neorealists recognize that the international system is more than its constituent parts (Waltz 1979: 39):

> A systems approach will be needed, if outcomes are affected not only by the properties and interconnections of variables but also by the way in which they are organized. If the organization of units affects their behavior and their interactions, then one cannot predict outcomes or understand them merely by knowing the characteristics, purposes, and interactions of the system's units. The failure of the reductionist theories . . . gives us some reason to believe that a system's approach is needed.

A systemic approach to the democratic peace recognizes that we cannot simply aggregate the number of democratic states or the number of democratic dyads to predict aggregate levels of conflict and cooperation in the system (Ray 2001). Rather, the democratic nature of the system generates causal properties that alter all states' behavior at the monadic and dyadic levels.

In this chapter, I review normative approaches to the democratic peace, highlighting the major theoretical arguments and empirical findings at the dyadic and systemic levels of analysis. I also describe several norms of behavior that the democratic community of states has promoted, including (1) third-party conflict management, (2) respect for human rights, (3) cooperation through international organizations, and (4) territorial integrity. I argue that the normative perspective of the democratic peace cannot be fully appreciated unless we consider all of the ways democracies have altered norms of interstate interactions. The absence of war between democracies is a big piece of this puzzle, yet we must also look at foreign policy behavior beyond interstate conflict to appreciate how democratic norms arise and evolve in the international system. The normative democratic peace approach also highlights the dynamics of the international system, showing that the influence of democracy on peace is gaining momentum as the system itself becomes more democratic.

Perhaps the best evidence we see for the normative systemic democratic peace is the adoption of democratic norms of behavior by autocratic states (Mitchell 2002). While domestic democratic institutions are important mechanisms for explaining interstate interactions, as the bargaining model of war emphasizes, they are insufficient for thinking about broader shifts in the context within which bargaining occurs in world politics. Rationalist, institutional approaches to the democratic peace cannot explain why states without democratic institutions adopt democratic norms of behavior or why the influence of democracy on interstate conflict and cooperation is stronger in some time periods relative to others. In this chapter, I argue that we can think about the systemic democratic peace as a type of normative order that helps to define possibilities for interactions in world politics (Raymond 2000).

NORMATIVE EXPLANATIONS
FOR THE DEMOCRATIC PEACE

The influence of norms in international relations has been the subject of rigorous debate, particularly among neorealists, neoliberals, and constructivists. Neorealists focus on the material structure of the international system, asserting that norms, if they exist, merely reflect the underlying material distribution of power. Neoliberals and regime theorists have recognized the potential for norms to influence the behavior of states, although they "concentrate on explicit contractual arrangements (such as those embodied in regimes) intended to resolve collective action problems" (Kowert and Legro 1996: 455). Constructivists, on the other hand, have recognized a much greater role for norms and ideas in international politics. Agents and structures are mutually constituted; norms do more than simply regulate behavior. "Constructivists . . . argue that states develop norms to provide structure to their relations and that these norms help constitute the identity and interests of states by creating standards of appropriate behavior" (Flynn and Farrell 1999: 510).

While the definition of norms employed by scholars in these areas varies, "there is general agreement on the definition of a norm as a standard of appropriate behavior for actors with a given identity" (Finnemore and Sikkink 1998: 891). Some distinguish between regulative and constitutive norms; the former order and constrain behavior, while the latter help to create and define new actors or interests. "Norms either define ('constitute') identities in the first place . . . or prescribe or proscribe ('regulate') behaviors for already constituted identities. . . . Taken together, then, norms establish expectations about who the actors will be in a particular environment and about how these particular actors will behave"[3] (Jepperson, Wendt, and Katzenstein 1996: 54). Many international norms prohibit certain behaviors such as piracy, slavery, the killing of whales (Nadelmann 1990), the use of land mines (Price 1998), and chemical weapons (Price and Tannenwald 1996; Price 2007), while others encourage behaviors such as decolonization (Goertz and Diehl 1992c); peaceful dispute resolution (Russett 1993); respecting territorial boundaries (Kacowicz 1994; Zacher 2001; Hensel, Allison, and Khanani 2009); respect for human rights (Keck and Sikkink 1998); and women's suffrage (Finnemore and Sikkink 1998).

A persistent question in the literature on international norms involves the origin and evolution of norms. "Why, of the variety of norms available at any given time to govern behavior in particular choice situations, does one rather than another become a widely accepted standard of behavior?" (Florini 1996: 363). While some scholars have examined the process by which norms emerge (Nadelmann 1990; Finnemore 1996; Florini 1996; Zacher 2001), they have not typically considered the changing proportion of democratic states in the international system as a potential source of norm formation (although see Risse-Kappen 1995; Wendt 1999; Mitchell 2002).

Kant envisioned the emergence of democratic norms in the international system in his famous work on "Perpetual Peace" ([1795] 1991: 99–105). He identified three key conditions for perpetual peace: (1) republican forms of government domestically,[4] (2) an international federation of free states, and (3) a principle of cosmopolitanism, or universal, hospitality. He asserted that the categorical imperative to end warfare could only be reached through the spread of a domestic and international "rule of law," whose principles are founded on individual freedom, legal equality, and separation of executive and legislative powers. A republican form of government built on these principles creates the freedom to act morally. "The history of the human race as a whole can be regarded as the realisation of a hidden plan of nature to bring about an internally—and . . . externally—perfect political constitution as the only possible state within which all natural capacities of mankind can be developed completely" (Kant [1784] 1991: 50). Kant concluded that democracy leads to peace in the international system by decreasing the uncertainty that arises in a state of anarchy. Kant believed that democracies would extend their domestic rule of law to an international rule of law, such that the norms characteristic of democratic interaction would extend to the international arena (Doyle 1986).

Kant's ideas have influenced dyadic and systemic theories about how democracy influences the chances for interstate militarized conflict. Normative theories at both levels of analysis attribute the democratic peace to the unique ideas and norms that democratic states promote in their interstate interactions, including individual freedom and human rights, the protection of minority rights, equality of citizens in the political process, peaceful conflict resolution, and transparency of the political process (Risse-Kappen 1996). I discuss each of these theoretical literatures before discussing the specific norms that the democratic community promotes, such as third-party conflict management and ethical human rights policies.

Normative Democratic Peace Theories at the Dyadic Level

One of the earliest quantitative papers to clearly stake out a normative argument for the dyadic democratic peace was Maoz and Russett's (1993) influential paper on the topic. The authors built upon Kant's perpetual peace philosophy to construct two theoretical models of the dyadic democratic peace, a structural (or institutional) theory and a normative (or cultural) theory.[5] The normative model is based on two assumptions (Maoz and Russett 1993: 625):

Normative assumption 1: States, to the extent possible, externalize the norms of behavior that are developed within and characterize their domestic political processes and institutions.

Normative assumption 2: The anarchic nature of international politics implies that a clash between democratic and nondemocratic norms is dominated by the latter, rather than the former.

Based on these assumptions, Maoz and Russett (1993) argue that militarized disputes between states with strong democratic norms should not only be less likely to break out but also be less likely to escalate to higher levels of violence. The authors argue that the strength of democratic norms will be positively related to how long democratic institutions have been operating legitimately. They find strong empirical support for the normative model in an analysis of politically relevant dyads from 1946 to 1986, showing that democratic regimes that have been stable for longer periods of time and who employ lower levels of political violence against their citizens are significantly less likely to engage in militarized conflicts with other democratic regimes. When comparing structural features of regimes to the stability of democratic norms, Maoz and Russett (1993) find that democratic norms more consistently predict lower levels of interstate violence than domestic institutions.

William Dixon further develops the normative approach to the dyadic democratic peace by focusing on norms of bounded competition. "All modern democracies are openly competitive systems of governance where conflicting material interests and basic political values routinely clash over the proper course of public action. . . . Just as competition is a constant of democratic governance, so too is the presence of rules, procedures, or guidelines for setting its boundaries" (Dixon 1994: 15). Actors participating in a democracy agree not to use force to achieve a victory on a contested issue: "Contingent consent implies that within democratic societies political actors will prefer to follow nonviolent regulatory procedures and will expect competing actors to do likewise" (Dixon 1994: 16). Dixon suggests that this democratic norm of bounded competition extends to world politics. When two democratic states disagree over some international issue, they should be more likely to resolve the dispute peacefully because they realize that their opponent is operating under a similar norm of compromise and nonviolence. In addition, such conciliatory democratic norms should increase the chances of democracies adopting or agreeing to conflict management efforts, especially active participation by third parties (Dixon 1993). Dixon's (1993) analysis of post–World War II SHERFACS data strongly supports this hypothesis. He finds that third-party management in a given crisis phase is about 50 percent more likely if both dispute participants are highly democratic. A follow-up paper (Dixon and Senese 2002) shows similarly that democratic dyads are more likely to resolve militarized conflicts through negotiated settlements than nondemocratic dyads.

Gregory Raymond (1994) also emphasizes democratic norms that promote peaceful interstate dispute settlement. He focuses on legal norms that originate from domestic legal traditions in democratic societies. Democratic institutions create a norm of trust in legal procedures (Slaughter 1995; Simmons 1999), which helps to explain why democracies are more inclined to involve third parties in the resolution of disputes in ways that are binding (arbitration and adjudication) as opposed to nonbinding (good offices, mediation, inquiry, conciliation), whereas, lacking such norms, autocratic leaders are more apt to restrict third-party intervention (Raymond 1994: 27). Raymond's analysis of 206 dyadic disputes from 1820 to 1965 reveals that coherent democratic dyads were three times more likely to use binding third-party arbitration than nondemocratic dyads.

Hansen, Mitchell, and Nemeth (2008) find that contentious issues involving democratic adversaries are more likely to experience conflict management by international organizations. This finding is consistent with democratic states' trust in legalistic forms of dispute settlement, as many instances of adjudication are carried out through the judicial arms of international organizations, such as the United Nations and European Union. Similarly, Powell and Mitchell (2007) find that democratic states are significantly more likely to accept the compulsory jurisdiction of the World Court than autocratic states, a move that opens up democracies to adjudication of their interstate disputes by the court. Mitchell and Powell (2011) find that jurisdictional acceptance is influential even in situations where the World Court is not directly involved as a conflict manager. Civil law dyads that bargain bilaterally in the shadow of the World Court and jointly accept its compulsory jurisdiction are more likely to reach agreements and comply with agreements designed to resolve territorial, maritime, and river conflicts than pairs of states who negotiate bilaterally outside of the court.

Huth and Allee (2002) develop extensive empirical tests to compare accountability (institutional), norms, and affinity (regime similarity) explanations for the dyadic democratic peace. Using data on territorial claims from 1919 to 1995 to evaluate the three theories, they find empirical support for the normative model. Specifically, they show that leaders are more likely to seek out negotiations to resolve border disputes if they come from more established, less domestically violent democratic regimes, a finding that is similar to Maoz and Russett's (1993) earlier results. These findings suggest that states with strong nonviolent norms are less likely to use force to pursue their issue-related goals. Huth and Allee (2002) also find that recently established and highly repressive democracies are more likely to use force to resolve border disputes and more likely to escalate those conflicts to more severe levels. These patterns are consistent with the dyadic normative democratic peace theory, as more established, older democratic countries are more likely to negotiate peaceful settlements to contentious territorial disputes, while newer regimes with less entrenched democratic norms resort to the use of force more frequently. It also accords with Mitchell and Prins' (1999) discovery that militarized disputes involving newer, democratizing regimes are more likely to involve highly salient issues, such as border disputes, in comparison to militarized conflicts between fully democratic states.

While there is ample evidence to suggest that democratic norms influence the chances for militarized conflict and the peaceful tools that states select to manage interstate disputes, dyadic conflict studies in the past two decades have not emphasized this quality of regimes in empirical tests. Many conflict scholars utilize the Polity regime scale (democracy-autocracy), which captures the degree to which a regime is democratic (−10 to +10). On the other hand, this measure does not represent the stability of political regimes. In a study linking regime characteristics and civil war onset, Hegre et al. (2001) demonstrate that both the degree of democracy and the stability of a regime are important characteristics influencing states' intrastate conflict behavior. Maoz (2004) also shows the importance of regime stability as a predictor of interstate conflict, while also demonstrating that the manner through which a regime is established influences its future conflict propensities. He shows that political instability significantly increases the chances that a state or a pair of states will engage in repeated militarized conflicts. He also finds that regimes that were democratic at birth and were established through peaceful rather than revolutionary means are much more likely to remain pacifistic in their regime history. Normative tests of the democratic peace theory at the dyadic level remind us of the importance of taking into account regime history and regime stability, as democratic norms take time to become fully internalized into states' foreign policy practices.

Constructivists assert that it is misleading to simply code institutional features of regimes and correlate those factors with conflict behavior. There is also an ideational component to the dyadic democratic peace, in that states must view each other as belonging to their own security community for peace to prevail. Peceny (1997) illustrates this logic using the case of the Spanish-American War, showing that even though Spain was institutionally democratic, people in the United States did not view Spain as part of the global liberal society, which made it easier for them to justify their support for the war. Widmaier (2005) makes a similar argument about the near war between the United States and India in 1971, suggesting that President Nixon felt more in common with autocratic Pakistani leaders than the more democratic Indian ones, attitudes which fueled tensions between the two countries. These ideas accord with quantitative scholars' emphasis on regime stability and duration; just as it takes time for institutions to mature, it also takes time for states to be embraced by their established democratic counterparts in world politics. Feminist research on the democratic peace also points to variation in the quality of democratic regimes as important predictors of states' conflict behavior. States characterized by gender equality are more pacific, escalating and initiating interstate conflicts less frequently (Caprioli 2000), which is why feminists often equate the security and equality of women with state security more generally (Hudson and Den Boer 2002).

Normative Democratic Peace Theories at the Systemic Level

While studies of the normative democratic peace at the dyadic level emphasize how democratic norms influence interactions between pairs of states, the systemic democratic peace considers dynamic changes in the international system over time. This perspective often correlates the number of democratic states in the international system with the incidence of global war or militarized conflict. It is often assumed that peace in the international system follows logically from peace at the monadic or dyadic level, especially as the number of democracies increases over time. As noted earlier, the number of democratic states has risen substantially over time, with democracies now comprising a majority of states in the system. Furthermore, the last two hegemonic powers, the United Kingdom and the United States, are both fully democratic regimes. As Ikenberry (2001) notes, the democratic institutions of victor states in major wars influence the types of postwar orders that emerge, as democratic victors are more likely to put limits on their power through the creation of postwar institutions and security agreements.

The United States and Great Britain have also been entrepreneurs in the use of binding forms of dispute settlement, such as arbitration and adjudication. The successful use of binding techniques by these democratic major powers to resolve claims surrounding the Jay Treaty and damages wrought by the *Alabama* provided impetus for the Hague Conferences at the turn of the twentieth century and ultimately led to the creation of the Permanent Court of Arbitration and the Permanent Court of International Justice (Mitchell 2002). This combination of democratic values and material strength also aided in the successful transitions of autocratic regimes to fully functioning democratic systems, even in the presence of war in the regional or global neighborhood (Kadera, Crescenzi, and Shannon 2003). Democracies are also less likely to become the targets of external military interventions as the number of democracies in the system increases (Hermann and Kegley 1996: 454).

Initial examinations of systemic democratic peace hypotheses utilize an aggregation approach, seeking to determine if the distribution of democratic regimes at the monadic or dyadic level translates into different levels of war at the systemic level. Maoz and Abdolali (1989) evaluate the systemic democratic peace theory with autoregressive moving average (ARMA) regression models from 1817 to 1976. They find that the proportion of jointly democratic dyads in the system typically has a *positive* effect on systemic conflict (e.g., the number of militarized disputes begun and under way), contradicting the expectation of a peaceful system with an increasing proportion of democracies. Their results on war, however, support the systemic democratic peace proposition: "While more democracies made for more disputes and more dispute involvements (number of dyads involved in disputes), they tended to make for less war, and they tended to reduce the probability that a low-level militarized dispute would escalate to an all-out war" (Maoz and Abdolali 1989: 29–30). These findings for war are confirmed in a study evaluating the post–World War II era; the proportion of democracies in the system decreases the proportion of states participating in war (Crescenzi and Enterline 1999).

Gleditsch and Hegre (1997) criticize previous tendencies to assume either that an increase in the proportion of democracies globally will decrease the level of systemic conflict (which follows from the dyadic level) or that the spread of democracy will have no impact on the overall level of conflict in the system (which follows from the monadic level). The authors assume that non-democratic dyads have a lower propensity for war than mixed democratic-nondemocratic dyads (Raknerud and Hegre 1997). They model the relationship between regime types in the international system and systemic conflict as a function of (1) the probability of war in jointly autocratic dyads, (2) the probability of war in democratic-nondemocratic dyads, (3) the proportion of democracies in the system, and (4) the total number of nations in the system. If the probability of war is greater in mixed dyads than in jointly autocratic dyads, then the relationship between the proportion of democracies in the international system and the frequency of international conflict is parabola shaped. In other words, if the proportion of democracies in the system is low, then the initial effect of new democracies entering the system is an overall increase in the level of global conflict due to high chances for militarized conflicts in mixed dyads. This increases up to a threshold point, where the proportion of democracies is large enough to produce greater levels of systemic peace. The threshold point is a function of the probability of war in mixed and jointly autocratic dyads. Gleditsch and Hegre's (1997) model predicts an increasing historical level of democracy to have produced more war initially. Their empirical analysis provides some support for this predicted theoretical relationship, with the pre–World War II time period being associated with more democracy and more war, and the post–World War II time period being characterized by more democracy and less war in the international system.

Mitchell, Gates, and Hegre (1999) compare this parabolic relationship to a time-varying parameter model that allows for the relationship between democracy and war in the system to change over time. They argue that the relationship between democracy and war at the systemic level is endogenous and evolutionary (McLaughlin 1997; Mitchell 2002). War in the system increases the proportion of democratic states, which in turn reduces the amount of systemic war. The argument draws upon Kant's ([1784] 1991: 47) claim that war justifies the development of democratic governments and creates a more widespread peace, which is essential to the survival and improvement of republican constitutions.

Kant believed that the experience of civil and interstate war would compel human beings to improve the institutions of their governments and that these governments would in turn seek to protect those gains by promoting a democratic rule of law internationally (Huntley 1996: 58). Mitchell, Gates, and Hegre (1999) also point to the findings relating regime type and success in interstate war. If democracies are more likely to win the wars they fight (Lake 1992) and if losing states in wars are most likely to experience regime changes (Bueno de Mesquita, Siverson, and Woller 1992), then democratic regimes surviving in the aftermath of interstate wars will increase in the system over time. Mitchell, Gates, and Hegre (1999) find empirically that global levels of democratization are inversely related to the proportion of states at war, and that the pacifying effect of democracy on war became more pronounced over time.

Analyses of learning processes at the dyadic level confirm these systemic findings as well. Using a dyadic time-varying parameter model, Cederman and Rao (2001) find that militarized dispute probabilities for jointly democratic dyads have gotten smaller over time. Their nineteenth-century findings reveal some time periods in which dyadic democracy has a positive effect on militarized conflict, which provides indirect support to the parabolic relationship (Gleditsch and Hegre 1997). Mitchell, Gates, and Hegre (1999), on the other hand, find no significant relationship between systemic war and democracy in the pre–World War I time period. While both types of models agree that the pacifying effect of democracy is growing over time, they are in disagreement about whether democracy's influence on war was negligible or war inducing when the proportion of democratic states was small. Regardless of the earlier dynamic path, however, both models agree that the pacifying effect of democracy on war has strengthened over time.

Democratic peace scholars have also shown the importance of regional configurations of regime type when predicting monadic or dyadic conflict. Maoz (1996, 2004) finds that pairs of states located in more democratic and stable regions have a significantly lower risk for militarized conflict compared to dyads in more autocratic, unstable regions. Gleditsch (2002a) also shows that interstate war and militarized disputes are much less likely to occur in regions with more democratic states and higher densities of regional trade. Similar to Maoz's (2004) findings on the birth of regimes, Enterline and Greig (2005) confirm that democratic regimes that are created through a strong external imposition have more positive regional effects than regimes established through weak impositions. The presence of "bright beacons," or those states imposed through strong external impositions, reduces war in the region, encourages democratization of neighboring states, and enhances the economic prosperity of the entire region.

Theoretically, the move from a Hobbesian or Lockean system to a Kantian system is discussed in the literature extensively. Bull (2002) and Wendt (1999) describe competing ideas of international society or cultures of anarchy depending on the enemy images that states ascribe to each other. In the Hobbesian society, states view each other as enemies, the risk of international conflict is high, and states fear potential elimination when conflict ensues. In the Lockean or Grotian system, states view each other more as rivals, which keeps them on their security guard, while at the same time allowing for some forms of interstate cooperation. War may occur in the Lockean system, although norms of state sovereignty will protect states from their ultimate demise, even when they are on the losing side of a conflict. Eventually the system could become a Kantian society where states view each other as friends, seeing each other's security as their own. In the Kantian world, interstate disputes are resolved without the use or threat of force. Constructivists emphasize that anarchy is what states make of it (Wendt 1992); systemic-level empirical findings in the democratic peace literature confirm this idea, showing that the system is evolving toward a Kantian society.

NORMS PROMOTED BY THE DEMOCRATIC COMMUNITY

Normative approaches to the democratic peace make novel claims that democratic norms will ultimately dominate interactions in the international system. While democracies initially promote specific norms of behavior to protect their interests, these norms often become adopted by nondemocratic states too. The presence of democratic hegemonic states facilitates this process as well, as they serve as important entrepreneurs in the development and spread of new international norms. International organizations and nongovernmental organizations also play important roles in the spread of new global norms. Some of the democratic norms identified in the literature include peaceful (third-party) conflict management practices, respect for personal integrity rights, the creation of international institutions and international courts to promote cooperation and conflict management, and respect for state sovereignty and territorial control.

The normative democratic peace theory predicts that democratic norms of behavior, like peaceful conflict management and good human rights practices, will spread in the international system, influencing the behavior of all states. The more democratic the international system, the more likely that the norms governing interactions between states will change. In particular, the greater the proportion of democracies in the system, the more likely the traditional power politics "rules" of the international system will become replaced by more cooperative, conciliatory, and peaceful rules of interaction like we see between democracies. "Once a critical mass of liberal democracies emerges, the norms of the liberal pacific union may begin to generate socialization effects and cascade through the international system" (Harrison 2004: 531).

In Kant's language, the greater the proportion of republican governments in the world, the more widespread their international "rule of law," which is both created from their domestic rule of law and perpetuated by the peace among them. War serves to promote the spread of republican forms of government, and the overall strength and success of republics serve to further their growth and influence over time. Cooperation in economic and cultural spheres serves to strengthen the peaceful and cooperative systemic norms of behavior. As Harrison (2004) explains, nondemocratic states may adopt norms of the dominant liberal culture because they have incentives to reap the economic benefits of trade and investment. The expansion of the European Union (EU) offers an empirical example of this process at the regional level, as prospective member states often adopt the economic and social behaviors of liberal EU member states to gain entry into the economic community (Moravcsik 2000; Shannon 2005). Some international relations scholars view economic exchange and highly developed economies as the key force explaining the democratic peace (Mousseau 2000; Gartzke 2007).

In this section, I describe research on the spread of norms associated with the democratic community. By focusing strictly on militarized conflict, which is typical in many reviews of the democratic peace literature, conflict scholars lose sight of the larger tapestry of empirical findings that show us the importance of ideas and norms generating peace in the Kantian community. Democratic norms influence not only states' conflict behavior, but also a wide variety of cooperative actions ranging from human rights protection to respect for territorial borders to support for international institutions.

Third-Party Conflict Management

Much of the early democratic peace literature focused on peaceful conflict management strategies, seeking to understand how regime type conditions the way in which states settle interstate conflicts. Scholars identify a broad range of tools for interstate conflict management including bilateral negotiations, conflict management with the assistance of a third party (nonbinding and binding tools), and the use of force. This emphasis follows naturally from the focus on militarization of contentious issues, as much of the initial empirical analyses relating regime type and conflict focused on the monadic (state-year) or dyadic unit of analysis, with conflict onset as the key dependent variable. As noted earlier, William Dixon and Gregory Raymond developed arguments about why democratic countries would be more amenable to third-party conflict management in comparison to nondemocratic countries, with the rule of law and respect for domestic opposition carrying over into international interactions. Yet in some regards, their conceptual emphasis was in line with structural or rationalist democratic peace theories, as both scholars viewed institutional features inherent only to democratic regimes as producing distinct conflict management strategies.

This democratic-autocratic difference based approach has been carried forward in a lot of modern conflict management literature which views regime type as an important factor predicting the use and success of particular conflict management tools. The most general finding is that joint democracy promotes the use of peaceful strategies to resolve interstate conflicts (Dixon 1993, 1994, 1996, 1998; Raymond 1994; Huth and Allee 2002; Greig 2001, 2005; Terris and Maoz 2005; Allee and Huth 2006; although see Hensel 2001a; Mitchell, Kadera, and Crescenzi 2008; Beardsley 2010) as well as the success of those settlement attempts (Leng and Regan 2003). Furthermore, shifts toward democratization in the context of a dispute also bode favorably for successful peaceful dispute settlement (Greig 2001, 2005) and the termination of interstate rivalries (Hensel, Goertz, and Diehl 2000). Other features of domestic institutions influence conflict management strategies as well, with solid domestic political opposition increasing the likelihood of legalistic dispute settlement (Allee and Huth 2006) and recent elections in the target state raising the chances for peaceful talks (Huth and Allee 2002). These studies focus on monadic or dyadic attributes of regimes and relate these institutional features to differences in the types of conflict management strategies selected or to the probability of success with particular tools of conflict management.

Normative democratic peace scholars, on the other hand, view the increasing usage of third-party conflict management as an outgrowth of the emerging and powerful democratic community. As the proportion of democratic states has grown in the international system, so too have the number of international organizations, international courts, and nongovernmental organizations available as potential conflict managers. Modern conflict management studies examine the influence of these nonstate actors on interstate conflict and cooperation. This follows naturally from the broader liberal peace literature which views international organizations as one of the three legs of the Kantian tripod for peace; democratic regimes and trade constitute the other two legs (Russett and Oneal 2001). Yet democratic states are also more likely to mediate other states' interstate conflicts than are autocratic states (Crescenzi et al. 2011). Thus the international system has witnessed a significant increase in the supply of third-party conflict managers, both through international organizations and courts and through the spread of democratic state mediators and arbitrators.

Viewing third-party conflict management as one norm promoted by the democratic community, Mitchell (2002) builds upon Finnemore and Sikkink's (1998) norm life-cycle argument, noting that powerful democratic states served as entrepreneurs in the modern usage of third-party conflict management strategies. The United States and the United Kingdom pushed for increased usage of arbitration in the nineteenth and twentieth centuries and also played important roles in the negotiations to create the Permanent Court of Arbitration, the Permanent Court of International Justice, and the International Court of Justice. As a critical mass of democratic states emerged, the use of third-party conflict tools became more widespread, even among states that did not have democratic institutions domestically. International organizations and domestic peace groups also played a part in this process, encouraging leadership in the United States and Great Britain to promote peaceful tools for dispute resolution. Analyzing data on territorial claims from 1816 to 2001 in the Western Hemisphere, Mitchell (2002) finds that third-party conflict management is sixteen times more likely for nondemocratic dyads when the system is comprised of 50 percent democratic states (versus a system with no democratic countries). This finding shows that the structure of the international system influences the way that states resolve contentious issues, and that while regime type characteristics help us understand conflict management strategies, they cannot account for dynamic changes occurring at the systemic level or the democratic behavior of states that do not have democratic domestic institutions.

Powerful democratic states have served as norm entrepreneurs in the spread of new democratic norms of behavior. Not only have democratic states become more frequent in the international system, but the power they wield relative to the autocratic community has also grown substantially as well. The strength of the democratic community now exceeds the strength of the autocratic community, which also has important implications for the frequency and success of conflict management efforts as well as the success of fledgling democratic regimes (Kadera, Crescenzi, and Shannon 2003; Mitchell, Kadera, and Crescenzi 2008; Crescenzi et al. 2011). For example, Mitchell, Kadera, and Crescenzi (2008) find that third-party conflict management is utilized more frequently by states in the Western Hemisphere to resolve geopolitical issues as the strength of the democratic community increases. This is consistent with Mitchell's (2002) findings using a simpler measure of the proportion of democratic states in the system. They also find that democratic states and international organizations serve as active conflict managers more frequently in a system when the democratic community is strong. These results show the dynamic nature of the international system and its influence on conflict management attempts by states, as certain strategies such as adjudication and mediation are utilized more frequently in a system dominated by democratic states. Interestingly, Mitchell, Kadera, and Crescenzi (2008) find no significant dyadic relationship between democratic institutions and the use of third-party conflict management. Part of this observation has to do with potential selection effects, whereby democracies are able to resolve conflicts more frequently through bilateral negotiations due to their more transparent regimes (Lipson 2003). However, it also demonstrates the problems with simple aggregation of regime types from the dyadic level to the systemic level. Many of the cases of third-party conflict management in a strong democratic system occur in nondemocratic dyads, as these states are socialized into the conflict management practices of democratic states. The likelihood of specific conflict management strategies also changes over time as a result of the shift toward the Kantian system; thus we need to consider the systemic context more carefully when evaluating states' conflict management strategies.

Respect for Human Rights

The year 2008 marked the sixtieth anniversary of the Universal Declaration of Human Rights. While the global human rights regime has suffered some setbacks along the way, the international system has reached a point in history where states belong to more global human rights treaties than ever before and where individuals have recourse for prosecuting human rights abuses through a variety of courts and tribunals. These trends reflect the power of the Universal Declaration, as they attest to the institutionalization of the norms and practices embodied in that landmark document. Many types of human rights identified in the Universal Declaration are rights guaranteed in democratic political systems, including freedom of speech, the right of assembly, the right to vote, and the right to form and join political parties (Arat 2003). While individuals, advocacy groups, and NGOs promote these important human rights' protections, democratic countries also played a large role in the creation of these various instruments for the promotion of good human rights practices.

Broadly speaking, human rights are "a set of principled ideas about the treatment to which all individuals are entitled by virtue of being human" (Schmitz and Sikkink 2002: 517). Political scientists tend to conceptualize "negative" human rights in terms of violations of personal integrity rights, including extrajudicial killings, torture, disappearances, and political imprisonment. Most quantitative analyses employ either the political terror scale (Gibney and Dalton 1996) or the Cingranelli-Richards (CIRI) Human Rights Dataset (Cingranelli and Richards 1999). Both of these data sets are constructed on the basis of Amnesty International and US State Department country reports.

A plethora of research on human rights has shown democratic states to have significantly better human rights practices and lower levels of repression and genocide than nondemocratic states (for example, Poe and Tate 1994; Harff 2003; Davenport and Armstrong 2004). These norms have been transmitted to the international arena as well. The Universal Declaration of Human Rights, as noted above, is strongly influenced by the types of rights protected in democratic political systems. Democratic states have also been instrumental in the creation and promotion of human rights tribunals and international courts. The like-minded group of states, who pushed for a strong, independent prosecutor and mandatory jurisdiction for the International Criminal Court, were led by many established, democratic countries including Canada, the Netherlands, Belgium, Sweden, Norway, Australia, and New Zealand (Schabas 2011). This democratic leadership translated into a higher rate of ratification of the Rome Statute by democratic countries (Mitchell and Powell 2011). Democratic states who respect the rule of law have also resisted the United States' efforts to undermine the ICC, as they have been reluctant to sign bilateral nonsurrender agreements with the United States (Kelley 2007). More broadly, human rights treaties are found to be more effective at promoting good human rights practices when linked with preferential trade agreements (Hafner-Burton 2005). Democratic countries strike more trade agreements than nondemocratic states (Mansfield, Milner, and Rosendorff 2002), and thus it is natural that trade and human rights institutions would be utilized as complementary foreign policy tools.

Much like the findings for the systemic democratic peace, research on human rights shows these global norms to influence the behavior of states without democratic institutions. States wishing to join regional trade agreements, like the European Union, must show improvements on personal integrity rights (Moravcsik 2000). Leaders seeking to credibly commit to peace after their state has suffered a civil war can join the International Criminal Court to signal their future pacific intentions more clearly (Simmons 2009). Many accounts of the human rights regime adopt a constructivist framework, emphasizing the role of entrepreneurs and nongovernmental organizations in the promotion of sound human rights practices (Keck and Sikkink 1998). For example, a coalition of over eight hundred NGOs (CICC) was instrumental in the Rome negotiations for the creation of the ICC, distributing information and facilitating dialogue among states (Leonard 2005). NGOs and advocacy groups have also played important roles in publicizing human rights violations and putting pressure on governments to improve their behavior toward their citizens. In short, as the international system has evolved toward a Kantian system, protection of basic human rights has emerged as a global norm, with states improving the way in which they treat their citizens as well.

Cooperation through International Organizations

Intergovernmental organizations (IGOs) are part of the Kantian tripod for peace, as Kant envisioned a federation of free states as a crucial component of a perpetual peace. Russett and Oneal (2001) find virtuous circles in their quantitative analysis of the relationship between democracy, IGOs, and peace. First, they find that a higher density of shared IGO memberships reduces the chances for dyadic militarized conflict by 24 percent (p. 171). Second, they show that democratic states join more IGOs than nondemocratic states: "Shared democracy is associated with a 7 percent higher density of IGO memberships: twenty-one such organizations" (Russett and Oneal 2001: 217). On the other hand, militarized conflict between states lowers shared IGO ties, a pattern that is consistent with the negative effects of regional conflict on democratization (Maoz 1996). Russett and Oneal (2001) also find support for the systemic effects of democracy, IGOs, and trade on peace, with a one standard deviation increase in average democracy level in the system reducing dyadic conflict by 24 percent. Global trade levels have an even larger effect, reducing the probability of dyadic conflict by 35 percent for each standard deviation increase in average global trade dependence (Russett and Oneal 2001: 182–83).

Mitchell and Hensel (2007) show that international organizations improve the chances for compliance with peace agreements both actively, through their direct involvement as conflict managers, and passively, through an increase in shared IGO memberships between disputants. As active conflict managers, IGOs' success rate depends on the tools they employ to manage interstate conflicts. Agreements brokered by an IGO and reached through binding procedures, such as arbitration and adjudication, have much higher success rates than nonbinding settlement attempts by IGOs (e.g., mediation) or negotiations involving the disputants themselves (e.g., bilateral talks). In terms of the passive effect of IGOs, an increased web of shared ties in international organizations increases the chances for nonbinding third-party conflict management (Hensel 2001a) and active intervention by IGOs (Hansen, Mitchell, and Nemeth 2008).

Mitchell and Hensel (2007), focusing on IGOs that call for peaceful dispute settlement in their charters, find that shared membership in these organizations increases the probability of agreement over contentious issues by .147 and the probability of compliance by .246 when increasing shared IGOs from its minimum to its maximum. Security organizations have similar effects, with shared alliance ties between disputants increasing the chances for third-party mediation (Terris and Maoz 2005); peaceful dispute settlement (Dixon 1993, 1994; Dixon and Senese 2002; Mitchell and Hensel 2007); and increasing states' shared IGO memberships (Russett and Oneal 2001). Collective security agreements involving democracies are more typically designed with consensual and compromise-oriented decision-making procedures and rules, as illustrated in the case of the North Atlantic Treaty Organization (NATO) (Risse-Kappen 1996: 368).

IGOs comprised of democratic members have advantages for promoting peaceful and successful dispute settlement as well. Pevehouse and Russett (2006) find that IGOs densely populated with democratic states promote peace between members more strongly than IGOs comprised of more regime heterogeneous states. Hansen, Mitchell, and Nemeth (2008) find that IGOs with more democratic members are very capable of helping disputing member states strike peaceful agreements when they intervene as active conflict managers. In conclusion, not only do democracies cooperate through international organizations more frequently than nondemocracies, but these institutional ties also reap many benefits for member states, helping them to resolve outstanding conflicts more successfully and avoid future militarized disputes.

As noted above, democracies also support international courts more readily than do nondemocratic states, and they join regional and global free-trade organizations more often. Democracies are more likely to establish institutions, both security and economic agreements, in the aftermath of large wars that they have won in comparison to autocratic victors (Ikenberry 2001). In short, there is ample evidence that democratic states view the creation and use of international organizations as an important part of their overall foreign policy agenda.

This norm of cooperation through international organizations has spread to nondemocratic states as well, consistent with the systemic democratic peace theory. A good example is provided by changing patterns of state support for international courts over time. Early courts, such as the Permanent Court of Arbitration and Permanent Court of International Justice, were utilized by less than a third of all countries, whereas courts created more recently, such as the International Criminal Court and the World Trade Organization Dispute Settlement Understanding receive much broader state support, with over three-fourths of all states joining these institutions. Autocratic governments have become much more willing to join international organizations, as the economic and security benefits of doing so outweigh the sovereignty costs of joining. This is occurring despite the potential costs to repressive leaders who accept the jurisdiction of courts like the ICC, as the prosecution of Sudanese president Bashir illustrates.

Territorial Integrity

Another norm that democracies have transmitted to the international system is a respect for territorial boundaries. Kacowicz (1995: 265) asserts that

"well-established democracies do not fight each other since they are conservative powers, usually satisfied with the territorial status quo within and
across their borders." He argues that well-established democracies are satisfied with the territorial status quo for two primary reasons. First, as democracies become more institutionalized, the number of nationalist and irredentist
claims outside homeland territorial boundaries will decrease. Mitchell and
Prins (1999) confirm this pattern in an examination of the issues at stake in
militarized disputes between democracies, as there are very few instances of
territorial MIDs involving fully democratic states. Kacowicz's second argument stems from work on power transition theory; democracies have tended
to be the most powerful states in their regions, often creating the regional
status quo. Thus they are more likely to be satisfied with the status quo, creating a situation where democracies have few or no incentives to fight each
another. Lemke and Reed (1996) also attribute peace between democracies
to their satisfaction with the international status quo.[6] Gibler (herein) and
Rasler and Thompson (2005) challenge the causal direction of this claim, arguing instead that the peaceful settlement of land borders reduces the militarization of the state and creates space for democratic institutions to develop.

The territorial integrity norm reflects in part a decline in the benefits of
territorial conquest as states engage in increased economic exchange, trade,
and investment (Brooks 1999; Rosecrance 1999). Democratic states were key
players in pushing for territorial integrity norms in the postwar settlements
after World War I and World War II, norms which have effectively removed
successful territorial aggrandizement from the international scene (Zacher
2001; Hensel, Allison, and Khanani 2009). Zacher (2001) emphasizes that
territorial integrity became a norm through its enshrinement in important
organizations, such as the League of Nations and United Nations. Hensel,
Allison, and Khanani (2009) also attribute the territorial integrity norm to the
increasing importance of the legal norm, *uti possiditis juris*, or the preserva-
tion of colonial borders following independence. In a series of judgments, the
International Court of Justice upheld this legal principle, strengthening the
sanctity of colonial borders.

The emergence of a territorial integrity norm is reflected in data collections
of territorial disputes, as new claims to territory have declined, especially in
the past century (Hensel, Mitchell, et al. 2008). Early signs of this trend could
be found in Holsti's (1991) compilation of issues surrounding interstate wars
over the past five hundred years, as he found territory to be affiliated with
the fewest wars in the post–World War II era.[7] Democratization of one or
both disputants also helps to end interstate rivalries, many of which involve
competitive claims to contiguous land borders. Shannon (2009) finds that
interventionist IGOs with more resources at their disposal are more active

in helping member states resolve territorial disputes, a finding consistent with Boehmer, Gartzke, and Nordstrom's (2004) claim that interventionist, security IGOs are best positioned to prevent their members from engaging in militarized conflict. Thus while the democratic membership of an IGO influences its conflict management efforts, other institutional features of organizations matter as well. Highly institutionalized IGOs are more active and more successful as global conflict managers. In some senses, though, these institutional conflict managers become less needed over time as new challenges to land borders become less frequent in the Kantian culture.

CONCLUSION

In this chapter, I review the literature on the normative democratic peace. I argue that normative approaches help us to explain behaviors that are hard to understand when focusing only on domestic institutional features, a strategy typically taken in the rationalist approach to the study of war. Once liberal states reach a critical mass in the international system, they can effectively promote liberal norms of behavior such as peaceful conflict management, cooperation through international organizations, respect for international law, and respect for good human rights practices. Thus the system is more than its parts, as Waltz (1979) argued. But it is also more than power politics; the success of liberal regimes over the past two centuries has created a system whereby liberal norms are systemic norms, an evolutionary process that has boded well for the peace and security of all mankind.

NOTES

I am grateful to John Vasquez and conference participants for useful comments.

1. The monadic level of analysis focuses on whether democracies are more peaceful overall in world politics; the dyadic level of analysis examines whether democracies are more peaceful in interactions with other democracies compared to interactions with nondemocratic states; the systemic level of analysis ponders whether an international system filled with democratic states is more peaceful than a system filled with mostly nondemocratic states (Gleditsch and Hegre 1997).

2. According to the Polity IV project (http://www.systemicpeace.org/inscr/inscr .htm), 94 of 163 countries (57.7 percent) had democracy scores of six or higher (on a scale from zero to ten) in 2009. Freedom House records 89 of 184 countries (48 percent) free and 48 of 184 countries (26 percent) partially free in the most recent 2010 survey (http://www.freedomhouse.org/template.cfm?page=546&year=2010).

3. For good summaries of how to define norms, see Goertz and Diehl (1992c) and Raymond (2000).

4. "The key characteristics of the republic are the retention of sovereignty by the citizens who compose it and the incumbent separation of legislative and executive powers" (Huntley 1996: 48).

5. In this chapter, I do not review the structural approach to the democratic peace, focusing instead on the contribution of normative democratic peace theories. The structural approach emphasizes the features of democratic regimes that slow decision-making processes for war and encourage peaceful dispute settlement, including checks and balances, division of power, and public opinion (Russett 1993). The rationalist version focuses on the size of the winning coalition and selectorate as important factors influencing states' foreign policy behavior (Bueno de Mesquita et al. 1999, 2003).

6. Lemke and Reed (1996: 145) define the status quo in the international system as "the rules, norms, and accepted procedures that govern international relations."

7. Although Vasquez (1993, 1995) reminds us that territorial disputes that occur, even if smaller in numbers overall globally, are often catalysts for the steps to war.

Chapter Nine

A Market-Capitalist
or a Democratic Peace?

Michael Mousseau

"History has proven," said George W. Bush, "that democracies do not fight their neighbors," aping his predecessor, Bill Clinton, who claimed that they "don't attack each other."[1] Yet history has not been kind to this view; just as the Clinton administration began promoting democracy as a strategy for global peace in 1993, the first clear-cut war between two democratic nations began: the Kargil War between India and Pakistan, initially a dispute that eventually escalated to war in 1998. Nor has the accumulating evidence been kind to the democratic peace. Studies have shown that a capitalist peace may supersede the democratic one, and that it is far more substantial; while the democratic peace achieved fame with its claim of an absence of wars between democratic nations—with "wars" defined as militarized conflicts with at least one thousand battlefield-connected fatalities—the capitalist peace can boast an absence of any battlefield-connected fatalities among capitalist nations (Mousseau 2009).

This chapter reviews the literature on a capitalist peace and explores the prospect that the capitalist peace may supplant the democratic one. Other chapters in this volume by Sara McLaughlin Mitchell and Douglas Gibler cover important events and challenges in the democratic peace research program, so this chapter begins with what may be the next stage in this research program: the capitalist peace. Two kinds of capitalist peace theories are distinguished: free-market theories equate "capitalism" with freer markets and are in the neoclassical liberal economic tradition (Weede 1996, 2005; Gartzke, Li, and Boehmer 2001; McDonald 2007, 2009); social-market capitalist peace theory suggests that advanced capitalism may be a product of state intervention (Mousseau 2000) and has roots in traditional critiques of the liberal tradition (Polanyi ([1944] 1957). The divergent causal mechanisms of the capitalist peace theories are then applied to the case of the Falklands/Malvinas War fought between

Argentina and Great Britain in 1982. This case shows considerable discrepancy among the theories on the meaning of "capitalism." The subsequent section finds that only the social-market definition of "capitalism" has the potential to account for what most observers usually think of when they think of "capitalist peace": the peace among the wealthy democracies of Europe, North America, and the Pacific Rim. Finally, the insignificance of the democratic peace is corroborated: from 1961 to 2001 about half of all democratic nation years did not have advanced capitalist economies, and these democracies had their normal share of deadly conflicts; the advanced capitalist nations, in contrast, had none.

The implications of the capitalist peace are far from trivial. The democratic peace drew widespread attention when it emerged a generation ago in part because it presented itself as the foremost stylized fact of international politics. It thus offered the most promising clue for scholars seeking to crack the puzzle of war. If the capitalist peace subsumes the democratic one, then scholars of war must revise their research bets: rather than explore how governing institutions might affect war and peace, we must set our sights on economic institutions.

CAPITALISM, DEMOCRACY, AND WAR

Comparative research has well established that wealth and democracy correlate (Lipset 1959), so early investigators of a democratic peace—the observation that democratic nations rarely fight each other, even though they frequently fight other nations—were careful to examine the possibility that economic factors might account for it. Influential studies by Stuart Bremer (1992) and Zeev Maoz and Bruce Russett (1992) tested for wealth as a potential confounding variable; yet both found democracy significant even after controlling for development. Later Russett and colleagues tested for international trade (Oneal et al. 1996), finding that it too did not overturn the democratic peace, and then launched a series of highly influential studies identifying what they called a "Kantian peace" of democracy and trade, named after eighteenth-century philosopher Immanuel Kant (Russett and Oneal 2001).[2] Russett and Oneal (2001) firmly placed their research program in the classical liberal tradition, arguing that the benefits of trade reduced the gains from conquest, and the impacts of democracy and trade on peace were *complementary*: each factor contributed to a decreasing probability of militarized conflict among nations.

A complementary relationship must be contrasted with a confounding one. In a confounding pattern, the third variable is offered as accounting for the second as well as the dependent variable (Blalock 1979: 468–74). Whereas Russett and Oneal offered trade as *complementary* to the democratic peace,

Erich Weede offered it as *confounding* (Weede 1996), dubbing the impact of trade on democracy and peace a "capitalist peace" (2005). In the tradition of Weede, and in contrast to Russett and Oneal, most theories of capitalist peace posit capitalism as a confounding variable in the democratic peace—a factor that may render the impact of democracy on peace spurious.

There are two main kinds of capitalist peace theories. Free-market theories equate "capitalism" with freer markets and link peace with trade (Weede 1996, 2005), fewer regulations on foreign investment (Gartzke et al. 2001), or smaller government (McDonald 2007, 2009). Social-market capitalist peace theory, in contrast, defines a "capitalist economy" as one where most citizens regularly use the market for jobs, goods, and services, and does not equate capitalism with less regulated markets or smaller government (Mousseau 2000). The two kinds of capitalist peace theories also have quite divergent core assumptions: free-market theories tend to have roots in classical and neoclassical liberal theories of politics and economics, such as Norman Angell (1911) and Friedrich Hayek (1989), and the rationalist bargaining theory of war (Fearon 1995), which assumes an anarchic and inherently competitive world. Social-market theory, in contrast, is more closely rooted in Karl Polanyi's ([1944] 1957) critique of neoclassical liberal theory and treats preferences, anarchy, and conflict endogenously.

Free-Market Theories of Capitalist Peace

The Trade Model

The correlation of economic development with stable democracy is well established (Lipset 1959), and neoclassical liberal theory has long claimed that free markets promote economic development (Hayek 1989) and, as such, increase the incentives for peace among nations (Angell 1911). Linking the two trends, Erich Weede offered that since trade may promote both peace and development, trade might account for the peace among democracies (1996, 2005). The state of evidence has not been kind to this viewpoint, however. Economic development does not appear to be highly correlated with trade (Mousseau 2010: 186), and democracy remains a significant force for peace after consideration of it (Russett and Oneal 2001).

The Capital Openness Model

To explain the peace among the wealthy democracies (Mousseau 2000), Gartzke (2007) offered the existence of what he called three "pillars" of "capitalist peace": development, foreign policy preferences, and openness to foreign investment. However, only the third pillar of capital openness, originally explicated by Gartzke, Li, and Boehmer (2001), is actually "capitalist" by most definitions of the term, and most attention has been focused here (e.g., Dafoe 2011; Dafoe and Kelsey 2010).[3]

Gartzke and colleagues (2001) showed how open capital markets can avert war. Because investors see risks in war, a nation on the brink of war with open capital markets is likely to face capital flight. Leaders in a dispute that bear this loss of capital thus signal their resolve, yielding information for adversaries with which they can choose to back down. In fact, it seems that interstate dyads with higher levels of capital openness are less likely to have militarized conflicts (Gartzke et al. 2001). Gartzke has also reported the democratic peace as insignificant after controlling for his three "pillars" (2007), but this result has been shown to be erroneous (Choi 2011; Dafoe 2011). It is also unlikely that capital openness might explain the democratic peace because neither Gartzke nor anyone else (to my knowledge) has shown how capital openness might cause democracy. Absent some explanation for how a third factor (capital openness) might explain the second (democracy), we cannot interpret a relationship as confounding because our observation could just as well be a result of reverse causation, with democracy causing capital openness (Blalock 1979: 474).

The Public Sector Model

The bargaining theory of war has shown that, under certain conditions, a dispute will escalate to war if, among other things, there is a lack credibility of commitments to peace (Fearon 1995). If nations in dispute could somehow improve their credibility, war could be averted. Patrick McDonald (2007, 2009) has shown how governments whose revenues are comparatively dependent on domestic taxation may have more credibility than those more dependent on revenues from the public ownership of property. Governments of nations with large portions of their economies owned by the state are less dependent on raising taxes to wage war and thus may be less constrained by their publics from waging it. If all foreign policy decision makers know this, the commitments of nations with smaller public sectors should be more credible than the commitments of those with larger ones. In fact, it seems that nations with large public sectors are more likely than others to have militarized conflicts (McDonald 2007, 2009). McDonald (2009) claims that his capitalist peace is stronger than the democratic one, though it does not fully account for it.

* * *

The free-market theories of capitalist peace share several characteristics. First, all equate "capitalism" with free markets and adopt—sometimes only implicitly—the economic liberal assumption that smaller government, lower taxes, and deregulation cause economic development (Hayek 1989). Weede assumes that free trade and development are strongly linked (1996); Gartzke seeks to explain "the absence of war among states in the developed world" (2007: 166); and McDonald introduces his private sector peace with reference to entering the debate linking peace with "modernization and economic development" (2007: 569).

Second, all of the free-market theories of capitalist peace are firmly in the mainstream neorealist/neoliberal tradition in the study of international relations that treats anarchy exogenously and assumes an inherently competitive world where states are the primary actors. Because war is costly, liberals assume war does not pay and thus explain the fact of war as occurring by mishap, resulting from weak information or an inability of nations to credibly commit to peace (Fearon 1995; Keohane and Martin 1995). In this way capitalist nations are assumed to be in perpetual conflict like everybody else; they are just better at avoiding militarized conflict because with trade the cost of war is greater than its gains (Weede 1996), free markets signal resolve (Gartzke et al. 2001), or small public sectors make the commitments of nations more credible (McDonald 2007). Violence is averted not because of common interests but because it is not profitable, and free markets make this calculation clear to all. As we will see below, the social-market model of capitalist peace makes none of these assumptions.

Social-Market Theory of Capitalist Peace

One of the primary weaknesses of realist and liberal theories of international relations is that they treat preferences exogenously. Since actors—states and citizens—are assumed to want the same things (whether it is money or security), variance in war and peace tends to be explained by such things as miscalculation, misinformation, and mistrust rather than divergent preferences. Economic norms theory departs from this realist-liberal tradition in the field of international relations by identifying how preferences can vary among states and individuals, and how these divergent preferences can explain war and peace. This is achieved by drawing on the well-known fact of two kinds of economies in history—contract intensive and contract poor (Polanyi [1944] 1957; North, Wallis, and Weingast 2009)—and deducing bounded norms from these divergent socioeconomic ways of life (Simon 1955). In so doing, economic norms theory shows how the neoliberal viewpoint—that war is not rational—may apply only within and among contract-rich societies; war can be quite rational among contract-poor nations and between contract-rich and contract-poor ones.

By definition a contract-rich economy is one where most citizens normally contract with strangers in the market to obtain their incomes, goods, and services. In contract-poor economies, in contrast, citizens are more dependent upon favors reciprocated among friends and family. The primary insight of economic norms theory is that because bigger and wealthier markets offer more opportunities to contract compared with smaller and poorer ones, citizens in contract-intensive economies must have common interests in each other's equal rights (to contract) and welfare (to buy things). They must also have an interest in the government ardently protecting free choice in contracting, at home and abroad, and their government continuously doing whatever it takes to promote market growth, at home and abroad. The latter can include government spending and redistribution policies, as well as foreign aid. To trust strangers in contract, citizens also have an interest in their government enforcing private contracts and the rule of law reliably and impartially. As a result, in contract-rich socioeconomies, the liberal democratic rule of law is legitimated from below.

While many theories of democracy assume that preferences for equal rights, the impartial rule of law, and economic growth are inherent and universal, economic norms theory identifies how these preferences may be *learned* in a contract-rich economy. In a contract-poor economy, individuals are far less dependent on an impersonal market than they are on good relations with friends and family, who are in turn linked with various groups. Citizens thus have interests not in the welfare of strangers but in the welfare of their groups. Organized along patron-client lines, groups can take a variety of forms, including neighborhood associations, gangs, mafias, labor unions, religious sects, political parties and movements, ethnic groups, tribes, and clans. Clients rely on the goodwill of patrons for physical and economic security, as patrons distribute these securities according to the level of loyalty of each client. Patrons, in turn, look to the state as they seek physical and economic security for their clients. Because a gain in state rents for one group is necessarily a loss for another, groups are in constant conflict over distributive gains, and this may explain why contract-poor states are often weak, corrupt, and dysfunctional (Mousseau 2002–3, 2012).

Within and among contract-rich "capitalist" nations, wars cannot happen because they require the harming of others, and citizens in these economies are always better off when others in the market are better off: there is not much opportunity to be had from those who are dead or poor. Since each nation's economic growth contributes to a larger global marketplace, and citizens reward and punish their leaders according to how well they produce market growth at home rather than according to how well their economy is growing relative to other nations, there are few relative-gains concerns within and among contract-rich nations. In fact, because all are better off with a stronger rather than weaker global economy, compared with contract-poor nations, contract-rich nations easily cooperate on trade issues and on the defense and promotion of global law and order.

In contract-poor political economies, in contrast, war, civil and foreign, can be rational. Because citizens are loyal to their groups rather than their states, it is relatively easy for group leaders to organize insurgency and rebellions, and they are obligated to their clients to do so if it appears that their group is not getting its preferred share of state rents. As a result, states are not only weak, but terrorism is also made possible because the terrorizing or genocide of an out-group is a cost-effective means for deterring it from competing over state rents (Mousseau 2002–3, 2011). Foreign war serves two purposes. First, it can be in the economic interests of the ruling coalition of in-groups, with the cost of war imposed on disenfranchised or repressed out-groups. Second, foreign tensions can help unify disparate in-groups at home, reducing the costs of buying their loyalty or repressing them.

While the economic norms model as presented thus far has assumed instrumental rationality—that citizens identify their interests based on the information available to them in their everyday life—the theory works just as well, perhaps better, with the recognition of bounded rationality. Introduced by Herbert Simon in the 1950s, bounded rationality draws on the fact that it is not rational to be rational; many goals can be reached more efficiently by forming decision-making habits, or heuristics, for situations that arise routinely (Simon 1955). As applied here, individuals routinely dependent on trusting strangers in contract will develop the habits of trusting strangers and preferring universal rights, impartial law, and liberal democratic government. Individuals in contract-poor economies will develop the habits of trusting and caring for others within their in-groups, abiding by the commands of group leaders, and distrusting those from out-groups, including their states. In this way, citizens in highly capitalist economies will perceive an interest in freedom and democracy and promoting these institutions for everyone, even though most, acting on bounded norms rather than on instrumental rationality, do not know why they have these universalistic liberal values. Individuals in contract-poor economies, in contrast, will be comparatively more susceptible to the appeals of those who offer strong in-group identities and warn against the threats of outsiders, even though most, acting on bounded norms rather than on instrumental rationality, do not know why they are susceptible to such fears or why they place such great value in loyalty to their groups and group leaders.

Comparing the Social-Market and Free-Market Models

The social-market theory of capitalist peace, as deduced from economic norms theory, is quite unlike the free-market models. Foremost, "capitalism" is not equated with unregulated markets or small government. A capitalist economy by definition consists of profit-maximizing actors linked in free and voluntary contracts, but this in no way precludes the state from regulating contracts or from propping up market growth with heavy spending. Indeed, rather than advanced capitalism being assumed to emerge spontaneously (Hayek 1989), it is allowed that contract-intensive economy may arise most often when political authorities make the decision to promote and sustain market growth with government spending, redistribution, and regulation. In fact, nations with contract-intensive economies have a long history of government interventionism aimed at propping up their markets (Polanyi [1944] 1957; Gurr, Jaggers, and Moore 1990).

Second, while the free-market models treat preferences exogenously in the tradition of mainstream neorealist and neoliberal theories of international relations, economic norms theory treats preferences endogenously: capitalist citizens and leaders perceive interests in equal law and order; contract-poor citizens and leaders perceive interests in having power over others. Third, while the free-market models are state-centric in the tradition of mainstream neorealism and neoliberalism, the social-market model predicts preferences across levels of analysis, including individuals, groups, and states. Fourth, while the free-market theories define peace negatively, as the absence of militarized conflict, the social-market model defines peace positively, as actual friendship among citizens and states rooted in common interests.

Fifth, perhaps the greatest difference between the models is in their scope. The free-market models are medium- or small-sized theories: they offer explanations for how nations may avoid militarized conflict in a presumed competitive/conflict-ridden world where anarchy is taken as a given. The social-market model, in contrast, deduced from economic norms theory, is a far larger theory of global politics and does not treat anarchy as a given. Economic norms theory informs us that the very concepts of government having a monopoly on violence, the rule of equal law, and even the system of sovereign states are all possible outcomes of the rise of capitalism (Mousseau 2000, 2009).

In this way, economic norms theory is not just a theory of relations among nations; it is a theory *of* international relations. As used to describe contract-intensive economy, "capitalism" means to engage in contracting, with parties enjoying free choice. This is the opposite of imperialism, which means to take through coercion. Just as individuals and firms in capitalist nations need an impersonal, impartial, and reliable enforcer of contracts at home that protects the freedom to contract, in order to trade outside their borders individuals and firms need an impersonal, impartial, and reliable enforcer of contracts in other countries that protects the freedom to contract. Citizens and governments of capitalist nations thus prefer other peoples to have governments that also hold the monopoly on violence, and the very concept of sovereignty as used today—government with a monopoly on the use of force over a geographic space whose legitimacy is recognized by outsiders—may be, like liberal democracy, an epiphenomenon of capitalism.

In contrast, contract-poor orders have relations among actors that are inherently imperial: most everyone is in a hierarchy, with inferiors perpetually owing tribute to superiors in exchange for protection. Sovereignty can have no real meaning because there is little perceived interest in legal equality among units or in the state holding the monopoly on violence. If imposed or influenced from outside, the norm of sovereignty is copied but not internalized. This may explain why the problems of civil and interstate war, terrorism, and failed states plague the developing world, as this region has comparatively fewer contract-rich economies, and, as such, the very idea of sovereignty is widely misunderstood (Mousseau 2012).

This insight is supported in history: most if not all anarchic-like systems of states that have existed—the Classical Greek, Renaissance Italian, and Westphalian European—emerged, and the first two fell, with the rise and fall of capitalism. Today most of the less-developed nations have contract-poor economies, and in many of these the government does not hold the monopoly on violence. Externally, many governments act as clients to more dominant states, offering loyalty to their metropoles or Washington in exchange for financial aid and then distributing this aid domestically on a personalist basis according to degree of loyalty to the ruling in-group. This suggests that efforts to fight corruption in many developing countries are impractical absent a transition to contract-intensive economy.

Finally, the social-market model has accrued a much larger list of successful novel predictions compared with the free-market models. The evidentiary successes of the free-market models have been limited to predicting fewer militarized conflicts among nations that trade (Weede 1996), have open capital markets (Gartzke et al. 2001), and have larger private sector ratios (McDonald 2007). The social-market model has successfully predicted the economic conditionality to the democratic peace (Mousseau 2000), the overturning of the democratic peace (Mousseau 2009), and cooperation (Mousseau 2002) and common preferences (Mousseau 2003) among nations; within nations it has successfully predicted variance in social trust (Mousseau 2009: 61), state respect for human rights (Mousseau and Mousseau 2008), public support for terrorism (Mousseau 2011), and civil war (Mousseau 2012).

THE FALKLANDS/MALVINAS WAR

The centuries-old dispute between Great Britain and Argentina over sovereignty of the Falklands/Malvinas Islands in the South Atlantic escalated to war in 1982 when the government of Argentina forcibly occupied the islands,

and the British government responded by sending a naval task force to reoc-
cupy them. The war has been called an enigma to capitalist peace theory,
since it was unprofitable for the British (Gomsrud, Gates, and Strand 2009).
It is true that the war itself could not have been profitable for either country,
but whether it poses a challenge to the capitalist peace depends on what we
mean by *capitalism*.

The trade model (Weede 1996) defines *capitalism* as trade dependency—
total foreign trade in a dyad divided by a nation's GDP—with high levels of
interdependency causing both nations in a dyad to refrain from fighting. Thus
whether the Falklands/Malvinas War poses a challenge to this model depends
on whether the countries had above-average levels of trade interdependency.
In fact they did: the level of trade interdependency in the Argentine-British
dyad over the five-year period prior to the conflict (1976–1981) was 0.52
percent, a bit higher than the global mean over this period of 0.25 percent.[4]
While this difference is not statistically significant, it is clear that if "capitalist" dyads are defined as having above-average levels of trade interdependency, this is an anomalous case of intercapitalist war. The trade model also
assumes that nations will fight only if the gains of war are greater than its
costs. Most agree that the costs of the war for the victor, Great Britain, were
far higher than the potential gains from this war, which has been described
by Argentine poet Jorge Luis Borges as "a fight between two bald men over
a comb" (Rees 2006: 98).

The capital openness (Gartzke et al. 2001) model relies on signaling facili-
tated by open capital markets to prevent war among capitalist nations. Thus
whether the Falklands/Malvinas War poses a challenge to this model depends
on whether both countries had comparatively open markets. In fact they did:
the Argentine-British dyad had significantly fewer regulations on foreign
investment than other dyads during the five-year period leading up to the
war, and this difference is significant (.05, one-tailed test), meaning that the
odds of this result being due to chance are less than 5 percent.[5] Indeed, both
governments were pushing deregulatory and free-trade policies at the time of
the onset of the war.

Dafoe and Kelsey (2010) offer that the Falklands/Malvinas War offers a
specific test of the capital openness model. This is because the long distance
from the British Isles to the South Atlantic meant that the British task force
could not arrive and actually start the war for several weeks, allowing for
a period of negotiation and, given the visibility of the impending conflict,
what they call "market-mediated" signaling. Yet while the British bore the
economic costs of stock market variability and some decrease in the value of
the pound during this period, the Argentine junta, led by Leopoldo Galtieri,
seems to have failed to read these as signals of British resolve (Dafoe and

Kelsey 2010). The Falklands/Malvinas case thus appears as an anomaly for the capital openness model.

The public sector model (McDonald 2007) suggests that the commitments of nations with large public sectors are less credible than others, and these nations should be in more militarized conflicts than others. Thus whether the Falklands/Malvinas War poses a challenge to this model depends on whether both countries in this war had comparatively small public sectors. In fact both had large ones: over the five-year period prior to the war, the global average size of public sectors was 11.4 percent; Argentina's was 23.2 percent, and Great Britain's 12.2 percent. Since neither country was capitalist by this definition, the Falklands/Malvinas War does not pose a challenge to the public sector model: neither country's economy could have rendered the foreign policy commitments of their governments particularly credible.

The notion that Great Britain lacks a capitalist economy raises the question of whether the size of the public sector genuinely indicates "capitalism," given that Great Britain is normally thought of as the epitome of a capitalist state. It is also questionable whether lack of credibility played any role in this war, given that most historians would consider the war a function of the lack of indivisibility of the issue involved rather than a lack of credibility of commitments. The war happened not because either country distrusted the commitments of the other. It happened because the countries disagreed on a fundamental issue: the British insisted they could not reward the use of force; the Argentines insisted they must (Freedman and Gamba-Stonehouse 1991).

The economic norms social-market model (Mousseau 2000) of capitalist peace defines capitalism as contract-intensive economy, the condition when many citizens normally contract in the impersonal market to obtain their incomes, goods, and services. Direct data on contracting in life insurance have been compiled under the auspices of the World Bank (Beck and Webb 2003), and a high level of life insurance contracting indicates a highly institutionalized norm of contracting in a society because, compared with most other sectors, to contract in life insurance requires a great deal of trust that the other party will fulfill the terms of the contract after death (Mousseau 2009: 65; North, Wallis, and Weingast 2009: 159).

Table 9.1 lists all nations with above-median levels of life insurance contracts in force over the period of available data from 1960 to 2000.[6] As can be seen, defined in this way the United Kingdom appears to have had a contract-intensive economy throughout this period. Argentina, in contrast, does not appear in the table. While it approaches the median in the year 2000 and may have a contract-intensive economy today, it almost certainly had a contract-poor economy in the 1980s. It thus appears that the Falklands/Malvinas War of 1982 pitted a contract-rich nation against a contract-poor one.

Table 9.1. Nations with Contract-Intensive Economies, 1960–2000

Australia	1960	Austria	1973
Belgium	1960	Israel	1973
Canada	1960	Ireland	1979
Denmark	1960	South Africa	1979
Netherlands	1960	Singapore	1982
New Zealand	1960	South Korea	1983
Norway	1960	Taiwan	1984
Sweden	1960	Spain	1986
Switzerland	1960	Italy	1987
United Kingdom	1960	Cyprus	1988
United States	1960	Portugal	1991
German Federal Republic	1961	Greece	1992
Finland	1963	Chile	1993
Japan	1963	Malaysia	1994
France	1965	Slovenia	1995

Note: Years after 1960 indicate transition years to contract-intensive economy.

Economic norms theory predicts that governments of nations with contract-poor economies have particular incentives in foreign policy. Recall that these governments are often coalitions of in-groups, with each group having some force capability and thus an ability to threaten the state, with state rents allocated among coalition members according to relative power (in democratic contract-poor nations, the ability to use force can be augmented with seats in the legislature). Out-groups, receiving few if any rents, must be repressed by the ruling in-groups. However, some segments of society can be in the middle—neither highly repressed nor bought off with state rents. This stratum often includes a small, frequently urban middle class, many of whom may not be well connected with any group. This is particularly likely when a nation is in the middle range of economic development, as Argentina was at the time. As a means to hold power, loyalty is far cheaper than repression. Because citizens in contract-poor economies habitually fear outsiders and grant loyalty to their group leaders, the leaders of contract-poor nations have particular incentives for convincing their citizens that their nation *is* their in-group. This is most easily done with nationalist discourse reinforced with foreign tensions.

At the time it initiated the conflict, the Galtieri regime was widely unpopular, with Argentina in the midst of a devastating economic crisis and large-scale civil unrest (Levy and Vakili 1992). Most historians agree that by occupying the islands, the Galtieri regime hoped to gain popularity by drawing on Argentine patriotic feelings, which "dared the Military Government to use force in support of valid national 'aspirations' related to 'territorial integrity'" (Freedman and Gamba-Stonehouse 1991: 4). Considering the poor economic value of the islands for Great Britain, and the great distance involved, the junta calculated that their temporary military advantage could enable a settlement resulting in Argentine sovereignty.

However, the Argentines grossly misestimated how the British would perceive their interests. While sovereignty over the islands was negotiable, Prime Minister Margaret Thatcher could not be seen to "reward Argentine aggression" (Freedman and Gamba-Stonehouse 1991: 240). This attitude was shared by the United States, another nation with a contract-intensive economy, which desperately wanted to avoid a war, but not at the cost of a settlement that "could be widely read as any kind of significant reward for the use of force" (Freedman and Gamba-Stonehouse 1991: 166).

The Falklands/Malvinas War is entirely consistent with the social-market model of capitalist peace (Mousseau 2000). The war was launched by the regime of a contract-poor nation seeking popular domestic support during a time of crisis. While the diversionary theory of war literature has long emphasized such motives in war making, economic norms theory informs us that contract-poor nations are far more susceptible to this malady than contract-rich ones, particularly when facing internal crises. Indeed, it is hard to recall a case where popular opinion in a contract-rich society can be said to have favored the use of force for "national aspirations" related to "territorial integrity."

Economic norms theory also explains the British decision to fight. While some might think that "capitalist peace" means that capitalist nations are averse to war, economic norms theory makes no such claim. Rather, this theory informs us that contract-rich nations perceive their interests differently from contract-poor ones and, like everyone else, will fight for their interests. Contract-rich nations perceive interests in, and will fight for, global law and order. Readers with contract norms might interpret this goal as idealistic or even altruistic—and thus perhaps not credible—but this is because these readers share the value of law and order. Economic norms theory informs us that not everyone benefits from law and order, and the capitalist nations will fight for it not because they are altruistic, but instead because global law and order lies at the backbone of global markets and thus sustained economic growth at home. I suggest that this is one of the core motivations of the United States and other capitalist nations for rallying the coalition that fought Iraq in the Persian Gulf War of 1991: annexation of a sovereign nation and the taking of its property put at severe risk the countless commitments, contractual and public, that are at the core of the global capitalist economy.

In this way Great Britain fought the Falklands/Malvinas War for economic growth at home, even though the war itself cost far more than any conceivable direct gain from possessing the islands. Indeed, Margaret Thatcher was perfectly willing to negotiate sovereignty over the islands; she just could not be seen to reward the use of force, a view shared by the United States. The important audience that might "see" Britain rewarding the use of force was not the British public; it was the global business community and authorities in contract-poor nations—otherwise why would the United States share the same concern? British and US leaders feared that to be seen rewarding the use of force would signal that taking things by force was allowed, and this could result in major disinvestment from developing countries, a possible collapse of global markets, and ultimately less economic growth at home. No leader of a contract-rich society can lead a war rally cry for preventing an economic recession, but they can rally support for a war on the capitalist principle of not rewarding the use of force, which is a core value in contract culture and which lies at the core of capitalist economics at home and abroad. In this way the British fought the war on behalf of all contract-rich nations, and this is why no contract-rich nation could conceivably side with Argentina in this conflict, and why many of them assisted the British in various ways.

The Argentine junta, on the other hand, could not withdraw without some sort of reward. Aware of and sharing contract-poor habits and mind-sets, the junta leaders knew their leadership role depended on their image as protectors of the Argentine "in-group" and that withdrawal without preconditions would shatter this image and cause them to be forcefully removed from power.

The Argentine strategy of negotiation also fits the expectations of economic norms theory. In exchange for peace, the Argentines repeatedly offered the British access to minerals on the islands. This is expected from those accustomed to the zero-sum-like struggles that epitomize the domestic politics of contract-poor nations, where everything is assumed to be a crude struggle over material wealth. The generals could not seem to accept that the British were not fighting for mineral rights or other direct profits, as US secretary of state Alexander Haig had to stress "again" that "the attitude of the British Government had nothing to do with economic interests in the area" (Freedman and Gamba-Stonehouse 1991: 196).

The case of the Falklands/Malvinas War challenges some, but not all, models of capitalist peace. By the standards of the trade (Weede 1996) and capital openness (Gartzke et al. 2001) models, this war was fought between two capitalist nations—a clear-cut anomaly. By the standards of the public sector model (McDonald 2007), neither state was capitalist, so the case cannot be anomalous. The war does not pose a challenge for the social-market model, which also offers a full explanation for it: it accounts for why the Argentine junta attacked, how they miscalculated British reactions, why the British fought "over a comb," and why the junta leaders could not conceive of the British motive as anything other than a quest for natural resources.

WHAT IS "CAPITALISM" ANYWAY?

When asked to identify the advanced capitalist nations that might be in peace, most observers of global affairs probably think of the liberal democracies with advanced economies in Western Europe, North America, and the Pacific Rim. Yet the case of the Falklands/Malvinas War illustrates that at least some measures of capitalism may not actually capture it. The trade (Weede 1996) and capital openness (Gartzke et al. 2001) models identify both Argentina and Great Britain as "capitalist," while the public sector model (McDonald 2007) considers neither "capitalist." Only the social-market model (Mousseau 2009) seems to fit what is probably the most intuitive sense of "capitalism" in this case, identifying Great Britain, but not Argentina, as capitalist at the time of the Falklands/Malvinas conflict.

The most basic way to test if variables indicate a common underlying dimension is to test their correlations. Table 9.2 reports the pairwise correlations of the capitalist variables at the dyadic level. As can be seen, none of them are highly correlated. Private sector (McDonald 2007) is almost perfectly unrelated with all the other capitalist variables.[7] Trade (Weede 1996) and capital openness (Gartzke et al. 2001) are also unrelated ($r = 0.16$). Only contract-intensive economy is related with more than one other factor: there are moderate correlations with capital openness ($r = 0.39$) and trade ($r = 0.32$).[8]

The lack of strong correlations among the four factors purporting to indicate capitalism informs us that they are not measuring the same underlying concept. Factors that do not relate with each other cannot be reflecting a common dimension, so at least three of the four factors purporting to indicate capitalism are gauging something else. Because private sector (McDonald 2007) is least related with the others, it is the least likely measure to be representing an underlying dimension of capitalism. Conversely, because contract-intensive economy (Mousseau 2009) is most related to the other factors, it is the most likely factor reflecting the underlying dimension of capitalism.

Table 9.2. Pairwise Correlations of the Capitalist Peace Variables at the Dyadic Level

Pairwise Combinations	Pearson Correlations	Number of Observations
Trade and Private Sector	0.03	119,898
Capital Openness and Private Sector	0.01	81,882
Private Sector and Contract-Intensive Economy	0.13	120,852
Trade and Capital Openness	0.16	154,276
Capital Openness and Contract-Intensive Economy	0.39	154,528
Trade and Contract-Intensive Economy	0.32	321,441

To gauge which factors, if any, mirror our intuition that the capitalist coun-tries are the liberal democracies with advanced economies, I constructed an interaction term of economic development and democracy, in line with the way these terms are usually gauged in the democratic peace literature.[9] The "developed democracy" term can take on high values only if both nations in a dyad are democratic and have advanced economies. As can be seen in table 9.3, most of the capitalist variables are only weakly related with devel-oped democracy, with correlation coefficients at or less than 0.20. It is hard to overstate the importance of these results: the dyads we normally think of as "capitalist"—the developed democracies—are *not* substantively more likely than other dyads to be trade interdependent (Weede 1996), have open financial markets (Gartzke et al. 2001), or have large private sector ratios (McDonald 2007). The only capitalist variable that appears to reflect the wealthy democracies is contract-intensive economy (Mousseau 2009), which correlates moderately with developed democracy at 0.51.

The association of contract-intensive economy with the advanced nations of Europe, North America, and the Pacific Rim is also supported by a look at table 9.1 above. The usual "capitalist" suspects appear in the table when the period of observation begins in 1960: Australia, Belgium, Canada, Denmark, the Netherlands, New Zealand, Norway, Sweden, Switzerland, the United Kingdom, and the United States. In the 1960s, Finland, France, Germany (West), and Japan transitioned to contract-intensive economy, confirming that these states were not market-capitalist when they fought against the market-capitalist powers in World War II (France fought on both sides in this war). After the transitions of Austria, Ireland, Israel, and South Africa in the 1970s, many of the remaining countries are those often identified as having gone through successful economic and/or democratic transitions in the 1980s and 1990s—in order, Singapore, South Korea, Taiwan, Spain, Italy, Cyprus, Portugal, Greece, Chile, Malaysia, and Slovenia.

While some of these cases might be surprising for some, overall they probably fit with the intuitions of most observers when thinking of the capi-talist nations and those with recently emerged markets. It is also consistent with economic norms theory that none of these countries have transitioned

Table 9.3.   Correlations of the Capitalist Peace Variables with Developed Democracy

Dyadic Measures	Pearson Correlations	Number of Observations
Trade	0.20	316,753
Capital Openness	0.16	154,304
Private Sector	0.20	119,830
Contract-Intensive Economy	0.51	318,230

backward, away from democracy, and only one country, Singapore, has managed to stay nondemocratic for a long period of time after it transitioned to contract-intensive economy.

CAN THE DEMOCRATIC PEACE SURVIVE?

Can capitalism explain the democratic peace? To account for the impact of democracy on conflict, capitalism must correlate with both democracy and conflict (Blalock 1979: 468–74). Table 9.4 reports the correlations of the four capitalist variables with democracy. As can be seen, most of them correlate only weakly with democracy: trade (Weede 1996) correlates at only 0.18, capital openness (Gartzke et al. 2001) at only 0.14, and private sector (McDonald 2007) at only 0.20. These low correlations make it clear that these free-market factors do not hold much promise of overturning the highly robust democratic peace. Only contract-intensive economy is moderately correlated with democracy at 0.47, and thus the social-market model of capitalist peace stands the strongest chance of challenging the reign of the democratic peace.

As discussed above, most nations with contract-intensive economies are also democratic, as economic norms theory predicts, but about half of all democratic nations have had contract-poor economies (when aggregated annually). So if we want to know if capitalism—contract-intensive economy—can account for the democratic peace, these contract-poor democracies are the crucial test cases; if democracy is a direct and independent cause of peace among nations, then these countries should be in peace. To investigate this question I collected data on militarized interstate conflict from the Correlates of War Militarized Interstate Dispute data set (Ghosn, Palmer, and Bremer 2004).[10] Since war happens between nations, the appropriate unit of analysis for this test is the nondirectional interstate dyad, aggregated annually.

Table 9.5 examines the onset of militarized conflicts with fatalities over the period that all data are available from 1961 to 2001.[11] The first column reports the number of each dyadic type: both democratic and both contract-poor

Table 9.4. Correlations of the Capitalist Peace Variables with Democracy

Dyadic Measures	Pearson Correlations	Number of Observations
Trade	0.18	316,753
Capital Openness	0.14	154,304
Private Sector	0.20	119,920
Contract-Intensive Economy	0.47	318,360

Table 9.5.   Capitalism, Democracy, and Fatal Militarized Conflict, 1961–2001

Dyad Types	Dyad Years	Fatal Conflict Years	Conditional Probability	χ^2	Significance
Both Democratic, Both Contract Poor	11,267	9	0.0008	0.557	0.455
Both Contract Rich	8,897	0	0.0000	5.729	0.017
All Other Dyads	297,754	190	0.0006		

(11,267) and both contract-rich (8,897). The third row reports the number of all other types of dyads in the sample (297,754), which serves as the null set. The second column reports the number of fatal conflict onset years in each row, and the third column shows the conditional probability of fatal conflict for each row—the second column divided by the first. Column four reports the chi-square coefficient comparing each row with the null set, with tests of significance reported in column five.

The crucial test is in the first row: are dyads where both states are democratic and both contract-poor less likely than others to have fatal conflicts? It appears they are not; the probability of fatal conflict among contract-poor democracies (.0008) appears higher than that of the null set (.0006). While this difference from the null set is not significant ($p = .455$), it does indicate that, if anything, contract-poor democracies are *more* likely than other states to fight each other. In contract-rich dyads, in contrast, not a single fatal militarized conflict appears to have occurred, and this peace is significant ($p < .017$). From table 9.5 there is no support for the contention that democracy causes peace. Contract-intensive economy, however, is a robust force for peace.[12]

As discussed above, most nations with contract-intensive economies are also democratic, just as economic norms theory predicts. Indeed, with the exception of Singapore, all the cases of nondemocratic rule with contract-rich economy are cases of short lags from transitions to contract-intensive economy to transitions to democratic rule. Examples include South Korea and Taiwan in the 1980s. The rarity of cases of non-joint-democratic contract-rich dyads (only 17 percent of the contract-rich dyad years in table 9.5), combined with the rarity of fatal conflicts in contract-rich dyads, is exactly the pattern we would expect if the democratic peace is spurious. The confounding variable, contract-intensive economy, must account for the second variable, democracy, as well as the dependent variable, militarized conflict. So it is the very success of the theory that causes too few cases of nondemocratic contract-rich dyads from which to generalize their absence of fatal conflicts.

CONCLUSION

This chapter explored the state of theory and evidence on the capitalist peace and its prospects for explaining the democratic peace. Two kinds of capitalist peace theories were distinguished, the free-market and the social-market, yielding four observable causal mechanisms: trade, capital openness, and size of private sector as free-market theories, and contract-intensive economy as the social-market theory. Analyses of these causal mechanisms indicate that the free-market theories are not viable explanations for the democratic peace or the peace among the advanced industrial nations, primarily because none of them correlate substantially with democracy or developed democracy; they do not even correlate much with each other. Only the social-market measure of contract-intensive economy correlates moderately with democracy and developed democracy. Application of the theories to the case of the Falklands/ Malvinas War yields similar results: this war appears as an anomalous case for the trade (Weede 1996) and capital openness (Gartzke et al. 2001) models, while the public sector model (McDonald 2007) identifies Britain as a non-capitalist state; only the social-market model (Mousseau 2000) offers an account for this conflict. Finally, analyses of fatal militarized interstate disputes from 1961 to 2001 corroborate that the democratic peace is spurious, with contract-intensive economy the more likely explanation for both democracy and the "democratic" peace.

The free-market theories also face problems of internal and external validity. Regarding internal validity, to account for a peace between developed nations, all of these theories critically assume that free markets cause economic development. Yet the scientific evidence tells us this is not so (Gurr, Jaggers, and Moore 1990). Regarding external validity, for all but the most myopic observers of global affairs it is clear that the peace among the advanced capitalist nations is much more than restraint due to the high cost of killing each other (Weede 1996), fear of each other's resolve (Gartzke et al. 2001), or the credibility in their commitments (McDonald 2007). These theories may be correct, but it is apparent that these nations do more than just tolerate each other; they are friends. This is evident from the fact that whenever a capitalist economy takes a turn for the worse, the other capitalist nations seek to boost it back up, overcoming collective action problems with negotiations enhanced by shared norms of equity and law. The capitalist nations are not better balancers: they do not balance. They do not simply read each other's signals better or send or receive better information: they know that other capitalist nations will never attack them. Indeed, the very image of war today between France and Germany is comical, yet until they became market capitalist only five decades ago these two nations slaughtered each with seeming zeal roughly every generation.

Once the origins and nature of capitalism are grasped, it is easy to see the direction this world may be heading in. Once capitalism gets a footing in a national economy, voters begin demanding ever-increasing market growth, causing capitalism to both endure and expand. At home the marketplace expands as greater portions of society are increasingly included as vibrant actors in the marketplace, as has been exemplified by the historical pattern of older capitalist societies making the shift from equal rights for only white male landowners in the eighteenth century to equal rights for everyone in the latter twentieth century. Continuing voter demands for market growth also cause capitalist states to fervently seek new markets, and thus these states prefer all other states to be both capitalist and rich. At the same time, capitalist states generally defeat clientelist empires in war, as capitalist economies are stronger, their citizens are more loyal to their states (rather than to groups or personalities), their bureaucracies are more effective (for enforcing contracts), and the norms of individualist and independent thinking in capitalist culture promote innovation and improvisation in citizens and soldiers. In this way, since it was exogenously triggered in fifteenth-century Europe, capitalism has been a cause of both states and wars, yet it is ultimately the surest cause of peace and friendship among individuals, groups, and states. If we can manage to avoid killing ourselves and our planet in the centuries-long process of global transformation, the weight of the evidence informs us that social-market capitalism will in the end bring us permanent peace and prosperity.

NOTES

1. George W. Bush, White House press release, "President and Prime Minister Blair Discussed Iraq, Middle East," http://georgewbush-whitehouse.archives.gov/news/releases/2004/11/20041112-5.html (retrieved October 2, 2010); Bill Clinton, "1994 State of the Union Address," *Washington Post*, http://www.washingtonpost.com/wp-srv/politics/special/states/docs/sou94.htm (retrieved October 5, 2010).

2. Russett and colleagues subsequently added a third leg of the Kantian peace, international organizations, but membership in international organizations proved to be less robust than the first two legs (Russett and Oneal 2001).

3. Another reason to focus on capital openness is that Gartzke's other pillars do not seem theoretically developed. Gartzke argues that industrialization (not development per se) reduces the incentives for conquering territory, since resources can be traded in free markets (Gartzke 2007: 172). But he does not explain why nonindustrialized economies cannot also engage in trade, why industrialized economies, such as the Soviet Union's, are assumed to have free foreign markets, or why it is not profitable to take territory that contains rich resources. For the pillar of preferences, Gartzke of-

fers only the unsupported assertion that "developed countries also retain populations with common identities, cultural affinities, and political, social, and economic ties" (2007: 172). In terms of theoretical innovation, Gartzke's "capitalist peace" is best understood as the capital openness model of Gartzke, Li, and Boehmer (2001).

4. Following Russett and Oneal (2001), trade dependency for i is gauged as exports$_{ij}$ + imports$_{ij}$, with the resultant divided by the gross domestic product of i. Trade interdependency is gauged as the lower of i and j. Trade data were obtained from Gleditsch (2002b).

5. Results obtained using the capital openness (the lower of both states in a dyad) variable kindly provided by Erik Gartzke.

6. Missing data are assumed to reflect contract-poor economy. Noncontractual clientelist transactions are customarily not recorded, since they are framed as favors, and governments of clientelist economies do not normally construct bureaucracies for collecting economic data, in part because there is little to record, and in part because their incentive is to conceal economic data since they are constrained to distribute state funds to supporters, often illegally. Governments of nations with contract-intensive economies, in contrast, are constrained by voters to collect and report economic data, in part because of the capitalist norm of recording contractual transactions (for enforcement purposes), and in part to pursue continued growth in their markets (Mousseau 2012).

7. McDonald (2009: 84) claims that an increased probability of militarized conflict should appear if only one state in a dyad has a large public sector. To be consistent with the directional expectations of the other capitalist variables at the dyadic level, I reverse the scale of McDonald's measure and test the lower of both states in the dyad, which I call "private sector." I thank Patrick McDonald for sending me his data.

8. In tables 9.2 through 9.5, contract-intensive economy is measured with the natural log of life insurance contracts in force, the lower of both states in the dyad, with missing values imputed using secondary sources. For details see Mousseau (2012).

9. Economic development is measured as the natural log of GDP per capita in constant US dollars (Gleditsch 2002b). Democracies are identified in standard form as states scoring greater than six in the Polity2 measure obtained from the Polity IV data set (Marshall and Jaggers 2003).

10. Specifically, I obtained the Dyadic Militarized Interstate Disputes Dataset, version 1.1 (EUGene corrected version dyadmid602) (Maoz 2005), to identify those dyadic disputes where the states confronted each other directly. Only the original (day 1) disputants in militarized conflicts are considered.

11. The 1961 to 2001 period results from lagging the independent variables one year behind the dependent variable to reduce the risk of reverse causality.

12. Of the nine fatal conflicts in democratic dyads in table 5, three are between India and Pakistan, two between Ecuador and Peru, two between Greece and Turkey, one between Cyprus and Turkey, and one between Mali and Niger.

Chapter Ten

The Implications of a Territorial Peace

Douglas M. Gibler

The strongest relationship we have discovered in international relations is not the fact that democracies do not fight each other. Instead, issue type seems to be a better predictor of international conflict. Almost every single study that controls for issue type finds that territorial issues often lead to international disputes and wars, tend to recur, and are difficult to resolve. These issues are much more dangerous than other types of issues over which leaders and states contend. Nevertheless, though the conflict-proneness of these issues is well documented, we still do not know much about why territorial issues are so different from other types of international issues.

I argue that most territorial issues constitute threats to homeland territories, and these threats are different from other issues because they force domestic centralization of power within the state. The logic of the argument has three parts. First, territorial threats are highly salient to individuals in threatened countries, and leaders must respond by promoting the security of the state. Second, threatened territories must be defended by large, standing land armies, and these armies can then be used as forces for repression during times of peace. Finally, domestic political bargaining is dramatically altered during times of territorial threat. Opposition forces in both democracies and nondemocracies respond to the salience of the issue by joining the leader in promoting the security of the state. The leader then has a favorable environment within which to institutionalize greater executive power and also a greater ability to aggressively bargain against the rival. Consequently, the leader also has strong incentives to continue the conflict.

Combined, these three centralizing forces explain why conflicts and non-democracies cluster in time and space, and this in turn implies why peace and democracy cluster as well. States that have removed territorial issues from their agenda are more likely to democratize, and, by settling these issues, these states are likely to be at peace. This is why we observe that democracies do not fight each other. The importance of territorial issues is again demonstrated by the identification of the democratic peace as the spurious result of a larger, territorial peace.

My 2007 article in *International Studies Quarterly* laid the foundation for the spuriousness argument. Since then I have tested the argument using alternate specifications of territorial threat (Gibler and Tir 2010; Gibler and Braithwaite n.d.) and have extended the argument to other empirical regularities associated with the democratic peace (Gibler and Wolford 2006; Miller and Gibler 2011; Gibler and Miller forthcoming). I believe this is the first theory to subsume the many findings associated with democracies into a broader theory that is not derivative of the particular characteristics of these types of regimes. The theory also provides important implications for better understanding domestic political bargaining (Hutchison and Gibler 2007; Gibler, Hutchison, and Miller 2009; Gibler 2010b, 2012; Gibler and Randazzo 2011). I discuss these studies here, developing first the argument for why territorial issues are so salient to domestic populations.

HOW TERRITORIAL ISSUES AFFECT DOMESTIC POLITICS

We know well that territorial issues are linked to an increased rate of disputes and war. Completely underdeveloped, however, are explanations of why territorial issues are so salient to the states that fight these conflicts. Unlike other types of issues, I argue that territorial issues often constitute direct threats to individual lives and livelihoods, and this triggers many of the basic biological and psychological responses to threat that are endemic to humans. Indeed, for an individual in a threatened country, territorial issues may overshadow all other environmental factors that determine such basic political attitudes as personal identity and tolerance for others.

Territorial Issues and the Individual

The Correlates of War project provides a straightforward classification of various issue types—territory, regime, policy, and other issues define separate categories of militarized interstate dispute (Jones, Bremer, and Singer 1996). Other classifications follow similar patterns. For example, Holsti (1991) examines the wars since Westphalia (1648) with a twelve-part list of issue types, but his typology can easily be aggregated into the basic categories of territory, regime, and policy.[1] This suggests that similar types of issues occur over time, and, importantly, it provides a consistent basis for comparisons of the effects of issue type on international conflict and the states who fight.

Territorial issues are different from other issues because they trigger multiple biological and psychological responses by individuals in threatened states. First, targeting land also directly targets individuals' lives and livelihoods. Thus, unlike most other types of conflict, territorial conflicts affect humans' strong biological drive for survival. Territorial issues also activate individuals' attachment to their own homeland, which is often made even more important by group attachments to regional territories. Group attachment is complemented in turn by the psychological dimensions of conflict: threats to territory enable the in-group/out-group comparisons that are at the heart of many individual political values, including identity choice. Once these in-group and out-group dynamics are established, secondary values such as political tolerance, trust, and other democratic values become more difficult to maintain (Hutchison and Gibler 2007; Hutchison 2011). Taken as a whole, then, territorial conflicts comprise an issue type that is highly salient for the individual.

Land and Economic Well-Being

In primitive societies, land was the primary source of food, shelter, and other resources necessary for survival, and in many ways that still holds true for individuals in developing countries. Competition for scarce resources means that groups who hold particular pieces of land thrive, while those who do not, suffer. The problem of constantly worrying about survival has dwindled for most with modernization, but land ownership still comprises a key economic resource in even the most developed countries. Indeed, it oftentimes represents an individual's most valuable asset. Land still provides shelter, and, with a strong legal system, private property can be leveraged into higher-order goods and services or the tools needed for personal wealth creation. Threats to the territories of the state therefore also carry threats to individual property, which translates into threats to individual lives and livelihoods that are only mildly attenuated by the level of economic development within the state.

Territorial conflicts are often doubly dangerous because of their possible indirect effects on individual fortunes. For example, the likelihood of being proximate to active fighting is much higher for individuals in states targeted by territorial issues. This is just the nature of territorial conflict itself. Occupation and control of territory is the goal of the conflict, and therefore the targeted territory becomes a battleground itself. These effects will be exacerbated in those conflicts that use primitive supply techniques in which the army literally feeds off the land. Intense conflicts also sap the resources available to the area to manage the public health and relocation issues that follow the end of fighting (Ghobarah, Huth, and Russett 2003). Thus, the average individual residing in or near disputed territories has reason to fear the start of conflicts over the land since most status quos are better than the likely outcome of nearby conflicts.[2]

Attachments to Land

Territory also holds more than economic value for most individuals. Vasquez (1995) argues that there is a biological basis for the salience of territorial issues in individuals. According to this argument, humans are "soft-wired" to have certain predilections when exposed to external stimuli such as threat. Constituting neither instinct nor drive, humans are instead socialized to treat violence as an appropriate means of resolving disputes over land. This tendency explains the empirical association between threats to property and aggressive behavior in the individual. It is also consistent with a substantial anthropological literature that suggests humans are like other animals who use aggressive displays to hold and gain territories (Wilson 1975; Goodall 2000).

Aggregated to the society or state level, the human tendency toward aggressive displays when property is threatened is used to explain the strong, positive correlation between territorial issues and war. Individuals, leaders, and societies as a whole learn that war is a preferred method of distributing political goods such as territory. Power and war thus determine land ownership, at great cost to those who fight, of course.

In-Group Definition

Vasquez's (1993, 2009) territorial explanation of conflict has clear theoretical roots in the early social psychology literature, specifically the work of Georg Simmel and Lewis Coser. Building on Simmel's (1955) hypothesis that conflict is a socialization mechanism, Coser (1956: 38) extended the socialization hypothesis to argue that "conflict serves to establish and maintain the identity and boundary lines of societies and groups." In this sense, external threat serves to increase the internal cohesion of a group. Thus, territorial threats that target the state increase nationalist responses among ordinary citizens, and these encourage popular rallies in support of the leader. But why would territorial issues and not other conflicts control this sociopsychological response?

Conflicts over regime status may sometimes create the same in-group versus out-group dynamic that results from territorial issues, but one condition must first be met for this to occur on a large scale within the targeted country. The average individual has to have some type of bond with the regime. Absent this, the average individual is presented with conflicting cross-pressures. Threats from outside the state compete with threats from the regime to define group comparisons. If the external threat promises liberation, or at least some sort of positive change in domestic policy, then the dynamics of group definition become quite complicated and inconsistent. If, however, regime status is equated with wholesale political change directed against the entire state, then the average individual would fear conflict, fear change, and thus identify with the threatened nation. Only the few regime conflicts that target the entire state—both regime and people—are capable of eliciting such in-group versus out-group definitions.

The Politics of Issue Salience

These arguments all suggest that territorial issues resonate with individual citizens differently than other types of conflict. Territory affects base survival instincts and also the more developed socio-psychological attachments to land derived from group identities. This issue salience imposes an interesting dynamic upon the domestic politics of the state.

To demonstrate the importance of territorial threat for individuals, table 10.1 provides an adaptation of an empirical study of political tolerance I conducted with Marc Hutchison (Hutchison and Gibler 2007). The dependent variable is whether individuals are likely to provide a response to a World Values Survey questionnaire that suggests they would be tolerant of their least-liked group within the country—i.e., individuals would allow someone from their least-liked group to hold office or demonstrate against the government. The best predictors of tolerant responses have traditionally been measures of democracy.

Model 1 provides a baseline estimate of individual-level effects on political tolerance. The addition of a general conflict variable in model 2 does not alter these effects; general conflict also has little effect on tolerance itself. However, when models 3 and 4 include specifications for the type of external threat, a clear pattern begins to emerge. For example, in model 3 the external threat variable is disaggregated by issue type, and there is a strong, negative relationship between disputes over territory and political tolerance ($\beta = -0.53$, $p < .05$) but no significant relationship with nonterritorial disputes. Thus, these results suggest that territorial and nonterritorial disputes have different substantive effects on tolerance levels. This finding is consistent with

Table 10.1. Multilevel Models of Political Tolerance across Thirty-Three Countries

	Model 1 N = 17,977 Coefficient	Model 2 N = 17,977 Coefficient	Model 3 N = 17,977 Coefficient	Model 4 N = 17,977 Coefficient
Individual Level				
Democratic Activism	0.15* (0.02)	0.15* (0.02)	0.15* (0.02)	0.15* (0.02)
Political Interest	0.07* (0.03)	0.07* (0.03)	0.07* (0.03)	0.07* (0.03)
Conformity	−0.22* (0.04)	−0.22* (0.04)	−0.22* (0.04)	−0.22* (0.04)
Democratic Ideals	0.10* (0.03)	0.11* (0.03)	0.11* (0.03)	0.11* (0.03)
Free Speech Priority	0.26* (0.04)	0.26* (0.04)	0.26* (0.04)	0.26* (0.04)
Gender (0 = male)	−0.29* (0.06)	−0.29* (0.06)	−0.29* (0.06)	−0.29* (0.06)
Age	−0.01* (0.001)	−0.01* (0.001)	−0.01* (0.001)	−0.01* (0.001)
Education	0.11* (0.02)	0.11* (0.02)	0.11* (0.02)	0.11* (0.02)
Ideology (high = left)	0.01 (0.02)	0.01 (0.02)	0.01 (0.02)	0.01 (0.02)
Macro Level				
Militarized Interstate Disputes (1 yr.)		−0.003 (0.18)		
Territorial Disputes (1 yr.)			−0.53* (0.09)	
Nonterritorial Disputes (1 yr.)			0.11 (0.10)	

Targeted Territorial Disputes (1 yr.)				−0.60* (0.26)
Targeted Nonterritorial Disputes (1 yr.)				−0.04 (0.44)
Nonterritorial Territorial Disputes (1 yr.)				0.05 (0.73)
Nontargeted Nonterritorial Disputes (1 yr.)				0.14 (0.25)
Democratic Duration		0.005 (0.005)	0.004 (0.004)	0.004 (0.004)
Economic Development (log)		0.14 (0.18)	0.13 (0.14)	0.12 (0.13)
Ethnic Fractionalization		0.20 (0.99)	0.34 (0.88)	0.39 (0.74)
Random Effect				
Variance Component	0.67	0.50	0.43	0.42
d.f.	32	28	27	25
χ²	1635.2	940.1	848.9	814.9
Prob.	0.000	0.000	0.000	0.000

Source: 1995–1997 World Values Survey; table adapted from Hutchison and Gibler 2007: 137, table 2.
Notes: Entries are full maximum likelihood coefficients and standard errors estimated with HLM 6.02. The unit of analysis is individual responses to World Values Survey questionnaires; these are aggregated by country in the macro-level models. The robust standard errors are listed under the coefficients in parentheses.
* $p \leq .05$

the claim that territorial disputes are more salient than nonterritorial disputes to individuals and is also consistent with Simmel's (1955) and Coser's (1956) expectation of increased conformity in the face of hostility.[3]

We used multilevel modeling to asses these relationships, and one of the key statistics of interest in this type of estimation is the variance component for each model, which indicates the amount of variance left unexplained by the predictors included in the model. Using this statistic, we were able to compare across models to determine whether changes in the specification of the macro-level variables improved the overall goodness of fit. This technique was particularly helpful for testing the hypotheses regarding the inclusion of the macro-level variables, especially those measuring external threat, and whether macro-level specification was necessary to adequately explain individual responses to questions of tolerance. For example, further specification of the external threat variable not only confirmed the relationship between threat and tolerance but also yielded a notable increase in the explanatory power of the overall tolerance model. In comparing models 2 and 3, we found a significant decrease in the variance component, indicating that further specification of the external threat variable provided a more complete understanding of the relationship between threat and political tolerance.

In model 4, we again changed the specification of the external threat variables and compared the difference between targets and nontargets of militarized disputes. Critical to our analysis was the number of times each state was targeted by either territorial or nonterritorial disputes. As expected, we once again found that territorial issues decreased political tolerance ($\beta = -0.60$, $p < .05$), while nonterritorial disputes have no effect on political tolerance. However, most importantly, territorial issues only decreased political tolerance when the state was the target. In those cases in which the states were not targets of territorial disputes, the effect of conflict on political tolerance was negligible. Furthermore, territorial disputes in the final model had a stronger substantive impact on aggregate tolerance levels. These results suggest that while territorial disputes are more salient than other issue types, the effect is most pronounced for targeted states, as this variable appears to drive the overall statistical relationship. The results clearly reinforce the contention that domestic publics react more strongly to threats over territory.

These results suggest important changes in individual attitudes when states are threatened by territorial issues. Previous explanations of tolerance had almost uniformly considered the presence of democracy and democratic institutions as key determinants of tolerant individuals. However, the addition of the conflict variables, especially the presence of territorial targeting, eliminated the statistical significance of democracy in these models of political tolerance. This explains a long-standing conundrum for tolerance studies—among democracies, why are individuals from Australia, New Zealand, and the United States so much more tolerant on average than citizens in Israel? The difference is threat. Island states and countries in pacified regions rarely have territorial threats, while Israel has been under threat since its inception as a state.

Territorial Issues and the Structure of the Military

Territorial conflict, unlike other types of conflict, has the occupation of land as its primary goal. Of course, in order to occupy land, countries that initiate territorial conflicts must construct armies capable of both defeating the enemy and also holding the land once it has been taken. Note the differences across conflict types, though, especially with regard to possession of the status quo in the dispute. Prior to challenge, the land is physically held by the targeted states. In most other types of disputes, the status quo is more ephemeral, relating to the stated policy position of the target. This position can be changed much more easily than possession of land, but more importantly for my argument, policy positions can be defended by means other than occupation. Simply increasing the costs of conflict enables better defense of the policy position, providing deterrence, and if conflict does occur, the combat is not strictly land based. Territorial issues, conversely, force defense by land possession, and this makes standing land armies a necessary tool for this type of conflict.

Threat Location and Military Type

There are two key determinants of domestic military structure: type and location of threats to state interests. Threats to far-flung interests such as trade routes should lead to the construction of navies and air forces for defense since no occupation of land is required, only protection of the policy interests of the state.

This is also true for states with vast colonies. Land occupation is technically necessary for colonial disputes but not to the extent that this type of threat would, by itself, affect the military structure of the state. If threats are posed by indigenous forces, the technology advantage of a major state compared to the local population often makes a small land force and navy enough to put down the conflict. If another major state initiates the threat, then the locus of conflict shifts to wherever the major states are positioned, and the conflict devolves to major state versus major state and forces the use of militaries appropriate to that particular dyadic conflict. Regardless, the very nature of the colonial holding—that it is abroad—suggests that whatever occupying force is necessary in the conflict is physically removed from the state for the duration of the conflict. In most cases, colonial holdings actually weaken the repressive power of the elites at home.[4]

Threats from far-flung states may also target locations in or contiguous to the state. This has been especially true recently as many nondemocratic regimes have been targeted by major states. In these cases the location of the conflict necessitates the construction of at least some land army force to repel the threat (or maintain order). However, the primary goal for the defender is repelling the threat. Therefore, the threatened leader uses whatever forces are best designed to thwart an invasion or conquering force. Armies have no intrinsic advantage over other types of forces in these cases, unless they provide a cost-effective means of damaging the challenger.

Threats made by contiguous states are usually more serious because of their location, which makes force projection much easier. Contiguity also conditions at least some of the targeted state's defenses, but this varies by type of threat. For policy disputes or for disputes over trade, repelling the intentions of the initiator is paramount, and again, the mix of forces does not necessarily presuppose an army-led force. In fact, air forces or other quick-strike forces may be best equipped to provide maximum deterrence. Since the goal of the threat is not land occupation, and any territorial acquisitions are for the goal of policy change, the incentives for the targeted state are to repel and damage the challenging force.

Issues and Military Type

Territorial threats made by contiguous states are different, however. The added costs of occupying and holding the land make large armies indispensable for these types of threats. The goal of the challenger is to take the land, and in order to do this, the challenger constructs an army for occupation. Conversely, the target seeks to hold the territory against land attack and therefore builds an army capable of maintaining occupation. Possession is the goal for both states.

Issue types are also likely to affect threat duration. According to Vasquez (1993: 147), states will continue to fight over territorial issues until one side is decisively victorious and can claim the land, or a compromise is negotiated that is acceptable to both parties. Remaining are the cases of recurrent conflict, when one state tries to defeat the other but does so only nominally. These cases tend to fester. Short of decisive victory, the losing state has every incentive to maintain its army and attempt a challenge when the conditions best warrant such an attack. The winning state understands this logic and maintains its army's presence as well. Thus, territorial conflicts tend to recur (Hensel 1994), and the presence of militarized states across tense borders maintains.[5]

TERRITORIAL ISSUES AND THE STATE

Thus far I have argued that territorial issues are salient for individuals and make large land armies necessary for the defense of the state. Both of these factors combine to impose a strong, centralizing force on domestic politics in territorially threatened countries. The large land army gives elites the resources necessary to repress other segments of society, and the territorial issue itself makes political centralization within the regime likely. Collectively, these reactions to territorial threat make autocracy likely in territorially threatened states. Absent territorial threat, democracy may take hold.

Repressive Bargaining between Elites and the Poor

The economic nature of large land armies reinforces the trend toward greater concentration of power in the hands of the elite within society. Standing armies require high levels of taxation as well as a broad centralization of authority—to acquire, arm, equip, feed, and otherwise maintain the troops. High taxation and centralization both contribute to a widened gap between the fortunes of the elites and the poor as compared to the status quo. High levels of military spending and frequent conflict also depress domestic consumption and economic growth. This makes the costs of adopting democracy and conceding to the poor's redistributive demands far higher than the costs of using the army to pursue a strategy of exclusion and suppress competing social groups.

The Centralization of Political Power

Territorial threat also encourages political centralization within the institutions of the state. As I argue above, individuals in threatened territories are likely to seek security. The consequences of this attitude change are such that most leaders—both in and out of power—will turn their attention to security and support the state against the now common foe. As opposition forces move to support the leader, the favorable political climate provides the executive in power a unique opportunity to institutionalize its increased political power. Checks against the leader fade as the regime centralizes authority.

This type of centralization happens in both democracies and nondemocracies (Gibler 2010b). While opposition forces in nondemocracies often must remain silent until the opportunity for regime change presents itself, the opposition in democracies tends to be quite vocal. Nevertheless, opposition leaders in both types of regimes must be responsive to their own bases of political support. When such an important issue as territorial threat affects the average individual, the opposition must shift or maintain a position of security against the common threat. This quest for security therefore often results in the opposition supporting the leader, who is actively defending the state as well.

Repression only amplifies this effect. Just as elites may use the military structure of the state to extract greater rents from society, so too may leaders turn the military against opposition forces, even when the opposition includes the ranks of the economic or political elite of society (Gibler 2012: ch. 4). In fact, the mere threat of military repression may be enough to quell opposition unrest in most cases, and in this way regimes in territorially unsettled environments reach a type of autocratic equilibrium. Only the removal of the threat and the elimination of the political power of the military would be enough to encourage democratization.

Territorial Threat, Regime Type, and Militarization

This argument suggests strong correlations between authoritarianism and territorial threat, democracy and territorial peace. Still, the concepts are distinct. For example, not all states free from territorial threat will be democracies. States with settled borders may still lack the economic or political factors that encourage democratization. Conversely, territorial threat may sometimes force political centralization within established democracies. Each of these possibilities assures that the correlation between settled borders and democracy will remain imperfect.

Consider first the large literature on democratization. Over fifty years ago Lipset (1959) demonstrated the role of wealth in predicting states likely to be democratic, and the literature has since consistently affirmed that wealth and democracy are strongly linked.[6] Indeed, this is one of the strongest findings in the comparative literature on democracy. But wealth is not necessarily affected by an absence of territorial threat. Resolved borders do not put raw materials in the ground, educate the workforce, or create strong property rights systems. While states with settled borders are not likely to have politically powerful militaries, standing land armies, and domestic forces that push for centralization of the state, the lack of territorial threat does not immediately translate into greater wealth for society or competitive middle-class interests. The poorest states that have otherwise resolved their borders may therefore still remain nondemocratic if other components of democracy are absent. This is the case for many sub-Saharan states that accepted their colonial borders upon independence in the early 1960s but have remained nondemocratic since. Mired in civil wars and poverty, few of these states have been able to democratize even while territorial threat remains low across the continent (Lemke 2002: ch. 7). There are other notable exceptions to this probabilistic argument as well (see Gibler 2012: ch. 2). Nevertheless, the implications are clear: external territorial threat leads to domestic political centralization, and this often causes an association between authoritarian governments and conflict.

THE TERRITORIAL PEACE AND INTERNATIONAL CONFLICT

The key contention of the territorial peace argument is that resolving territorial issues leads to the decentralization of power within the state. Since decentralization also increases political competition within the state, democratic transitions are most likely to occur in stable regions in states with stable borders. Of course, if democracies are most likely to be found in regions without dangerous territorial issues confronting them, then this would explain why democracies almost never fight each other. The democratic peace is really a subset of a much larger territorial peace.

Clear Borders and Peaceful Dyads

I provided the first test of the argument that variations in the occurrence of territorial issues explain the well-documented peace between democracies in Gibler (2007). At that time the large peace-to-democracy literature had difficulty overcoming problems associated with endogeneity. Peace could cause democracy, but democracy could also cause peace. Separating the causal sequence of the two concepts is really difficult to do in a convincing way. Further, one of the leading democratic peace arguments had embraced the peace-to-democracy criticisms within its own broader framework of a Kantian peace, arguing that the reciprocal effects of democracy on peace were still powerful even if peace leads to decentralized political power within the state (Russett and Oneal 2001).

I decided to try to eliminate questions of endogeneity in the peace-to-democracy literature by focusing on geography. I therefore tried to identify likely territorial threats with a measure that was not dependent upon conflict itself. Building on Schelling's (1960) argument that geographic salients ease coordination, I inferred that international borders that follow easily identified geographic markers are likely to be more stable than borders that do not. Geography adds a status quo bias to border placement coordination that is difficult to overturn. If my assumptions were correct and geographic salients are correlated with a lower likelihood of territorial conflict, then the endogeneity problem would be solved since democracies are unable to change geographic landmarks in any meaningful way.

Deciding on which landmarks to measure proved difficult since there is no simple measure that accounts for all possible geographical salients. I therefore used several indicators such as differences in mountainous terrain between contiguous states and the presence of similar ethnic groups on both sides of a border. I also assumed that historical maps may prove useful for border delineation. Major states whose colonies bordered the colonies of other major states would be more likely to take care in defining their borders, and therefore the countries that inherited those borders would be more likely to have clearly defined borders. When combined with several behavioral measures of border strength—capability differences, the presence of neighboring civil wars, the age of the border, and the length of peace in the dyad—these geographic measures provided a set of border strength indicators that correlated well with territorial conflict but remained mostly isolated from the possible pacifying effects of joint democracy. I found that contiguous dyads that had the same colonial master were more likely to have territorial claims as were dyads with sharp terrain differences. Interestingly, borders that divided similar ethnicities were unlikely to have territorial claims. These statistical results are provided in table 10.2 (adapted from Gibler [2007: table 3]), in a model that predicts dyadic dispute onset.

The first model provides a baseline and demonstrates that democracy reduces the likelihood of conflict, even after controlling for wealth, parity, and contiguity. Somewhat surprisingly, parity is not statistically significant in this model, though the sign is in the expected direction (positive). Models 2 through 4 add border control variables and vary the sample size to assess the effects of the Cold War. Now, with the border controls added, the parity variable is statistically significant ($p < .05$) and in the expected direction in each model, while wealth and contiguity remain unchanged.

The border variables confirm the importance of territory. Contiguity, peace years, and civil war in at least one state of the dyad all increase the likelihood of MID initiation. Similarly, an international border that divides an ethnic group also has a higher chance of experiencing conflict. The dyadic duration and colonial master variables are not statistically significant in any of the three models, and while the terrain differences measure is significant in only one model (for the post–Cold War years), the sign is in an unexpected direction (negative).

Finally, the key variable for these analyses is the democracy indicator, which is not statistically significant in any of the models of conflict that

Table 10.2. The Effect of Borders on Joint Democracy and Conflict (logit regression models with standard errors in parentheses)

Dependent Variable Temporal Domain Spatial Domain	MID Onset 1946–1999 All Dyads (nondirected)	MID Onset 1946–1989 All Dyads (nondirected)	MID Onset 1990–1999 All Dyads (nondirected)	MID Onset 1946–1999 All Dyads (nondirected)
Lowest Democracy Score in Dyad	−0.005 (0.002)**	0.003 (0.004)	0.007 (0.006)	0.004 (0.003)
Smallest GDP of Dyad (logged)	0.087 (0.028)**	0.320 (0.039)***	0.339 (0.071)***	0.252 (0.033)***
Border Strength Variables				
Capability ratio within dyad (weaker/stronger)	0.105 (0.101)	0.484 (0.121)***	0.660 (0.240)**	0.511 (0.108)***
Years since last MID outbreak		−0.060 (0.004)***	−0.033 (0.004)***	−0.052 (0.003)***
Civil war onset in at least one state of dyad		0.804 (0.193)***	1.009 (0.298)***	0.829 (0.161)***
Duration of dyad (years since youngest state's entry into state system)		−0.001 (0.001)	0.002 (0.002)	0.001 (0.001)
Contiguous Dyad	3.988 (0.057)***	3.386 (0.113)***	3.398 (0.218)***	3.360 (0.099)***
Border Salient Variables				
Same colonial master before independence		0.128 (0.118)	−0.159 (0.267)	0.110 (0.107)
Ethnic border (border separates ethnic group from its brethren across the border)		0.278 (0.101)**	0.638 (0.184)***	0.326 (0.088)***
Terrain differences (logged ratio of percent mountainous/more mountainous)		−0.019 (0.044)	−0.173 (0.084)*	−0.031 (0.039)
Constant	−6.785 (0.053)***	−5.656 (0.075)***	−6.698 (0.166)***	−5.863 (0.067)***
Number of Contiguous Dyads	504,376	255,196	109,583	364,779
LR χ^2	3,631.25***	2,793.52***	923.84***	3,696.08***
Pseudo R^2	0.199	0.227	0.272	0.234

Source: Adapted from Gibler 2007: table 3.
*$p < 0.10$, **$p < 0.05$, ***$p < 0.01$

include the border controls. Of course, even if level of democracy were significant, the sign demonstrates a positive relationship between level of democracy and conflict in each fully specified model. This finding obviously supports the proposition that democracy has little or no effect on conflict once controls are included for stable borders, especially considering the inclusiveness of these models, each with over 100,000 dyadic cases. Indeed, these findings suggest that joint democracy is really a subset of a larger territorial peace.

Testing the Argument with Different Specifications

Of course these findings are provocative since they challenge a large body of literature with a substantial number of findings supporting the democratic peace. I have therefore tested the argument using multiple specifications of both territorial peace and territorially unstable borders. First, in a piece I wrote with Jaroslav Tir, we used border specifications based on peaceful transfers of territory (Gibler and Tir 2010). Not all international borders are the same. In the 2007 article, I argued that stable borders correlate well with the existence of geographic salients. In the work with Tir, we identified peaceful borders using the existence of prior territorial transfers that were mutually agreed upon by the states involved. By focusing the analysis on international borders that have been altered by mutual consent, we identified a set of border cases that are likely to have a greater degree of legitimacy since the neighboring states have demonstrated positive motivation, trust, and credible commitment toward territorial dispute resolution.

Our results provide strong support for the argument that settled international boundaries decrease the level of threat to the territorial integrity of states. We demonstrated that peaceful transfers are prominent among the factors increasing the rate of transitions to democracy.[7] We also found that there is empirical support for the expected processes that lead to democratization. First, peaceful transfers reduce the chances that a state will be targeted in the future by military force over its border; this confirms that peacefully adjusted borders are indeed more settled. Second, when examining the effects of peaceful transfers, we confirmed a link to substantially lower levels of militarization within the country during future years. These findings reinforce the contention that settled borders are associated with political decentralization and liberalization within the state.

A second alternate specification leverages the tendency for conflicts to recur spatially and temporally to test the territorial peace theory. In work with Alex Braithwaite (Gibler and Braithwaite n.d.), we found that territorial "hot spots" occur frequently, indicating geographic dependence in the data on conflict (see also Braithwaite 2005). Moreover, these hot spots provide a good, behavioral indicator of territorial threat in the region and eliminate a reliance on geographic salients. Substituting the behavioral hot spot indicator of territorial threat in models predicting fatal MID onset, we found that the presence of a territorial hot spot is linked to both the occurrence of joint democracy and conflict. In fact, the inclusion of the territorial hot spot indicator also eliminated the statistical significance of joint democracy as a predictor in a common model of international conflict. We only found pacifying effects for joint democracy in regions that already lack territorial conflict. In other words, the pacifying effects of joint democracy may only be present in conflicts that do not involve territorial issues.

The core of the territorial peace argument has thus been affirmed in three separate studies with alternate codings of the key explanatory variable (see also a similar study in Owsiak 2012). This of course suggests a robustness to the findings associating territorial issues, democracy, and conflict, while also providing confirming evidence for the argument that the process of state development matters greatly for the international conflict literature. The next step, then, is extending the argument to other findings associated with the democratic peace research program.

EXTENDING THE ARGUMENT TO EXPLAIN OTHER EMPIRICAL REGULARITIES

The democratic peace research program has followed the initial discovery of an association between democracy and peace with a host of extensions (Small and Singer 1976; Rummel 1983). Bueno de Mesquita et al. (2003: 218–19), for example, suggest that regime type may also provide an explanation for, among other things, the tendency of democracies to fight nondemocracies; the tendency for democracies to fight less costly, shorter wars in which they are likely to be victorious; and the tendency for democracies to negotiate their disputes rather than fight. Many of these findings can also be explained as a function of the territorial peace.

Issue Type, Conflict Selection, Duration, and Victory

For example, the findings that democracies, when they do involve themselves in conflict, tend to fight and win shorter wars at lower costs can also be explained by the types of issues facing democracies. The democratic peace literature argues that elected leaders fear punishment at the polls, so they tend to carefully select their targets. Once involved in conflict, these leaders use all their resources to fight hard and win since defeat in conflict is likely to bring punishment at the next election. However, a territorial peace explanation of these conflicts provides a different view of these findings. Since territorial conflicts with neighbors have been selected out of the issues facing democratic leaders, the sample of disputes that involve democracies differs fundamentally from those that involve authoritarian leaders. Direct threats to the territorial composition of the state necessarily preoccupy a targeted state and confine its conflicts locally. Once these threats are resolved, the decisions for dispute onset or dispute escalation become matters of choice. Thus, democracies are likely to fight short wars, at lower costs, which they can win (Gibler and Miller forthcoming). All leaders would like to win their wars while expending fewer costs. The difference is that territorial peace states have greater flexibility in which to do so.

Disputes between democracies are quite different from the conflicts that affect other regime types. For example, Mitchell and Prins (1999) found that most disputes between democracies involve "fisheries, maritime boundaries, and resources of the sea." Rarely do mature democracies fight over territorial issues that are likely to be salient to the public at large. Huth and Allee (2002: 281) provide similar evidence that democracies rarely fight over territorial issues, as their study finds that "there were no cases of democratic challengers and targets waging war against each other over disputed territory." In fact, democracies in their study were almost always less aggressive than other regime types when bargaining over territorial issues at lower stages of dispute. The only exception to this involved new democracies, which were found to be much more belligerent than other regime types. Together, these findings suggest that mature democracies rarely, if ever, fight over territorial issues. The findings further suggest that this empirical regularity is not a function of regime since new and less-developed democratic regimes still have territorial disputes and aggressively bargain over them.

Issues, Negotiations, and International Norms

Democracy is also supposed to affect the likelihood of negotiated settlements to end militarized disputes. Dixon (1994) provides the clearest articulation of this theory which argues that the norm of bounded competition is common to all democracies, even though social and cultural norms as well as institutional mechanisms vary from state to state. Rivals in democracies openly compete for scarce resources and policy outcomes, but they do so with rules and restraints that normatively restrict political actors from using coercion or violence. A "contingent consent" follows from this universal democratic norm. Aware that unregulated competition creates intolerable risks and uncertainty for all, political elites trust each other not to use force or violence during the electoral contest or any time after it. Since leaders, democratic leaders especially (Joffe 1990), view international politics as an extension of democratic politics, this norm of bounded competition surfaces in international disputes. When two democracies are locked in the early phases of an interstate conflict, the leader of each democracy is secure in his or her knowledge that the leader of the other state is bounded by the same norm. When a democratic leader is confronted by an autocrat, the democrat does not believe that the autocrat is bounded by any norm, and nothing remains to restrain escalation. This normative perspective generates a unique answer to the paradoxes of the democratic peace. Democratic leaders do not trust autocracies but trust each other to the point where they peacefully negotiate settlements to their disputes before war is an option.

This normative perspective constitutes the theoretical backdrop for the empirical support linking democratic dyads and peaceful dispute settlements, such as arbitration, mediated settlements, and mutual compromises. If the territorial peace argument is correct, however, state development paths should affect this observation of democratic differentness with regard to negotiation and settlement as well. Again, states must settle their territorial disputes early in order to become democratic. Removal of these territorial issues then biases the sample of contentious issues for democracies toward cases that are much less likely to include territory and other issues salient to the homeland. Lower salience then leads to easier conflict management and makes negotiated settlements more likely.

As work I conducted with Steve Miller demonstrates, this is indeed the case (Miller and Gibler 2011). Using techniques similar to the work on conflict victory and duration above, we find that, when issues are unspecified in the estimation, the pacifying influence of joint democracy on negotiated compromises is confirmed. However, when the model is fully specified to include territorial issues between neighboring states, the pacifying influence of jointly democratic dyads disappears. The same happens when we split the sample according to contentious issue (territorial versus nonterritorial). These differences confirm the argument that dangerous territorial issues have been sampled out of the issues facing democratic dyads. The disputes that do involve democracies are easier to handle and more amenable to negotiation.

Other Extensions of the Argument to International Relations

Extending the territorial peace argument even further, the conflicts that a state may select itself into typically do not involve border issues. Instead, disputes for states at territorial peace involve less salient issues of imperialist claims and matters of policy and regime preferences around the international system, and when the issues are of minor importance to elites and publics, the need to handle disputes with power politics is reduced. This is why there tends to be an association between democracy and a host of other international outcomes. For example, in the alliance literature, democratic alliances tend to endure and serve as credible threats. In the audience cost literature, democracies are supposed to be able to credibly signal their intentions (Schultz 2001). However, rather than focusing on a regime-based explanation of these regularities, the territorial peace explanation would assume that there is significant variation in the types of issues that affect these states. Democracies face less dangerous threats to the state, and this in turn leads to alliances that are rarely threatened and democratic audiences that rarely care about foreign policy issues, which makes audience costs exceedingly rare in these states (Gibler and Hutchison n.d.). Thus, the territorial peace argument not only predicts the likelihood of conflict, but it also provides expectations on the content of the issues fought over.

THREAT AND DOMESTIC POLITICS: THE PERSISTENCE OF DEMOCRACY

The territorial explanation is, at heart, an explanation of the domestic politics of the state under duress. As such, the theory provides a unique explanation of the bargaining that takes place among subnational actors. For example, much of the comparative literature considers the strong correlation between democracy and wealth. Wealth either increases the likelihood of democratic transitions (Boix and Stokes 2003; Epstein et al. 2006), or democratic transitions are random and those that take place in wealthy countries persist (Przeworski 2000). The territorial peace argument can inform this debate.

One of the main causes of democratic reversals is external threats to the state. Within the territorial peace framework, salient threats to the state should cause political centralization domestically as the political elite anticipate and sometimes take advantage of the reactions of their threatened populations (Gibler 2010b). Note the mechanism though. The threat causes a political environment that favors domestic centralization. The key, then, to finding when democracies under threat are likely to endure is to turn to those institutions that are more resilient to electoral threats. In a forthcoming study, I therefore examined the ability of independent judiciaries to block executive power grabs during international conflicts (Gibler and Randazzo 2011). Independent judiciaries are unique because, if viewed as legitimate within the state, these institutions protect the regime during times of electoral stress. As an institution, most are isolated from the domestic power changes that can result when state territories are threatened.

The model of centralization outlined here relies on changes in the domestic bargaining power of various actors as a mechanism for regime centralization. International conflict advantages the executive vis-à-vis other domestic actors, and eventually power is concentrated in the executive as democratic principles are eroded. The causal mechanism relies on the opportunity given the executive by international crisis, as this threat, when coupled with popular backing, allows the executive to supersede the constitution in favor of expediency.

An independent judiciary can affect this process in two ways. First, established judiciaries are likely to deter executives from using the crisis as an opportunity to gain power. An executive facing an international crisis will likely not risk additional political decisions that may cause the questioning of its authority. This weak form of judicial independence creates few judicial annulments, but the court does buttress the political power of other societal and governmental interests against executive incursions. A stronger form of judicial independence manifests when the executive is overtly checked with annulments as the court favors minority rights and participatory democracy. In either case the executive is constrained by the court, and democracy maintains. Established judiciaries are probably one of the best institutional guarantees for providing a bulwark against executive-led political centralization.

The empirics support the stabilizing nature of judiciaries. Using forty-one years of data (1960–2000) identifying judicial constraints across 163 different countries, we found that the presence of an independent judiciary is consistently associated with regime stability.[8] Specifically, our analyses suggested that established judiciaries help prevent all types of regime changes toward authoritarianism for samples that included all regime types. When the sample was limited to democracies only, independent judiciaries still predicted fewer negative regime changes, but large-scale changes remained unaffected by the courts.[9] In the end, independent judiciaries did stop political centralization caused by territorial threats. However, judiciaries were incapable of halting centralization during intense, long-term threats, such as those resulting from territorial rivalries.

This type of study suggests the importance of connecting theories of dyadic, interstate relations with the domestic processes within the state. The territorial explanation of conflict provides important answers for which issues are likely to affect political bargaining most, and these issues carry implications for the structure of institutions and individual attitudes within the state. Marrying theories of international conflict to domestic politics demonstrates the importance of independent judiciaries and other veto players for creating an environment that sustains democratic governance. This is of course a much more nuanced explanation of the peace-to-democracy thesis.

FINAL THOUGHTS: ISSUE EVOLUTION
ACROSS THE INTERNATIONAL SYSTEM

The territorial peace theory is broad and applicable to many different literatures. I have used the theory to explain empirical regularities as disparate as the likelihood of party polarization across countries, how this affects changes in the number of veto players able to check the power of the leader, and how this is in turn related to international conflict. Further, these advancements are based on a new understanding of when popular opinion is likely to be intolerant and when individuals are likely to support their leader with rally-round-the-flag behavior. All of these theories have previously remained isolated arguments and, to varying degrees, plagued by inconsistent results. However, treated comprehensively as interrelated mechanisms, strong and consistent findings confirm the overarching theory and its many implications.

As a field, we are beginning to realize that territorial issues matter for individuals, governments, and polities in general. The next step in this research program will develop the mechanisms by which territorial issues affect different aspects of the state. We are also beginning to uncover the ways in which territorial issues become conflicts between states. Future research should build on this momentum and try to account for variations in the number and types of territorial disputes across time and space in the international system. This type of research is fundamental for understanding the distribution of international conflict and democracy in different regions.

The research I have discussed here demonstrates that issues matter (Mansbach and Vasquez 1981). An important implication of these findings is that there is substantial spatial and temporal variation in the types of issues and types of regimes that populate the international system at any given time. This is important for a literature that has become dependent upon cross-sectional time-series analyses of dyadic data. For example, King (2001) essentially argues that the failure to account for variations in hostility levels across dyads—a form of issue salience variation—renders almost all large-N, quantitative conflict studies prone to omitted variable bias since variation of the historical animosity within the dyad remains unmeasured. After all, any peaceful years between, for example, India and Pakistan are not exchangeable with the peaceful years between the United States and Canada, without first accounting for the level of hostility that exists in the dyad. The territorial peace argument suggests that there is a reason for this variation, and it is based on state and regional development paths. Established democracies—those states most likely to be at territorial peace—will not face the same types of issues as new states or states in dyads with continually contested borders.

Finally, territorial peace theory makes a strong argument for reconsidering some of the foreign policy practices of the major players in the current international system. For example, the United States and Britain continue to emphasize peace and democratization abroad, but my theory suggests that neither will take hold without firm, settled borders. Even development provides little hope for democratization unless the pertinent territorial issues are resolved first. This suggests that an even greater emphasis should be placed on peace between Israel and its neighbors, between Iraq and Iran, between Afghanistan and Pakistan, and between the Spratly Islands, as well as in the myriad other ongoing territorial conflicts. Rather than maintaining democracy as the solution for conflict and development, territorial dispute resolution needs to come first.

NOTES

1. Territorial issues are listed in the two categories labeled strategic territory and, simply, territory. Policy issues include the categories commerce/navigation, protect religious confreres, enforce treaty terms, balance of power, and so forth. Finally, regime issues include dynastic/succession claims, state/regime survival, and national liberation/state creation.

2. By comparison, it seems difficult to connect an increased individual wariness with threats to foreign policy decisions or to the regime status within the state. Most regime disputes, for example, concern foreign governments that are targeting the leadership of nondemocratic, mostly authoritarian states. (Indeed, only 5 of 103 regime challenges targeted democracies between 1816 and 2001, according to version 3.1 of the Correlates of War Militarized Interstate Dispute [MID] data. Of the remaining cases, 56 targeted states were at or below −5 on the combined Polity IV scale.) Under an authoritarian government, most individual citizens would benefit in the long term following some type of regime change; at the very least, most would expect the chance of benefitting through regime change. This is perhaps why targeting countries have sometimes assumed that mass support would follow their attempts to impose some type of regime change on their rivals.

3. The tolerance measure we used only asked respondents to exercise judgments toward a generalized list of unpopular groups in most of the countries in our sample. Thus, we did not have a direct measure of the tolerance for groups that are the source of the external threat to each country. Of course, the absence of this direct measure probably biased our results against finding a correlation between external threat and political tolerance. That we still observed a connection between territorial threat and least-liked groups should underscore the strength of the overall relationship.

4. North and Weingast (1989) argue, for example, that the powerful British king had to compromise with his parliament precisely because the bulk of the military force was abroad. The navy could not force increased revenues from the lords. Similarly, Friedberg (1988) argues that a more modern Britain was unable to maintain its global supremacy, thanks largely to its many, far-flung colonial holdings.

5. Other types of issues are unlikely to affect threat duration in quite the same way. Policy and trade disputes are more likely to be time and place specific, as conflicts end once there has been either a change in or confirmation of the status quo. Those conflicts that do recur—over regime type, perhaps—are still unlikely to engender the same type of military structure as territorial disputes. So, militarized states may tend to be found proximate to recurrent policy or regime disputes, but the land army will probably not be as politically dominant within the state.

6. This relationship has been repeatedly confirmed, but the cause of the wealth-democracy link remains debated. Przeworski and various coauthors (Przeworski et al. 1996; Przeworski and Limongi 1997; Przeworski 2000) contend that wealth does not cause democratization but instead provides the antidote to all types of antidemocratic reversions. According to this argument, democratic transitions occur for myriad reasons that are often unrelated to economic development, but high levels of state wealth (usually measured by GDP) provide strong societal protections against reversions from democracy. Wealth is also generally found when other important domestic determinants of democracy are present. Wealthy states have a strong middle class that makes autocratic repression more difficult (Moore 1966; Rueschemeyer, Stephens, and Stephens 2000), and more generally, an increase in the number of powerful actors within society can be found in wealthier states, which makes a competitive, democratic equilibrium more likely (Olson 1993). Ultimately, though the role of wealth in establishing democracy continues to be questioned (Boix 2003; Boix and Stokes 2003; Epstein et al. 2006), no one seems to doubt that wealth prevents reversions from democracy.

7. Importantly, we also demonstrated that our analyses are not by-products of the argument that democracy leads to peaceful transfers; our analyses clearly affirm that democratic regime type has no appreciable influence on the likelihood of peaceful transfers in the dyad.

8. It is important to note that our analyses also confirmed that these results were not spurious to traditional correlates of democracy such as wealth and development history. Nor are independent judiciaries endogenous to polity changes.

9. Newly established independent judiciaries were associated with large-scale reversions (magnitude of 4 or more on the Polity IV scale) in both democracies and nondemocracies. Our examination of the data suggested that this last finding resulted mostly from placement of the courts in difficult political environments, adding additional support to the argument that the power of the court grows over time. These results also indirectly confirm the ability of external threat to lead to domestic centralization—if external threats lead to increased popularity and a political environment that favors the leader, then only checks that are removed from popular will, such as unelected judiciaries, can mitigate the effects of political centralization.

Part III

REFLECTIONS AND CONCLUSIONS ON THE SCIENTIFIC STUDY OF PEACE AND WAR

Chapter Eleven

War Making and State Making

How and Where Does It Fit into a Bigger Picture?

Karen Rasler and William R. Thompson

Students of war are interested, almost reflexively, and very often exclusively, in causes. Why do wars occur? What factors make war more or less likely? While we would be the last authors to urge abandoning the elusive hunt for causation, there is also a case to be made for looking at war impacts. In general, what difference do wars make? War impacts are important in their own right—that is, understanding the effects of war should be as important as understanding the causes of war. But switching the emphasis from what drives war to what war drives is not necessarily a separate question. In some instances, war effects influence the nature and likelihood of subsequent wars. Or, expressed differently, war effects can also be war causes. The relationship between war making and state making is a case in point. War makes states, and states make war in a reciprocal dialectic. This is hardly a novel observation. The war making–state making literature is expanding, but not without some causality problems of its own.

The "war making–state making" phrase has been around for more than a generation, but it remains to be precisely delineated. In this chapter, we focus primarily on reciprocal interactions between the development of state institutions and warfare and, in particular, on the diverse reactions to Tilly's (1975, 1985, 1992) initial formulation of the relationship. Accurately or not, the late sociologist Charles Tilly is most associated with the argument that wars and state making are intertwined. A better case could be made for Otto Hintze who wrote about these issues in the late nineteenth and early twentieth centuries. But Tilly's work on this subject is where most contemporary analysts begin their arguments. Nonetheless, we do not adhere strictly to a narrow definition of war making and state making. We argue that the core relationship overlaps with related topics such as economic growth, democratization, and the democratic peace. We offer a framework that connects these topics and some of their still outstanding analytical puzzles. However, our framework will show that much more work is still required before these puzzles can be resolved.

"War made the state and the state made war" demands explication because it means a variety of things to different analysts. Part of the problem is that the phrase leaves considerable room for theoretical interpretation. There is also ample disagreement about to which actors, regions, and behavior it most applies. For instance, Tilly (1975), who coined the phrase, initially thought it applied to European developments in the second millennium CE but not to the Third World—a point seconded by an array of Middle Eastern, African, and Latin American scholars.[1] Later, Tilly (1985) argued that the relevant processes were best modeled as interactions among war making (eliminating external rivals), state making (eliminating internal rivals), protection (eliminating enemies of clients), and extraction (acquiring resources to execute the first three types of activities). Alternatively, Bruce Porter (1994) asserted that these processes were best represented as a triangular flow of one-way relationships among capital, bureaucracy, and arms. Eventually, Tilly (1992) would put forward a third model that differentiated the impact of war and war preparations according to whether they took place in coercive or capital-intensive areas. Mayhew (2005) extended this approach by theorizing about how war shaped policy changes, new issue developments, electoral shifts, and changes in party ideologies. All of these works indicate that the relationships linking war making and state making involve many causal paths, scope conditions, and different theoretical perspectives and preferences. Nor do all scholars view the domain of war making–state making processes in precisely the same way. Nor can these arguments be reduced to the simple statement that participation in warfare leads to larger, expanded, or more complex states.

Despite this diversity, we offer a broad framework for interpreting war making–state making relationships. The framework (Thompson 2006; Levy and Thompson 2011) links six coevolving sets of processes: war, political organization, military organization, weaponry, the threat environment, and political economy. Significant changes in any one of these foci will have major reverberations that alter the others. In this respect, these six foci coevolve over time but not without variety and qualification.

In addition to describing this framework, we will also examine how our framework and the war making–state making linkage fits into larger questions about the causes of war. We believe that the war making side of the linkage occurs in a variety of contexts, but the state making side is always part of each context—either explicitly or implicitly. We propose to make it more explicit. In addition, we will argue that war making influences subsequent war making by altering the institutional capabilities of the actors involved. Hence, if states are stronger as a result of war, they may increase their future war participation, while the opposite may occur if states are weakened by their prior war involvement.

THE FRAMEWORK

Our framework links six sets of factors, listed in table 11.1, that are the most influential in explaining the linkages among phenomena that pertain to war, including its emergence, escalation, and transformations. In this chapter, we are more concerned with escalation and transformations. Warfare, which often serves as a conduit for the reciprocal influences of the other five factors, is defined quite generally as sustained and coordinated combat between groups. Although war is conceptualized broadly, we want to encompass bellicose behavior over many thousands of years. Right now, however, we are most interested in combat between states (external warfare) and within states among organized opposition groups (often but not always internal warfare).

Military weaponry focuses on the technologies and instruments used to wage warfare, ranging from spears to nuclear bombs. Weaponry is wielded by military organizations that are in one way or another subordinated to political organizations of varying complexity. Our contemporary interest in political organizations tends to focus on more complex organizations that we now call states, but war behavior has been occurring for millennia and the complexity of

Table 11.1. Six Coevolutionary Factors and Their Definitions

Coevolutionary Factors	Definition
Warfare	Sustained and coordinated combat between groups.
Military weaponry	Technology employed to inflict damage in warfare.
Military organization	Institutions specializing in the planning, coordination, and execution of combat.
Political organization	Institutions specializing in authoritative decision making for groups (bands, chiefdoms, states).
Threat environment	Distinctive characteristics of the operational milieu in which people are faced with the possibility of physical damage from enemies (e.g., the proximity of grassland plains sustaining horse-riding nomads, the presence and proximity of multiple strong states, or relative insulation from attack due to bodies of water that are difficult to cross).
Political economy	a) Strategies for organizing economic production (hunting/gathering, agrarian, industrial, postindustrial).
	b) Relative scarcity of resources.

combat groups has varied over time—not always linearly. In fact, sometimes war today resembles warfare manifested many generations earlier.

Meanwhile, the remaining two factors of our framework, threat environment and political economy, refer to broader environments that shape the interactions among the first four factors. Since the threat environment varies across time and space, we anticipate varying responses by states. For instance, Eurasian states that were exposed to frequent nomadic attacks were forced to focus their defenses against light cavalry tactics. Those Eurasian states that were able to protect themselves against nomadic horsemen were in a position to develop gunpowder weaponry even though it required a number of centuries before it could be sufficiently lethal to predominate on the battlefield. In short, those states exposed to nomadic cavalry attacks experienced a much different threat environment than other states that were less vulnerable.

Political economy plays two critical roles in this model. First, it refers to the predominant strategy for economic production. Levy and Thompson (2011), for instance, maintain that warfare in and between preagrarian, agrarian, and industrial societies will not be identical. The most obvious distinction is that industrialized weaponry and military organizations are much more lethal, even though preagrarian warfare might have been proportionally more devastating on local populations, given the small size of warring groups. The second meaning of political economy denotes the degree of resource scarcity. Greater resource scarcity will expand the incentives for warfare, especially when increased scarcity occurs abruptly with climate changes.

Figure 11.1 sketches one way to view the relationships among the six factors.[2] It depicts a coevolutionary theory that shows major changes in any one of these six factors will reverberate and affect the behavior of the remaining factors. These coevolutionary processes include environment

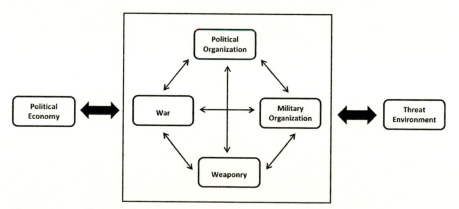

Figure 11.1. Six Coevolutionary Factors Involved in War-Related Phenomena

factors (threat and political economy) that define the context in which organizational warfare takes place. Organizational warfare, therefore, is affected by changes in the environment. In turn, such warfare can also alter the environment. A good illustration of such a process can be found in the democratic peace arguments. As political organizations in a system transition from autocratic to democratic forms, scholars argue that conflict will increase between autocracies and democracies over ideological issues but decrease between democracies. Only when the system is predominately or perhaps exclusively democratic would we expect an overall reduction in warfare. From this perspective, changes in the regimes or forms of political organizations have altered which actors go to war.

Our discussion on the coevolution of these six types of processes does not tell us where to draw the line precisely between what is germane to war making and state making and what is not. It does, however, suggest a way to organize the relevant theoretical and empirical works on the subject. The question is which of the many causal pathways depicted in figure 11.1 should be addressed, since many of them are not equally interesting or salient. Since a lion's share of the research on the war making–state making relationship deals mostly with the linkages between war and political organizations, we will emphasize this coevolutionary process over the others. Nevertheless, we contend that drawing boundaries among these processes is somewhat arbitrary. This is a crucial part of our argument. If we observe these processes interacting in broad and complex ways, we probably need to reexamine how we take state actors for granted in developing our explanations of war onset. Nor can we easily sideline the category of war impacts as something of interest but not immediately germane to why states go to war. States go to war within contexts that influence the probability of warfare, just as states going to war can alter the contexts within which states operate.

THE WAR↔POLITICAL ORGANIZATION CONNECTION

The reciprocal linkages between war and political organizations/states, no doubt, constitute the core focus in the war making–state making literature. Yet, as we have said before, many of these relevant topics fail to fit neatly within this rubric because they reflect processes that have been filtered through military organizations, weaponry, and others. Hence, our discussion will inevitably stray across other linkages.

The basic aphorism about war making and state making can be dissected in two obvious ways: (1) states make war, an uncontroversial observation, and (2) war making is the principal path to state making, a much different observation and one to which scholars are most likely to react positively or negatively. Charles Tilly, who originated the aphorism, was mostly interested in the war-as-the-principal-path-to-state-making argument.[3] Therefore, we organize a substantial portion of the pertinent literature around scholars' responses to Tilly's assertion. We find that there are three types: (1) Tilly, for the most part, was right; (2) Tilly was right about the history of European state making, but his argument no longer holds, especially outside Europe and North America; and (3) Tilly was wrong about European history, and consequently war making is not a principal path to state making then or now.

"Tilly Was Right" Arguments

One time-honored way to expand or to consolidate the size of the state is through military conquest. Thus, war is a policy instrument that is integral to state formation as long as other actors ultimately accept the outcomes of military victory and territorial occupation as legitimate endeavors. This is part of Tilly's "war making" activity—states defeating external rivals and neutralizing their threat by absorbing all or some of their territory. International relations scholars usually start the clock on modern international politics in 1494 or 1648. In the former case, the French movement into Italy triggered a coalition of states opposed to the French expansion and a long-running rivalry between Hapsburgs and Valois/Bourbons over hegemony in Western Europe. After a protracted contest between "English" and "French" dynastic claims for control of the French state, remaining political issues concerned the territorial expansion of the French state. In the latter case of 1648, decades of bloodletting in central Europe, at least in part over which territories Protestants and Catholics would be allowed to control, had played itself out without a decisive outcome that signaled a clear-cut Protestant or Catholic victory. At the same time, it was clear that Protestant states had survived and in some cases had expanded their territorial control. Moreover, state sovereignty, or so the mythology goes, was also firmly established in 1648 in contrast to the vagaries of ill-defined imperial borders. State making in modern international relations thus began with either the onset (1494) or the temporary termination of war making activities (1648).

Some of the scholars who support the war making–state making connection throughout history (that is, past and present) tend to focus on the continuation of these types of activities long after 1494 and 1648.[4] Most of these scholars (including Tilly) converge on the ruler's need to create a monopoly of violence by eliminating rivals within state boundaries. They also argue that this behavior is precisely what is taking place in many of the newer states today and why external warfare is less critical to state making than internal warfare.[5] Nonetheless, there are also clear cases of external warfare leading to the creation of stronger states in the global South, even if the occurrences are not numerous.

Helling (2010), for instance, compares the unusual case of Somaliland to Somalia, which basically disintegrated, partially as a function of war making. In contrast, Somaliland's recent route to state making follows the familiar European path where rulers established their monopoly over violence, built administrative infrastructures, and negotiated elite bargains— all within the context of war. Working in the same region, Clapham (2000) draws attention to the ability of Ethiopia and Eritrea to raise taxes and organize armies for warfare—something unusual in sub-Saharan Africa. While he is not fully convinced that these state making activities were due to war making per se, he does appreciate the nation building payoffs of war making at least for the Eritrean case.

In the Asian context, Taylor and Botea (2008) argue that war making enhanced state making in Vietnam but not in Afghanistan. They contend that the difference between the outcomes in the two cases had more to do with ethnic homogeneity and, especially, revolutionary ideology—which were present in Vietnam but less so in Afghanistan. They assert that revolutionary ideology was critical in motivating state bureaucrats to build extractive and coercive agencies. Moreover, national identities were easier to create in the relative absence of ethnic competition and conflict. In contrast, Callahan (2003: 3), who examines the many decades of military rule in Burma/Myanmar, expresses no caveats:

> Warfare creates the conditions under which elites and social forces negotiate, create, revitalize, reorganize, and rethink the patterns and practices of governance.

Yet it is not clear that military rule in Burma/Myanmar can be equated with a strong state. There is no question, however, that the state became more coercive over time.

In the Middle East, Barnett (1992) compares Israel and Egypt—neither of which is a stranger to warfare. Israel is found to have fared better on state making than Egypt in their mutual wars. What intervened, according to Barnett, was the mix of state strategies that Israel and Egypt utilized to prepare for war. He asserts that states can rely on accommodational (entailing modest changes), restructural (major changes to increase available resources), or international (redistributing the costs of warfare to foreign actors) strategies to prepare for external warfare. Although states are likely to rely on a mixture of all three strategies, as did Israel and Egypt, those states that avoid or minimize painful restructural strategies are less likely to absorb the full impact of war preparations on subsequent state making. Hence, the comparative impact of wars on

Israel's and Egypt's state strength did not yield a clear outcome between a strong versus a weak state. Instead, Barnett found that both states experienced substantial political and economic instability due to their strategic choices, but overall Israel's state structures were better enhanced than Egypt's.

Still another approach is taken by Thies (2004, 2005, 2007), who has examined multiple regions. Thies argues that the Tilly relationship works if we substitute rivalry for warfare in the developing world since warfare is less frequent and is likely to have less impact. In other words, participation in interstate rivalries will generate similar extraction benefits for state making that were earlier credited to war making. Hence, states that have external rivals are more likely to develop domestic strategies for mobilizing state resources in order to contend with external rivals, while states without external rivals are much less likely to do so.[6]

"Tilly Was Right about European History but the Relationship No Longer Holds" Argument

For many scholars, the real core of the war making–state making relationship is the idea that to make war states had to improve their ability to extract resources in order to pay for the war making. States needed the "sinews of war" to pay and feed their soldiers, and to buy military equipment to defend their garrisons against their opponents. To acquire them, decision makers developed strategies for extracting resources from their international and domestic environments. To the extent that they were successful in mobilizing resources and developing competitive military capabilities, rulers found that the costs of engaging in warfare increased over time. Hence, rulers routinized and increased their revenues through domestic taxation, just as they searched for assistance from external allies. Consequently, recurring warfare resulted in a "ratchet effect" on the resources that rulers mobilized. Each subsequent war expanded the tax base and rate to pay for more troops, military equipment, and ultimately the destructiveness of combat. Although the new, war-induced extraction rates were unnecessary in the postwar era, they rarely returned to their prewar levels.

War-induced ratchet effects on public debt, tax collections, state revenues, and state expenditures have been found readily in the fiscal accounts of European and North American states. It is less clear that similar effects are discernable in the fiscal records of many Third World states, especially the ones that have been most involved in warfare.[7] Nonetheless, there are several reasons why we might not observe a ratchet effect. One reason is that Third World war participants are more likely to rely on external than on internal extraction efforts. Superpower patrons, at least in the Cold War years, were quick to rearm their clients in war. Hence, Third World rulers were less likely to raise monies at home for their war efforts and were less inclined to do so. Moreover, the general nature of the threat environment has changed. While defeated European states could be absorbed by their victors in earlier times, this result is less likely to occur today when there are norms against absorbing territories of defeated foes (Fazal 2007). Meanwhile, Third World wars have often been too short or too inconclusive to produce the ultimate costs of defeat. So, newer states rarely disappear as an outcome of war losses. Hence, decision makers know that their state's existence is relatively protected and that they will not have to face the full consequences of military defeat. In most cases, contemporary decision makers do not perceive themselves as fighting for the very survival of their states. As a result, their wars are frequently less intense. Of course, since relatively weak states lack the capabilities to conduct intense warfare, they are less likely to generate stronger states as they pursue war making policies.

There are two reasonable responses to the argument that war making and state making worked in Europe but are not likely to work the same way in other regions. One response is to accept the "fact" that things have changed fundamentally. Hence, we should reject the war making–state making relationship for contexts in the developing world. A second response is that the relationship should be redefined with greater specificity. For instance, war intensity could be a critical conditional variable. The one element that differentiates the European wars from more contemporary warfare in the developing world is their escalating intensity and lethality over time. When we say that European warfare made European states, we are really talking about hundreds of years of escalating warfare and their successive impacts on political organizations. Relatively strong European states in the twentieth and twenty-first centuries survived wars that had become increasingly total in terms of their resource mobilization and mass participation. Perhaps more intense wars are likely to have more extensive impacts on state making than are less intense wars.

If this is the case, Tilly's argument could be modified to take into account that it was not so much European warfare itself but the increasing intensity and lethality of that warfare over time that produced more complex state making. Therefore, our inability to observe consistent war making–state making relationships in regions outside Europe may be the absence of an upward spiral of frequent and escalating warfare that we observed in Europe from 1494 to 1945. In fact, probably the only comparable instance to the European experience is the Warring States Era in China that preceded the creation of the Han Empire. This period also led to the creation of a strong Chinese state.[8]

Evidence for this argument shows up in several places. For example, Rasler and Thompson (1985a, 1985b, 1989) have demonstrated that global wars involving Europe and North America were more likely to exert strong impacts on increasing the size of public debts, state expenditures and revenues, and military organizations than nonglobal wars. More recently, Centeno (2002) argued that one of the reasons that Latin American states remain weak today despite their past war experience is that their wars were limited in scale and scope. His research implies that limited wars produce smaller impacts on state making. Combining both of these perspectives, Levy and Thompson (2011) conclude that it was the intensification of European warfare that created strong states, and the historical absence of such warfare in other parts of the world indicates that strong states are less likely to reside in these areas.

In short, we maintain that it is feasible and necessary to elaborate the war making→state making theory by introducing more variables. Certainly, the evidence above suggests that the first modification should be war intensity→state making, rather than the direct bilateral relationship between war and state making. Barnett (1992) suggests another intervening variable: state strategies of resource extraction. Taylor and Botea (2008) advance two more possible variables involving the role of revolutionary ideology and national identities. For that matter, scholars who argue that the international environment has changed substantially for developing states today in comparison to early modern Europe offer a potentially important fourth variable. That is, the international threat environment may also mediate the war→state making relationship.

Still another perspective is advanced by Gongora (1997), who argues that the use of industrialized weapons by nonindustrialized states makes these states more heavily dependent on external support in comparison to European states and rulers who, according to Tilly, relied more heavily on generating internal support in order to survive war making. Gongora's thesis suggests that weaponry is the key intervening variable (war weaponry→state making).

"Tilly Was Wrong" Argument

There are two types of arguments that reject the Tilly model. Both essentially argue that war making is given far too much credit for state making because other processes were as important, or even more important. Among the social scientists, Spruyt (1994) is the leading challenger. His model does not eliminate war making altogether but definitely subordinates it to the status of an intervening variable. Spruyt believes that economic change and rulers' reactions to these economic changes preceded the growing concern that they had for warfare after 1400. Between 1000 and 1300 CE, however, feudalist institutions were created, contingent on bargaining between rulers and elites, to deal with or to best exploit the changing political-economic circumstances (1000–1300 CE) associated with problems of trade, monetization, and expanding economic growth. Those institutions rooted in sovereign and territorially based states provided better strategies of survival than city-states or city leagues. Although Spruyt argues that war did not determine which institutional response would survive, he does acknowledge that rulers came to realize that territorial states could raise more revenues and soldiers in the long run and therefore were more efficient and successful in war. So, institutional survival was not determined by combat per se but ruler perceptions about which types of institutions were likely to be superior in war making. Hence, rulers of small states managed to survive as long as they kept to the fringes of European warfare.

Spruyt (1994) asserts that his approach complements rather than rivals traditional war making–state making perspectives. We agree with this view, especially when we situate the Spruyt argument in the context of environmental changes that preceded the increasing European emphasis on war making. Hence, the theoretical emphasis now shifts from state making in general to state making of a given era and place. Once territorially based, sovereign states became established (Spruyt's main interest), they were then well placed to make war (Tilly's main interest). However, Spruyt's work suggests that there might be another rival variable to war's influence on state making, and that is rulers' responses to economic changes. The question then becomes which variable has stronger explanatory power for changes in state making. Alternatively, the better question is whether we have to choose between them. Spruyt started with the assumption that war making was less important in state making in order to make his point about the more important role of economic changes. Yet we remain open to the possibility that multiple stimuli will affect state making and that their effects will vary over time and place.

A second set of criticisms emanate from historians of early modern Europe (Glete 2002; Gunn, Grummitt, and Cools 2007; Burkhardt 2010; Gunn 2010; Parrott 2010; Teschke 2010). They believe that the sociological models of war making–state making in European history are not well substantiated by the reality of early modern Europe. They argue that the process by which weak states in the medieval era became stronger states in the early modern and modern era occurred more unevenly and less linearly than sociological models suggest. They also lament the absence of theorizing about historical exceptions, cultural influences, local variations, and other such variables. Finally, these historians emphasize that in the early modern period, the distinction between internal and external warfare was blurred. Thus, theories that focus on the decisive role of external warfare not only miss the greater significance of internal warfare but also overlook the contributions that other variables make to state making. Their bottom line is that we should be wary of elevating external warfare as the major shaper of early European state making.

Some of these criticisms, no doubt, are related to the historians' unwillingness to embrace generalizations, which are preferred by social scientists. But, their criticisms raise two points. One is that if we wish to pursue war making as the major stimulus for state making, we need to do a better job of comparing and contrasting the effects of war making on state making with other factors that may or may not vary by time period and geographical space. In other words, it is not enough to ask whether war is or was the main stimulus to state making. What other stimuli are generalizable and comparable? Can we empirically compare the explanatory strengths of multiple stimuli? Finally, we also need more detailed analyses of the effects of war making on historical cases in Europe and elsewhere. We already have some important studies, but we need more to improve our understanding of how the various stimuli work.

Beyond the Central War Making↔State Making Relationship

At the same time that we focus on whether war making makes for stronger or weaker states, we should consider other questions as well. In particular, one that remains firmly within the war political organization rubric is whether there is a relationship between war and political organizational format or regime type. For instance, there is the argument that democratization emerged in varying degrees as a result of bargaining among rulers, elites, and mass populations over the provision of increased resources to the ruler for making war. In exchange, rulers sometimes made deals that surrendered a portion of their sovereign powers. War making thus fueled democratization in some places.

Yet, in other places, the demands and stresses of surviving in a highly competitive environment encouraged the concentration of political resources and power within state institutions. For example, the rise of absolutist regimes in early modern Europe has been traced to rulers' need for expensive weapons and larger armies in order to defend against local rivals in a hostile neighborhood.[9] But there are other incentives as well. The emergence of totalitarian regimes in the twentieth century, for example, have been traced to rulers who want to catch up quickly to other states who have greater political and economic advantages, as well as to avenge losses from World War I (Porter 1994). Still another incentive can be found in contemporary garrison states where rulers have relied extensively on violence to repress local opposition groups (Cohen, Brown, Organski 1981; Gurr 1988).

These types of interpretations reverse the causal arrow between war and state making. A very familiar one to students of world politics is the democratic peace contention: that is, that democracies do not tend to fight other democracies.[10] In this argument, the causal path is that dyadic regime type influences war. But it can be argued that war can explain regime type. Specifically, variation in threat environments helps to explain which states are more or less likely to democratize. As depicted in figure 11.1, there is a large reciprocal causal arrow between threat environment and other variables such as war, political organization, military organization, and weaponry. While the standard approach to explaining democratization concentrates on domestic processes (e.g., literacy, wealth, elite bargains), the contention is that the role of the external environment should be considered as equally important. The essential argument is that democratization is more likely to occur in less threatening external environments, while autocratization is more likely to emerge in more threatening environments. Now, the question is which comes first? Democratic peace theorists maintain that dyadic regime type influences war, while some war making–state making theorists believe that regime type is a function of the threat environment and war.[11] This causal arrow question is also debated among theorists who believe that there is a reciprocal relationship between war and regime type.[12]

Yet there is now increasing empirical evidence that democratic peace arguments that advance the regime type→war relationship are on less sound footing. For instance, the first crack in the foundations of the argument appears when analysts discovered that economic development was a significant factor in the relationship. Recent evidence shows that less-developed democratic states do not demonstrate the same reluctance to fight other democratic states that is shown by more developed states (Hegre 2000; Mousseau 2000; Mousseau, Hegre, and Oneal 2003). A second crack emerges with arguments that the dyadic-regime-type–war relationship masks more fundamental relationships associated with industrial/capitalist economies and war making propensities. The evidence shows that when democratization itself is the focus (rather than democracy per se), it tends to be influenced by major changes in the prevailing political economies both domestically and internationally. Hence, political-economic changes→democratization→war.[13]

Yet a third crack in the democratic peace edifice is reflected in the findings that link warfare propensities to another dimension of state making: border settlements. Dyadic states with settled borders are unlikely to fight one another, and the relationship may hold regardless of the regime types involved.[14] Of course, settled boundaries may not be independent of other factors such as economic development or age in the system. Nonetheless, it is conceivable that our recent and widespread obsession with regime type may prove to be a theoretical dead end—at least vis-à-vis questions about which states fight others and why.

Besides the questions about the causal relationships between war, state making, and regime type, broader questions about war and economic change exist as well. Tilly (1992) emphasized that intervening variables in the war making–state making relationship had to include state approaches to capital-intensive or coercive-intensive economic strategies as well. In short, war making and state making have implications for economic growth both in the short and long term, and, in turn, economic growth has implications for war and state making.

Despite the presence of some studies that have investigated the effects of war on economic growth, we have few findings that encompass all states and all time periods.[15] Outstanding issues still persist about whether there are likely differences between short- and long-term effects—the former are often negative, but the latter are sometimes found to be positive. One way in which war can have long-term positive effects is via the introduction of new technologies which might have been slower to develop otherwise. Unfortunately, this story has yet to be told systematically. Then, there are also the issues about distinctions among different types of war (e.g., global, interstate, and internal). Do all wars impact economic growth the same way, or, as is more likely, do different types of war have different types of impacts?

What we really need, however, are more studies that link war and economic growth to other processes such as state making. One such example is Sobek and Thies' (2010) attempt to integrate war, economic development, and political development through simultaneous modeling.[16] They find that war impacts economic and political development differently. The effect on political development is negative in the short and long term, but the impact on economic development is positive in the short term and negative in the long term. They also find that political development influences war in the short (negatively) and long (positively) term, while economic development affects political development in much the same fashion (negative in the short term and positive in the long term). Some of these findings do not match well with other relationships found in earlier works, but then the earlier findings were not based on simultaneous modeling. Hopefully there will be more attempts to integrate the analysis of multiple war and state making processes.

Another and different type of study is provided by Stubbs (2005), who makes a strong case for situating the contemporary economic success of Japan, South Korea, Taiwan, Hong Kong, Singapore, Malaysia, and Thailand in the context of a series of hot and cold wars that shaped the economic and political institutions of these seven states. He observes a unique sequence of war impacts. First, World War II was mainly destructive. Subsequently, the

Korean War and the early part of the Cold War stimulated developmental outcomes that reinforced the state's ability, along with its economy, to better oppose real and anticipated communist attacks.

Later, Vietnam and the Cold War became associated with a push toward industrialization. As external threats diminished, states came under pressure to reform and redistribute societal resources. Eventually, political institutions liberalized in some but not all of these Asian tigers. Although none of these seven states experienced the same developmental paths, they did develop within a similar geopolitical environment. The bottom line is that state making and economic growth occurred together along with war, and that each of them had reciprocal influences on each other.

What Do We Know and Not Know?

We have good reasons to believe that strong states make war differently (although we may not agree fully on what those differences are) than weak or failed states do. We also know that there is ample evidence to suggest that war and preparations for war have influenced a variety of processes including state making, democratization, and economic growth. On the other hand, there is contradictory evidence that indicates that war and the mobilization for war have not had these effects. More importantly, there is simply much that we do not know just yet. We need to develop deeper causal theories and mechanisms explaining the war making–state making relationships. A host of possible and plausible intervening variables have been suggested—war intensity, topography, ethnic homogeneity, capitalist or coercive state strategies, interstate rivalry, revolutionary ideology, state-elite bargaining strategies, variations in threat environment, industrialized weaponry, and norms against state death. Yet, in most instances, they remain to be tested systematically, either by themselves or in direct comparison to the others that are listed here.

We advocate multivariate tests as opposed to bivariate ones. We have good reasons to believe that war making and state making are embedded in a larger, complex web of activities that encompass inequality, taxation strategies, economic growth, and changes in regime type. A good example of such an approach is Gibler (2007), who situates his argument about the relationship between borders, war, and the democratic peace within an ambitious field of variables. One set of variables focuses on linkages among external threat, economic growth, capital mobility, inequality, and redistributive processes. Another set of variables connects external threat to militarization, government centralization, taxation, and repression costs. These two sets come together around government centralization, taxation, and capital mobility and, at a later point, converge to influence regime type. This work reminds us that we need to develop more ambitious theories that encompass wider parts of the domain pertinent to war making. In fact, it is fair to say that we do not yet know just how large this pertinent domain actually is. Without a doubt, it will be some time before we are in a position to understand its full scope. Perhaps the most efficacious strategy is to go beyond the core war making–state making focus without taking on everything at once. Even so, we will still need ambitious theories to guide our more selective strategies.

What Difference Does War Making–State Making Make to Our Efforts to Explain War?

Whether war making is *the* major or *a* major or even just a *sometime* contributor to state making is an interesting question. Yet, however the question is posed, it may not be fully clear what difference it makes to explaining war behavior. Many scholars who have examined the war making–state making relationship have not been particularly interested in the "causes of war" question. State making, after all, is mostly interesting to comparative scholars who seek to explain various trajectories of state development. However, knowing that states possess varying complexity and effectiveness does not help us to understand what states do with their complexity and effectiveness. In this vein, the war making–state making question may be entirely peripheral to questions about why wars occur.

Although others may indeed agree that war making and state making are peripheral to our understanding of what causes wars, we think a strong case can be made for why this relationship is central to war onset. The critical link is states' capabilities which influence rulers' decisions to initiate or respond to attacks. That capabilities matter to war initiation and victory are well-established propositions. For instance, in an earlier review of the role of capabilities in explaining war, Geller (2000b: 259) states that "explanations of war and peace usually grant a primary position to the power of states and to their relational balances." He goes on to discuss a number of pertinent research programs such as status, relative power cycle, capability balance, power transition, long cycle, polarity, and capability concentration in which capability figures prominently as an explanatory factor. One could also add the many empirical studies that control for capability balances and major power status automatically. To this set, add the many studies that have focused on differentiating strong, weak, and failed states. If all these analyses have capability considerations at their core, we need to be concerned with how states develop (or fail to develop) their capabilities to go to war. It is not something to be assumed, taken for granted, or modeled as a binary variable.

Moreover, wars will have feedback effects on the actors that are most involved and will likely influence the probability of subsequent wars. If engaging in war makes for stronger states, the wars that they engage in are apt to become increasingly influenced by the participation of stronger states. Wars become more lethal, involve more people, range over more space, and may also last longer. Stronger states can extract more resources to pay for larger armies and navies. They can also mobilize larger segments of their populations to participate in warfare, directly or indirectly. Finally, the participation of stronger states on opposing sides will mean that the issues at stake in the conflict will not be settled quickly.

Yet, we have reason to believe that all states do not benefit identically or even similarly from war participation. A number of European and North American states that survived their serial encounters with warfare did indeed become unusually strong. However, many states elsewhere have not become as strong. This pattern points to a possible clue about contemporary warfare. The region(s) with the strongest states no longer war with each other. Despite a few exceptions, European states on the whole have become more unlikely to go to war with other European states. Regions that have very few strong states, on the other hand, either go to war infrequently or tend to fight very short and frequently inconclusive battles. How do we explain this? One possibility is that the war making–state making relationship is curvilinear. Weaker states lack the capabilities to fight external foes long and hard. Considering that these states are still struggling to secure a monopoly of force at home, we should expect to see internal warfare as the norm for weaker states. Meanwhile, long wars that require the mobilization of large numbers of people in conventional combat should be extremely rare in weak states. In marked contrast, stronger states have developed sufficient capabilities to inflict major damage on their adversaries should it come to that. But, as the costs of warfare between stronger states have become increasingly high, stronger states are more reluctant to fight wars with their counterparts. Nor are they all that likely to become embroiled in internal warfare. Nonetheless, stronger states can still be expected to fight weaker states and to become involved in their internal warfare.[17]

Finally, we assert a third reason for the centrality of the war making–state making relationship. We believe that understanding the impacts of war is just as important as, if not more important than, explaining the causes of war onset. Collectively, scholars have argued long and hard about why wars occur. We need to show equal concern for how wars have made a difference to society both in the past and in the present.[18] We believe that explaining state making should be fairly fundamental to our analyses of war behavior.

Although it may not be the most interesting or salient dependent variable for students of international politics, state making will continue to be important so long as states are still around.

Therefore, in terms of our framework (in figure 11.1), the war↔political organization relationship should remain the core focus. However, it is extremely difficult to overlook the reciprocal linkages between political economy, war, and the threat environment. Opening this vein of research is likely to expand our agenda even more dramatically because war and economic change are pervasive sources of societal change. In sum, we expect that the domain of war making–state making analyses will remain elastic as we probe the full extent of war-induced change.

NOTES

1. In a 2003 chapter, Tilly seemed to back away from this scope limitation when he argued that non-European developments might be similar to the European experience. Meanwhile, there is ample evidence that the argument can be applied to North America (Rasler and Thompson 1989; Bensel 1990; Skocpol 1992; Porter 1994; Sparrow 1996; Katznelson and Shefter 2002).

2. We could draw more arrows in figure 11.1, but for now we will keep it simple.

3. We choose to emphasize Tilly's focus on war making–state making, but other earlier and related arguments were put forward by Ardant (1975), Braun (1975), Hintze (1975), and Finer (1975).

4. Although the historical illustrations are usually European, the war making–state making linkage can be extended to the very beginning of warfare (Cioffi-Revilla 2000) and yet equally apply to US developments.

5. While ample amounts of internal conflict are ongoing today, the question about whether states are made or destroyed by internal warfare is a different question altogether.

6. Rasler and Thompson (2009) do not find corroboration for this claim in their examination of extraction rates. They argue instead that one might better anticipate that rivals in the global South will privilege military interests and preferences, handicap economic development, and slow the pace of democratization. Empirically, the 2009 study looks at tax extraction and military spending and finds no support for a systematic rivalry impact on tax extraction. Military spending, however, is significantly and positively affected.

7. This argument is found in Herbst (2000), Heydemann (2000), al-Khafaji (2000), Reno (2003), and Leander (2004).

8. Were it not for the intervention of a non-European state (or two, depending on how one views the Soviet Union) in the upward spiral of European warfare, it is conceivable that only one strong state would have emerged in Europe. Europe also possessed another characteristic that was missing in the Chinese Warring States Era. European great powers were either sea powers or land powers. When a land power

attempted to become the European regional hegemon, the sea powers organized successful blocking coalitions.

9. See and compare Bean (1973), Ames and Rapp (1977), Tilly (1992), Downing (1992), and Ertman (1997).

10. Russett and Oneal (2001) remains the standard reference on the democratic peace.

11. Various types of arguments and evidence are put forward by Layne (1994); Midlarsky (1995); Gates, Knutson, and Moses (1996); Thompson (1996); Mitchell, Gates, and Hegre (1999); and Rasler and Thompson (2005).

12. See Mousseau and Shi (1999); Crescenzi and Enterline (1999); James, Solberg, and Wolfson (2000); Oneal and Russett (2000); and Reiter (2001).

13. Economic interpretations of the democratic peace are hardly monolithic. See Weede (2003), Gartzke (2007), McDonald (2009), and Mousseau (2009).

14. See Gibler (2007; this volume), Rasler and Thompson (2011), and Owsiak (2012) for supportive empirical studies of this contentious border issue.

15. See, for example, recent works by Imai and Weinstein (2000); Anderton and Carter (2001); Murdoch and Sandler (2002); Koubi (2005); and Yamarik, Johnson, and Compton (2010).

16. An earlier effort along similar lines is Colaresi and Thompson (2003).

17. These arguments are advanced at greater length in Levy and Thompson (2011).

18. For more general reviews of war impacts, see Thompson (1993); see Kier and Krebs (2010) for war impacts on democracy.

Chapter Twelve

Future Directions in the Scientific Study of Peace and War

Peter Wallensteen

The seminal Correlates of War research program is now in its fifth decade and continues to generate increasingly complex insights on the conditions that result in interstate war. The number of books, book chapters, articles, and papers that have been produced is impressive. There is no other coherent program of this sort that can look back at a similar track record. To this should be added the scores of professors and teachers at universities around the world who owe their training, dedication, and personal advancement to this remarkable program. The Correlates of War project was conceived as a challenge to established commonsense ways of thinking about international relations, and it turned into an academic revolution of the entire field of peace research, international studies, and political analysis. This chapter departs from the idea that the most appropriate way to contribute to the program's further evolution is to focus on the validity of the chosen approach in some basic regards, particularly in view of achieved results and the way the world appears in the 2010s. It raises issue on the concept of the international system, key actors in the making of war (and peace), and the relations between different types of conflict. This chapter concludes with some reflections on a possible new research program on the Correlates of Peace.

EVOLUTION OF THE INTERSTATE SYSTEM

A basic idea underlying the Correlates of War project was the significance of the international system as a system. The connection to the new ideas of system analysis that were formative in the 1960s is obvious and close. Properties of this system were seen to harbor the ultimate causes of war. This concern was driving some key features of the project, but it did not preclude other approaches. The data generated have turned out to be useful also in analysis that differs dramatically from system analysis. In some key aspects, however, the system approach has remained.

This can primarily be seen in the concern for delimiting the system. Which entities are members, and which units are not? There is a continuous need for such system delimitation. The advent of the UN as a global organization simplified the efforts. The close to two hundred internationally recognized states are definitely core actors in such an international system. The UN in this way helps the effort, although there are another twenty state entities with international recognition that are difficult to handle (ranging from Kosovo and Western Sahara, with diplomatic recognition by three to four dozen other states, to Somaliland with none, but still a more functioning state than, say, Western Sahara). Still, the actual number of participants in the international system is vastly higher. The Uppsala Conflict Data Program (UCDP) Non-State Conflict data set lists more than one thousand entities for a much shorter period than COW covers. The system delineated in COW can perhaps be described as one that focuses on the state systems and relates to other actors as they become relevant for the state actors. It is possible that such a more precisely delimited interstate system could be separated from a global system that has many more types of actors (Small and Singer 1982: 35–36; Wallensteen 2002: ch. 10; Sarkees and Wayman 2010: ch. 1).

More importantly, it raises the question of whether the system is the same one when comparing 2011 to 1816. In other words, is it a unitary system that has remained unchanged in basic dimensions? Clearly there are states in this system, and that provides for a degree of continuity. There are, however, differences that may affect the propensity to initiate war. Some obvious differences are the following:

- Political leaders come into office and are controlled in new ways (democracies were not even a handful in 1816, but constitute at least half of all states in 2011, when rule of law is also a stronger principle than earlier).
- The type of interaction in the system is different (ships and horse rides have been changed to cars, airplanes, and fast trains).
- The dimensions of interdependence are different (the global market is comprehensive; production depends on constant, instantaneous, and safe delivery across vast distances).
- The intensity of information flows is different (going from an eighteenth-century horse-based postal service to twenty-first-century reliance on instant mail, Internet, and social media).
- Major powers and their capabilities have changed dramatically, resulting in concentration in some dimensions (nuclear weapons, global intervention capacity), but also vulnerability in others (small arms, terrorist tactics).

- Dramatic demographic changes since 1816, with a world total population at about 1 billion, compared to almost 7 billion in 2010, and where all of Europe in 1816 had a smaller population than Indonesia in the early 2000s.

The assumption of comparability is still built into any analysis that treats the entire epoch as one unit, but it may be interesting to challenge this notion. This is not an original point, of course. A number of users apply COW data in ways that may indicate that the system actually changes in some fundamental respects.

Some examples, drawn from this volume, suggest that there are important variations in the use of the entire time span, the two hundred years since 1816:

- There is more escalation to war after 1945 (Hensel herein).
- Arms buildup and escalation to war show no relationship during Cold War period (Sample herein).
- The effect of alliances is strongly positive for the 1816–1945 period but negative for the Cold War period. It turns out to be positive again for the post--Cold War period (Kang herein).
- The deterrent effect of defensive alliances ceases to be statistically significant after 1900 (Benson herein).

There are some changes that are undeniably clear—for instance, the advent of nuclear weapons—but it is of course true that the importance of this factor cannot be understood if there is no previous period to compare to, for instance.

- There was no escalation from dispute to war during the Cold War, but there was one instance in the post–Cold War period, suggesting an increased danger of more wars among such states (derived from Geller herein).
- Rivalry development will vary through the period (derived logically from Valeriano herein).
- Norm development will increase with the number of democracies, thus creating new conditions in the international system (derived from Mitchell herein).
- The settlement of territorial issues will stabilize democracies, which thus are increasing over the period (derived from Gibler herein).
- More social-market economies will lead to more peace (Mousseau herein).

This may in fact suggest that there are arguments for differentiating between different system characteristics. Singer observed already in 1972 that this could have some merits for particular types of scientific investigation. Typically, he also noted that such changes between periods had to be "ascertained empirically and not accepted on faith, since each generation tends to exaggerate and misperceive the differences between its own time and that of previous generations" (Singer 1972: 8). It is easy to agree with Singer, and that is why it is interesting that a host of studies have made significant empirical observations that point to such variations in the system. Intellectually it makes a lot of sense, however, to investigate whether correlations could go in one direction at certain times and in the opposite way at others. The alliance-war connection is a case in point, where it was observed early on that it was more connected to major wars in the twentieth century than in the nineteenth, as reported by Kang (herein) but also by others, on older versions of the data. It may, however, only mean that the rigid type of alliances we saw before World War I and World War II failed to deter, whereas the flexible ones during the nineteenth century did. Why there would be such differences is intriguing and thus a good puzzle for researchers to solve.

I have previously argued for three periods, namely (1) 1816 to the end of nineteenth century, (2) from the late nineteenth century to 1945, and then (3) from 1945 to 1989, and I would now like to add (4) the post–Cold War period (Wallensteen 1981, 1984, 2011). This differentiation is primarily built on the number of major powers, arguing that this reflects a variation in the concentration of power, and that this is such an important factor that entire world dynamics change; that is, we can talk about separate systems. However, at these particular junctures there are also other historical changes. For instance, the changes after 1945 seem as great as—or even greater than—those after 1816, which actually is the starting point for the COW interstate system. The changes can be observed on many dimensions, covering political changes based on shifts in geographical control, military capabilities, economic power, and ideological dynamics. Thus, there appear to be many strong logical and historical reasons for delineating separate systems. The strongest may actually be between the periods before and after the Second World War.

However, the original COW conception of the interstate system argues against such a distinction. The "founding fathers," Melvin Small and J. David Singer, write clearly that if a system builds on the same territorial area and the same social entities, it is the same system (Small and Singer 1982: 35). With that view the cutoff at 1816 also can be debated; it could as well be 1649 (after the Westphalian peace agreements) or 1714 (when the treaties constituting the Peace of Utrecht were concluded ending the Spanish War of Succession). In that perspective, shifting major power constellations and other indications of change are only "attributes" of the system, not the markings of system changes.

It is interesting to ask what would then constitute a separate and different system. Clearly, the period before the European states, say the time of a strong Catholic Church (the Middle Ages in European history), would be one, as the social entities are different. The period from 1500 until 1789 may also have been a separate system, as dynasties as well as the pope were actors that often were more important than the states.

These were, of course, fairly regional systems, confined to the European continent. As such, they would be comparatively well documented, but there should at the same time have been different interstate or interentity systems in, say, East Asia, South Asia, Southeast Asia, sub-Saharan Africa, and different areas of the Western Hemisphere. The "global system" of 1816 (Small and Singer 1982: 35) was much less concentrated than the global system of today. The period since 1816 may be marked by the forceful pulling together of all such separate systems into one loosely but still more integrated system than had previously been seen. In fact, much of the nineteenth century's history was exactly about that: the imperial expansion emanating from some few centers in Europe and acquiring control by superior force over the rest of the world. It was a short-lived imperial movement, largely achieved by the end of the nineteenth century and quickly breaking up less than fifty year later, after the Second World War. This gives further arguments for a different delimitation of the periods or systems. The major powers, in particular, changed in composition in terms of geo-, real-, kapital-, and idealpolitik variables (Wallensteen 1981, 2011).

Of course, there can be debates over distinctions based only on the number of major powers. The original COW definition related to the major powers of the system, and it has been observed that they have changed in number and composition at four particular junctures (1816, 1895, 1945, and 1990). For instance, COW added two new major powers around 1990 (Germany and Japan). China, however, was seen as a major power already in 1950 rather than from the early 1990s, something one can discuss. System changes, however, go beyond the mere numbers. One could argue that much more changed when the "leadership" of the system changed. It points in the direction of the internal operations of the states as well as the type of rivalry this could generate among the major powers, for instance.

Let me relate this argument to two additional reflections and then try to reach a preliminary conclusion on the utility of thinking about consecutive systems.

WARS BETWEEN STATES AND WARS WITHIN STATES

In line with the system approach, the focus on COW has been on interstate relations. There are good reasons for that, but this is not possible to derive simply from the sheer number of the different types of war. Sarkees and Wayman (2010) make that clear. Their effort to reform the definition of intrastate wars and their application of this to the full post-Napoleonic era is a major achievement and points in a new direction for the COW program. It brings it closer to the UCDP ambition of having an integrated definition of war, no matter between what parties. The results are also similar, but of course COW covers a period that is three times as long. Sarkees and Wayman (2010) demonstrate that there are 91 interstate wars between 1816 and 2007, compared to more than 330 intrastate wars; that is, intrastate wars are more than three times as common for the whole period. The prevalent focus on interstate war has been explained from another concern: the importance of preventing another interstate conflagration like World War I and World War II. The Cold War made such an occurrence more likely, and thus this was a realistic understanding and a relevant focus. The post–Cold War period, however, gives rise to other priorities for research, for instance, the dangers of devastating civil wars. The international dimension of this is also clear, as there are various effects derived from such wars (refugee flows, arms flows, terrorism, etc.). Frequencies—even when measured for a long period—are not necessarily a good guide to the future, and thus there is no reason to drop any of these types of conflict. The new data instead provides an argument for studying possible connections between the two. That could be seen as a new challenge for COW. With the project's insights on interstate relations as a basis, hypotheses could be developed on the connections between different configurations of power and their impact on the likely occurrence of intrastate conflict and war.

This means, however, that there has to be an epistemological shift away from a system theory approach, building on states with equal properties, to inject a more asymmetrical perspective. The argument could follow a logic like this one: Major powers are not only concerned about challenges stemming from other major powers; they are also attentive to minor disputes, particularly in their own "sphere" of influence. They could be perceived as "tests" by the other side, or as "denials" of the willpower of the majors. There are many additional ways of thinking of such asymmetric relations. It would suggest that in times of heavy rivalry and unclear interstate power relations, there will be more concern for interstate relations, thus leading to lesser involvement in intrastate conflict, which consequently also might be fewer (as there is less interest in supplying weapons from major powers, for instance). In periods of less rivalry, such intrastate conflicts will have more attention, and support in different forms will flow more generously. In terms of frequencies, for instance, there would be a variation.

To demonstrate the fruitfulness of such an approach, we can use the new COW data. Sarkees and Wayman (2010) have made a heroic effort in redoing all the codings for intrastate wars in COW, increasing the total number dramatically. It certainly provides a new picture of the era since 1816, and this image has considerable face validity. It is also interesting to see that this work also separates between different types of intrastate wars, based on motives and goals (Sarkees and Wayman 2010: 339), in ways that strongly remind one of the distinctions in the UCDP data between conflicts over the control of territory versus over government (Wallensteen 2002 gives the theoretical explanation for this; it has been applied in UCDP at least since Wallensteen and Axell 1993). Bringing the intrastate war data together with the interstate war results is table 12.1 (Wallensteen 2011).

Table 12.1 shows that interstate wars were not the most frequent type of war in any of the periods. As mentioned above, they seldom are more than one-quarter of all conflicts. However, they may have a higher potential of escalating to major wars, thus being a legitimate concern. The results in table 12.1 are, however, consonant with the hypothesis that major power rivalry will be inversely correlated with interstate conflict. The interregional period is the one with the most major powers, the unclear relations in terms of power distribution, and also the most interstate conflicts (still not more than a third of all wars). The global period with the balance of power between the major powers, then, resembles the previous period of balance of power: the post-Napoleonic nineteenth century. The balance of power systems may have been different (highly polarized and stable during the Cold War, highly flexible and with shifting alliances during the nineteenth century). For the leading elites, the issue of interventions in various situations in "distant" places was a major concern in both of these periods. The dangers of another world war

Table 12.1.   Historical Systems, Inter- and Intrastate Wars; Correlates of War Data, 1816–2007

System	Time	Length of Period, Years	Number of Interstate Wars	Number of Intrastate Wars	Intrastate War of All Wars (%)
Eurocentric	1816–1895	80	27	103	79.2
Interregional	1896–1944	49	30	59	66.3
Global	1945–1989	45	29	111	79.3
Post–Cold War	1990–2007	18	9	61	87.1

Source: Sarkees and Wayman 2010.
Notes: The column to the right includes all intrastate war as percentage of all intra- and interstate wars for each period. The totals for interstate wars are 95 and for intrastate wars 334 (not 335 as reported in Sarkees and Wayman 2010: 341).

might have been seen as contained through different mechanisms. First, it was done by the flexibility of the alliance patterns in the nineteenth century (no allies were completely committed to a particular alliance; there could always be shifts—indeed COW data show that alliances were of a much shorter duration in this period). Second, the fear of nuclear war in the Cold War increased attention to internal conflicts elsewhere, as demonstration of commitments to the resolve of the alliance.

Furthermore, table 12.1 shows that the present period is markedly different from any of its predecessors: almost nine out of ten wars are internal to a state in the period since 1990. The features of the international system that explain this can be discussed. If we describe it as a unipolar system, it implies that the lack of rivals also means that there is less interest in internal conflicts from a strategic perspective. Instead, a humanitarian concern may have taken its place. This, then, would be entirely new to global affairs. And indeed, the period since 1989 is full of new concepts pointing to this: principles of humanitarian intervention, responsibility to protect, conflict prevention, democracy promotion, gender and peace, peace building, climate change and peace. The research agenda has become different, and that reflects a changed reality away from nuclear weapons, balance of power and terror, second- and first-strike capabilities, credibility of alliances, détente, confidence-building measures, arms control, and other concepts that often were central to Cold War analysis. These notions still retain significance, of course, as the nuclear weapons have not disappeared but instead have spread to more actors. However, they are lower down on a busy policy agenda, and on researchers' agendas.

These findings challenge conventional thinking and lead to new questions of research, not the least the one suggested by Rasler and Thompson (herein) that fewer interstate wars will make for more weak states, thus creating increasing intrastate conflict, unless there can be other ways of building strong states.

These reflections support each other. It might be meaningful to describe the periods as four different systems, even to the point that one may wonder how much can be learned from one system to the next. One could, for instance, argue along the following lines. The intense rivalries of the second period were different from those of the first period. The interregional period was dominated by an internally driven ambition of unlimited expansion on the part of several major powers, even at the expense of the interests of other major powers. To the "old" dominants, it was no longer possible, for instance, to accept power transitions as it was in the first period. Negotiations and deals that were typical of the nineteenth century, including the partition of countries, no longer worked, even though they were attempted (as in Ethiopia in 1935–1936 and Munich in 1938). Similarly, the third, global system saw dynamics that were different from the interregional (second) period, although the parallels were frequent in public rhetoric. In fact, the global system may have been very different and also ended in a completely different way (where détente polices played a central role). This, then, would suggest that the lessons from the Cold War might not have much to say to the political actors of the post–Cold War era. Preventive war and preemptive strikes, for instance, have a completely different meaning. Politics may no longer be a matter of replacing a leader in an intransigent country, without concern for legitimacy and processes. This would be an argument that supports the analytical distinctions between different systems, for the entire post-Napoleonic era. In a way this gives a good argument for studying the full period after 1816, as this allows comparisons along the temporal dimension. One conclusion is that scholars would benefit from studying the whole epoch, but do that while searching for different patterns through the era, not just for similarities and generalities. However, this also leads to a third reflection: what about the "extrasystem" actors?

WARS WITH THE "OUTSIDERS"

It is time to bring in the war making that goes on outside the "central" interstate system (Small and Singer 1982: 36). What is often seen as the periphery seldom has been part of the COW analysis. The dangers of another world war between the strongest members of the international system made this focus reasonable during the Cold War. However, looking at the full war picture today, it means not incorporating a significant element of war activity. The situation for analysis now has changed thanks to the new data on "extrastate wars" produced by Sarkees and Wayman (2010: 193–336). Table 12.2 uses the same system categories as table 12.1 but now relates interstate wars to

Table 12.2. Historical Systems, Inter- and Extrastate Wars; Correlates of War Data, 1816–2007

System	Time	Length of Period, Years	Number of Interstate Wars	Number of Extrastate Wars	Extrastate War of All Wars (%)
Eurocentric	1816–1895	80	27	98	78.4
Interregional	1896–1944	49	30	42	58.3
Global	1945–1989	45	29	18	38.3
Post–Cold War	1990–2007	18	9	5	35.7

Source: Sarkees and Wayman 2010.
Notes: The column to the right shows extrastate war as percentage of all extra- and interstate wars for each period. The totals for interstate wars are 95 and for extrastate wars 163.

extrastate wars. The generic definition of this category of war is that it involves "the fighting by a state system member outside its borders against the
armed forces of an entity that is not a member of the interstate system." Often
this covers actors that are ethnic or tribal, but also terrorist groups (e.g., al-
Qaida). We would expect important differences among the four systems also
with respect to this factor. Table 12.2 brings that out very clearly.

The differences over time are remarkable and give further support for
including this category into the analysis. The extrastate wars are not only
many more than the interstate wars, but their number also brings out the
importance of including colonialism in scholarly work on war. Table 12.2
shows that three-quarters of all uses of armed force outside a state's borders
were in colonial wars during the 1800s. Certainly this would support a notion
that European relative "peace" was related to colonial expansionism. Keeping influence in the system by acquiring territory in faraway places (from the
center's perspective) was obviously an important goal for many of the leading
states. It also resulted in considerable rivalry between them, with increasing
dangers of spilling over into interstate war. Furthermore, table 12.2 shows
that colonial wars continued right up to the Second World War, suggesting
that the idea of the value of colonialism did not really end until that very war.
In the post-1945 world, extrastate wars are fewer even than interstate wars,
which in turn (as was demonstrated in table 12.1) were much fewer than
intrastate conflicts. The extrastate wars of the post–World War II period are
also often related to independence struggles initiated by actors representing
the colonized peoples (liberation movements). The creation as well as elimination of colonialism was related to considerable warfare.

The data of table 12.2 strongly suggests that the periods are very different
and that the priorities of leading decision makers with respect to war may
have varied considerably throughout this period. Again, we could make a
hypothetical argument such as the following. If the main priority for international action in much of the nineteenth century focused on military "expedi-
tions" for colonial expansion, it may have given the major powers an interest
in managing conflicts in their own neighborhoods with more caution, and
through alliance politics rather than confrontations. The agenda of decision
makers may have been different, although governments may have had a division of labor between, say, "foreign affairs," dealing with other major powers, and "colonial offices," dealing with the typical asymmetric conflicts of
the day. From the point of view of military staff, however, war planning had
to consider the use of scarce resources for either purpose.

Furthermore, tables 12.1 and 12.2 point to the importance of one particular
break, the one at the end of the Second World War. The year 1945 emerges
as an important turning point, parallel to the one in 1816. The fact, however,

that we have data for the entire period is the only way to make clear that there are such marked differences. It makes it important to continuously introduce a control variable in computations in the study of the causes of war. It is likely, as has already been documented, that this will affect many of the results about the onset and magnitudes of war.

Still, the arguments focus on the major actors, the big powers. They are seen as highly cohesive and pursuing purposeful policies with respect to international action. However, that might be troubling and leads us to consider the domestic side of major power action.

WARS FROM "WITHIN" THE STATE

A basic notion in the state system conception is that the building blocks of the system, the states, remain the same. They have a stable quality that makes it possible to think of the system as comparable over time. Certainly, their names may change, and so may their territory, but on the whole their basic characteristics remain the same throughout the period. Indeed, this is true for many of the major powers. Only a few have disappeared, most notably Austria, which first became Austria-Hungary and then divided into present-day Austria, Hungary, and a number of other successor states. However, the very struggle for survival of this particular entity may have been a key variable in explaining some of the wars, not the least the outbreak of World War I, and thus the threat perceptions of such "weak" major powers may have particularly strong effects on the operation of the system.

By many criteria, Britain and France should also be seen as less than major powers today, but that is rarely the case. The extent of their influence now, however, is very different from 1816 or their peak of power at the beginning of the twentieth century.

The addition of new actors, surpassing some of the older ones, leaves a clear mark on the system. China was not seen as a system member in 1816 (only since 1860, Sarkees and Wayman 2010: 19) and is today the world's second-largest economy. Italy and Japan are states that were not counted in 1816, were of crucial importance one hundred years later, but were dropped as major powers in the Second World War, and are of lesser importance for international security as we approach the hundredth anniversary of the outbreak of World War I.

Furthermore, we may today see a set of emerging states with increasing capabilities in economic terms as well as in regional significance. India and Brazil both aspire to leading positions, including seats on the UN Security Council, and can muster considerable support for their aspirations.

These shifts among major powers relate to the internal dynamics of these countries. Domestic power is the basis for a state's leaders and is likely to be their absolute main concern. History is likely to be an important source for legitimacy for such regimes. It is remarkable to see the extent of intrastate confrontations that even major powers have been exposed to. For instance, some major powers have been known to be fragile along ethnic lines (as was the case of Austria-Hungary), and others have had repeated experiences of localized ethnic revolts (Russia and China throughout the period, and the United Kingdom with Irish revolutionaries). Still others have seen regimes replaced through popular insurrections or coups (France in 1830, 1848, 1870, and 1958; Austria in 1848; Germany in 1919 and 1933; and the Soviet Union in 1991), and some have had the formative experiences of civil war (China at many occasions in this period, the United States in the mid-nineteenth century, and Russia in 1917–1921). Exactly what effect this experience will have on a country's way of reacting to new threats or emerging interstate conflicts is not easily determined. There can be variations between universalist and particularist approaches (Wallensteen 1984, 2011). Those suggesting the former outcome would argue that a country with a fractured internal political life would prefer to have a benign external environment as external conflict involvement might generate internal strains. However, there is also an argument for a particularist approach saying that the regime would like to preempt possible challenges from the outside that may instigate internal uprising. Even how regimes deal with internal conflicts may vary in important ways, ranging between cooperative and repressive strategies. Indeed, the external environment may very well influence also the choice of domestic strategy. In other words, there is a rich field of inquiry in how interstate issues relate to intrastate situations. This provides an additional new field of international peace research. The new information from COW as well as the detailed data at UCDP covering the post–World War II period allows for such important and pathbreaking studies.

The point here, however, is not only that there is permanency as well as shifts in the composition of the leaderships. It is also that the shifts in themselves will have an impact on the frequency of interstate war (and possibly also on intra- and extrastate wars).

TOWARD THE CORRELATES OF PEACE

Exploring the temporal dimension and expanding the universe of wars for analysis suggests an important new direction in the search for correlates of war. For instance, the finding that rivalry termination leads to a concern for interstate peace building points in that direction (Diehl and Goertz herein). However, the focus is on explanations of war. The underlying hope, however, has all along been to find conclusions for peace. If we know the origins of war, the argument goes, preferably across time and space, we would also have general insights into how to create peace. When the central variables have been identified, it then becomes a matter of developing the right strategies for peace. However, even if we know that arms races might lead to war, or that certain types of alliance patterns among major powers increase the risk of war, this is not the same as knowing what to do. The arguments in favor of arms buildups or alliances are not only based on peace but also on security. The risks may be understood by decision makers, but the risks in changing strategy may be seen as higher. Thus, there is a need also to think about and do research on the alternatives. What would be appropriate strategies for ending arms races or replacing alliances with more inclusive organizations, for instance? Most of all, we would need to demonstrate that this results in gains both with respect to the likelihood of lasting peace and for immediate security concerns.

These examples are drawn from the interstate system. There are probably considerable lessons to be drawn from détente policies, as a way of reducing tension between major powers and creating openings for agreements. But it may be a very narrow peace, one that could build on continued domestic repression, for instance. This is why intra- and extrastate conflict patterns also have to be part of the analysis. Would détente policies also favor internal changes that enhance peace and security within major powers? The reform policies in the Soviet Union initiated in the mid-1980s required relaxation in tension with the West. The West was willing to provide that, which in turn contributed to make reform policies undermine communist rule from the inside, as witnessed in Europe in 1989. It also led to the ending of a number of extrastate wars where Cold War tension had resulted in protracted conflict (e.g., in Namibia, Afghanistan, and Cambodia). The reduction in external tension, in other words, may contribute to internal changes, which also may contribute to changes in interstate relations. Such complicated relationships point to the importance of thinking in terms of correlates of peace. Actions for peace have been undertaken throughout the period and should, in principle, also be possible to study in a systematic way. Data on war endings are already available and give some clues, but new data may have to be generated.

A related observation is that not all areas or states of the world are equally involved in all types of conflict. For interstate and extrastate wars, we might see a much more concentrated pattern of war participation (some few major powers appearing in proportionally high numbers), while intrastate wars may display a different pattern (for one, the total number of such wars is higher than the other two categories put together). Thus there are states and regions that display different patterns. If they are made the focus of analysis, new insights might be gained. A case in point is the new project on "East Asia in Peace?" starting from the empirical observation that East Asia has seen thirty years without war since 1980, after having experienced decades of war before that (Tønnesson 2011). Obviously, peace is generated in a different way in East Asia than, say, in Europe. Again, profound insights might be discovered.

This points to the importance of thinking of peace building, not just as a matter of intrastate peace building, reflecting the many and repeated experiences of intrastate war, but also interstate peace building. How should regional dynamics be changed so as to allow not only for one particular state to recover, but also for that recovery to be supported by simultaneous developments in neighboring countries? The changes from the intrastate wars in Central America of the 1980s to relative peace since the mid-1990s rested on the idea of regional and parallel developments.

Thus, the Correlates of War needs a corollary program on the Correlates of Peace. This is a testimony to advances in the study of war. We know more about the way wars come about. We also need to know how to make peace from this. And peace, furthermore, has to be understood as a broad and inclusive peace. It is quality peace that is in demand, and scientists need to respond to this challenge.

NOTE

This chapter has benefited from the comments at the "What Do We Know about War?" workshop, University of Illinois, Urbana-Champaign, October 15–16, 2010, as well as the panel presentation on the same theme at the International Studies Association Convention, Montreal, Canada, March 17, 2011. In particular, comments by Zeev Maoz and Stein Tønnesson are gratefully acknowledged. The responsibility for the content, however, rests solely with the author.

Chapter Thirteen

Normal Science and Open Questions

Reflections on the Study of Peace and War, 2001–2011

Zeev Maoz

John Vasquez pointed out eleven years ago that we have "islands of find-ings" about the factors that either increase or decrease the probability of war (Vasquez 2000). I think this is an understatement of the knowledge we have about the factors that affect the likelihood of war. We have a fair amount of cumulative evidence regarding how territorial conflict, enduring rivalries, arms races, alliances, power transitions, and democratic peace help answer Bremer's question, "Who fights whom, when, and why?" (Bremer 2000).

The good news is that ten years later, we have generated considerably more knowledge on these matters. This is due to better data, increased sophistica-tion in research methods, and careful replication and extension of existing knowledge. In effect, the principal characteristic of the research on war and peace over the last decade has been its "normal science" nature. Much of the research on these factors has expanded these islands of knowledge. The bad news is threefold. First, these are still islands—the connection between them on either a theoretical or empirical level is weak to nonexistent. Second, the expansion of empirical knowledge within this normal science came largely at the expense of a more profound theoretical understanding of the process leading to (or away from) war. Third, the repeated focus on questions that had been rehashed (and some in my view had been answered quite convincingly) came at the expense of exploration of some central puzzles on war and peace that have been left largely unexplored.

In the following pages, I discuss what I consider to be the main achieve-ments of the research on war and peace over the past two decades. The main focus is on the reasons for such progress. I then examine some of the pitfalls and shortcomings of research on war and peace. Finally, I will outline some of the key challenges for scholars in the coming years. These are one person's assessments, and they can and should be questioned. Nevertheless, it would

271

be a good idea to consider some or all of these points when teaching courses on the scientific study of war and peace, and when contemplating research on these issues in the future.

MAIN ACHIEVEMENTS OF RESEARCH
ON WAR AND PEACE, 2001–2011

The key observation about war and peace research over the last decade is that it evolved into a normal science. Much of the research on these topics in previous decades has been largely scattered in terms of its theoretical and empirical foci. In contrast, the current decade saw a large number of studies building on and extending previous studies. This is reflected in substance, method, and replication. The key factors that had been found to be correlated with the probability of war and peace have been repeatedly tested and retested over the past decade. In some cases, the level of confidence in previous results was elevated. In other cases, debates on certain empirical results persist. By and large, we can confidently say that we know more about the correlates of war today than we knew a decade ago. This does not mean, however, that the overall level of knowledge has expanded by orders of magnitude. Rather, we have made linear improvement in our knowledge thanks to new and expanded data, better and more sophisticated methodologies, and more disciplined research. I outline some of these key islands of knowledge.

First, an important research focus—unfortunately not represented in this volume—concerns the bargaining literature on war. This literature views war as a bargaining failure—an inability or unwillingness of states to reach an agreement on a division of one or more assets (Fearon 1995). Since this literature is reviewed in greater detail elsewhere (Maoz and Siverson 2008), I do not elaborate on it here. I will point out, however, some of the main advances in this line of research. The initial approach focused on war as a risky lottery that can emerge as one of the possible outcomes of a bargaining process. These studies—originating with the observation that states on both sides enter into combat with the belief that they can get from war more than what they could get from negotiations (Blainey 1988)—viewed war outbreak as an end result. Their focus was on modeling the conditions under which this outcome emerged as an equilibrium (Fearon 1995; Powell 1999, 2002).

The development of this literature in the last decade consisted of three related trends. First, several extensions of the basic bargaining model included insertion of domestic political factors into the bargaining equation (Schultz 2001) and more sophisticated analyses of the role of information, audience costs, and commitment issues (Powell 2006). Second, recent bargaining models combine prewar bargaining with war bargaining, focusing on the idea that states that decide whether to accept a settlement before the war starts are engaged in a process of strategic anticipation regarding the management and termination of the war. This process defines not only their choice of war as opposed to a prewar settlement; it also affects the strategies they use to manage the war and their decision of whether, how, and when to terminate it (Filson and Werner 2002, 2004; Slantchev 2003, 2004; Powell 2004; Smith and Stam 2004). These models showed how different factors that enter into war-related calculations—such as estimates of resolve and capabilities, or regime type—affect the probability of war outbreak and the duration and outcomes of war. Second, empirical tests of these models provided support for the key propositions. Such tests show that the likelihood of victory for initiators of war diminishes as the war prolongs. They also offered explanations for war initiation under conditions of capability inferiority (Slantchev 2004). More general tests of expected utility and game theoretic models of wars yielded mixed results (Bennett and Stam 2004), although a great deal of empirical research remains to be done in order to test some of the key propositions of such models.

The value of the bargaining models of war should be quite evident at this point. First, they outline a decision-related calculus by rational leaders in which war is seen as a failure of bargaining. The more recent versions of these models allow for bounded rationality approaches to enter the picture. However, they also envision prewar bargaining to be affected by strategic anticipation of the war outcomes. This anticipation is revised as the war progresses. The combination of prewar bargaining with war management models is extremely useful. It allows a broader understanding of the war process than previously envisioned. On the other hand, the problems with this literature are also significant (Maoz and Siverson 2008: 175–76). In terms of war outbreak, these models may account for the logic that drives dyadic wars, or wars that are expected to be dyadic. They do not account for expectations of actors regarding third-party behavior in the manner that early rational choice models of war (e.g., Bueno de Mesquita 1981) have done. Nor do they provide insights about war joining.

The quantitative literature has made several strides. First and foremost, most analyses of the new decade were performed on new and improved data sets on topics that have been the center of research in the previous period. These include data sets on rivalries (Thompson 2001; Klein, Goertz, and Diehl 2006); alliances (Gibler and Sarkees 2004; Leeds 2005a); territorial, river, and maritime issues (Hensel, Mitchell, et al. 2008); international organizations (Pevehouse, Nordstrom, and Wranke 2004); and trade (Barbieri, Keshk, and Pollins 2008; Gleditsch 2002b). This was accompanied by updates of the COW capability, national entities, diplomatic representation, and the Polity data set (Marshall and Jaggers 2004). All the variables included in these data sets featured prominently in the quantitative literature of the 1990s. They continue to be the principal correlates of wars in the studies of this volume as well as in the major publications of the first decade of the twenty-first century.

Second, we have seen significant increase in the sophistication of the methods used to estimate models of war outbreak. In particular, the extant studies of war outbreak have paid more attention to possible violations of the assumptions underlying the simpler models of war of the previous decade. Since most analyses of these issues used the nation year or dyad year as the principal unit of analysis, time dependence and unit dependence are a particular threat to inferences in such cases. Fixes for possible violations of these assumptions—such as the binary time-series cross-sectional (BTSCS) approach proposed by Beck, Katz, and Tucker (1998)—were employed. Other methodological controversies included the control variables issue (Achen 2005; Oneal and Russett 2005; Ray 2005). In most cases, however, robustness tests vindicated the inference drawn from the earlier analyses of dangerous dyads (Bremer 1992) or the democratic peace (Maoz and Russett 1993; Russett and Oneal 2001).

Third, additional replications of previous research allowed us to better define the limits of our knowledge. For example, the lack of a monadic democratic peace was better refined in analyses examining directed dyads (e.g., Peceney, Beer, and Sanchez-Terry 2002; Reiter and Stam 2003) with better regime classification than the ones given in the classical Polity data set.

SOME DRAWBACKS

Normal science has its uses if it helps advance knowledge even within a given paradigm, and even if this advancement of knowledge is only marginal. However, some of the aspects of this normalcy have and should be called into question. Several problems that had plagued research on war in the previous decade tend to afflict much of the research of the current decade. Some of these problems may explain the persistence of important controversies in the literature. I would like to highlight here three issues: (1) a continued disconnect between theory and testing, (2) methods that rest on problematic or even flawed assumptions, and (3) excessive focus on the dyadic unit of analysis resulting in lack of attention to context.

Some of the leading models of the causes of war imply a more or less complex process that spells out a sequence of "steps" or processes leading to war. A major example is the "steps-to-war" approach spearheaded by Vasquez (Vasquez 1993; Senese and Vasquez 2008). The idea is quite compelling. There are some underlying issues that create a potential for conflict among states. Chief among them are territorial issues. These issues create an atmosphere of tension, particularly if they entail unilateral or bilateral claims. This tension causes states to prepare for war—by arming themselves. They also create continued hostility and suspicion that induces a rivalry. In order to deal with such security threats, states seek alliances. These alliances in some instances may serve as deterrents, but in others they increase tensions. Such tensions give rise to disputes. These disputes are far more likely to escalate to war, the more "steps" or factors that increase tension are present. So the theory spells out a dynamic process. Some factors—such as democracy and economic interdependence—may offset tensions, but it is not clear how this happens both in theory and in empirical research.

However, the tests of this theory (e.g., Senese and Vasquez 2008) are essentially static, broken down into a set of binary tests or multivariate analyses in which all variables are introduced simultaneously. This creates not only a significant disconnect between the dynamic nature of the theory and the empirical tests; it dilutes the theory and may in fact lead to erroneous inferences. Even if all of the factors entailed in the steps-to-war model turn out to be related empirically to war outbreak (and they generally are), we do not know if the sequence matters. In fact, what is required here is a set of tests that employs either structural equation models or selection processes.

A similar problem characterizes some of the debates that mark studies in this volume. Consider the arms race/rivalry debate. Sample (this volume) characterizes this debate nicely: "The steps-to-war thesis contends that arms races, as one step on the realist road to war, have an independent impact on the likelihood that two states will go to war. . . . Much of the rivalry literature to date, in contrast, has argued that arms races have no independent causal relationship with war. Rather, they emerge as symptoms of an ongoing rivalry, so that there may be a statistical relationship between arming and war when the dynamics of the rivalry are not taken into account, but the relationship largely disappears when they are." However, here too, the question of whether rivalries lead to arms races which increase the probability of war or whether arms races increase the probability of rivalry (or whether the process is recursive) is not really tested.

Yet another example concerns some arguments on whether democracy is a cause of peace or whether the relationship between democracy and peace reflects a spurious relationship (see, for example, Thompson 1996). Two chapters in this volume make the spurious correlation argument (Mousseau, Gibler, this volume). However, the tests they present or review do not allow any meaningful inference with respect to their claims. To test the claim that the settlement of territorial disputes generates decentralized polities which in turn avoid conflict with each other requires a structural equations model or a selection approach. The same applies to the capitalist peace argument. The only test of the Thompson (1996) proposition in a dynamic setting was Maoz (2006), which in fact provided support for the democratic peace thesis.

Testing dynamic models that entail staged processes within single-equation models is not only methodologically unsound; it is substantively misleading. While this practice could be explained as a characteristic of an exploratory stage of research, it is no longer suitable to a maturing field. Creating a stronger connection between theoretical claims and empirical tests presents, therefore, a key challenge of this literature in the coming years.

Another aspect of the "normal science" nature of the research on war over the past decade was the nearly exclusive focus on the dyad as the principal unit of analysis. For many purposes, the dyadic level is the proper unit. But this focus carries several adverse implications. Here are some points. First and foremost, while BTSCS fixes allowed overcoming some of the issues associated with longitudinal models, there is an important issue of complex spatial dependence. Specifically, both of the factors that may account for behavior in a given dyad or the dyadic behavior itself might be—and typically are—affected by the dependence of the dyad in question on other dyads or sets of dyads. The complexity of such dependence stems from the characteristic of the network or networks that emerge from sets of dyadic relations (Cranmer and Desmarais 2011; Cranmer, Desmarais, and Menninga 2012). Because of that, models that attempt to explain dyadic behavior without conceptualizing and accounting for complex dependencies are not only methodologically problematic; they are also substantively questionable.

A related problem with the near exclusive focus on dyads is the neglect of systemic processes that emerge from a web of dyadic relations but that also have an important impact on dyadic relations. Consider, for example, the effect of dramatic shifts in the structure of the international system and their effects on some of the key factors of the steps-to-war model. We typically take territorial issues to be an important underlying cause of rivalries, militarization and arms races, and latent hostility. So one would think that the presence, absence, or severity of territorial claims is a key exogenous variable in the process leading states to war (e.g., Vasquez 1993; Hensel, Mitchell, et al. 2008; Senese and Vasquez 2008). However, many of the territorial claim cases emerged with the rise of new states. New states tended to rise following processes of imperial collapse. Some—but not all—of these imperial downfalls came in the wake of major wars. So the number and nature of territorial claims are not really exogenous to the steps-to-war process; systemic shocks may have a profound effect on that as well. The important linkage between state making and war making that Rasler and Thompson (this volume) discuss is also subject to such systemic processes that affect the type and magnitude of state formation and state collapse.

Likewise, certain types of dyadic factors (on both the right-hand side and the left-hand side of the war equation) may induce systemic processes. We know that democratization has dyadic effects. We also know that democratization comes in cycles (Starr 1991; Starr and Lindborg 2003). So the cross-level connection between democracies and war may have systemic implications that are not visible if we examine the systemic democratic peace proposition in simple aggregate terms (Maoz 2011: ch. 8). One of the key implications of network analytic approaches in international relations research is its potential for creating systematic linkages across levels of analysis. This offers new opportunities for resolving long-standing puzzles in war research (Maoz 2011, 2012).

Finally, and this is a long-standing complaint of mine (Maoz 2009b), we have not yet focused in any systematic manner on what I consider to be a key puzzle in war research, namely, the fightaholism phenomenon. Specifically, it is an established fact that a small fraction of all states is responsible for a vast majority of the wars in the system. The same states tend to fight over and over again (typically against the same enemies). On the other hand, a majority of all states have not fought at all throughout their history. The huge inequality in the distribution of wars over states is a structural phenomenon that calls for new approaches and new theories focusing on structural tendencies of states. The paucity of research on this topic continues to be a problem in war research.

CONCLUSION

The balance sheet of war research during this decade is not as good as it was a decade ago. The improvements in methods, data, and models are indeed impressive, but this progress is outweighed by the failure to meet the central challenges of the research in previous years. In particular, four challenges need to become the center of attention of war research in the coming decade.

1. *Systematic modeling of dynamic processes leading to and away from war.* We need to move away from single-equation models of war where all factors that are said to account for the process leading states, dyads, regions, or systems to war are thrown into the right-hand side. This approach misrepresents the substantive content of various theories. Moving

to multi-equation models (either structural equations or selection models) poses serious methodological challenges, but past experience suggests that such challenges could be successfully confronted. Both methodological innovations of the recent past and substantive insights that may emerge from this shift may yield important results. Alternative research strategies given such complexity are agent-based models. These models can overcome some of the methodological complications of multi-equation models. They have also several distinct advantages. First, they can better capture causally hypothesized sequences. Second, they can provide a better approximation to experimental designs in that they allow for analysis of counterfactuals which data-based approaches do not. Finally, they can capture complexities that are masked by statistical models.

2. *Dealing with complex dependencies.* In this case, too, the focus on dyadic units seems to have reached the point of diminishing marginal returns. The failure to incorporate complex dependencies into our analysis of dyads and the assumption that dyadic behavior is independent of network-related context is not only methodologically problematic; it is substantively questionable. The solution to this problem is not only the adoption of such network analytic methods as exponential random graph models (ERGMs) (Cranmer and Desmarais 2011). A more profound understanding of how networks affect dyadic behavior is needed. The growing impact of network research on international relations (Hafner-Burton, Kahler, and Montgomery 2009; Maoz 2011: ch. 1) suggests some ways of dealing with these problems, but other strategies can and should be explored.

3. *Exploring cross-level effects and implications.* We need to spend a greater effort in exploring both cross-level causes and cross-level implications in the study of war. Here, too, network approaches may offer a great deal of potential. Previous cross-level puzzles in war research—such as the democratic peace puzzle or the interdependence-conflict puzzle—were the stuff of acute debates in the discipline. However, recent research applying network models and measures made substantial advances in resolving them (Maoz 2009a, 2011: ch. 8). Understanding the impact of systemic shocks on the causes or correlates of war—especially those which we treat as underlying causes—is an important task of future research.

4. *Explaining inequalities in the propensity to fight.* The a priori probability of war is not the same across states. The structural tendency of some states to fight repeatedly and of others to systematically avoid conflict is—in my view—the single most important puzzle in the study of war. We need to pay much more attention to this puzzle. Failure to make significant headway in resolving it would make many of our other findings relatively unimportant when all is said and done.

We certainly know more about war than we knew a decade ago. We know significantly more about war than we knew two decades ago. However, this progress should not make us complacent; the challenges that lie ahead are as significant as the progress we have made. The good news is that we have much better data, much better tools, and models to confront such challenges. Our graduate students and young scholars are better trained both theoretically and methodologically than we have been; they also have better tools at their disposal than we had ten, twenty, or thirty years ago. So the outlook is promising.

NOTE

For the sake of full disclosure, my criticism of war research in the last decade refers to my own research as well as to others' scholarship. I do not consider my research to be an exception to the critical observations made here.

Chapter Fourteen

The "Paths-to-War" Concept

Jack S. Levy

The chapters in part 1 of this volume focus on "factors that increase the probability of war," including territorial contiguity and disputes, alliances, arms races, rivalry, and related variables. The implicit logic underlying most of these analyses, individually and collectively, is that the more of these factors that are present and the higher their magnitude, the higher the probability of war. The more intense a territorial conflict, rivalry, or arms race, the greater the probability of war.[1] In addition, a higher value of one variable can compensate for a lower value of another variable. Thus, these factors collectively constitute an additive linear model of the probability of war.

The chapters in part 2 focus on "factors that promote peace" and include discussions of the deterrent role of nuclear weapons and of the democratic peace, including related hypotheses about the market capitalist peace and the territorial peace.[2] The implicit causal logic underlying these chapters is different from that in part 1. The form of the relationship between the independent variable and the onset of war is not additive and linear. The authors do not argue that the more democratic a state (or a pair of states), the greater the probability of peace, or that the greater the number and destructiveness of nuclear weapons, the greater the probability of peace. Instead of more being significantly better, some is enough. The argument is that dyads consisting of two minimally democratic states never (or almost never) go to war with each other, and that a reasonably secure nuclear deterrent, however modest, prevents war between the two parties.

Moreover, the presence of more than one of these factors does not significantly increase the likelihood of peace. Adding a nuclear deterrent to each side of a democratic dyad does not make them significantly more peaceful. Joint democracy is close to a sufficient condition for peace, regardless of what other factors are present. The same is true for nuclear deterrents. The factors in this section do not just "promote" peace; they very nearly guarantee it. Collectively, these factors do not constitute an additive linear model. Instead, peace within a dyad can arise *either* from two democratic states *or* from two reasonably secure nuclear deterrents. These are two alternative paths to peace.

Thus the form of the hypothesized causal relationships between independent and dependent variables differs in parts 1 and 2 of this volume. Hypotheses in the first are additive and linear, whereas those in the second are not. The first proposes what is essentially a single path to war, consisting of the additive combination of many different variables, whereas the second suggests several analytically distinct paths to peace.[3]

EQUIFINALITY AND MULTIPLE PATHS TO WAR

The idea of multiple causal paths goes back to general systems theory and the concept of *equifinality*).[4] Bertalanffy (1968) contrasted open systems, which interact with other systems and with the external environment, with closed systems, which do not. In closed systems, such as a clock or a planetary system, the final state is determined unequivocally by initial conditions (and by the laws of behavior in the system). In open systems, such as social and biological systems, an end state can be reached from different initial conditions and in different ways. This is the principle of equifinality—the existence of different causal paths or trajectories to the same outcome.

Although the concept of equifinality has been influential in biology, developmental psychology, organizational theory, archaeology, anthropology, and a number of other disciplines, it has received only scattered attention in the literature on war and peace, which has been dominated by the implicit assumption of an additive linear process. This is reflected in the common use of regression models, and also in qualitative work that attempts to assess the relative causal weight of different variables in the processes leading to war.

One can find occasional references to the concept of multiple paths to war, along with theoretical analyses that clearly refer to the concept without explicitly naming it. In their typology of deterrence failure, George and Smoke (1974) identified several different ways in which deterrence can fail, precipitating war. Lebow (1981: 23) identified three types of international crises, each "with distinctive origins, patterns of development, and probabilities of resolution." In his typology of different types of misperceptions, Levy (1983) suggested hypotheses about the different causal paths through which each can contribute to war (or to peace). In a subsequent study he emphasized equifinality and several distinct causal sequences leading to war (Levy 1989:

296). Fearon's (1995: 381) analysis of "rationalist theories of war," which identified three "general mechanisms" or "causal logics" that can lead to war between rational unitary actors (private information and incentives to misrepresent that information, commitment problems, and indivisible issues), can also be thought of as identifying analytically distinct paths to war.[5]

Vasquez has further developed and applied the concept of multiple paths to war. In his book *The War Puzzle*, Vasquez (1993: 7) argued that there are different types of war and different causal sequences leading to each, and that "to explain war requires identifying the various paths that lead to war."[6] He developed a "realist road to war" that involved the combination of a territorial dispute and states' use of "realist practices" (alliances, arms races, and coercive threats) to resolve disputes on favorable terms. Vasquez emphasized that his "steps-to-war" model focuses on "one path, for one type of war, in one historical era." He acknowledged that there are other paths to war, including a path involving disputes over policy (rather than over territory).

Hinting at one source of multiple paths to war, Bremer (1995: 21) argued that war, as a rare event, is "often generated by a particular concatenation of not-so-rare events," and consequently "there are several different and unique paths to war rather than one." From a different analytic perspective, Suganami (1996: 190) argued that "wars come about in different ways," driven by "a wide variety of mechanisms" or "causal processes" and captured by different narratives.

Scholars have also applied the multiple causal paths concept to outcomes besides the outbreak of war. Stinnett and Diehl (2001) identify distinctive behavioral and structural "paths to rivalry," and Valeriano (this volume) constructs a "steps-to-war" model of rivalry.[7] Valeriano and Vasquez (2010: 566) and Vasquez et al. (2011) identify multiple paths through which war might spread. In their article "The Equifinality of War Termination," Stanley and Sawyer (2009) argue that shifting domestic coalitions and Bayesian bargaining define alternative causal paths to war termination. Levy and Thompson's (2011: ch. 2) argument that war originated in different places at different times under different conditions suggests that there were multiple paths to the origins of war nearly ten millennia ago.

The concept of paths to war is sometimes used in a more idiographic way to refer to a sequence of events leading to a particular war or perhaps to alternative causal interpretations of the outbreak of a particular war. When historians argue that "each war is unique" or that "the number of causes of war equals the number of wars," they presumably mean that each war comes about through a unique causal path. When policy analysts identify alternative scenarios through which a particular war might occur in the future, they implicitly assume that there are multiple paths to war. Cronin (2010), for example, identifies three paths through which a war might break out on the Korean Peninsula: accidental escalation, the breakdown of deterrence, or a sudden regime change or collapse.

Although references to the paths-to-war concept are increasingly common, scholars have yet to come up with a fully satisfactory conceptualization of what the term means and how it might be used to construct better theories and guide empirical research. As Vasquez (2011b: 134) states, "It is one thing to assume that there are various paths to war, but it is quite another to identify and document them." The remainder of this essay is an exercise in conceptual clarification, in the hope of moving the discussion of paths to war a few steps forward.

WHAT IS A "PATH TO WAR"?

I begin this discussion of what a path to war is with a brief discussion of what it is not. To say that there are multiple causal paths does not simply mean that an event or outcome has multiple causes. Monocausal models are a thing of the past, and today nearly all theories of war and peace incorporate multiple variables. The issue is not the number of causal variables, but the existence of several analytically distinct causal paths or sequences. Most linear regression models include many independent variables, but their additive nature, and the fact that more of one factor can compensate for less of another, suggests a single path rather than several analytically distinct causal paths.[8] Nor is it useful, in historical explanation, to equate a causal path with a particular set of conditions, decisions, actions, and events leading to a particular historical outcome. As Vasquez (2011b: 135) argues, "A path to war is not simply an idiographic historical listing of events thought to bring about a particular war." For the path-to-war concept to be useful for social scientific analysis, a given path must be generalizable beyond a particular case. Otherwise, the multiple paths-to-war concept would be equivalent to the argument that there are as many causal paths to war as there are wars, significantly diminishing the theoretical utility of the paths-to-war concept.[9]

I provisionally define *causal path* as a combination and/or sequence of factors that leads, with high probability, to a particular outcome. The idea of multiple causal paths to war means that there is more than one combination or sequence of factors that leads to war with high probability. This is similar to but not identical to Vasquez's (2011b: 135) definition: "Different paths to war embody different variables that singly or in combination greatly increase the probability of war. Any given path to war delineates the sequence of events, actions, decisions, and/or conditions that bring about war in general."

The combinatorial/conjunctural/interactive form of the causal relationship is critical to the paths-to-war concept. As Bremer (1995: 21) argued, we must "be skeptical of models that assume simple additivity. . . . What counts is not the value of any particular condition but rather the interactive effect of all conditions." The importance of interaction effects is also implied by Beck, King, and Zeng's (2000) argument that a particular set of variables has a large impact on dyads with a high *ex-ante* probability of war but a much smaller impact on the vast majority of dyads. This leads Bennett and Stam (2004: 213) to write that if explanations for war are "highly contingent and interactive . . . then the approach of including multiple independent factors in additive fashion will surely prove inadequate." This appears to be the basis of their argument that "there is no single story of war" (p. 201).

HOW MANY CAUSAL PATHS?

My definition of a causal path raises a number of questions. One is how broadly a path should be defined. Consider the steps-to-war model, as further refined by Senese and Vasquez (2008). Does the "realist road to war" constitute a single path to war? Or do territorial disputes constitute one path to war, territorial disputes between rivals another, territorial disputes between rivals that form outside alliances still another, and so on? Or consider domestic politics. Is there a single "domestic path to war," or should we identify distinctive paths constituted by diversionary behavior, pressure from influential economic or ethnic groups, the impact of institutional transparency on signaling, and identity conflicts?

A closely related question is whether a causal path is defined by a particular combination of variables, or whether the temporal sequence of variables is important. Senese and Vasquez (2008) and Vasquez (2011a) define distinct paths to war in terms of different combinations of variables, but they do not (as yet) include the different sequences in which the same combination of variables might occur. Is it one path to war if states with a territorial dispute first form outside alliances and then initiate an arms race, and another path if they initiate an arms race and then form outside alliances?

Vasquez (2011b: 137) is right to argue that the order and sequence of the steps to war might make a difference, because the occurrence of one step might increase the likelihood of a second step. But this raises another issue. The more narrowly a path to war is defined, the greater the number of paths to war. This involves some difficult trade-offs between parsimony and complexity. After a certain point, identifying more paths to war moves us further away from parsimonious theory closer to the view that each war is unique,

defined by a unique causal path. There is no single answer to the question of
how far we should go in decomposing a broad causal path into a number of
more specific paths within it, but there is a clear criterion—the theoretical and
empirical utility of the resulting classification. For Vasquez and Valeriano
(2010: 296), "the real utility of a classification . . . is whether it can guide
empirical research." For Levy and Thompson (2010b: 214), "The question
is not how many paths to war there 'really are,' but what definition is most
useful in helping us understand the causes of war."

The issue is empirical as well as conceptual. Presumably, the introduction
of the paths-to-war concept is only useful to the extent that it can advance our
understanding of variations in war and peace in time and space. If all paths to
war are equally likely to arise and equally likely to lead to war, then it would
be hard to argue that the identification of distinct paths to war has any value.
Thus one of Vasquez's many contributions is to demonstrate that different
paths to war within the realist road to war have a different probability of arising and, once in place, have a different probability of leading to war (Vasquez
and Valeriano 2010; Valeriano and Vasquez 2010; Vasquez 2011a, 2011b).

One possible middle ground—one way of balancing the trade-offs
between parsimony and complexity—is to adopt a nested hierarchical
framework with a limited number of "first-order" paths, more specific
"second-order" paths nested within each, and possibly "third-order" paths
nested within them. This is how I interpret Vasquez's steps-to-war model.
The realist road is a first-order causal path to war that includes a number
of second-order paths defined by different combinations of key variables,
with different sequences of variables defining third-order paths within each
combination. This maintains some degree of parsimony while permitting
considerable complexity within it.

That still leaves the question of order and sequence. I agree in principle
with Vasquez (2011b: 135) that the concept of a causal path implies some
sense of a dynamic process (Bremer 1995; Diehl 2006), implying that a path
involves a causal sequence and not just a combination of variables.[10] The
more complete the theoretical specification of the causal mechanisms leading
to conflict, the better, subject to one important constraint: the conceptualization must remain generalizable, in the sense that we must be able to identify
multiple empirical cases for most theoretical paths. My hunch, however, is
that going beyond combinations to focus on sequences would leave us with
too many causal paths, with few historical cases per path. Consequently, I am
inclined to focus on combinations of variables rather than on specific causal
sequences, and I define causal path as a combination of variables with a high
probability of war.

One implication is that a combination of variables that correlates highly with war would be a path to war, even in the absence of a fully specified causal mechanism or sequence. Twenty-five years ago I would have said that democratic dyads constituted a path to peace, even in the absence of a strong theoretical argument underpinning the observed correlation. I would say the same thing today with respect to other combinations of factors that correlate highly with either war or peace (overwhelming power preponderance within a dyad, for example).

THE "HIGH PROBABILITY" CRITERION

If a causal path involves a combination of variables that lead to war with high probability, we must specify what we mean by "high probability." Should we define a causal path to include *all* the factors that "cause" a war to occur? If so, do we mean the complete set of conditions and processes that are jointly sufficient for war? Or should we define a causal path as a set of factors that make war highly probable? If the latter, what threshold of probability is appropriate? This question raises some difficult issues.

It would be useful to start with the ideal-type case of strict sufficiency, with a path to war defined as a set of variables that are jointly sufficient for war. The concept of multiple paths to war, then, would involve two or more sets of variables, each of which is jointly sufficient for war.[11] We can think about this in terms of the "INUS" conception of causation (Mackie 1965: 246): a factor is an INUS cause if it is an "*insufficient* but *necessary* part of a condition which is itself *unnecessary* but *sufficient* for the result."

A good example from comparative politics is Moore's (1966) argument that the path to democracy in early modern Europe required a strong bourgeoisie and an aristocracy that either aligned with the bourgeoisie or that had been historically weakened. In this model, there is one necessary condition for a democratic pathway (a strong bourgeoisie) and two INUS conditions (alliance between the bourgeoisie and the aristocracy, or a weak aristocracy), generating two causal pathways to democracy. This can be represented as follows:

$$Y = X \times A + X \times W$$

where Y = democratic pathway, X = strong bourgeoisie, A = alliance between bourgeoisie and aristocracy, and W = weak aristocracy, using × for the logical AND and + for the logical OR.

This is a simple model with two causal paths. There are presumably more than two possible paths to war, with no single factor common to all paths (unlike X in the above model), so that no single factor is either necessary or sufficient for war. If war could be modeled as a combination of INUS causes, each factor would be a necessary component of a set of variables that would be jointly sufficient for war, but no single combination of variables would be necessary for the outcome.[12] Many readers will recognize this causal model as reflecting multiple conjunctural causation, which Ragin (1987) has modeled using Boolean algebra and described as qualitative comparative analysis (QCA).

Most international relations scholars would agree that if a set of factors is jointly sufficient for war, they collectively constitute a path to war. Those who conceive of war in probabilistic terms and incorporate an error term into their models would argue, however, that this standard is too demanding and would leave us with few if any paths to war, undermining the theoretical utility of the concept. Thus it is preferable to lower the threshold and say that a combination of factors constitutes a path to war if it makes war highly probable.

Although some define both necessary and sufficient conditions in exclusively deterministic terms (Lieberson 2001), others define these concepts in probabilistic terms, often (but not always) accompanied by the language of "nearly" or "almost always" (Dion 1998; Ragin 2000; Goertz and Starr 2003). It is often said, for example, usually with minimal qualification, that joint democracy is a sufficient condition for peace (Gleditsch 1995; Russett and Starr 2000: 96). I have no problem with a probabilistic conception of necessary and sufficient conditions, though I prefer the language of nearly necessary and nearly sufficient. If a factor or set of factors leads to an outcome with 95 percent probability, then to call it a nearly sufficient condition is more informative than to describe the relationship as probabilistic, which covers an enormous range of probabilities.

Even if we conceive of sufficiency in probabilistic terms, we are still faced with the fact that international relations scholars have been able to identify very few lawlike propositions about international conflict, relatively few combinations of variables that lead to war even with a high probability. Although a disproportionate number of wars involve territorial disputes, most territorial disputes do not lead to war (Vasquez 2011a, 2011b). War is a relatively rare event, and most combinations of factors do not lead to war under most conditions. Moreover, even those combinations of factors that have the highest probability of resulting in war can also result in other outcomes. Many argue, for example, that in crisis situations some strategies are riskier (more war prone) than others, and that careful crisis management can reduce the probability of war (George 1991). Context, contingency, and idiosyncrasies are important. In a crisis situation, individual belief systems, risk orientations, time horizons, and personalities can push toward war or toward peace.[13] These considerations lead to the argument that "war is in the error term" (Gartzke 1999).

We can describe this pattern with another concept from systems theory, *multifinality*, in which similar initial conditions lead to different outcomes.[14] Equifinality and multifinality each create enormous difficulties for the task of developing universal or unconditional laws of behavior (Most and Starr 1987), including problems applying linear models to social behavior (Bremer 1995; Ragin 2000; George and Bennett 2005).[15] This issue needs far greater attention, as it is one of the most serious methodological hurdles confronting students of the causes of war. In his attempt to suggest the complexity of analyzing war, Bremer (1995: 25) likened the task of understanding the puzzle of war to that of opening a combination lock. Knowing the combination of numbers, and even their sequence, is not enough. In addition, one must know the rules for dialing the numbers (e.g., how many complete rotations before each number). He also suggested that to "pick" the lock required an understanding of "what is inside it and how it works."

One interpretation of Bremer's argument is that an understanding of war requires opening up the "black box" of decision making. This is almost certainly necessary (but not sufficient) for the understanding of the outbreak of individual wars. Whether that can be done in a more general theory of war, in a way that satisfies social scientific concerns for a reasonable degree of parsimony, raises a more difficult set of issues.

NOTES

1. As the chapters in this volume by Kang and Benson each suggest, the relationship between alliances and war is more complex.

2. Rasler and Thompson have a different focus, and I exclude their chapter from this discussion.

3. The fact that part 1 focuses on explanations for war and part 2 on explanations for peace is coincidental. One can easily imagine a linear probabilistic explanation for peace (consisting of low values of all the variables in a linear model of war onset), or multiple paths to war, as discussed below.

4. Alternatively, one might trace the multiple causal paths argument back to the development of path analysis by the geneticist and biometrician Sewall Wright (1920).

5. Fearon (1995) acknowledges the existence of nonrational and nonunitary logics that can lead to war.

6. Many qualitative methodologists propose the identical analytic strategy, in the form of "typological theory" (George and Bennett 2005: ch. 11) or "explanatory typologies" (Elman 2005).

7. Young and Levy (2011) specify several alternative paths through which economic rivalry might lead to war.

8. In contrast to a "compensatory" decision rule, in a "noncompensatory" decision rule, benefits on one dimension cannot compensate for losses on another (Redlawsk and Lau, forthcoming).

9. More accurately, if we defined a causal path as a particular set of conditions or sequence of events leading to a particular war, and if we included additional paths through which a given war could have started even if a few things had been different, then the number of causal paths to war would be far greater than the number of wars.

10. Some causal sequences might involve a causal chain consisting of either necessary or sufficient conditions or both (Goertz and Levy 2007: 23–29).

11. A particular war is overdetermined if two or more of these sets of conditions are present, because eliminating one set of conditions would not eliminate war.

12. Contrary to Bremer's (1995: 21) argument, seconded by Geller (2004: 233), that complex combinatorial causation requires us to "give up the notion of necessary/ sufficient causation," those concepts can be quite useful as part of more complex causal relationships.

13. On time horizons, see Streich and Levy (2007).

14. This is the opposite of equifinality, in which different initial conditions lead to the same outcome.

15. King, Keohane, and Verba (1994: 87–89) acknowledge that equifinality complicates the analysis of mean causal effects but do not explore its implications for research design in any detail. They say only that equifinality can be incorporated into their conception of causality and that one must be careful to precisely specify the counterfactual conditions associated with each causal effect. On the analysis of counterfactual arguments in case studies, see Levy (2008).

Chapter Fifteen

Peace Science as Normal Science

What Role for Geography in the Coming Revolution?

Colin Flint

For the community of scientists involved in the project known as peace science, there are many aspects of its current status, and their activities, that suggest that the taken for granted needs to be investigated in a critical fashion. The positive aspect of the condition of peace science is the maintenance of an impressive project of normal science. For peace scientists themselves, the enterprise that they are engaging in may appear normal, almost taken for granted. It is, however, quite extraordinary—a sustained project of normal science with an essential and morally laudatory goal, constructing peace (Vasquez 2009: 10). It is hard to think of a comparable project in the social sciences. The fusion of data collection and hypothesis testing, aided and abetted by an active system of journals, professional organizations, and conferences, has maintained an organized and sustained analysis of the causes of war.

However, perhaps these strengths are also an area of weakness. Normal science builds knowledge, but it also constrains the development of questions. The intense evaluation of hypotheses and the need to construct data that can evaluate them can promote an insularity in which increasingly nuanced consideration of these questions becomes the only way to produce new knowledge (Kuhn 1970; Lakatos 1978a, 1978b). In conjunction with such insularity can come recognition that the ontology and epistemology that defines the normal science project limits scientific inquiry. Related to these two scientific issues is the tendency to drift into increasingly academic speculation at the cost of losing sight of real-world applicability. The condition of peace science displays some characteristics that suggest it is at a juncture defined by tensions of, on the one hand, maintaining the ongoing normal science project and, on the other hand, defining a new approach that is based upon a new ontology and epistemology.

In this short essay I discuss two elements of the peace science project that are at the heart of this tension. The first is an epistemological question of the universalism of the relationships pursued by peace science (Senese and Vasquez 2008: 62–63), and is provoked by discussion of the need for temporally specific models (Houweling and Siccama 1985). The second is an ontological question regarding the assumption of the independence of observations in regression models and the burgeoning interest in social network analysis (Flint et al. 2009; Hafner-Burton, Kahler, and Montgomery 2009; Maoz 2010). To tie these two strands together I introduce a discussion of geography. Starting with a critique of the common usage of geography in peace science as a simple operationalization of contiguity or distance, I illustrate how contemporary academic geography can serve as a framework for taking context seriously and, at the same time, for grounding social network analysis in physical settings. I conclude the essay by discussing how a spatialized social network approach can be used to expand and update the range of issues peace science can engage, and thereby enhance its policy relevance.

EPISTEMOLOGICAL AND ONTOLOGICAL CONSTRAINTS AND OPPORTUNITIES

The twin considerations of meso-level and network-based models expose deep faults, and perhaps underlying misgivings, of the peace science project. The scientific goals and practices of peace science were originally defined by a search for relationships between the correlates of war that, if robust and consistent, can be understood to approach the status of laws (Singer 1979, 1980), and then in terms of probability (Bremer 1992, 1995). Fundamental to this approach is a sense that the relationships are universal: what we know about war is not expected to be specific to historical-geographical contexts. The basis of the data collection efforts of the peace science community has been to collect variables on units of analysis that are deemed to remain consistent from 1816 to the present day. The generic modeling technique is an analysis that includes dyad years across the same time period. In other words, the meaning of alliance or rivalry or regime type is expected to be consistent between, say, 1818 Western Europe and 2010 sub-Saharan Africa. Though natural science can make arguments that the laws of physics may be consistent across such time-space contexts, the very fact that peace science studies politics (acts that purposefully change society) should give pause for thought as to whether power relations act in a consistent manner across different contexts.

A call for models that are specific to historical-geographical contexts challenges this assumption of universal relationships and the related search for laws (Houweling and Siccama 1985). But rather than this being seen as a setback for peace science, it should be framed as an opportunity. Defining the appropriate temporal and geographic scope of models requires consideration of the structures, actors, and processes that have interacted in a particular way to define a specific context. This definition must involve an understanding of what is "coming together" and stays related over particular times and spaces. What at first glance may appear as conflicts that are simple to parameterize, such as World War II, can quickly become problematic once the stress is made upon connectivity (Flint 2011). By relying upon state actors and dyads, the analytical bounds of such a conflict are usually defined in peace science by declarations of war and amnesties. However, the processes of conflict are much broader and involve nonstate actors as well.

Dyad-year-based regression analysis encourages us to think of conflicts as separate interactions between states, rather than being a particular manifestation of ongoing political processes. The temporal span of conflict processes does not match dyad years, and the scope of relations involved in conflict and peace formation are more expansive than dyads. This does not mean that the dyad-year model is inappropriate for all questions, and it should of course be recognized that the dyad-year unit of analysis has produced important knowledge about the processes of war. However, dyads are simply one link within a broader set of linkages. Furthermore, if we think of conflict as process, then we need to think more seriously about the appropriate temporal metric or time horizon. Certainly there is no sense that calendar years have any meaning as the measure of political processes, they are likely simply arbitrary.

Recognition that dyads and years are merely the bricks of bigger structures is a pathway to an important ontological shift. The growing sense within peace science of the need to take temporal context seriously should not terminate with a move to temporally specific models, or even worse a proliferation of dummy variables denoting time periods. Instead, a major theoretical exercise is necessary to define the criteria for identifying meaningful temporal-geographic contexts. Theorizing the temporal and geographic scope of conflict processes would lead to meso-scale models that identify causal relations within geographic-historical settings. Such an exercise would simultaneously challenge the universalism of peace science models while advancing the discipline by forcing us to theorize contexts that underlie an epistemology based upon the mutuality of political agency and the formation of contexts within which agency is mediated. This approach emphasizes that connectivity is the means and product of political behavior. In sum, an epistemology of context-specific models and an ontology based upon connectivity support each other.

GEOGRAPHY: THE RISK OF SPATIAL FETISHISM

Though there are likely many pathways toward such a theorization, geography and spatialized social networks offer a direction. The goal is to utilize geography to connect the notion of context with the political science concept of "opportunity" (Siverson and Starr 1991) and hence form a conceptualization and operationalization of what can be called contexts, or surfaces, of opportunity.

The discipline of geography has gone through many paradigm shifts (Johnston and Sidaway 2004) and currently has no coherent normal science project. Instead, emphasis is upon (1) ideas of the social construction of space and society, (2) the role of the contingency of human behavior, and (3) the understanding of geographic settings as both product and medium of human activity (Gallaher et al. 2009). This situation has emerged from a long-term trend challenging the very same spatial approach that peace science has recently embraced.

Post–World War II academic geography followed the trend of social science and explored ways of becoming a "science" (Johnston and Sidaway 2004). The move away from turgid regional descriptions was necessary for the development of the discipline, and in its place came a search for spatial laws of social relationships and their analysis through statistical methods, the so-called quantitative revolution. The foundation for this spatial scientific epistemology was an abstract ontology of the isotropic plane, a flat featureless space in which objects were placed in relation to each other on the basis of mathematical calculations (Chorley and Haggett 1967). It was a science, it was based on math, and it utilized the new adoption of computers; but the worlds it engaged were distinct and abstractly separate from real-world settings.

In the wake of the quantitative relationship came approaches that wanted to reinsert real people and real places into academic geography, based on the accusation of "spatial fetishism" (Soja 1980). Spatial fetishism refers to the idea that space is somehow separate, pre-given, or autonomous from social processes. In other words, the distribution of industrial plants, for example, is unconnected to processes of capitalism. The agency that lay behind the spatial patterns identified by early spatial science was, at best, implicit and was a function of simplistic cost-benefit calculations that did not consider social relations. The location of factories was unrelated to the multiple forms of power, social institutions, and collective identity that are the very essence of society.

The identification of spatial fetishism, and the new social theoretic directions it inspired, can be seen in a quite simple term that has been used to frame introductory approaches to geography: pattern and process. A geographic tendency to "map" is of explanatory value if the pattern of a phenomenon is used to understand the social processes that cause the phenomenon itself.

The significant implication for peace science is that distance and contiguity are not social processes that cause phenomena, such as wars. Hence, adopting them as "explanatory variables," in and of themselves, is problematic. Put starkly, distance is not a social process. Rather, and as Zeev Maoz put it at the conference upon which this book is based, the theoretic intention is to see "geography as political."

Geography, measured as distance or contiguity, and also to include terrain, should be seen as a mediator of social processes and not a social entity in and of itself (O'Loughlin 2000). For example, a rivalry between two states is likely to be mediated by the distance between them. It can be theorized, or it may just be common sense, that the closer rivals are to each other, the greater the likelihood for interaction and, therefore, conflict. But of course such mediation is related to many other things, such as social and technological capacities for interaction. It follows that the relationship is dynamic in that changing social relations can change the mediating role of geographic factors.

Other geographic concepts are also currently underutilized in peace science. Geographic scale was the foundation for a revitalized political geography in the 1980s. Its original conceptualization was very similar to the idea of levels of analysis that has been an important part of the ontology of peace science. However, Taylor's (1981) original identification of the local, nation-state, and global scales has been critiqued in a theoretical debate that has emphasized the need to see scales as social constructs rather than rigid analytical categories (Herod 2010). A neat compartmentalization of scales that are seen as nested and distinct from each other is a poor reflection of social activity. Rather, an act of war is simultaneously a local, national, and global act (let alone other relevant scales such as the individual and the household). For example, the global political agenda of the United States, its attempts to construct and maintain a unipolar interstate system, involves the simultaneous development of (dyadic) bilateral relations, the nature of political systems of some states, and the securitization (sometimes involving combat) of particular regions and places within such states.

Similarly, the separation of processes of conflict into monadic, dyadic, and systemic levels of analysis is an analytical construct that denies the way in which actions of war are simultaneously causing, and the product of, processes at a multitude of scales. One way forward with this ontological problem of creating analytical constructs that do not reflect the actual operation of social processes is to rephrase the analysis to see the relative importance of processes that can be conceptualized as operating primarily within one scale or level. The technique of hierarchical linear modeling would allow for an exploration of such an approach, namely that processes at all levels are operating simultaneously, though some may have more explanatory impact than others. This would be a way of recognizing that the monadic, dyadic, and systemic levels are analytical constructs that must be modeled to reflect the actual behavior of actors, and that the scope of processes cannot be readily compartmentalized into epistemologically based categories.

CONFLICTSPACE: A GEOGRAPHY OF CONNECTIVITY AND CONTEXT

Along with other social science disciplines, including peace science, geographers have increasingly adopted social network analysis as a tool (Wasserman and Faust 1994). The discussion of social networks in geography is related to engagement with Bruno Latour's (2007) actor network theory. The two are very distinct and not necessarily compatible. In tandem they have driven geographers toward two important developments: (1) understanding social agency as being mediated by webs of relationships within which actions are both mediated physically and given social meaning and (2) deprioritizing the state as the unit of analysis and primary actor. In peace science, the emphasis upon networks has been more ontological, through an emphasis upon systemic relations between states (Maoz 2010; Vasquez et al. 2011). The processes being analyzed remain the rational decision of states, but in a different realm of interaction, something that is beyond the dyadic.

However, the implications of social network approaches to peace science are wider and deeper if the interaction between ontology and epistemology is explored. At the heart of social network analysis is the understanding that no actor is fully independent. The assumption of independence of observations is a fundamental building block of the dominant epistemology of peace science and related methodologies. Despite recognition of this disparity between methodological assumptions and the social world being modeled (Houweling and Siccama 1985), there has been limited engagement with the implications. Rather, spatial analysis has been adopted as the means to include new explanatory variables (distance and contiguity) rather than as a pathway toward recognizing the invalidity of an epistemology based on assuming independence of observations when modeling very much related actors.

The emphasis in social network analysis upon connectivity has important implications for peace science. It builds upon the dominant adoption of dyads, which on the one hand has focused analysis upon relations between states, while on the other hand, and in a contradictive sense, it has retained the assumption of independence of observations through its dominant application within regression-based models. The strength of social network analysis is the identification of relations between two actors, a subset of actors or cliques, and the whole system of actors. This ontology understands the behavior of actors as a function of their relations with others. Peace science has adopted this understanding through the construction of many dyad-based variables: alliances, rivalries, territorial disputes, and so forth. The ontological switch that social network analysis requires is that such bi-actor relations are an inadequate representation of the way actors behave and the situation, or context, within which they must make calculations.

The way in which a network of actors provides a context of relations within which actors behave refocuses peace science toward the role of the environment within which an action takes place. Originally proposed by Sprout and Sprout (1965), the idea of modeling the context of actions was continued through Siverson and Starr's (1991) "opportunity and willingness" model. Most peace science has emphasized the analysis of "willingness," or the decision-making activities of states. The notion of "opportunity" has not been developed theoretically. If it has been modeled, it has been in a simplistic way, with unsophisticated understandings of geography (distance, contiguity, and terrain) being the apparent operationalizations of contextual settings (Gleditsch 2002a). The result has been a mismatch in the theoretical sophistication of what is meant by willingness, or agency, compared to how we understand opportunity, or context. Opportunity and willingness are in a relationship akin to a structure and an agent. It is inadequate to try and model opportunity, or structure, through the addition of another independent variable in a regression analysis in which the explanatory variables are measures of agency. Opportunity or context is not something that can be modeled in an additive sense through one measure in a multivariate analysis. The opportunity and willingness concept, which is highlighted by social network analysis through the identification of bilateral relations within a network of relations, requires an epistemology within which opportunity and willingness are combined from theoretical conceptualization, through analysis, and to interpretation.

Contemporary geographic thinking provides an avenue toward conceptualizing environment or opportunity. Geographers have consistently promoted the need for an understanding of context. However, the idea of context was poorly theorized for a long time and led to accusations that any contextual effect found in spatial models was merely a function of a misspecified model (King 1996). Recently, a combination of theoretical and methodological advances means that geography has the ability to help define and model environment.

First, the tradition of dyadic analysis, and its recent expansion to networks, in peace science can be connected to the focus on relational power in geography (Allen 2003). Though relational power is based upon the ideas of actor network theory, the understanding that power is a relation rather than a material entity, or something that is exercised rather than possessed, begs the questions of interaction that dyads and networks are in place to illustrate. One of the best examples from peace science is targeted alliances (Leeds et al. 2002): power is exercised through institutionalized commitments that identify another state as a threat and promise mobilization of many actors against that state in particular circumstances. Though the military capacity of all of the actors involved is part of the decision-making process, they only matter when the relations between states are taken into consideration and the resources are mobilized. The ability for dyadic and network analysis to inform theoretic debates about relational power is an interesting development in and of itself. In addition, an emphasis upon relations begs questions about the set of actors with which relations are informed; or put another way, the context of opportunity for political relationships.

Though networks offer potential for such an exploration of the context of opportunity, networks have been critiqued for the very same issues of abstraction from real geographic settings that were mobilized to critique the spatial analysis of the quantitative revolution (Hess 2004). Geographers have called for consideration of the way in which network relations are embedded within real-world settings.

The need to see networks as just one component of context or environment parallels theoretical claims to engage the multiple spatialities of politics (Leitner, Sheppard, and Sziarto 2008). Political actors operate within a number of settings simultaneously, settings that can be seen as the combination of scalar, network, and territorial geographies. It is with such a goal that the ConflictSpace project at the University of Illinois at Urbana-Champaign has been developed through collaboration between geographers and political scientists (Flint et al. 2009; Vasquez et al. 2011). The initial focus of the project has been upon the diffusion of war and has combined spatial analysis and social network analysis to model the interaction between network relations and neighborhoods (measured by contiguity) in explaining the timing of states entering an ongoing war. The combination of network and physical space to understand contexts of opportunity is necessary because considering just one element of context produces too many false predictions.

The ConflictSpace approach provides a more complete and realistic modeling of the opportunity context of a state by acknowledging that actors are simultaneously embedded within geographic contexts and networks of political relations that mediate the decision-making process of actors. This setting is operationalized through spatial variables and social network analysis. Furthermore, the setting or context is not static, as it is a product of the behavior of the actors being modeled. Hence, geography is not pre-given and exogenous but a continually evolving component of the processes being investigated (Flint et al. 2009). In the case of World War I, as new states joined the war, other states found themselves the neighbors of a combatant state, and, with regard to networks, rivalries developed over the course of the conflict (Vasquez et al. 2011). In sum, the geography identified by the ConflictSpace project is of a complex and dynamic context of opportunity that is made of multiple spatial settings that are simultaneously constructed by the behavior of actors while simultaneously mediating those activities. Such an approach builds an understanding of geography as an ongoing construct of conflict behavior that mediates actions, not as a pre-given, static, and exogenous variable.

CONCLUSION: MAINTAINING RELEVANCE

Finally, it is worthwhile considering the potential contribution of a spatialized social network analysis beyond the confines of ontological and epistemological questions. One of the admirable aspects of peace science is its commitment to engaging the real world and informing discussion of policy that may prevent war and promote peace. However, this commitment requires peace science to keep pace with developments in the real world, but without being drawn into faddish analysis or the politicization of its findings. The most pressing question for peace science regards its continued focus upon interstate war. War is no longer a matter of state-versus-state antagonisms, and hence the actors that are brought into the analysis must expand. This matter has been addressed elsewhere in this book, so I will not belabor the point about needing to include nonstate actors.

However, the recognition of the role of nonstate actors provokes another set of questions; namely, can we retain attention upon the set of issues that are understood to be drivers of war once we expand the set of participants in wars to include nonstate actors? As part of its commitment to normal science, peace science has focused on the set of processes that are highlighted in this book: alliances, rivalries, regime type, and so forth. These are all state-centric and not readily translatable to analysis that reflects the contemporary interaction of state and nonstate actors.

Put another way, the issues that are commonly understood to be the underlying causes of contemporary conflict are conspicuous by their absence within the paradigms of normal peace science. Climate change, the sustained poverty of the majority of the world, the legacies structuring a postcolonial world, the processes of globalization, access to water, and religious identity are all themes that other disciplines have embraced. They are also issues that policy makers and the general public perceive to be causes of war, or "security threats." If the goal is to promote peace through understanding war, our scientific explanations must keep pace with the changing practices of war.

Consideration of such pressing issues promotes theoretical, ontological, and epistemological opportunities for peace science. Theories need to expand beyond what are seen as the rational actions and calculations of territorial states. Ontological developments need to go beyond the addition of nonstate actors to a framing of the relevant context of opportunity of a diversity of actors, depending upon the issue at hand. For example, if the issue is access to water in a particular river basin, then the scope of the conflict and actors involved should be defined by the impacted stakeholders. In terms of epistemology, such an issue-based approach requires that we think of actors as connected or related through the issue at hand, rather than as independent actors, as in an epistemology that sees a regression analysis as the appropriate and final outcome. Hence, a network approach that also reflects the geographic embeddedness of actors has much potential (Hess 2004), especially when coupled with an ontology that sees actors and their contexts of opportunity as mutually constructed and dynamic. These intertwined theoretical, ontological, and epistemological issues must be addressed if relevance is to be maintained. Processes of war have always involved state and nonstate actors, territorial-based political entities, and those best thought of as operating as networks with less territorial constraints, and war has for the large part been a multilateral, multiactor, multi-issue process.

My engagement with peace science has, to some degree, been motivated by the commitment to informing society in a way that can promote peace. However, a stark question to the peace science community is whether the laudable goal of peace science, to understand the processes of war to inform policies to build peace, is a driver of the peace science community's actions or just lip service. An audit would easily come to the conclusion that the primary focus is on academic practices, building reputations and publishing records that allow one to advance from PhD student to full professor. This is an inward-looking exercise that is all about regression coefficients rather than framing policy briefs to statesmen. In a sense this is understandable; peace science is a community of professional academics required and motivated to advance through the criteria the profession has defined. Though the obvious response is that the policy recommendations require the scientific analysis, the current imbalance is stark. It is time for either (1) truth in advertising or (2) a long hard look to see if and how policy relevance can be obtained. Both scientific progress and policy relevance are obtainable if theoretical focus upon pressing issues is matched with ontological and epistemological changes that situate the war- and peace-making behavior of a diversity of actors within contexts of opportunities that reflect real-world power structures. Focus upon the interaction of the multiple spatialities confronted by actors within networks of many social relations that are embedded within actual physical geographic settings is one such way of analyzing contemporary expressions of opportunity and willingness.

Chapter Sixteen

What Do We Know about War?

John A. Vasquez

Despite claims that interstate war is on the wane, it is still a very serious social problem. The post–Cold War era, where most of this decline is alleged to have been evidenced, saw the United States fight in the Persian Gulf, the former Yugoslavia, Afghanistan, and Iraq. New territorial wars and clashes have arisen from the collapse of the Soviet Union, that between Russia and Georgia being the most recent. Africa, which had been previously seen as comparatively free of interstate war (see Lemke 2002), albeit with plenty of internal conflict, saw Congo have Africa's "first world war." The statistical conclusion about the decline of interstate and, especially, territorial wars, is really a function of the benchmark that one takes. Interstate wars are down since the Second World War, but not that different from the pre-1914 era (i.e., 1816–1913) (see Henehan and Vasquez 2011; see also Wallensteen 2006; Sarkees and Wayman 2010). Hensel (herein) also finds little decline in the proportion of territorial issues involved in fatal militarized interstate disputes (MIDs) or wars after 1945 and a slight increase after the end of the Cold War.

If war is to be mitigated, the factors that cause it must be identified. The chapters in this book summarize the current state of scientific knowledge about the role of territory, alliances, arms races, interstate rivalry, and nuclear capability in bringing about or preventing interstate war. In addition, three chapters look at the factors that promote peace. The emphases in these chapters should not be taken to mean that other factors, like economic variables, play no role; it is only to say that the book has emphasized those factors about which the most is known in terms of current scientific research.

It must be emphasized that scientific knowledge is always a work in progress. What is "known" today may be overturned tomorrow. This is particularly true in young sciences, such as international relations, in which the data and research are limited. Although this research has not produced the kind of knowledge found in the physical sciences, it should not be concluded, as perennial skeptics would, that we know nothing. In some areas, our knowledge may even be more precise than in the physical sciences—for example, we can do better in predicting war than seismologists do in predicting earthquakes. Their predictions typically state that a major earthquake can be expected in a certain area of the earth's crust (which has certain characteristics) within the next fifty years. Some of the research reported in this book does better and predicts that pairs of states that have certain characteristics will have a high probability of going to war within five years and that others will have a very low probability. The knowledge in this book, while probabilistic and tentative, is not without utility. This does not mean that we do not still have a long way to go before we reach the level of knowledge in the mature physical sciences, but neither does it mean that we know no more than Thucydides.

With these caveats in mind, the remainder of this chapter will turn first to what we know about the factors that increase the probability of war. Next, the much more limited research on what we think we know about the factors that promote peace will be reviewed. In each instance, not only will the main findings be summarized, but the major questions that need to be answered to deepen our knowledge further will be noted.

FACTORS PROMOTING WAR

The first thing to keep in mind is that most of the research reported in this book is confined to interstate war (i.e., warfare between formally recognized states). While some of this research goes back to 1495, most of it deals with the post-Napoleonic system after 1815. What have we learned about these wars and the factors that bring them about?

Territorial Disputes

If we look at the characteristics of militarized interstate disputes that give rise to war, we find that states that have territorial disputes have a higher probability of going to war than would be expected by chance. This hypothesis, which has been extensively probed in the last decade, now has substantially more evidence supporting and elaborating it. The central finding is that territorial disputes have a greater probability of escalating to war than other kinds of disputes, namely regime or policy disputes, which are the only other ways in which disputes are classified in the data. Vasquez and Henehan (2001) show that this is the case for both the 1816–1945 and 1946–1992 periods using three different samples of MID data (disputes, dyadic disputes, and dyad history), as well as for major-major, major-minor, and, with the exception of one sample, minor-minor dyads. Subsequent research by Senese and Vasquez (2008) using the updated MID 3.02 data to 2001 confirm this finding across three periods—1816–1945, 1946–1989, and the post–Cold War period (1990–2001).

Earlier research by Hensel (1996) and Senese (1996) showed that territorial disputes are more prone to war and to conflict than nonterritorial disputes, without breaking down the nonterritorial category. Senese (1996) finds that territorial MIDs are more apt to result in fatalities, which implies that leaders and their followers are more willing to spill their blood over these issues than others. Hensel (2000) has a similar finding. He finds that states that have previously made a territorial claim (without yet threatening or using force; i.e., there is no MID) are more likely to have a fatal MID.

Similar findings have been produced using the International Crisis Behavior (ICB) project data. Ben-Yehuda (1997, 2004) finds that crises involving territorial questions are more apt to have violent management techniques and are more apt to escalate to war. Colaresi and Thompson (2005), in a test of the steps-to-war explanation, find that spatial rivalries (i.e., those over territory) are more apt to end in war (after two crises and an arms race) than other types of rivalries. This leads them to conclude that territorial disagreement has a high likelihood of escalating to war.[1]

Hensel (1996, 2000) provides some clues as to why territorial disputes are so war prone. He finds that when states are faced with territorial disputes, they are more likely to respond to these challenges in a militarized manner. Likewise, Mitchell and Prins (1999: 174n13) find that territorial disputes are more apt to be reciprocated than nonterritorial disputes. Hensel (1996) also finds that territorial disputes, once initiated, have a high probability of recurring. Both of his findings indicate that states often find territorial disputes to be of high salience and are willing to risk increased escalation to support their stand. On the basis of the above evidence, it can be concluded that territorial disputes increase the probability of war. However, since many territorial disputes do not escalate to war, it would be erroneous to assume that they are a sufficient condition for war.

Lastly, if territorial disputes are so war prone, then they should leave an imprint on the historical record. Vasquez and Henehan (2001) find that a little over half of the interstate wars fought from 1816 to 1992 have their origins in the escalation of territorial MIDs. Vasquez and Valeriano (2010: 300) find that the modal war from 1816 to 1997 is a dyadic war between neighbors over territory. This is consistent with the territorial explanation of war (see Vasquez 1993: ch. 4), which states that territorial disputes are a main source of war.

One of the common criticisms in the last decade of the above sort of research is that the relationship between territorial disputes and war does not take account of possible selection effects. In other words, it could be the case that some unknown X factor is bringing about both a territorial MID and war. Using a Heckman or two-stage probit model, Senese and Vasquez (2008: ch. 3) look at whether the presence of a territorial claim would predict both the onset of an MID and whether that first stage would wipe out the significance between having a territorial MID and escalation to war within five years. They find, using Huth and Allee (2002) data for the 1919–1995 period, that having a territorial claim increases the likelihood of having some sort of MID, but that controlling for this first stage does not eliminate the relationship between having a territorial MID and escalation to war. This and other tests indicate that there is no selection effect for this variable.[2]

Another possible source of selection is whether contiguity could predict both MID onset and escalation. Contrary to the contiguity explanation that explains neighbors' fighting because they have the opportunity to have more interactions and hence more wars, the territorial explanation maintains that any set of states (whether or not they are neighbors) will have a greater probability of going to war if they are disputing territorial claims through the threat or use of force. This suggests that neighbors become involved in war usually because they are fighting over territorial disputes.

Both Hensel (2000) and Vasquez (2001) provide evidence to show that both contiguous and noncontiguous states have severe conflict (fatal MIDs and wars) if territory is at stake and less conflict if territory is not at stake. These analyses provide additional evidence consistent with the territorial explanation as opposed to the contiguity explanation. Hensel (herein: tables 1.5 and 1.6) provides an update of some of this research and finds that while both territorial issues (claims) and contiguity are important for the onset of an MID, when controlling for the salience of the territorial claim or failed negotiations, the effect of contiguity is wiped out. The most definitive evidence, however, comes from Senese (2005), who, using a two-stage probit model, finds that contiguity increases the likelihood of some sort of MID occurring, but it is the presence of a territorial MID and not contiguity that increases the probability of war.

Although territorial disputes as a whole are more likely to escalate to war, that does not mean that all types of territorial disputes are equally prone to war. Huth (1996) finds that territorial issues (claims) involving ethnic questions are most likely to escalate, followed by strategic territory, with territorial issues involving economic questions being the least likely to escalate.[3] Huth and Allee (2002) have confirmed this earlier finding for the 1919–1949 period. Second, Hensel, Mitchell, et al. (2008), using a different data set, have also found that ethnic issues are more likely to produce an MID, at least for the Western Hemisphere and Western Europe.

The major new findings on the types of territorial disputes that are war prone show that intangible issues are more apt to escalate to war than tangible issues. This hypothesis which is common in the conflict resolution literature had not been tested previously with regard to territorial disputes. Hensel and Mitchell (2005) find that intangible territorial issues are more apt to escalate to an MID than tangible ones.

The above treats the question of whether certain types of territorial issues are more war prone than others in terms of substantive characteristics. The other factor that can be used to categorize territorial issues is the process by which they are handled. One of the key process characteristics that distinguish territorial MIDs that escalate to war from those that do not is whether they recur. This hypothesis is implicit in Hensel's (1996) early findings. Senese and Vasquez (2008) find that for the 1816–1945 period, recurring territorial disputes has a separate and independent effect on MIDs escalating to war from rivalry (which generally involves having at least six MIDs [over any issue] within twenty years). This relationship disappears in the Cold War period (rivalry wipes out the significance of recurring territorial disputes). However, there is limited evidence that recurring territorial disputes has a separate and independent effect from rivalry for the brief post–Cold War era, 1990–2001 (see Senese and Vasquez 2008: 146–48, 162). Senese and Vasquez (2008: ch. 5–6) also find for the 1816–1945 period that if one or both sides in a dispute have made an outside alliance, their MID is more apt to escalate. The same is true if they are engaged in a rivalry, and if they are engaged in an arms race.

While territorial disputes increase the probability of war breaking out, they do not make war inevitable. Indeed, most territorial, maritime, and river issues give rise to peaceful attempts at settlement and not MIDs (Hensel, Mitchell, et al. 2008: 135; see also Hensel 2001a: 100–102, tables 3–5; Hensel herein: table 1.7). The more salient the issue, the more likely that both peaceful attempts and MIDs will result. Elsewhere (Vasquez 2009: 349), I have interpreted this to mean that the more salient a territorial issue, the more likely decision makers are to feel pressured "to do something" about the issue. Therefore, the finding that salient issues often lead to peaceful attempts to settle does not necessarily contradict the finding that territorial disputes are also more likely to go to war than other types of disputes. Indeed, Hensel, Mitchell, et al. (2008: 134–35) and Hensel (2001a: 86–89) find that when peace attempts fail, they increase the likelihood of MIDs, and when MIDs fail to settle the issue, actors turn to peace attempts.

Once research on territorial disputes and war began to produce findings, it naturally gave rise to research on the relationship between peace and territorial disputes. Vasquez (1993: 146) argues in the territorial explanation of war that when territorial boundaries between neighbors are settled, long periods of peace can occur. This is one of the major testable differences between the territorial explanation of war and realism. The latter sees the struggle for power and conflict as endemic; once a territorial issue is settled, some other sort of issue should arise. The early research provided some support to the claim that settling territorial disputes could result in peace. Kocs (1995) finds for the 1945–1987 period that neighbors that have legally accepted their borders and do not have existing territorial claims are considerably less likely to have a war than those that do not have settled borders. This means that after borders are settled new issues are not arising to provide a different source for war. Consistent with this pattern is a finding by Huth (1996: 72, 86, 90–91, 182), also for the post–World War II period (1950–1990), that states tend not to raise a territorial claim if doing so violates a previous agreement that settled the boundary.

Both of these studies are limited to the Cold War period. Owsiak (2012) extends the temporal domain to 1816–2001 and has a more systematic measure of settled borders. He finds that once two states settle their borders, they are less likely to go to war with each other or to have a militarized interstate dispute. This holds for both democratic and nondemocratic dyads. Further evidence consistent with the above is Hensel (2006), who finds that settling a territorial issue (claim) significantly reduces the likelihood that any future MID (either territorial or nonterritorial) will arise. This speaks to the notion that territorial issues and disputes poison a relationship, and therefore settling them can place relations on a new basis. Indirect evidence to support the peace claim comes from research on peaceful eras and dyads. Henehan and Vasquez (2011) find that the historical periods that have no wars among major states—1816–1848, 1871–1895, and 1919–1932—have few or no territorial MIDs. The major finding on peaceful dyads, of course, is that joint democracies never (or rarely) fight wars with each other, and there is growing evidence that one reason joint democracies do not fight each other is that they have few territorial disputes (see the section below on factors promoting peace).

Given these findings, what do we think we know at this point?

- States that are involved in territorial disputes have a higher probability of going to war than states involved in nonterritorial disputes.
- Since both neighbors and noncontiguous states that contend over territorial disputes are more apt to go to war than neighbors and noncontiguous states

that contend over nonterritorial disputes, territory rather than contiguity is a more important underlying factor associated with war.
- Territorial disputes that go to war tend to be over ethnic questions and strategic territory rather than over economic questions, which are more apt to be settled peacefully.
- Intangible rather than tangible territorial issues are more prone to escalating to an MID and to war.
- Territorial disputes that recur, or that occur in the context of the disputants having a rivalry, an outside alliance, or being engaged in an arms race, are much more likely to escalate to war in the 1816–1945 era.
- Once neighbors recognize their borders as settled and mutually acceptable, the probability of having a war or even an MID goes down.

What are some of the queries that theoretically informed research in the future needs to answer to produce more cumulative knowledge about the role of territory?

- Why do states raise territorial issues in the first place (see Hensel herein), and how do disagreements over territory become MIDs?
- A related area for future research is the construction of an empirical and theoretical typology of territorial disputes that clearly distinguishes which are apt to escalate to war and which are not.
- What is the impact of decisively settling territorial disputes on the subsequent relations of states?
- What is the impact of external territorial MIDs on domestic politics?

Alliances

The role of alliances has long been an area of inquiry (see Morgenthau 1948; Singer and Small 1966; Choucri and North 1975; Levy 1981). Theoretically, much of the discussion on alliances has been centered on realism and its critics. Realists have generally seen alliances as a practice that can avoid war, if they balance capability. Critics, going back at least to Woodrow Wilson, have seen alliances as part of a power politics syndrome of behavior that encourages war.

Early research saw alliance formation somewhat associated with war involvement. Levy (1981) looking at major states from 1495 to 1975 found, except for the nineteenth century, that alliances involving at least one major state tend to be followed by war within five years (see also Singer and Small 1966). These findings are contrary to the classic realist notion that alliances can balance power and thereby reduce the probability of war. Whether this is because the alliances in question failed to balance, or whether having balanced war occurred anyway, cannot be determined without additional research. Levy (1981) also finds that many wars in his sample occur without a preceding alliance, which indicates that alliances are not a necessary condition of war. On the basis of this early evidence it can be concluded that, with the exception of the nineteenth century, alliances involving major states are much more frequently followed by war than by peace (see Vasquez 1993: 158–77).

Nonetheless, these findings basically show that sometimes alliances are associated with war and sometimes they are not. Gibler (2000) develops a typology of alliances that uncovers which of the alliances are dangerous and which are followed by peace. He finds that alliances that consist of a coalition of states that are major (as opposed to minor) states, that have been successful in their last war, and that are dissatisfied with the status quo are more apt to be involved in war within five years after signing an alliance, mostly because they pose threats.[4] Maoz (2000) also attempts to answer why some alliances are followed by war while others are not. His main finding is that alliances seem to operate differently and have different effects depending on whether they are made by democratic or nondemocratic states or by major or minor states.

Much of alliance research in the last decade has focused on the claim of the steps-to-war explanation that having an outside alliance increases threat perception and hence escalation to war once an MID breaks out. Senese and Vasquez (2008: ch. 6) find for the 1816–1945 period that if one or both sides have a politically relevant ally[5] this increases the probability that an MID will escalate to war.

For the Cold War (1946–1989), there is a fundamental shift. The type of alliance that Senese and Vasquez (2008) see as most war prone—when both sides have outside allies—now reduces the likelihood of war. This supports more of a realist notion. It is also consistent with what is known about the Cold War. Whatever may be the cause of this irenic effect, it seems to be confined to the Cold War period, since Senese and Vasquez's limited analysis of the post–Cold War period (1990–2001) suggests that the belligerent effect of outside alliances has returned.

One of the new areas of research in the last decade is based on the release of ATOP data. One of the reasons for collecting these data was the feeling that existing Correlates of War studies treated all alliances alike regardless of the specific obligations set out in the treaty (Leeds, Long, and Mitchell 2000). In particular, Leeds et al. were concerned that Sabrosky's (1980) conclusion that a little over 25 percent of allies were reliable was an unwarranted inference. In a reanalysis of Sabrosky (1980), they find, contrary to

him, that allies are reliable when they commit in writing to defend a state—
about 75 percent enter the war.

ATOP data have also been used to examine the question of whether certain
types of alliances deter successfully. Leeds (2003) maintains that it is primarily defensive pacts with specific obligations that should be seen as deterring.
She looks at MID onset and finds that states with an outside defensive pact
tend to have fewer MIDs initiated against them than those without such alliances. Nonetheless, according to this study, while MIDs are reduced, they
still occur, so the effect is probably better, or at least more conservatively,
described as a muting effect rather than one of successful deterrence.

Since Leeds (2003) finds this pattern for the 1815–1944 period, this raises
questions about the Senese and Vasquez (2008) findings that alliances are
war prone, although it must be kept in mind that their dependent variable is
war onset, and her dependent variable is MID onset. Leeds (2005b) looks
directly at the question of war onset. When this is the dependent variable, she
finds no statistically significant relationship, which means defensive alliances
with explicit commitments do not deter war. At the same time, however, she
does produce some evidence consistent with Senese and Vasquez (2008) that
defensive alliances are related to war diffusion. When defensive alliances are
present in disputes, allies live up to their commitments and are likely to intervene. Then she finds that multiparty disputes are more apt to escalate to war
than two-party disputes, a finding confirmed independently in other studies
(see Petersen, Vasquez, and Wang 2004).

More recent research has questioned Leeds' (2003) research design and
findings on deterrence of MIDs and wars. Benson (herein) raises serious
questions about the use of a dyad-year research design that may accentuate
greatly the impact of a few alliances. Further, and perhaps more importantly,
Benson (2011) finds problems with the typology Leeds (2003) uses for classifying defensive alliances that are the subject of the deterrence claims. He
reclassifies the data using Smith's (1995) scheme to produce more precise
categories that capture whether the obligation to defend is conditional or unconditional and whether the objective is compellence or deterrence. Benson
(2011) finds that the compellent alliances and active deterrent alliances are
conflict prone. Only the passive deterrent alliances reduce conflict, and these
are not a large percentage of alliance cases.

Kang (herein) also looks at Leeds (2003) with a more direct comparison
to the findings of Senese and Vasquez (2008). First, he finds that Leeds'
claims about the muting effect of defensive alliances only apply to the post–
Cold War era, 1989–2001, and then primarily for defense pacts with minor
states. In the Cold War, no significant effect for defense pacts is found. In
the 1816–1945 period, a state that has a defense pact with a major makes

it more likely that it will have an MID initiated against it. These findings show that the relationship between defense pacts and MID onset vary by historical period and by type of state (major or minor). It will require further research to tease out the precise impact, but for now it is clear that even for defensive alliances with explicit obligations, the likelihood of deterrence of MIDs is fairly circumscribed.

Additional questioning of Leeds' (2003) results is the focus of Kenwick (2011) and of Powers and Vasquez (2011). They seek to avoid some of the pitfalls of a dyad-year design by coming up with a longitudinal experimental design that examines each dyad with a defensive alliance before and after the alliance is made. The latter is seen as a treatment, and if deterrence is successful, the number of MIDs (and wars) before the treatment should be higher than after, and the reverse if it is not. They compare the five years before and after.

Kenwick (2011) finds for the 1815–1944 period (the subject of Leeds' 2003 study) that there are thirty-one defensive alliances that have fewer MIDs after than before and eighty-two that have more than before. This suggests that deterrence failure in terms of just muting the number of MIDs is more predominant (and statistically significant). Kenwick (2011) has one finding that is consistent with Leeds (2003). When only exclusive defensive alliances are examined, he finds eleven instances of fewer MIDS (deterrence success) and six with more MIDs. This result, however, is statistically insignificant.

Building on Kenwick (2011), Powers and Vasquez (2011) look at the question of war onset. Their findings are similar to those of Kenwick, even though they compare the number of wars before and after the treatment. They find only five cases of deterrence success when thirteen should be expected, twenty-one cases of deterrence failure when thirteen should be expected, and two cases where war both precedes and follows the defensive alliance treatment (which they take as an indicator of deterrence failure). A sign test shows that the difference is statistically significant.

In light of the above research, what do we think we know about alliances and war?

• Except for the nineteenth century, alliances involving major states tend to be followed by war within five years.
• Alliances that consist of major states that are dissatisfied or have been successful in their last war have a higher probability of being followed by war within five years than would be expected by chance. These findings by Gibler (2000) account for the differences between the nineteenth and twentieth century.

- Most wars involving major states have not been preceded by the formation of an alliance; therefore, alliances are not a necessary condition of war.
- Leeds (2003) has uncovered some evidence that defensive alliances have a muting effect on subsequent MIDs, but that once an ally is attacked, states will live up to their commitments and the MID will expand. Such multi-party MIDs are more war prone.
- More recent research finds that the cases supporting Leeds' claims about deterrence working to reduce MID onset are much more limited than previously thought, both in terms of the temporal domain and the types of actors involved.

These and other findings in the literature suggest a number of unanswered questions that should guide future research:

- In light of Maoz's analysis (2000), how do alliances composed of democratic states differ in their impact on the probability of war (and militarized disputes) compared to alliances composed of nondemocratic states?
- To what extent can system characteristics, including norms, strip war-prone alliances of their bellicose effects?
- Do alliances followed by war fail to prevent war because, as realists would suggest, they (1) fail to balance power or (2) fail to make a credible commitment that leads potential opponents to doubt that the alliance is reliable?
- What factors occur within five years after the signing of an alliance that can either increase or reduce the probability of war?
- What effects do alliances that score high on status, success, and dissatisfaction have on increased armament levels between disputants, repeated MIDs, and the making of counteralliances?
- What effect does making an alliance have on the domestic political environment of the signatories and possible targets, particularly the balance between hard-liners and accommodationists?
- Does the causal sequence of wars that break out without a preceding alliance differ in a theoretically significant manner from the causal sequence of wars that are preceded by an alliance?

Rivalry

Leng (1983) was one of the first to show that for many pairs of states their first crisis does not escalate to war, but that frequently repeated crises will escalate to war. He argues that to treat each crisis as independent, as many studies have done, is to fail to incorporate within research designs the idea that the onset of war is a process that comes out of the interaction of states taken over time. Leng (1983) believes that when crises recur between the same disputants, the behavior and outcome in one crisis has an impact on the next one, because decision makers learn from their previous bargaining behavior (see also Leng 2000). In Leng's early analysis, he uncovered two important patterns: (1) while war does not always occur during the first crisis, it usually does by the third, and (2) the reason this happens is that states (both the previous winner and loser) escalate their interactions as they move from one crisis to the next. Likewise, there are findings in the ICB project that dyads that have a number of crises have a greater disposition to employ violence and a greater likelihood that a crisis will escalate to war (Brecher, James, and Wilkenfeld 2000: table 3.2).

Leng's analysis set the stage for distinguishing dyads in terms of whether they had recurring disputes. Goertz and Diehl (1992a) and Wayman and Jones (1991; see also Wayman 2000) were among the first to see the importance of adjusting research designs to take account of what they labeled interstate rivalry. Rivalries became an important subject of study for both theoretical and methodological reasons. Up until this time, most scholars had compared and quantitatively analyzed individual disputes and crises without controlling for the particular states involved. It makes sense theoretically that one should study relations between states over time, rather than disputes one at a time, since it is probably the underlying relations between the states that are governing the onset of disputes and what happens within them (see Wayman 2000). Scholars began to realize that, methodologically, MIDs were not statistically independent, and to analyze them this way, as they had been doing, was underestimating relationships (see Goertz and Diehl 2000).

Until recently (Valeriano 2003), little research has been conducted on why states become rivals. Vasquez and Leskiw (2001: 308–9) show that states contending over certain kinds of disputes—namely, territorial disputes—are more apt to become enduring rivals and more apt to go to war than other types of rivalries. Tir and Diehl (2002) and Colaresi, Rasier, and Thompson (2007: 203–13; Valeriano herein) have similar findings. This pattern emerges because territorial disputes tend to recur, and they recur because they are not settled but typically result in stalemate (see Hensel 1998; Goertz, Jones, and Diehl 2005).

Bremer (2000) explains this as a result of the underlying issue not being resolved. When more issues are involved, it follows that stalemates are more likely, since the more issues, the less likely it is there will be a resolution (see James 1988; Brecher 1993). The same is true when more actors are involved in a dispute. Empirical research provides some evidence that the more issues involved, the more likely a stalemate (Dreyer 2010; Diehl and Goertz herein), and the more actors involved, the more likely escalation to war (Petersen et al. 2004; see also Brecher 1993).

Valeriano (herein) shows that there are other factors than the underlying issue that make for rivalry. He finds that states that make outside alliances and have arms races are apt to have repeated MIDs and thus become first proto- and then enduring rivals. As he shows (Valeriano herein), these are statistically significant relationships. He sees engaging in such power politics practices as a series of steps to rivalry.

Valeriano (2003; herein) also adds to our knowledge about the timing and sequencing of the steps to rivalry. He finds that alliance making comes early in a relationship that ends up as a proto- or enduring rivalry. Conversely, mutual military buildups come later. Lastly, in a very original analysis, Valeriano (2003) demonstrates empirically that rivals tend to escalate their interactions across MIDs. Leng (1983) had suggested such a pattern, but only tested for it on a selected small sample. Valeriano (2003) provides a systematic test with a new measure on the full set of proto- and enduring rivals. He finds that proto- and enduring rivalries that exhibit an increase in the level of hostility as they go from the early MIDs in a given stage to the later ones have a greater propensity for war. Valeriano (2003) calls these dyads that have an increase of hostility across their MIDs "escalating rivalries."

A number of important findings have been produced on interstate rivalries. First, interstate conflict in the form of MIDs is not evenly or randomly distributed across pairs of states in the international system but clustered within certain dyads (Diehl and Goertz 2000). More importantly, Diehl and Goertz (2000: 199) find that states that are rivals have a greater propensity to go to war. Indeed, 49.4 percent of the wars that occurred from 1816 to 1992 arose from enduring rivalries. Likewise, Colaresi, Rasler, and Thompson (2007: 88–89) find in an analysis of principal rivalries that about three-fourths of all wars are linked to rivalries. A related finding is also produced in ICB data, where Brecher and Wilkenfeld (1997: 832–33) find that states engaged in protracted conflict (repeated crises) have a higher likelihood of going to war.

In the last half decade, research has moved beyond bivariate analyses to examine how rivalry interacts with other variables. Most of this work has taken place within the steps-to-war framework. Senese and Vasquez (2008: chs. 5 and 6) look at the impact of rivalry while controlling for the presence of other steps to war—territorial disputes, outside alliances, and arms races. They find that rivalry has a separate and independent effect and is not simply a function of the other steps. They also find that rivalry is important for increasing the probability of escalation to war in both the 1816–1945 and the 1946–1989 (Cold War) periods, whereas two of the other factors—outside alliances and arms races—are not potent factors during the Cold War. This means that rivalry is a persistent factor associated with the probability of war.

In terms of explicit (statistical) interactions, Senese and Vasquez (2008) find (for 1816–1945) a significant interaction between the presence of territorial disputes and rivalry, which means that rivals have an enhanced probability of going to war in the presence of territorial disputes. Nonetheless, Senese and Vasquez (2008: 147–48) find that it is not just repeating territorial disputes that drive the relationship between rivalry and war. They provide some evidence that recurring territorial disputes (four or more) have a separate and independent effect from rivalry in the 1816–1945 period.[6]

Some of these findings are also produced using the ICB data set. Colaresi and Thompson (2005) find that with two or more crises (some indication of rivalry), states that have an external alliance and an ongoing arms race have an enhanced likelihood of war. In a similar vein, Colaresi, Rasler, and Thompson (2007) find that strategic rivals that are contiguous and contest territory are highly prone to war. These tests based on separate data sets—MID and ICB—suggest that various steps to war are not so much confounded with each other as they are mutually reinforcing, with the more steps each side takes the more likely war.

The study of interstate rivalry is important not only for its findings but for its theoretical insights about how to study war. Because disputes and wars are clustered by dyads, this suggests that scholars should compare pairs of states and specifically their *relations* to understand why these disputes and wars occur. Likewise, studying conflict termination should be done in the context of what makes rivalries persist and what makes them end.

It would be illusionary, however, to think that domestic politics plays no role in the persistence of rivalries. Early on, Lowi (1967) discussed the importance of domestic actors who exaggerate threats in bringing about hostile relations like those of the Cold War. Domestic actors are undoubtedly key to understanding the psychological factors that bring about hostility and rivalry (see Thies 2001). Colaresi (2005) has documented the role of "outbidding" by domestic hard-liners both in terms of escalating hostility and preventing peaceful settlements. This is similar to the role of "spoilers" in civil wars (Stedman 1997).[7]

In terms of rivalry termination, Bennett's (1996, 1997) work has provided important research and data. Rather than simply using a certain number of years without an MID, as Wayman (2000) and Diehl and Goertz (2000) do, he argues that a rivalry ends when the underlying issue the parties are contending over is resolved. Using this definition, Bennett has produced a set of termination dates that are more historically informed than we have previously had (but see Diehl and Goertz herein for some criticisms of this approach).

A pressing question related to termination is whether rivalries can be managed to reduce the probability of war. What quantitative research exists suggests that conflict resolution techniques may have limited utility (see Bercovitch and Diehl 1997; Diehl and Goertz herein). Nevertheless, there are some hopeful findings. Gibler (1997a) finds that states that settle their territorial disputes have a longer period of time between disputes and less intense disputes under certain conditions.

What have we learned about rivalry?

- Most enduring rivals go to war, and over half of the interstate wars come out of rivalries. Understanding rivalry seems to be a key to understanding war.
- Rivalry has a separate and independent impact on the probably of war compared to territorial disputes, outside alliances, and arms races, and is important for both the 1816–1945 period and the Cold War.
- States become rivals if they have territorial disputes, make outside alliances against each other, and engage in arms races.
- Conflict resolution techniques have limited success in ending rivalry, but there is some evidence indicating that settling underlying territorial issues can do so. Regime change is also associated with certain cases of rivalry termination.

Still a number of unanswered questions remain:

- What causes recurring conflict and the effects it produces?
- What processes make rivals go to war? As disputes recur, they seem to have an impact on each other. Exactly what that impact is, however, needs further research, but it is thought to produce an increase in hostility, threat perception, and some form of escalation, all of which increases the probability of war.
- How do rivalries end, and why do they last as long as they do?
- What is the role of domestic politics in the origin and persistence of rivalry? What is the domestic impact of recurring disputes within each state (e.g., on the balance of hard-liners and accommodationists)?

Arms Races

Some of the earliest work in peace science was devoted to measuring and modeling arms races (see Richardson 1960; Zinnes 1976), with only a few statistical analyses (Choucri and North 1975; Smith 1980). The major spurt of research only occurs with the publication of Wallace (1979), which shows that serious disputes that occur in the context of arms races have a statistically significant likelihood of escalating to war. This research generates both an empirical and methodological debate between those, like Wallace, who believe that arms races are dangerous and promote war, and realists, who see arms races as not inherently leading to war. Diehl (1983), who is the main critic, provides a clearly replicable measure of arms races, which he more conservatively labels mutual military buildups, and makes several changes in the research design that reduce the strength of the relationship but do not entirely eliminate its significance (see also Weede 1980). Since this debate is reviewed extensively in Sample (herein; see also Sample 2000; Vasquez and Henehan 1992, 103–6), it will not be discussed further here.

What is important is that Sample (1997) resolves the debate by showing that most of the mutual military buildups that Diehl sees as not going to war are of two sorts: either (1) they go to war within five years or (2) they occur in the nuclear era. Providing for a five-year window and controlling for nuclear weapons Sample finds a statistically significant relationship between mutual military buildups and the escalation of an MID to war. Her later work (Sample 1998b) goes on to show that the hostile spiral model is more accurate than the deterrence model. At the same time, she finds that the presence of nuclear weapons has a dramatic effect by lowering the likelihood that escalation will occur (see Sample 2000: 177).

The work up to 2000 focuses exclusively on arms races between major states. In Sample (2002), evidence between mutual military buildups and escalation to war is broadened by the collection of data on minor states. Sample (2002) shows that the arms race relationship also holds for minor-minor states for the 1816–1945 period. It does not hold, however, for the Cold War. Nor does it hold for major-minor dyads, which makes sense given their great disparity in capability.

In this research, Sample does not examine the relationship between arms racing and the other steps to war. Senese and Vasquez (2008) provide some research on this. They find that arms races in the prenuclear era have a separate and independent effect from alliances, rivalry, and territory, and that the impact of arms races is so high that they make war almost inevitable once a militarized dispute emerges in their presence. Although arms races can be extremely dangerous, they are fairly rare. Only a few wars are preceded by arms races (see Diehl 1983; Vasquez and Valeriano 2010). However, these wars are quite severe and include both World War I and World War II.

One of the criticisms of arms race research is that it might be prone to a selection effect since much of the research looks at arms races in the context of an ongoing MID (see Diehl and Crescenzi's 1998 criticism of Sample and her 1998a response). Gibler, Rider, and Hutchison (2005) address this issue by collecting arms race data based on the presence of a strategic rivalry

(Thompson 1995, 2001). Their analyses show that strategic rivals have a significantly greater likelihood of both having an MID and going to war in the presence of an arms race. Their analyses also suggest that what makes arms races associated with war is that during arms races the number of MIDs more than doubles—making the chances of war much higher simply because there are more MIDs (see Gibler, Rider, and Hutchison 2005: 144). If sustained (cf. Colaresi, Rasler, and Thompson 2007: 235, 265), this is an important new finding on the dynamics that bring about war.

Despite the above work, the claim of Diehl and Crescenzi (1998) that it is really rivalry that is responsible for MIDs escalating and not mutual military buildups has not been directly tested until just recently. Rider, Findley, and Diehl (2011) provide some evidence to support the claim. Even so, they still cannot entirely eliminate the significance of mutual military buildups despite several attempts. Unfortunately, the importance of this study is limited by the fact that certain well-known lessons about arms races and MID escalation to war are ignored in the construction of the research design. For example, there is no control for historical era even though it has been shown by Sample (1997) that the bellicose effect of arms racing is confined to the pre-1945 era. Likewise, no control is made for the presence of nuclear weapons, nor is a five-year window employed (on these and other problems, see Sample 2011). All these omissions bias the research design against finding a relationship between mutual military buildups and MID escalation to war. In a reexamination of these findings, Sample (2011, see also herein) shows that controlling for historical era and the presence of nuclear weapons restores the significance of arms racing in the presence of rivalry.

Sample (herein) pursues in greater depth the question between arms races, rivalry, and escalation to war, and the relationship between these variables and various measures of shifts in capability. She employs two conventional measures of rivalry—Thompson (2001) and Diehl and Goertz (2000) enduring rivalry—and a new measure of intense rivalry based on when states form alliances targeting an opponent (for which she uses ATOP data). She also extends her mutual military buildup data from 1992 to 2001.

Her first test is an aggregate data analysis that shows that mutual military buildups are significantly related to an escalation to war when controlling for rivalry in the 1816–1945 period. She then conducts a split population test. She finds that outside of rivalry, mutual military buildups significantly increase the likelihood that dyads with MIDs will go to war for the pre-1946 period. If the effect of arms races were totally due to rivalry as Rider, Findley, and Diehl (2011) and Diehl and Crescenzi (1998) argue, such a finding should not appear. Next, she examines the relationship between mutual military buildups and escalation within the population of rivals. For strategic rivals (Thompson) and enduring rivals (Diehl and Goertz), mutual military buildups are still significant (although for the latter only at the .10 level).[8] The ATOP measure of intense rivalry, however, wipes out the significance of mutual military buildups.

How does one explain the latter, which is inconsistent with the other findings? The most reasonable explanation is that the ATOP measure is picking up other advanced steps to war that already incorporate the impact of arms races. In other words, by the time rivals form targeted alliances against each other, there is a good chance that they are far along a path to war, and whether they have an arms race at this stage has limited or no impact on the probability of war because its impact is already incorporated in the ATOP measure. This implies that the ATOP measure is picking up something in addition to rivalry. Nonetheless, research on the interrelationships of the steps is just beginning, and as more data on the timing and sequence of steps is collected, this alternate hypothesis will undoubtedly receive further scrutiny.

What conclusions can be made about arms races and war in light of the research in the last thirty years?

- There is a statistically significant relationship between the presence of a mutual military buildup and the outbreak of a dispute that escalates to war, if a five-year window of opportunity is examined.
- This probability of war breaking out in the presence of a mutual military buildup can greatly increase in the presence of certain other factors, such as territorial disputes, outside alliances, rivalry, and certain shifts in capability.
- Conversely, the presence of nuclear weapons greatly mutes the impact of mutual military buildups.
- There has not been much research on the effect of arms races directly (i.e., without MIDs as an intervening variable) on the outbreak of war. What little there has been is consistent with the finding that arms races significantly increase the probability of war.

Although progress has resumed in this area of inquiry since Sample (1997), some questions still remain:

- Do arms races increase the probability of war simply because they increase the number of MIDs?
- There is a need to identify and collect other indicators on military buildups—such as instituting conscription, extending the time of military service, increasing the number reserves, purchasing new types of weapons, and increasing the stockpile of certain kinds of weapons. Such indicators

may also be useful in identifying arms races in the nineteenth century, which with present measures appears not to have many arms races.

- What effect does arms racing have on the domestic political environment?
- Research needs to be conducted on how arms races are linked to other factors thought to be associated with the outbreak of war; how are arms races related to alliance formation and alliance tightening, rivalry, and territorial disputes? This is part of a broader research concern on the sequences of the various steps to war and the question of endogeneity.
- Are there any theoretically significant differences between the way wars preceded by arms races break out and the way wars without preceding arms races break out?

Capability Distributions

The relationship between power and the onset of war has been one of the most discussed topics within the field. In the last decade, little new empirical work has been done in this area except for work on the balance of power and some applied studies on power transition, especially as they relate to the rise of China and other challengers to the United States. The most innovative work on capability has been on the role of nuclear weapons, which is the focus of Geller's review (herein).

The theoretical work on capability has been informed by realist analysis in its various forms, and a great deal of it has been widely contested, not only by critics of realism but by various theoretical perspectives within the realist paradigm, broadly defined. The findings have been varied and at times inconsistent but have provided a more complex and detailed picture of the role capability plays in the onset of war.

The basic and most consistent finding on capability is that relative equality in a dyad is associated with a dispute escalating to war, while great disparity in capability is associated with no war. Bremer (1992, 2000) finds that dyads that have only small or medium differences in capability are more likely to go to war. Geller (1993) finds, among enduring rivalries, that states relatively equal in military capability are much more likely to have wars than those where one side has preponderance. Similarly, Huth (1996: 115, table 10) finds that when there is a very large discrepancy in military capability, there is a lower probability that a state will escalate its territorial issues. To these data analyses can be added the host of studies that routinely control for capability and find that parity, not preponderance, is associated with war.

Of course, two of the most famous commentators on the balance of power—Gulick (1955) and Waltz (1979)—do not argue that a balance of power will prevent war, since sometimes war is necessary to maintain the balance. What Waltz (1979: 121) does argue is that systemic anarchy produces "balancing of power politics." The thrust of the best studies—both case studies (Kaufman, Little, and Wohlforth 2007) and data analyses (Levy and Thompson 2005, 2010a)—has not found a pattern of consistent overall balancing of capability, but has found that balancing occurs under certain circumscribed conditions.

The findings on power transition have been a little stronger. Organski and Kugler (1980) provide evidence to show that a power transition is a necessary condition for the biggest wars in the system (but also see Kim 1992 who raises questions about the generalizability of this finding). The strongest evidence in favor of the power transition and the related power parity thesis is that of Wayman (1996), who finds that a power transition within rival dyads increases the probability of war. In fact, war is most likely when there is a rapid approach toward power parity between rivals. One thing that needs to be kept in mind about this research is that the findings are strongest—indeed, only seem to hold—when the satisfaction of states is taken into account.

Most recent studies on power transition have been concerned with the implications of whether a coming transition might result in war, especially with the rise of China. Adherents of the power transition school have been especially diligent in avoiding an overly deterministic reaction (see Tammen et al. 2000). Likewise other theoretical approaches that see changes in capability have focused on this policy-relevant question (see Thompson 2008).

As with other quantitative studies on conflict, dyadic research has done better in producing results than studies of the system. Nevertheless, there may be some system-level effect if one examines the impact of systemic changes in capability on dyadic relations. Geller (1992; see also Thompson 1992) finds that shifts in the distribution of capability at the systemic level can interact with dyadic power shifts to increase the probability of war. Specifically, he finds that when a power transition at the dyadic level occurs in conjunction with a decreasing concentration of capability at the system level, war is more likely.

One clear finding on capability is that the strongest states in the system are the most war prone (Geller 2000a). Bremer (1980b) clearly demonstrates that major states are the most war prone and the most likely to initiate wars (see also Bremer 2000). Indeed, he finds that even among the strongest states, the stronger a state is the more wars it is apt to experience. The finding that the strong resort more frequently to the use of force is not a surprise to either realists or their critics.

A number of findings on the dyadic level show that strong states that have an advantage, particularly in terms of military capability, are more apt to initiate disputes and wars (Bueno de Mesquita 1981; Huth, Gelpi, and Bennett 1993). Similarly, Huth (1996: 115–56) finds that among states that have territorial disagreements, those that have a three-to-one military advantage tend not to compromise and instead "often adopt a firm negotiating position."

Nonetheless, it is important to note that for highly salient issues, dissatisfied states are not "deterred" from attacking stronger states unless there is close to a nine-to-one military advantage; Huth (1996: 87), for example, finds "many examples of very weak states disputing the borders of their powerful neighbors." Geller (2000a) finds that among enduring rivals, dissatisfied challengers have an equal probability of initiating war, regardless of whether they are stronger or weaker than their rivals.

The advent of nuclear weapons has been hypothesized to change the fundamentals of international politics and war. The so-called nuclear revolution (Jervis 1989a) is thought to be a function of the sheer destructive power of the weapons themselves, which coupled with mutual assured destruction (MAD) makes war irrational. The absence of any war between the US and USSR is attributed to the effect of nuclear deterrence. The fact that the Cold War was a "long peace" (Gaddis 1986) reverses one of the main findings on capability, namely, that the strongest states are prone to war. The reversal of such a firm pattern is an important piece of evidence for the nuclear revolution thesis.

Still, all this evidence is based on a single case, and the quantitative studies that find nuclear weapons reducing the likelihood of war (see Huth, Gelpi, and Bennett 1993; Asal and Beardsley 2007; Rauchhaus 2009; reviewed in Geller herein) are simply restating in aggregate form the well-known fact that the US and the USSR did not go to war. The relationship between nuclear weapons and peace could be a function of some other factor coterminous with the Cold War period, like the unique dynamics of the Soviet-American relationship or the deterrence impact of the world wars (which is what Mueller 1988 argues). A key is that nuclear deterrence worked with a number of irenic factors, so it is logically difficult to determine how great an impact should be attributed to nuclear weapons themselves (see Vasquez 1991: 214–22). What is agreed upon is that nuclear weapons have raised the "provocation threshold" (see Lebow 1981: 277), meaning that what used to provoke war in the past no longer does so now. Just how high that threshold is remains a matter of debate (for believers of deterrence, war will never occur).

Another piece of evidence that nuclear weapons has changed behavior deals with the "stability-instability paradox" (Snyder 1965). According to this hypothesis, because MAD makes war irrational, states use the threat of it to test resolve and play games of brinkmanship, of which chicken games are the most extreme example. This, of course, means that nuclear deterrence as a policy was not so much a way of avoiding war as it was a way of manipulating the risk of war to gain a bargaining advantage (Geller herein). Quantitative evidence has shown that nuclear states (compared to nonnuclear states) engage in more crises, and these escalate to higher levels of hostility (short of war). Geller (1990) is among the first to show this. Asal and Beardsley (2007) confirm this pattern, as does Rauchhaus (2009). Geller (herein) also points out that Pakistan's strategy in the 1999 Kargil War can be explained in terms of the stability-instability paradox.

While nuclear weapons have these impacts, other hypothesized effects have not materialized. The most important one is that nuclear weapons do not deter the initiation of crises. Even nonnuclear states do not seem to be inhibited in using force against a nuclear state. Kugler (1984) shows this in his study of US-Soviet-China crises, as Geller (herein) points out in his review. It is also clear that America's nuclear monopoly did not deter Stalin. Studies by Huth, Bennett, and Gelpi (1992) and by Gartzke and Jo (2009), which include many more cases, reconfirm this finding.

Another unexpected finding is that nuclear weapons have no impact on success or victory in a crisis; rather this seems to be a function of local conventional capability. Early studies on victory in militarized interstate disputes (Wayman, Singer, and Goertz 1983) and in war (Rosen 1972) show that overall capability (particularly economic capability) determines outcome. Recent studies show that the presence of nuclear weapons (in symmetric or asymmetric dyads) does not affect this relationship, in that nonnuclear factors have a greater impact on outcome (Kugler 1984; Blechman and Kaplan 1978; see Geller herein). Likewise, in a series of studies on deterrence (Russett 1963; Huth and Russett 1984), nonnuclear factors are also seen as more determinative.[9]

Further indicating the limited impact of nuclear weapons is their failure to prevent the Kargil War. This means that the danger of escalation from a conventional to a nuclear war first discussed by Kahn (1965) is not sufficient to deter a conventional war. Indeed, as Geller (herein) points out, the stability-instability paradox may actually play a role in this failure of nuclear deterrence. The fighting of a conventional war between nuclear states raises the possibility that even if nuclear deterrence works to prevent nuclear war in general, it may not do so in every instance, since any conventional war could get out of control. Yet preventing nuclear war in every instance is what needs to be done to avoid a nuclear holocaust. Such a concern is especially pressing in cases involving long-term rivals engaged in highly salient territorial disputes where there have been multiple wars as in South Asia and the Middle East.

In light of this research what have we learned about the role of capability in the onset of war?

- Major states are much more likely to become involved in wars than minor states, and they account for most of the interstate wars since 1815. This effect is reversed for symmetrical nuclear dyads.
- Parity between dyads is associated with war and preponderance, especially large preponderances, with the absence of war.
- Capability seems only important in bringing about war for states that have severe disagreements and are dissatisfied.
- Nuclear weapons have raised the provocation threshold for war and have most likely played a role in preventing total war among symmetric nuclear dyads. However, their destructive potential has encouraged games of brinkmanship and the manipulation of risk to gain bargaining advantages.
- Nuclear weapons and the doctrine of nuclear deterrence have failed to deter the initiation of severe crises or conventional war. Nor do they have a significant impact on who wins.

Despite the extensive studies conducted on the role of power in the onset of war, there are still things we would like to know:

- Is it worth researching broad questions like what aspects of capability, if any, are most important for bringing about war, or should capability variables be reduced, as has often been the case in recent years, to control variables?
- How are capability variables (including shifts) related to other factors that increase the probability of war, in particular, alliance formation, arms races, and repeated disputes?
- What are the characteristics of weaker states that initiate disputes and wars against stronger opponents? Do they have long-lasting territorial disputes and/or a domestic political environment dominated by hard-liners?

FACTORS PROMOTING PEACE

The most fundamental thing we know about peace is that it actually occurs in the international system; indeed, it is much more common than one would expect from reading realist international relations theory. Morgenthau ([1948] 1960: 38), the classic twentieth-century realist, asserted, "All history shows that nations active in international politics are continuously preparing for, actively involved in, or recovering from organized violence in the form of war." Waltz (1979: 121) maintained that such a pattern is due to the fact that the international system is anarchic.

Nevertheless, statistically, existing data on war and militarized disputes show that periods of actual fighting among recognized states have been relatively rare. As Geller and Singer (1998: 1) point out, in the post-Napoleonic period, 150 states never experienced even one war; an additional 49 had only one or two wars. Indeed by 1997 there were just 79 interstate wars (Vasquez and Valeriano 2010). Another way of making the same point is to examine the number of militarized disputes from 1816 to 2001 and compare that to the number that escalate to war. There are 3,511 dyadic disputes in this period, but only 320 of these escalate to war, which is 9.1 percent of the dyadic disputes (cf. Senese and Vasquez 2008: 59). This is not a high percentage of wars for dyads that have at least one MID.

The best evidence that states are not constantly at war is, of course, the democratic peace. As Ray (2000: 299) states, "One thing that 'we know about war' with unusual, or even unparalleled, confidence is that it almost never involves two democratic states in conflict against each other." A great deal of research has found that democratic states do not fight each other in interstate wars, with Levy (1988: 662) calling this pattern one of the few laws we have in political science. The landmark studies of democratic peace have been Rummel (1983), Doyle (1986), Maoz and Abdolali (1989), Maoz and Russett (1993), Russett (1993), and Ray (1995). Other research shows that pairs of democratic states not only do not fight each other but are also less likely to have militarized disputes (Bremer 1993; Russett and Oneal 2001) and are more likely to use conflict resolution to try to settle what militarized disputes they have (see Dixon 1994). Researchers also found that democratic dyads in ancient systems were not likely to fight each other (Weart 1998).

Despite this success, several researchers have challenged the findings, mostly questioning whether certain states can be dismissed as nondemocratic, whether other cases do not constitute wars between democratic states (see Elman 1997), and whether newly democratic states are peaceful (Mansfield and Snyder 1995). Others argue that the reason joint democracies do not fight each other is because they are states satisfied with the status quo (see Gartzke 1998; Gowa 1999).

There are two explanations of the democratic peace—the normative and the structural (Maoz and Russett 1993). The normative explanation maintains that democratic states share norms about how to deal with conflict that they externalize from their domestic politics. The structural explanation maintains that domestic constituencies and institutions restrain democratic leaders from going to war because war is generally not seen as in the interest of the common person. The explanations are not mutually exclusive, but both have been elaborated separately in the literature.

Mitchell (herein) gives a rationale for the normative explanation, which in recent years has been overshadowed by the structural explanation of Bueno de Mesquita et al. (2003). For her, the norms adopted by democratic states are so powerful that they can create a Kantian system or culture that will even influence nondemocratic states once democratic states reach a certain number (Mitchell 2002), which means that the democratic peace works not only at the dyadic level, but also at the system level. She finds that as the number of democratic states approaches a certain threshold in the global system, nondemocratic states adopt the more peaceful norms of democratic states, thereby producing a systemic effect. She demonstrates empirically that once democratic states constitute 50 percent of the states in the system, resorting to third-party conflict management is much more likely (Mitchell 2002).

Mitchell (herein) sees joint democracy promoting three norms, all of which help to explain why democracies do not fight each other: (1) the use of third parties to manage conflict, (2) respect for human rights, and (3) promotion of the territorial integrity norm (Zacher 2001), which means democratic states have few territorial disputes with each other (see Mitchell and Prins 1999). The acceptance of the territorial integrity norm also reflects a decline in the benefits of territorial conquest (see also Rosecrance 1986; Gartzke 2006). For Mitchell, these norms help mute the probability of war by providing alternatives to the use of force and keeping the most war-prone disputes—territorial disputes—off the agenda.

Raymond (2000) also argues that the democratic peace is a result, in part, of these states sharing norms about how to deal with conflict. Even when disputes emerge, democratic states are more apt than other pairs of states to resort to conflict resolution techniques, as Dixon (1994) shows (see also Raymond 1994). This is particularly true in how democratic states deal with very war-prone disputes, like territorial disputes (Huth and Allee 2002). In addition, democratic states are more apt to negotiate than to resort to force (Huth and Allee 2002). Bilateral negotiations are an important procedure for settling territorial issues. Hensel (herein: table 1.7) finds that over half of settlement attempts (whether by democracies or not) have been by using bilateral negotiations.

The structural explanation has gained more attention because of the formal models of first Bueno de Mesquita and Lalman (1992) and later Bueno de Mesquita et al. (1999), who developed a rational choice framework that looks at how differing "selectorates" and "win sets" of regimes affect their calculations about war. They provide evidence that states with institutional constraints are less likely to have wars with each other.

An important distinction to keep in mind about the democratic peace thesis is whether it is best cast at the dyadic level or the monadic—that is, whether democratic states are generally more peaceful than other types of states. The latter is consistent with the structural explanation, but not the normative explanation. Ray (2000) is not too sanguine about the monadic level, but he does provide some evidence, as well as a theoretical argument to support the claim, that democracies are in fact less war prone in general and hence truly pacific.

This is basically the Wilsonian version of the democratic peace. Some have argued that such a version of the democratic peace places insufficient weight on democratic bellicosity. While it may be true that democratic states do not fight interstate wars with one another, some democratic states, and specifically the United States, have used covert operations to overthrow duly elected governments. Forsythe (1992) provides a systematic test that supports the hypothesis that democracies do fight each other through the use of covert actions. Likewise, democratic states are subject to war fevers and can actively push their leaders toward wars that may have been avoidable, as in the Spanish-American War and the Crimean War (see Small 1980 and Richardson 1994, respectively).

Meanwhile, Russett and Oneal (2001) have systematically examined the other two pillars of liberalism—namely, that international organization and economic interdependence (including trade) reduce conflict and war (see also Oneal and Russett 1997). They find that democratic states tend to share a large number of joint memberships in intergovernmental organizations (IGOs) and to trade with each other. The work on shared IGOs is consistent with early peace research, which suggests that the mere presence of IGOs makes war less likely (see Wallace 1972) as well as more recent research (see Hensel, Mitchell, et al. 2008; Brochmann and Hensel 2009, 2011). Barbieri (1996, 2002), however, challenges the findings on trade and war.

More recent criticisms of the democratic peace have focused on why democratic states do not fight each other. Mousseau (2000) argues that the real reason democracies do not fight each other is not they that share norms or have restraining institutions but because of their capitalist economies. Unlike other capitalist explanations (Gartzke 2007; McDonald 2009), Mousseau emphasizes the market contract culture embodied within capitalism as the key causal factor. An intensive contract culture makes joint market-capitalist states more likely to resolve their disputes through negotiation. Mousseau (herein) provides new evidence to support this line of argument; he shows that the market-capitalist peace can account for more of the evidence than the democratic peace and that the contract-intensive culture explains both democracy and peace. While not as old as democratic peace research, Mousseau's and related work on the role of capitalism provides a promising alternative to democratic peace theory and research that will continue to receive wide attention.

Gibler (2007) argues that the reason democratic states do not fight each other is that they do not have territorial disputes (see also Vasquez 2000: 365) having settled their borders before they became democracies. Gibler (2007) provides evidence to show that neighbors that have stable borders do not fight each other and that this variable eliminates the significance of the joint democracy. The evidence on democratic states not having territorial disputes is consistent with earlier findings (Kocs 1995; Mitchell and Prins 1999; Huth and Allee 2002: 267; see also Gartzke 1998) and the claims of the territorial explanation of war (Vasquez 1993: ch. 4).[10] Gibler's use of this evidence to eliminate the significance of joint democracy, however, is an important and very original finding.

Gibler goes on to adopt Tilly's (1975, 1992) logic on state formation (see also Rasler and Thompson 1989) to argue that the democratic peace is spurious. He maintains that territorial disputes create an insecure political environment that leads to an increase in the centralization of the state. Gibler (herein) sees this effect as posing an obstacle for the development of democratic institutions. In a series of studies, he shows that the presence of an external territorial MID is significantly related to the absence of certain democratic characteristics, like the value of tolerance (see Hutchison and Gibler 2007). However, once territorial disputes are settled and the borders stable, centralization is apt to wane. For Gibler, a neighborhood with stable borders provides a benign environment for the emergence of democracy (presumably when other domestic and traditional correlates of democracy are present).

Gibler (2012) also cuts new theoretical ground by arguing that once major states settle their territorial disputes with neighbors, this frees up resources for entering disputes and wars with noncontiguous states. Because the stakes in such wars are not as serious in terms of their national security implications, democracies can choose their interventions carefully to increase their probability of winning. Lastly, it should be noted that there are important policy implications that Gibler has derived from the territorial peace, the key of which is that promotion of democracy (and peace) is best done by trying to resolve intractable territorial disputes.

Additional evidence that Gibler may be on the right track comes from recent studies by Rasler and Thompson (2010, 2011). They examine the impact of stable borders on the emergence of democracy and the absence of war between joint democracies in various regions. They find a similar pattern to that posited by Gibler using different data on stable borders (they used settled borders as indicated by Biger 1995) and a different research design (regions rather than dyads). They conclude that regime type is less important than most think, a sentiment that confirms some of their earlier skepticism about the democratic peace (Rasler and Thompson 2005). These studies, as made clear by Rasler and Thompson (herein), look at the impact of war on various political and economic processes including subsequent war, internal centralization, democracy, and peace. For Rasler and Thompson (herein), too much of the work on causes of war has not looked at the ways in which war has impacted the system and historical processes. In this way they see the findings of the territorial peace, as well as the capitalist peace, as part of a larger historical dynamic.

Peace however is not confined just to joint democracies. Peace research has shown that even among the most war-prone states in the system (i.e., major states), it is possible to have periods of peace. Wallensteen (1984) establishes that there are certain periods in the post-Napoleonic era that have no wars among major states. He finds periods of peace associated with major states attempting to establish "rules of the game." Henehan and Vasquez (2011) build on Wallensteen's work by showing that within his peaceful periods there are few or no territorial disputes between the major states. Still, when there are territorial disputes, they do not escalate to war, which suggests that norms are playing a role in resolving serious disputes.

Although Wallensteen's (1984) measure is subject to criticism because it is based on the coding of historians' judgments, it points to an important insight, namely, that norms have an impact on the probability of war. Even before Wallensteen (1984), there was research with more rigorous measures in support of the hypothesis. Kegley and Raymond (1982, 1990) find that when states accept the more restrictive *pacta sunt servanda* tradition of international law that sees alliance treaties as binding as opposed to the more permissive *rebus sic stantibus* tradition, wars and the occurrence of militarized disputes, especially among major states, are less likely.

What can be concluded about peace up to this point?

- Peace is possible and has occurred in the modern global system, even among the very war-prone major states.
- Despite the criticism and the possible statistical fragility of the finding, it does seem that democratic states rarely fight interstate wars with one another.
- There is some evidence, but not as extensive as the evidence for the democratic peace, that the reason democracies do not fight each other is that they do not have territorial disputes.
- Another reason democracies do not fight each other may have something to do with the characteristics of the capitalist economy they embody, especially their social-market culture, but this too needs considerable research.
- What limited evidence there is suggests that norms and attempts to establish rules of the game in the global system attenuate the outbreak of war among major states and reduce the number of militarized disputes.

This is not a great deal of knowledge, but then again considerably less research has been done on peace than on war. Nonetheless, these findings do suggest some fruitful topics and questions that would increase our knowledge:

- What are the characteristics (or correlates) of peaceful eras, peaceful systems, or zones of peace? Are peaceful eras or dyads less likely to have territorial disputes, or more likely to have norms or procedures that can settle these sorts of disputes?
- What specific kinds of norms are associated with peaceful systems? Are norms over certain issues (e.g., the transfer of territory) more essential to keeping the peace than others?
- What role do IGOs play in the establishment and maintenance of peace?
- Is there an economic foundation to peace (open markets versus autarkic empires, expanding global economy versus depression, economic interdependence, trade, lack of scarcity), and if so, what is it?

CONCLUSION: "ISLANDS OF FINDINGS"

Over sixty years ago, Harold Guetzkow (1950: 421) said, "The surest and quickest way to world peace is an indirect one—the patient construction over the years of a basic theory of international relations. From this theory may come new and unthought-of solutions to end wars and to guide international relations on a peaceful course." Guetzkow had thought it would be possible to construct "islands of theory" about different aspects of international behavior that could then be integrated into a basic theory. We are still very far away from even constructing islands of theory about the processes that lead to war, but this book has shown that we have identified what might be called "islands of findings," which can then be explained by existing or new theories.

While the findings reported in this chapter do not exhaust all that we know about war and about peace, they do encompass the kernels of knowledge that can be derived from the topics that have been the focus of this book. Each is a core of knowledge around which islands of findings can be built. These islands of findings themselves must be explained by midrange theories, which then must be integrated into an overall explanation of war. Explanations for these islands of findings may differ. The main purpose of this book has not been to appraise the various explanations or "theories" of war within the field but to identify a core of knowledge that any adequate theory of peace and war must explain. The islands of findings delineated in this chapter provide such a core and serve as a challenge to international relations theorists. They show that the scientific search for the sources of war and of peace has produced important and nonobvious findings and remains the best hope for uncovering the underlying forces that bring about war.

NOTES

1. Case studies on civil war also provide evidence that territorial issues are intractable and a source of internal violence; see Toft (2003) and Walter (2003).

2. An additional test found no correlation between the error terms of the two models.

3. Huth refers to his data as territorial disputes. To distinguish these from MIDs they are called territorial issues or claims here, because they do not necessarily involve the use of force. When they do, Huth says they have "escalated."

4. Gibler (1996, 1997b) finds that there is a unique type of alliance—the territorial settlement treaty—that settles territorial questions and is rarely followed by war; rather than posing a threat to any third state, these alliances eliminate the underlying source of threat.

5. Defined as a major state or minor state in the region or contiguous to one of the disputants.

6. It should be noted that dyads that have a great number of MIDs do not necessarily always go to war. Some dyads, like the US-USSR, exhibit a curvilinear relationship. This is found only for the Cold War period however (see Senese and Vasquez 2008: 202–3), which suggests it might be a function of nuclear weapons.

7. One of the things limiting research on domestic processes is the absence of data on domestic actors. In this sense, the collection of data on nonstate rivals by DeRouen and Bercovitch (2008) is a big advance.

8. But note that, since she posits direction, a one-tail test is warranted and would make the p value under .05.

9. The only study that is at variance with these is Beardsley and Asal (2009b) (cited in Geller herein), who find that nuclear states are more likely to win over a nonnuclear state.

10. It is also consistent with Reed (2000), who shows that joint democracies do not go to war because they have relatively few MIDs to begin with.

References

Achen, Christopher H. 2005. "Let's Put Garbage-Can Regression and Garbage-Can Probits Where They Belong." *Conflict Management and Peace Science* 22 (4): 327–39.

Akcinaroglu, Seden, Jonathan DiCicco, and Elizabeth Radziszewski. 2011. "Avalanches and Olive Branches: A Multimethod Analysis of Disasters and Peacemaking in Interstate Rivalries." *Political Research Quarterly* 64:260–75.

Allee, Todd, and Paul K. Huth. 2006. "Legitimizing Dispute Settlement: International Legal Rulings as Domestic Political Cover." *American Political Science Review* 100 (2): 219–34.

Allen, John. 2003. *Lost Geographies of Power*. Oxford: Wiley-Blackwell.

Altfeld, Michael F. 1984. "The Decision to Ally: A Theory and Test." *Western Political Quarterly* 37 (4): 523–44.

Ames, Edward, and Richard T. Rapp. 1977. "The Birth and Death of Taxes: A Hypothesis." *Journal of Economic History* 37:161–78.

Anderton, Charles, and John Carter. 2001. "The Impact of War and Trade: An Interrupted Time Series Study." *Journal of Peace Research* 38 (4): 445–57.

Angell, Norman. 1911. *The Great Illusion: A Study of the Relation of Military Power in Nations to Their Economic and Social Advantage*. 3rd ed. New York: Putnam.

Arat, Zehra. 2003. *Democracy and Human Rights in Developing Countries*. Lincoln, NE: iUniverse.

Ardant, Gabriel. 1975. "Financial Policy and Economic Infrastructure of Modern States and Nations." In *Formation of National States in Western Europe*, edited by Charles Tilly, 164–242. Princeton, NJ: Princeton University Press.

Asal, Victor, and Kyle Beardsley. 2007. "Proliferation and International Crisis Behavior." *Journal of Peace Research* 44:139–55.

Axelrod, Robert. 1986. "An Evolutionary Approach to Norms." *American Political Science Review* 80 (4): 1095–1111.

Barbieri, Katherine. 1996. "Economic Interdependence: A Path to Peace or a Source of Interstate Conflict?" *Journal of Peace Research* 33:29–49.

————. 2002. *The Liberal Illusion: Does Trade Promote Peace?* Ann Arbor: University of Michigan Press.

Barbieri, Katherine, Omar Keshk, and Brian Pollins. 2008. *Correlates of War Project Trade Data Set Codebook, Version 2.0.* 2008. Available from http://correlatesofwar .org (accessed October 29, 2008).

Barnett, Michael N. 1992. *Confronting the Costs of War: Military Power, State and Society in Egypt and Israel.* Princeton, NJ: Princeton University Press.

Barnett, Michael N., and Jack S. Levy. 1991. "Domestic Sources of Alliances and Alignments: The Case of Egypt, 1962–1973." *International Organization* 45 (3): 369–95.

Basrur, Rajesh M. 2007–8. "Do Small Arsenals Deter?" *International Security* 32:202–14.

Batcher, Robert T. 2004. "The Consequences of an Indo-Pakistani Nuclear War." In *The Construction and Cumulation of Knowledge in International Relations,* edited by Daniel S. Geller and John A. Vasquez, 135–62. Oxford: Blackwell.

Bean, Richard. 1973. "War and the Birth of the Nation State." *Journal of Economic History* 33:203–31.

Beardsley, Kyle. 2010. "Pain, Pressure, and Political Cover: Explaining Mediation Incidence." *Journal of Peace Research* 47 (4): 395–406.

Beardsley, Kyle, and Victor Asal. 2009a. "Nuclear Weapons as Shields." *Conflict Management and Peace Science* 26:235–55.

————. 2009b. "Winning with the Bomb." *Journal of Conflict Resolution* 53:278–301.

Beck, Nathaniel, Jonathan Katz, and Richard Tucker. 1998. "Taking Time Seriously: Time-Series-Cross-Section Analysis with a Binary Dependent Variable." *American Journal of Political Science* 42:1260–88.

Beck, Nathaniel, Gary King, and Langche Zeng. 2000. "Improving Quantitative Studies of International Conflict: A Conjecture." *American Political Science Review* 94 (1): 21–36.

Beck, Thorsten, and Ian Webb. 2003. "Economic, Demographic, and Institutional Determinants of Life Insurance Consumption across Countries." *World Bank Economic Review* 17:51–88.

Bennett, D. Scott. 1996. "Security, Bargaining, and the End of Interstate Rivalry." *International Studies Quarterly* 40:157–83.

————. 1997. "Measuring Rivalry Termination." *Journal of Conflict Resolution* 41:227–54.

————. 1998. "Integrating and Testing Models of Rivalry Duration." *American Journal of Political Science* 42:1200–1232.

Bennett, D. Scott, and Allan C. Stam. 2000. "EUGene: A Conceptual Manual." *International Interactions* 26:179–204.

————. 2004. *The Behavioral Correlates of War.* Ann Arbor: University of Michigan Press.

Bensel, Richard F. 1990. *Yankee Leviathan: The Origins of Central State Authority in America, 1859–1877.* Cambridge: Cambridge University Press.

Benson, Brett V. 2010. "ATOP Data, Alliances, and Deterrence." Paper presented at the "What Do We Know about War?" workshop, University of Illinois, Urbana-Champaign, October.

———. 2011. "Unpacking Alliances: Deterrent and Compellent Alliances and Their Relationship with Conflict, 1816–2000." *Journal of Politics* 73 (4): forthcoming.

Benson, Michelle A. 2005. "The Relevance of Politically Relevant Dyads in the Study of Interdependence and Dyadic Disputes." *Conflict Management and Peace Science* 22 (2): 113–33.

Ben-Yehuda, Hemda. 1997. "Territoriality, Crisis and War: An Examination of Theory and 20th Century Evidence." Paper presented at the annual meeting of the International Studies Association, Toronto, March 19.

———. 2004. "Territoriality and War in International Crises: Theory and Findings, 1918–2001." *International Studies Review* 5:85–105.

Bercovitch, Jacob, and Paul F. Diehl. 1997. "Conflict Management of Enduring Rivalries: The Frequency, Timing, and Short-Term Impact of Mediation." *International Interactions* 22:299–320.

Bertalanffy, Ludwig von. 1968. *General Systems Theory: Foundations, Development, Applications*. New York: George Braziller.

Biger, Gideon. 1995. *The Encyclopedia of International Boundaries*. New York: Facts on File.

Blainey, Geoffrey. 1973. *The Causes of War*. New York: Free Press.

———. 1988. *The Causes of War*. 3rd ed. New York: Free Press.

Blalock, Hubert M., Jr. 1979. *Social Statistics*. 2nd ed. New York: McGraw-Hill.

Blechman, Barry M., and Stephen S. Kaplan. 1978. *Force without War: U.S. Armed Forces as a Political Instrument*. Washington, DC: Brookings Institution.

Boehmer, Charles, Erik Gartzke, and Timothy Nordstrom. 2004. "Do Intergovernmental Organizations Promote Peace?" *World Politics* 57 (1): 1–38.

Boix, Carles. 2003. *Democracy and Redistribution*. New York: Cambridge University Press.

Boix, Carles, and Susan C. Stokes. 2003. "Endogenous Democratization." *World Politics* 55 (4): 517–49.

Boulding, Kenneth E. 1962. *Conflict and Defense*. New York: Harper.

Bowman, Isaiah. 1946. "The Strategy of Territorial Decisions." *Foreign Affairs* 24 (2): 177–94.

Braithwaite, Alex. 2005. "Location, Location, Location . . . Identifying Conflict Hot Spots." *International Interactions* 31 (4): 251–72.

Brams, Steven J., and D. Marc Kilgour. 1985. "The Path to Stable Deterrence." In *Dynamic Models of International Conflict*, edited by Urs Luterbacher and Michael D. Ward, 11–25. Boulder, CO: Lynne Rienner.

Braun, Rudolf. 1975. "Taxation, Sociopolitical Structure, and State-Building: Great Britain and Brandenburg-Prussia." In *Formation of National States in Western Europe*, edited by Charles Tilly, 243–327. Princeton, NJ: Princeton University Press.

Brecher, Michael. 1993. *Crises in World Politics: Theory and Reality*. Oxford: Pergamon.

Brecher, Michael, Patrick James, and Jonathan Wilkenfeld. 2000. "Escalation and War in the Twentieth Century: Findings from the International Crisis Behavior Project." In *What Do We Know about War?*, edited by John A. Vasquez, 37–53. Lanham, MD: Rowman & Littlefield.

Brecher, Michael, and Jonathan Wilkenfeld. 1989. *Crisis, Conflict and Instability.* Oxford: Pergamon Press.

———. 1997. *A Study in Crisis.* Ann Arbor: University of Michigan Press.

Bremer, Stuart A. 1980a. "The Contagiousness of Coercion: The Spread of Serious International Disputes, 1900–1976." *International Interactions* 9 (1): 29–55.

———. 1980b. "National Capabilities and War Proneness." In *The Correlates of War,* vol. 2, edited by J. David Singer, 57–82. New York: Free Press.

———. 1992. "Dangerous Dyads: Conditions Affecting the Likelihood of Interstate War, 1816–1965." *Journal of Conflict Resolution* 36 (2): 309–41.

———. 1993. "Democracy and Militarized Interstate Conflict, 1816–1965." *International Interactions* 18:231–49.

———. 1995. "Advancing the Scientific Study of War." In *The Process of War: Advancing the Scientific Study of War,* edited by Stuart A. Bremer and Thomas R. Cusack, 1–33. Luxembourg: Gordon and Breach.

———. 2000. "Who Fights Whom, When, Where, and Why?" In *What Do We Know about War?,* edited by John A. Vasquez, 23–36. Lanham, MD: Rowman & Littlefield.

Brito, Dagobert L., and Michael D. Intriligator. 1996. "Proliferation and the Probability of War: A Cardinality Theorem." *Journal of Conflict Resolution* 40:206–14.

Brochmann, Marit, and Paul R. Hensel. 2009. "Peaceful Management of International River Claims." *International Negotiation* 14 (2): 391–416.

———. 2011. "The Effectiveness of Negotiation over International River Claims." *International Studies Quarterly* (forthcoming).

Brodie, Bernard, ed. 1946. *The Absolute Weapon: Atomic Power and World Order.* New York: Harcourt Brace.

Brodie, Bernard. 1959. *Strategy in the Missile Age.* Princeton, NJ: Princeton University Press.

———. 1978. "The Development of Nuclear Strategy." *International Security* 2:65–83.

Brooks, Stephen G. 1999. "The Globalization of Production and the Changing Benefits of Conquest." *Journal of Conflict Resolution* 43 (5): 646–70.

Bueno de Mesquita, Bruce. 1981. *War Trap.* New Haven, CT: Yale University Press.

Bueno de Mesquita, Bruce, and David Lalman. 1992. *War and Reason: Domestic and International Imperatives.* New Haven, CT: Yale University Press.

Bueno de Mesquita, Bruce, James D. Morrow, Randolph M. Siverson, and Alastair Smith. 1999. "An Institutional Explanation of the Democratic Peace." *American Political Science Review* 93 (4): 791–807.

Bueno de Mesquita, Bruce, and William H. Riker. 1982. "An Assessment of the Merits of Selective Nuclear Proliferation." *Journal of Conflict Resolution* 26:283–306.

Bueno de Mesquita, Bruce, Randolph M. Siverson, and Gary Woller. 1992. "War and the Fate of Regimes: A Comparative Analysis." *American Political Science Review* 86 (3): 638–46.

Bueno de Mesquita, Bruce, Alastair Smith, Randolph M. Siverson, and James D. Morrow. 2003. *The Logic of Political Survival.* Cambridge, MA: MIT Press.

Bull, Hedley. 2002. *The Anarchical Society: A Study of Order in World Politics*. 3rd ed. London: Macmillan.

Bundy, McGeorge, and James G. Blight. 1987–88. "October 27, 1962: Transcripts of the Meetings of the ExComm." *International Security* 12:30–92.

Burkhardt, Jacob. 2010. "Wars of States or Wars of State-Formation?" In *War, the State and International Law in Seventeenth-Century Europe*, edited by Olaf As- bach and Peter Schroeder, 17–34. Burlington, VT: Ashgate.

Callahan, Mary P. 2003. *Making Enemies: War and State Building in Burma*. Ithaca, NY: Cornell University Press.

Caprioli, Mary. 2000. "Gendered Conflict." *Journal of Peace Research* 37 (1): 51–68.

Carlson, Lisa J. 1998. "Crisis Escalation: An Empirical Test in the Context of Ex- tended Deterrence." *International Interactions* 24:225–53.

Carter, David B., and Curtis Signorino. 2010. "Back to the Future: Modeling Time Dependence in Binary Data." *Political Analysis* 18 (3): 271–92.

Cederman, Lars-Erik, and Mohan Penubarti Rao. 2001. "Exploring the Dynamics of the Democratic Peace." *Journal of Conflict Resolution* 45 (6): 818–33.

Centeno, Miguel Angel. 2002. *Blood and Debt: War and the Nation-State in Latin America*. University Park: Pennsylvania State University Press.

Chan, Steve. 1997. "In Search of Democratic Peace: Problems and Promise." *Mer- shon International Studies Review* 41 (1): 59–91.

Chiozza, Giacomo, and Ajin Choi. 2003. "Guess Who Did What: Political Leaders and the Management of Territorial Disputes, 1950–1990." *Journal of Conflict Resolution* 47 (3): 251–78.

Choi, Seung-Whan. 2011. "Re-Evaluating Capitalist and Democratic Peace Models." *International Studies Quarterly* (forthcoming).

Chorley, Richard J., and Peter Haggett, eds. 1967. *Models in Geography*. London: Methuen.

Choucri, Nazli, and Robert North. 1975. *Nations in Conflict*. San Francisco: Freeman.

Cingranelli, David L., and David L. Richards. 1999. "Measuring the Level, Pattern, and Sequence of Government Respect for Physical Integrity Rights." *International Studies Quarterly* 43 (2): 407–17.

Cioffi-Revilla, Claudio. 1998. *Politics and Uncertainty: Theory, Models, and Appli- cations*. New York: Cambridge University Press.

———. 2000. "Ancient Warfare: Origins and Systems." In *Handbook of War Studies*, edited by Manus I. Midlarsky, 2:59–92. Ann Arbor: University of Michigan Press.

Clapham, Christopher. 2000. "War and State Formation in Ethiopia and Eritrea." Pa- per presented at the conference on La Guerre Entre Le Local et Le Global: Societes, Etats, Systemes. http://www.ceri-sciences-po.org.

Cohen, Yousseff, Brian R. Brown, and A. F. K. Organski. 1981. "The Paradoxical Nature of State Making: The Violent Creation of Order." *American Political Sci- ence Review* 75:901–10.

Colaresi, Michael P. 2001. "Shocks to the System: Great Power Rivalries and the Leadership Long Cycle." *Journal of Conflict Resolution* 45:569–93.

———. 2004a. "Aftershocks: Post-War Leadership Survival, Rivalry, and Regime Dynamics." *International Studies Quarterly* 48:713–28.

——. 2004b. "When Doves Cry: International Rivalry, Unreciprocated Cooperation, and Leadership Turnover." *American Journal of Political Science* 48 (3): 555–70.

——. 2005. *Scare Tactics: The Politics of International Rivalry.* Syracuse, NY: Syracuse University Press.

Colaresi, Michael P., Karen D. Rasler, and William R. Thompson. 2008. *Strategic Rivalries in World Politics: Position, Space, and Conflict Escalation.* Cambridge: Cambridge University Press.

Colaresi, Michael P., and William R. Thompson. 2002a. "Strategic Rivalries, Protracted Conflict, and Crisis Escalation." *Journal of Peace Research* 39:263–87.

——. 2002b. "Hot Spots or Hot Hands? Serial Crisis Behavior, Escalating Risks, and Rivalry." *Journal of Politics* 64:1175–98.

——. 2003. "The Economic Development–Democratization Relationship: Does the Outside World Matter?" *Comparative Political Studies* 36:381–403.

——. 2005. "Alliances, Arms Buildups, and Recurrent Conflict: Testing a Steps-to-War Model." *Journal of Politics* 67 (2): 345–64.

Conrad, Justin, and Mark Souva. 2011. "Regime Similarity and Rivalry." *International Interactions* 37:1–28.

Cook, R. Dennis. 1977. "Detection of Influential Observations in Linear Regression." *Technometrics* 19 (1): 15–18.

Cornwell, Derekh, and Michael P. Colaresi. 2002. "Holy Trinities, Rivalry Termination, and Conflict." *International Interactions* 28:325–54.

Coser, Lewis A. 1956. *The Functions of Social Conflict.* New York: Free Press.

Cox, Eric W. 2010. *Why Enduring Rivalries Do—or Don't—End.* Boulder, CO: First Forum Press.

Cranmer, Skyler J., and Bruce A. Desmarais. 2011. "Inferential Network Analysis with Exponential Random Graph Models." *Political Analysis* 19 (1): 66–86.

Cranmer, Skyler J., Bruce A. Desmarais, and Elizabeth J. Menninga. 2012. "Complex Dependencies in the Alliance Network." *Conflict Management and Peace Science* 29 (3): forthcoming.

Crescenzi, Mark J. C., and Andrew J. Enterline. 1999. "Ripples from the Waves? A Systemic, Time-Series Analysis of Democracy, Democratization, and Interstate War." *Journal of Peace Research* 36 (1): 75–94.

——. 2001. "Time Remembered: A Dynamic Model of Interstate Interaction." *International Studies Quarterly* 45:409–31.

Crescenzi, Mark J. C., Kelly M. Kadera, Sara McLaughlin Mitchell, and Clayton L. Thyne. 2011. "A Supply Side Theory of Mediation." *International Studies Quarterly* (forthcoming).

Cronin, Patrick. 2010. "Three Paths to War on the Korean Peninsula." Center for a New American Security. http://www.cnas.org/node/5525.

Dafoe, Allan. 2011. "Statistical Critiques of the Democratic Peace: Caveat Emptor." *American Journal of Political Science* 55:247–62.

Dafoe, Allan, and Nina Kelsey. 2010. "Observing the Capitalist Peace? A Test for Market-Mediated Signaling." Paper presented at the annual meeting of the American Political Science Association, Washington, DC, August.

Danilovic, Vesna. 2002. *When the Stakes Are High: Deterrence and Conflict among Major Powers*. Ann Arbor: University of Michigan Press.

Davenport, Christian, and David A. Armstrong II. 2004. "Democracy and the Violation of Human Rights: A Statistical Analysis from 1976 to 1996." *American Journal of Political Science* 48 (3): 538–54.

Deardorff, Alan V. 1998. "Determinants of Bilateral Trade: Does Gravity Work in a Neoclassical World?" In *The Regionalization of the World Economy*, edited by Jeffrey A. Frankel, 7–31. Chicago: University of Chicago Press.

Dehejia, Rajeev H., and Sadek Wahba. 2002. "Propensity Score-Matching Methods for Nonexperimental Causal Studies." *Review of Economics and Statistics* 84 (1): 151–61.

DeRouen, Karl R., and Jacob Bercovitch. 2008. "Enduring Internal Rivalries: A New Framework for the Study of Civil War." *Journal of Peace Research* 45:55–74.

Deudney, Daniel, and G. John Ikenberry. 1991–1992. "International Sources of Soviet Change." *International Security* 16:74–118.

Diehl, Paul F. 1983. "Arms Race and Escalation: A Closer Look." *Journal of Peace Research* 20:249–59.

———. 1985. "Contiguity and Escalation in Major Power Rivalries, 1816–1980." *Journal of Politics* 47 (4): 1203–11.

———. 1991. "Geography and War: A Review and Assessment of the Empirical Literature." *International Interactions* 17 (1): 11–27.

———. 1998. *The Dynamics of Enduring Rivalries*. Champaign: University of Illinois Press.

———. 2006. "Just a Phase? Integrating Conflict Dynamics over Time." *Conflict Management and Peace Science* 23:199–210.

Diehl, Paul F., and Mark J. C. Crescenzi. 1998. "Reconfiguring the Arms Race–War Debate." *Journal of Peace Research* 35:111–18.

Diehl, Paul F., and Gary Goertz. 1988. "Territorial Changes and Militarized Conflict." *Journal of Conflict Resolution* 32 (1): 103–22.

———. 2000. *War and Peace in International Rivalry*. Ann Arbor: University of Michigan Press.

———. 2010. "The Rivalry Process: How Rivalries Are Sustained and Terminate." Paper presented at the "What Do We Know about War?" workshop, University of Illinois, Urbana-Champaign, October.

Diehl, Paul F., Gary Goertz, and Daniel Saeedi. 2005. "Theoretical Specifications of Enduring Rivalries: Applications to the India-Pakistan Case." In *The India-Pakistan Conflict: An Enduring Rivalry*, edited by T. V. Paul, 27–53. Cambridge: Cambridge University Press.

Dinar, Shlomi. 2009. "Scarcity and Cooperation along International Rivers." *Global Environmental Politics* 9 (1): 107–33.

Dion, Douglas. 1998. "Evidence and Inference in the Comparative Case Study." *Comparative Politics* 30:127–45.

Dixon, William J. 1993. "Democracy and the Management of International Conflict." *Journal of Conflict Resolution* 37 (1): 42–68.

———. 1994. "Democracy and the Peaceful Settlement of International Conflict." *American Political Science Review* 88 (1): 14–32.

———. 1996. "Third-Party Techniques for Preventing Conflict Escalation and Promoting Peaceful Settlement." *International Organization* 50 (4): 653–81.

———. 1998. "Dyads, Disputes, and the Democratic Peace." In *The Political Economy of War and Peace*, edited by Murray Wolfson, 103–26. Boston: Kluwer Academic.

Dixon, William J., and Paul D. Senese. 2002. "Democracy, Disputes, and Negotiated Settlements." *Journal of Conflict Resolution* 46 (4): 547–71.

Downing, Brian M. 1992. *The Military Revolution and Political Change: Origins of Democracy and Autocracy in Early Modern Europe*. Princeton, NJ: Princeton University Press.

Doyle, Michael W. 1986. "Liberalism and World Politics." *American Political Science Review* 80 (4): 1151–69.

Dreyer, David. 2010. "Issue Conflict Accumulation and the Dynamics of Strategic Rivalry." *International Studies Quarterly* 54:779–95.

Dzurek, Daniel. 2000. "What Makes Some Boundary Disputes Important?" *IBRU Boundary and Security Bulletin* 7 (4): 83–95.

Ellsberg, Daniel. [1959] 1968. "The Theory and Practice of Blackmail." RAND P-3883. Santa Monica, CA: RAND Corporation.

———. 1960. "The Crude Analysis of Strategic Choices." RAND P-2183. Santa Monica, CA: RAND Corporation.

Elman, Colin. 2005. "Explanatory Typologies in Qualitative Studies of International Politics." *International Organization* 59:293–326.

Elman, Miriam Fendius, ed. 1997. *Paths to Peace: Is Democracy the Answer?* Cambridge, MA: MIT Press.

Enterline, Andrew J. 1998. "Regime Changes, Neighborhoods, and Interstate Conflict, 1816-1992." *Journal of Conflict Resolution* 42 (6): 804–29.

Enterline, Andrew J., and J. Michael Greig. 2005. "Beacons of Hope? The Impact of Imposed Democracy on Regional Peace, Democracy, and Prosperity." *Journal of Politics* 67 (4): 1075–98.

Epstein, David. L., Robert Bates, Jack Goldstone, Ida Kristensen, and Sharyn O'Halloran. 2006. "Democratic Transitions." *American Journal of Political Science* 50:551–69.

Ertman, Thomas. 1997. *Birth of the Leviathan: Building States and Regimes in Medieval and Early Modern Europe*. Cambridge: Cambridge University Press.

Fazal, Tanisha M. 2007. *State Death: The Politics and Geography of Conquest, Occupation and Annexation*. Princeton, NJ: Princeton University Press.

Fearon, James D. 1994a. "Signaling versus the Balance of Power and Interests: An Empirical Test of a Crisis Bargaining Model." *Journal of Conflict Resolution* 38:236–39.

———. 1994b. "Domestic Political Audiences and the Escalation of International Disputes." *American Political Science Review* 88:577–82.

———. 1995. "Rationalist Explanations for War." *International Organization* 49 (3): 379–414.

———. 1997. "Signaling Foreign Policy Interests: Tying Hands versus Sinking Costs." *Journal of Conflict Resolution* 41 (1): 68–90.

Filson, Darren, and Suzanne Werner. 2002. "A Bargaining Model of War and Peace: Anticipating the Onset, Duration, and Outcome of War." *American Journal of Political Science* 46 (4): 819–38.

———. 2004. "Bargaining and Fighting: The Impact of Regime Type on War Onset, Duration, and Outcome." *American Journal of Political Science* 48 (2): 296–313.

Finer, Samuel. 1975. "State and Nation-Building in Europe: The Role of the Military." In *The Formation of National States in Western Europe*, edited by Charles Tilly, 84–163. Princeton, NJ: Princeton University Press.

Finnemore, Martha. 1996. *National Interests in International Society*. Ithaca, NY: Cornell University Press.

Finnemore, Martha, and Kathryn Sikkink. 1998. "International Norm Dynamics and Political Change." *International Organization* 52 (4): 887–917.

———. 2001. "Taking Stock: The Constructivist Research Program in International Relations and Comparative Politics." *Annual Review of Political Science* 4:391–416.

Flint, Colin. 2011. "Intertwined Spaces of Peace and War: The Perpetual Dynamism of Geopolitical Landscapes." In *Reconstructing Conflict: Integrating War and Post-War Geographies*, edited by S. Kirsch and C. Flint, 31–48. Burlington, VT: Ashgate.

Flint, Colin, Paul Diehl, Juergen Scheffran, John Vasquez, and Sang-Hyun Chi. 2009. "Conceptualizing ConflictSpace: Towards a Geography of Relational Power and Embeddedness in the Analysis of Interstate Conflict." *Annals of the Association of American Geographers* 99 (5): 827–35.

Florini, Ann. 1996. "The Evolution of International Norms." *International Studies Quarterly* 40 (3): 363–89.

Flynn, Gregory, and Henry Farrell. 1999. "Piecing Together the Democratic Peace: The CSCE, Norms, and the 'Construction' of Security in Post–Cold War Europe." *International Organization* 53 (3): 505–35.

Forsythe, David P. 1992. "Democracy, War and Covert Action." *Journal of Peace Research* 29 (4): 385–95.

Freedman, Lawrence, and Virginia Gamba-Stonehouse. 1991. *Signals of War: The Falklands Conflict of 1982*. Princeton, NJ: Princeton University Press.

Friedberg, Aaron L. 1988. *The Weary Titan*. Princeton, NJ: Princeton University Press.

Gaddis, John Lewis. 1986. "The Long Peace: Elements of Stability in the Postwar International System." *International Security* 10 (4): 99–142.

———. 1991. "Great Illusions, the Long Peace, and the Future of the International System." In *The Long Postwar Peace: Contending Explanations and Projections*, edited by Charles W. Kegley Jr. New York: HarperCollins.

Gallaher, Carl, Carl T. Dahlman, Mary Gilmartin, Alison Mountz, and Peter Shirlow. 2009. *Key Concepts in Political Geography*. Thousand Oaks, CA: Sage.

Ganguly, Sumit, and William R. Thompson. 2011. "Conflict Propensities in Asian Rivalries." In *Asian Rivalries: Conflict, Escalation, and Limitations on Two-Level Games*, edited by Sumit Ganguly and William Thompson, 1–25. Stanford, CA: Stanford University Press.

Gartzke, Erik. 1998. "Kant We All Just Get Along? Opportunity, Willingness, and the Origins of the Democratic Peace." *American Journal of Political Science* 42:1–27.

———. 1999. "War Is in the Error Term." *International Organization* 53:567–87.

———. 2006. "Globalization, Economic Development, and Territorial Conflict." In *Territoriality and Conflict in an Era of Globalization*, edited by Miles Kahler and Barbara F. Walter, 156–86. Cambridge: Cambridge University Press.

———. 2007. "The Capitalist Peace." *American Journal of Political Science* 51 (1): 166–91.

Gartzke, Erik, and Dong-Joon Jo. 2009. "Bargaining, Nuclear Proliferation, and Interstate Disputes." *Journal of Conflict Resolution* 53:209–33.

Gartzke, Erik, Quan Li, and Charles Boehmer. 2001. "Investing in the Peace: Economic Interdependence and International Conflict." *International Organization* 55:391–438.

Gartzke, Erik, and Michael Simon. 1999. "Hot Hand: A Critical Analysis of Enduring Rivalries." *Journal of Politics* 61:777–98.

Gates, Scott, Torbjorn L. Knutson, and Jonathan W. Moses. 1996. "Democracy and Peace: A More Skeptical View." *Journal of Peace Research* 33:1–10.

Geller, Daniel S. 1990. "Nuclear Weapons, Deterrence, and Crisis Escalation." *Journal of Conflict Resolution* 34:291–310.

———. 1992. "Capability Concentration, Power Transition, and War." *International Interactions* 17 (3): 269–84.

———. 1993. "Power Differentials and War in Rival Dyads." *International Studies Quarterly* 37 (2): 173–93.

———. 2000a. "Explaining War: Empirical Patterns and Theoretical Mechanisms." In *Handbook of War Studies*, edited by Manus I. Midlarsky, 2:407–50. Ann Arbor: University of Michigan Press.

———. 2000b. "Material Capabilities: Power and International Conflict." In *What Do We Know about War?*, edited by John A. Vasquez, 259–77. Lanham, MD: Rowman & Littlefield.

———. 2004. "Toward a Scientific Theory of War." In *The Scourge of War: New Extensions on an Old Problem*, edited by Paul F. Diehl, 222–36. Ann Arbor: University of Michigan Press.

———. 2005. "The India-Pakistan Rivalry: Prospects for War, Prospects for Peace." In *The India-Pakistan Conflict: An Enduring Rivalry*, edited by T. V. Paul, 80–102. Cambridge: Cambridge University Press.

———. 2010. "Nuclear Weapons and War." Paper presented at the "What Do We Know about War?" workshop, University of Illinois, Urbana-Champaign, October.

Geller, Daniel S., and J. David Singer. 1998. *Nations at War: A Scientific Study of International Conflict*. Cambridge: Cambridge University Press.

Gent, Stephen, and Megan Shannon. 2011. "Bias and the Effectiveness of Third Party Conflict Management Mechanisms." *Conflict Management and Peace Science* (forthcoming).

George, Alexander L., ed. 1991. *Avoiding War: Problems of Crisis Management*. Boulder, CO: Westview.

George, Alexander L., and Andrew Bennett. 2005. *Case Studies and Theory Development in the Social Sciences*. Cambridge, MA: MIT Press.

George, Alexander L., and Richard Smoke. 1974. *Deterrence in American Foreign Policy*. New York: Columbia University Press.

Ghobarah, Hazem A., Paul Huth, and Bruce Russett. 2003. "Civil Wars Kill and Maim People Long After the Shooting Stops." *American Political Science Review* 97 (2): 189–202.

Ghosn, Faten, Glenn Palmer, and Stuart A. Bremer. 2004. "The MID3 Data Set, 1993–2001: Procedures, Coding Rules, and Description." *Conflict Management and Peace Science* 21 (2): 133–54.

Gibler, Douglas M. 1996. "Alliances That Never Balance: The Territorial Settlement Treaty." *Conflict Management and Peace Science* 15 (1): 75–97.

———. 1997a. "Control the Issues, Control the Conflict: The Effects of Alliances That Settle Territorial Issues on Interstate Rivalries." *International Interactions* 22:341–68.

———. 1997b. "Reconceptualizing the Alliance Variable: An Empirical Typology of Alliances." PhD diss., Vanderbilt University.

———. 2000. "Alliances: Why Some Cause War and Why Others Cause Peace." In *What Do We Know about War?*, ed. John A. Vasquez, 145–64. Lanham, MD: Rowman & Littlefield.

———. 2007. "Bordering on Peace: Democracy, Territorial Issues, and Conflict." *International Studies Quarterly* 51 (3): 509–32.

———. 2010a. "The Implications of a Territorial Peace." Paper presented at the annual convention of the International Studies Association.

———. 2010b. "Outside-In: The Effects of External Threat on State Centralization." *Journal of Conflict Resolution* 54 (4): 519–42.

———. 2012. *The Territorial Peace: Borders, State Development and International Conflict*. Cambridge: Cambridge University Press.

Gibler, Douglas M., and Alex Braithwaite. n.d. "Territorial Hot Spots: Assessing the Relationship between Conflict and Democracy in the Region." Department of Political Science, University of Alabama.

Gibler, Douglas M., and Marc L. Hutchison. n.d. "Territorial Issues, Audience Costs, and the Democratic Peace: The Importance of Issue Salience." Department of Political Science, University of Alabama.

Gibler, Douglas M., Marc L. Hutchison, and Steven V. Miller. 2009. "Territorial Threats, Civil Wars, and Identity Formation." Unpublished manuscript, University of Alabama, Tuscaloosa.

Gibler, Douglas M., and Steven V. Miller. Forthcoming. "Quick Victories? Territory, Democracies and Their Disputes." *Journal of Conflict Resolution*.

Gibler, Douglas M., and Kirk Randazzo. 2011. "Testing the Effects of Independent Judiciaries on the Likelihood of Democratic Backsliding." *American Journal of Political Science* 55 (3): 696–709.

Gibler, Douglas M., Toby J. Rider, and Marc L. Hutchison. 2005. "Taking Arms against a Sea of Troubles: Conventional Arms Races during Periods of Rivalry." *Journal of Peace Research* 42:131–47.

Gibler, Douglas M., and Meredith Sarkees. 2004. "Measuring Alliances: The Correlates of War Formal Alliances Data Set, 1816–2000." *Journal of Peace Research* 41 (2): 211–22.

Gibler, Douglas M., and Jaroslav Tir. 2010. "Settled Borders and Regime Type: Democratic Transitions as Consequences of Peaceful Territorial Transfers." *American Journal of Political Science* 54 (4): 951–68.

Gibler, Douglas M., and John A Vasquez. 1998. "Uncovering the Dangerous Alliances, 1945–1980." *International Studies Quarterly* 42 (4): 785–807.

Gibler, Douglas M., and Scott Wolford. 2006. "Alliances, Then Democracy: An Examination of the Relationship between Regime Type and Alliance Formation." *Journal of Conflict Resolution* 50 (1): 129–53.

Gibney, Mark, and Matthew Dalton. 1996. "The Political Terror Scale." *Policy Studies and Developing Nations* 4 (1): 73–84.

Gleditsch, Kristian Skrede. 2002a. *All International Politics Is Local: The Diffusion of Conflict, Integration, and Democratization.* Ann Arbor: University of Michigan Press.

———. 2002b. "Expanded Trade and GDP Data." *Journal of Conflict Resolution* 46 (5): 712–24.

Gleditsch, Kristian S., Idean Salehyan, and Kenneth Schultz. 2008. "Fighting at Home, Fighting Abroad: How Civil Wars Lead to International Disputes." *Journal of Conflict Resolution* 52 (4): 479–506.

Gleditsch, Kristian S., and Michael D. Ward. 2001. "Measuring Space: A Minimum Distance Database and Applications to International Studies." *Journal of Peace Research* 38:739–58.

Gleditsch, Nils Petter. 1995. "Geography, Democracy, and Peace." *International Interactions* 20:297–323.

Gleditsch, Nils Petter, and Håvard Hegre. 1997. "Peace and Democracy: Three Levels of Analysis." *Journal of Conflict Resolution* 41 (2): 283–310.

Glete, Jan. 2002. *War and the State in Early Modern Europe: Spain, the Dutch Republic and Sweden as Fiscal-Military States.* London: Routledge.

Goddard, Stacie E. 2006. "Uncommon Ground: Indivisible Territory and the Politics of Legitimacy." *International Organization* 60 (1): 35–68.

Goertz, Gary, and Paul F. Diehl. 1992a. "The Empirical Importance of Enduring Rivalries." *International Interactions* 18:151–63.

———. 1992b. *Territorial Changes and International Conflict.* New York: Routledge.

———. 1992c. "Toward a Theory of International Norms: Some Conceptual and Measurement Issues." *Journal of Conflict Resolution* 36 (4): 634–64.

———. 2000. "Rivalries: The Conflict Process." In *What Do We Know about War?*, edited by John Vasquez, 197–217. Lanham, MD: Rowman & Littlefield.

Goertz, Gary, Bradford Jones, and Paul F. Diehl. 2005. "Maintenance Processes in International Rivalries." *Journal of Conflict Resolution* 49:742–69.

Goertz, Gary, and Jack S. Levy. 2007. "Causal Explanation, Necessary Conditions, and Case Studies." In *Explaining War and Peace: Case Studies and Necessary Condition Counterfactuals*, edited by Gary Goertz and Jack S. Levy, 9–45. New York: Routledge.

Goertz, Gary, and Harvey Starr, eds. 2003. *Necessary Conditions: Theory, Methodology, and Applications.* Lanham, MD: Rowman & Littlefield.

Gomsrud, Lars Seland, Scott Gates, and Håvard Strand. 2009. "Surviving the Capitalist Peace: Leaders' Incentives and Economic Freedom." Paper presented at the fifth general conference of the European Consortium for Political Research, Germany, September 10.

Gongora, Thierry. 1997. "War Making and State Power in the Contemporary Middle East." *International Journal of Middle East Studies* 29 (3): 323–40.

Goodall, Jane. 2000. *Through a Window: My Thirty Years with the Chimpanzees of Gombe.* Boston: Mariner Books.

Gowa, Joanne. 1999. *Ballots or Bullets: The Elusive Democratic Peace.* Princeton, NJ: Princeton University Press.

Gray, Colin S. 1979. "Nuclear Strategy: The Case for a Theory of Victory." *International Security* 4:54–87.

Greig, J. Michael. 2001. "Moments of Opportunity: Recognizing Conditions of Ripeness for International Mediation between Enduring Rivals." *Journal of Conflict Resolution* 45 (6): 691–718.

———. 2005. "Stepping into the Fray: When Do Mediators Mediate?" *American Journal of Political Science* 49 (2): 249–66.

Grieco, Joseph. 2001. "Repetitive Military Challenges and Recurrent International Conflicts, 1918–1994." *International Studies Quarterly* 45:295–316.

Guetzkow, Harold. 1950. "Long Range Research in International Relations." *American Perspective* 4 (4): 421–40.

———. 1968. "Some Correspondences between Simulation and Realities in International Relations." In *New Approaches to International Relations*, edited by Morton A. Kaplan, 202–69. New York: St. Martin's.

Gulick, Edward V. 1955. *Europe's Classical Balance of Power.* New York: Norton.

Gunn, Steven. 2010. "War and the Emergence of the State: Western Europe, 1350–1600." In *European Warfare, 1350–1750*, edited by Frank Tallett and D. J. B. Trim, 50–73. Cambridge: Cambridge University Press.

Gunn, Steven, David Grummitt, and Hans Cools. 2007. *War, State and Society in England and the Netherlands.* Oxford: Oxford University Press.

Gurr, Ted R. 1988. "War, Revolution, and the Growth of the Coercive State." *Comparative Political Studies* 21:45–65.

Gurr, Ted Robert, Keith Jaggers, and Will H. Moore. 1990. "The Transformation of the Western State: The Growth of Democracy, Autocracy, and State Power since 1800." *Studies in Comparative International Development* 25:73–108.

Hafner-Burton, Emilie M. 2005. "Trading Human Rights: How Preferential Trade Agreements Influence Government Repression." *International Organization* 59 (3): 593–629.

Hafner-Burton, Emilie M., Miles Kahler, and Alexander H. Montgomery. 2009. "Network Analysis for International Relations." *International Organization* 63 (3): 559–92.

Halperin, Morton H. 1963. *Limited War in the Nuclear Age.* New York: Wiley.

Hansen, Holley, Sara McLaughlin Mitchell, and Stephen C. Nemeth. 2008. "IO Mediation of Interstate Conflicts: Moving beyond the Global vs. Regional Dichotomy." *Journal of Conflict Resolution* 52 (2): 295–325.

Harff, Barbara. 2003. "No Lessons Learned from the Holocaust: Assessing Risks of Genocide and Political Mass Murder since 1955." *American Political Science Review* 97 (1): 57–74.

Harrison, Ewan R. 2002. "Waltz, Kant and Systemic Approaches to International Relations." *Review of International Studies* 28 (1): 143–62.

———. 2004. "State Socialization, International Norm Dynamics and the Liberal Peace." *International Politics* 41 (4): 521–42.

———. 2010. "The Democratic Peace Research Program and System Level Analysis." *Journal of Peace Research* 47 (2): 155–65.

Harvard Nuclear Study Group [Albert Carnesale et al.]. 1983. *Living with Nuclear Weapons*. New York: Bantam.

Harvey, Frank, and Patrick James. 1992. "Nuclear Deterrence Theory: The Record of Aggregate Testing and an Alternative Research Agenda." *Conflict Management and Peace Science* 12:17–45.

Hassner, Ron E. 2003. "To Halve and to Hold: Conflicts over Sacred Space and the Problem of Indivisibility." *Security Studies* 12 (4): 1–33.

Hayek, Friedrich August Von. 1989. *The Fatal Conceit: The Errors of Socialism*. Edited by W. W. Bartley III. Chicago: University of Chicago Press.

Hegre, Håvard. 2000. "Development and the Liberal Peace: What Does It Take to Be a Trading State?" *Journal of Peace Research* 37:5–30.

Hegre, Håvard, Tanja Ellingsen, Scott Gates, and Nils Petter Gleditsch. 2001. "Towards a Democratic Civil Peace? Democracy, Political Change, and Civil War, 1816–1992." *American Political Science Review* 95 (1): 33–48.

Helling, Dominik. 2010. "Tilleyan Footprints beyond Europe: War-Making and State-Making in the Case of Somaliland." *St. Anthony's International Review* 6 (1): 103–23.

Henehan, Marie T., and John A. Vasquez. 2011. "The Changing Probability of Interstate War, 1816–1992." In *Territory, War, and Peace*, edited by John A. Vasquez and Marie T. Henehan, 179–94. New York: Routledge.

Hensel, Paul R. 1994. "One Thing Leads to Another: Recurrent Militarized Disputes in Latin America, 1816–1986." *Journal of Peace Research* 31:281–97.

———. 1996. "Charting a Course to Conflict: Territorial Issues and Militarized Interstate Disputes, 1816–1992." *Conflict Management and Peace Science* 15 (1): 43–73.

———. 1998. "Interstate Rivalry and the Study of Militarized Conflict." In *Conflict in World Politics: Advances in the Study of Crisis, War, and Peace*, edited by Frank P. Harvey and Ben D. Mor, 162–204. London: Macmillan.

———. 1999. "An Evolutionary Approach to the Study of Interstate Rivalry." *Conflict Management and Peace Science* 17 (2): 179–206.

———. 2000. "Territory: Theory and Evidence on Geography and Conflict." In *What Do We Know about War?*, edited by John A. Vasquez, 57–84. Lanham, MD: Rowman & Littlefield.

———. 2001a. "Contentious Issues and World Politics: The Management of Territorial Claims in the Americas, 1816–1992." *International Studies Quarterly* 45 (1): 81–109.

———. 2001b. "Evolution in Domestic Politics and the Development of Rivalry: The Bolivia-Paraguay Case." In *Evolutionary Interpretations of World Politics*, edited by William R. Thompson, 176–217. New York: Routledge.

———. 2006. "Territorial Claims and Armed Conflict between Neighbors." Paper presented at the Lineae Terrarum International Borders Conference, El Paso, TX, March.

———. 2010 "Territory: Geography, Contentious Issues, and World Politics." Paper presented at the "What Do We Know about War?" workshop, University of Illinois, Urbana-Champaign, October.

Hensel, Paul R., Michael Allison, and Ahmed Khanani. 2008. "Colonial Legacies and Territorial Claims: A Preliminary Investigation." Paper presented at the conference "National Territory and Sovereignty: Sixty Years since the Founding of the Nation," Seoul, Korea, August.

———. 2009. "Territorial Integrity Treaties and Armed Conflict over Territory." *Conflict Management and Peace Science* 26 (2): 120–43.

Hensel, Paul R., and Paul F. Diehl. 1994. "Testing Empirical Propositions about Shatterbelts." *Political Geography* 13 (1): 33–52.

Hensel, Paul R., Gary Goertz, and Paul F. Diehl. 2000. "The Democratic Peace and Rivalries." *Journal of Politics* 62 (4): 1173–88.

Hensel, Paul R., and Sara McLaughlin Mitchell. 2005. "Issue Indivisibility and Territorial Claims." *GeoJournal* 64 (4): 275–85.

Hensel, Paul R., Sara McLaughlin Mitchell, and Thomas E. Sowers II. 2006. "Conflict Management of Riparian Disputes: A Regional Comparison of Dispute Resolution." *Political Geography* 25 (4): 383–411.

Hensel, Paul R., Sara McLaughlin Mitchell, Thomas E. Sowers II, and Clayton L. Thyne. 2008. "Bones of Contention: Comparing Territorial, Maritime, and River Issues." *Journal of Conflict Resolution* 52 (1): 117–43.

Herbst, Jeffrey. 2000. *States and Power in Africa: Comparative Lessons in Authority and Control*. Princeton, NJ: Princeton University Press.

Hermann, Margaret, and Charles Kegley Jr. 1996. "Ballots, a Barrier against the Use of Bullets and Bombs." *Journal of Conflict Resolution* 40 (3): 436–60.

Herod, Andrew. 2010. *Scale*. New York: Routledge.

Herz, John. 1950. "Idealist Internationalism and the Security Dilemma." *World Politics* 2 (2): 157–80.

Hess, Martin. 2004. "'Spatial' Relationships? Towards a Reconceptualization of Embeddedness." *Progress in Human Geography* 28 (2): 165–86.

Hewitt, J. Joseph. 2005. "A Crisis-Density Formulation for Identifying Rivalries." *Journal of Peace Research* 42:183–200.

Heydemann, Steven. 2000. "War, Institutions, and Social Change in the Middle East." In *War, Institutions and Social Change in the Middle East*, edited by Steven Heydemann, 1–32. Berkeley: University of California Press.

Hill, Norman. 1945. *Claims to Territory in International Relations*. New York: Oxford University Press.

Hintze, Otto. 1975. "Military Organization and the Organization of the State." In *The Historical Essays of Otto Hintze*, edited by Felix Gilbert, 178–215. New York: Oxford University Press.

Ho, Daniel E., Kosuke Imai, Gary King, and Elizabeth A. Stuart. 2007. "Matching as Nonparametric Preprocessing for Reducing Model Dependence in Parametric Causal Inference." *Political Analysis* 15 (3): 199–236.

Holsti, Kalevi J. 1991. *Peace and War: Armed Conflicts and International Order, 1648–1989*. New York: Cambridge University Press.

Holsti, Ole, Robert North, and Richard Brody. 1968. "Perception and Action in the 1914 Crisis." In *Quantitative International Politics*, edited by J. D. Singer, 123–58. New York: Free Press.

Horn, Michael D. 1987. "Arms Races and the International System." PhD diss., University of Rochester.

Houweling, Henk W., and Jan G. Siccama. 1985. "The Epidemiology of War, 1816–1980." *Journal of Conflict Resolution* 29 (4): 641–63.

Hudson, Valerie M., and Andrea Den Boer. 2002. "A Surplus of Men, a Deficit of Peace: Security and Sex Ratios in Asia's Largest States." *International Security* 26 (4): 5–38.

Huntington, Samuel. 1958. "Arms Races Prerequisites and Results." *Public Policy* 8:41–86.

Huntley, Wade L. 1996. "Kant's Third Image: Systemic Sources of the Liberal Peace." *International Studies Quarterly* 40 (1): 45–76.

Hutchison, Marc L. 2011. "Territorial Threat, Mobilization, and Political Participation in Africa." *Conflict Management and Peace Science* 28 (3): 183–208.

Hutchison, Marc L., and Douglas M. Gibler. 2007. "Political Tolerance and Territorial Threat: A Cross-National Study." *Journal of Politics* 69 (1): 128–42.

Huth, Paul. 1988a. "Extended Deterrence and the Outbreak of War." *American Political Science Review* 82:423–43.

———. 1988b. *Extended Deterrence and the Prevention of War*. New Haven, CT: Yale University Press.

———. 1996. *Standing Your Ground: Territorial Disputes and International Conflict*. Ann Arbor: University of Michigan Press.

Huth, Paul K., and Todd Allee. 2002. *The Democratic Peace and Territorial Conflict in the Twentieth Century*. Cambridge: Cambridge University Press.

Huth, Paul, D. Scott Bennett, and Christopher Gelpi. 1992. "System Uncertainty, Risk Propensity, and International Conflict among the Great Powers." *Journal of Conflict Resolution* 36:478–517.

Huth, Paul, Christopher Gelpi, and D. Scott Bennett. 1993. "The Escalation of Great Power Militarized Disputes: Testing Rational Deterrence Theory and Structural Realism." *American Political Science Review* 87:609–23.

Huth, Paul, and Bruce Russett. 1984. "What Makes Deterrence Work? Cases from 1900 to 1980." *World Politics* 36:496–526.

———. 1988. "Deterrence Failure and Crisis Escalation." *International Studies Quarterly* 32:29–45.

Ikenberry, G. John. 2001. *After Victory: Institutions, Strategic Restraint, and the Rebuilding of Order after Major Wars*. Princeton, NJ: Princeton University Press.

Imai, Kosuke, and Jeremy M. Weinstein. 2000. "Measuring the Economic Impact of Civil War." Cambridge, MA: Departments of Government and Economics, Harvard University.

Intriligator, Michael D., and Dagobert L. Brito. 1981. "Nuclear Proliferation and the Probability of Nuclear War." *Public Choice* 37:247–60.

James, Patrick. 1988. *Crisis and War*. Montreal: McGill-Queen's University Press.

James, Patrick, Eric Solberg, and Murray Wolfson. 1999. "An Identified Systemic Model of the Democracy-Peace Nexus." *Defence and Peace Economics* 10:1–37.

———. 2000. "Democracy and Peace: A Reply to Oneal and Russett." *Defence and Peace Economics* 11:215–29.

Jepperson, Ronald L., Alexander Wendt, and Peter J. Katzenstein. 1996. "Norms, Identity, and Culture in National Security." In *The Culture of National Security: Norms and Identity in World Politics*, edited by Peter J. Katzenstein, 33–75. New York: Columbia University Press.

Jervis, Robert. 1979. "Why Nuclear Superiority Doesn't Matter." *Political Science Quarterly* 94:617–33.

———. 1984. *The Illogic of American Nuclear Strategy*. Ithaca, NY: Cornell University Press.

———. 1988. "The Political Effects of Nuclear Weapons: A Comment." *International Security* 13:80–90.

———. 1989a. *The Meaning of the Nuclear Revolution: Statecraft and the Prospect of Armageddon*. Ithaca, NY: Cornell University Press.

———. 1989b. "Rational Deterrence: Theory and Evidence." *World Politics* 41:183–207.

Joffe, Josef. 1990. "Tocqueville Revisited: Are Good Democracies Bad Players in the Game of Nations?" In *The New Democracies: Global Change and US Policy*, edited by Brad Roberts, 123–34. Cambridge, MA: MIT Press.

Johnson, Jesse, and Brett Ashley Leeds. 2010. "Defense Pacts: A Prescription for Peace?" Paper presented at the annual meeting of the International Studies Association, New Orleans.

Johnston, Ron J., and James Sidaway. 2004. *Geography and Geographers: Anglo-American Human Geography since 1945*. 6th ed. London: Arnold.

Jones, Daniel M., Stuart A. Bremer, and J. David Singer. 1996. "Militarized Interstate Disputes, 1816–1992: Rationale, Coding Rules, and Empirical Patterns." *Conflict Management and Peace Science* 15 (2): 163–213.

Kacowicz, Arie M. 1994. *Peaceful Territorial Change*. Columbia: University of South Carolina Press.

———. 1995. "Explaining Zones of Peace: Democracies as Satisfied Powers?" *Journal of Peace Research* 32 (3): 265–76.

Kadera, Kelly M., Mark J. C. Crescenzi, and Megan L. Shannon. 2003. "Democratic Survival, Peace, and War in the International System." *American Journal of Political Science* 47 (2): 234–47.

Kahn, Herman. 1960. *On Thermonuclear War*. Princeton, NJ: Princeton University Press.

——. 1962. *Thinking about the Unthinkable*. New York: Avon.

——. 1965. *On Escalation: Metaphors and Scenarios*. New York: Praeger.

——. 1968. *On Escalation: Metaphors and Scenarios*. Baltimore, MD: Penguin.

Kang, Choong-Nam. 2007. "Reassessing the Steps-to-War Explanation with Dyads' Power Status Condition." Paper presented at the annual meeting of the Midwest Political Science Association, Chicago, Illinois.

Kant, Immanuel. [1784] 1991. "Idea for a Universal History with a Cosmopolitan Purpose." In *Kant: Political Writings*, edited by Hans Reiss, 41–53. Cambridge: Cambridge University Press.

——. [1795] 1991. "Perpetual Peace: A Philosophical Sketch." In *Kant: Political Writings*, edited by Hans Reiss, 93–130. Cambridge: Cambridge University Press.

Kaplan, Morton. 1957. *System and Process in International Politics*. New York: Wiley.

Katznelson, Ira, and Martin Shefter, eds. 2002. *Shaped by War and Trade: International Influences on American Political Development*. Princeton, NJ: Princeton University Press.

Kaufman, Stuart, Richard Little, and William C. Wohlforth, eds. 2007. *The Balance of Power in World History*. New York: Palgrave Macmillan.

Keck, Margaret E., and Kathryn Sikkink. 1998. *Activists beyond Borders: Advocacy Networks in International Politics*. Ithaca, NY: Cornell University Press.

Kegley, Charles W., Jr., and Gregory A. Raymond. 1982. "Alliance Norms and War: A New Piece in an Old Puzzle." *International Studies Quarterly* 26 (3): 572–95.

——. 1990. *When Trust Breaks Down: Alliance Norms and World Politics*. Columbia: University of South Carolina Press.

Kelley, Judith. 2007. "Who Keeps International Commitments and Why? The International Criminal Court and Bilateral Nonsurrender Agreements." *American Political Science Review* 101 (3): 573–89.

Kenwick, Mike. 2011. "Analyzing Deterrence: Defensive Alliance Formation and Dispute Onset." Senior honors thesis, University of Illinois.

Keohane, Robert O., and Lisa L. Martin. 1995. "The Promise of Institutionalist Theory." *International Security* 20:39–51.

al-Khafaji, Isam. 2000. "War as a Vehicle for the Rise and Demise of a State-Controlled Society: The Case of Ba'thist Iraq." In *War, Institutions, and Social Change in the Middle East*, edited by Steven Heydemann, 258–91. Berkeley: University of California Press.

Kier, Elizabeth, and Ronald R. Krebs, eds. 2010. *In War's Wake: International Conflict and the Fate of Liberal Democracy*. Cambridge: Cambridge University Press.

Kim, Woosang. 1992. "Power Transitions and Great Power War from Westphalia to Waterloo." *World Politics* 45:153–72.

King, Gary. 1996. "Why Context Should Not Count." *Political Geography* 15 (2): 159–64.

——. 2001. "Proper Nouns and Methodological Propriety: Pooling Dyads in International Relations Data." *International Organization* 55 (2): 497–507.

King, Gary, Robert O. Keohane, and Sidney Verba. 1994. *Designing Social Inquiry: Scientific Inference in Qualitative Research*. Princeton, NJ: Princeton University Press.

Kissinger, Henry A. 1957. *Nuclear Weapons and Foreign Policy.* New York: Council on Foreign Relations/Harper & Row.

Klein, James P., Gary Goertz, and Paul F. Diehl. 2006. "The New Rivalry Data Set: Procedures and Patterns." *Journal of Peace Research* 43 (3): 331–48.

———. 2008. "The Peace Scale: Conceptualizing and Operationalizing Non-Rivalry and Peace." *Conflict Management and Peace Science* 28:67–80.

Kocs, Stephen. 1995. "Territorial Disputes and Interstate War, 1945–1987." *Journal of Politics* 57 (1): 159–75.

Koubi, Vally. 2005. "War and Economic Performance." *Journal of Peace Research* 42 (1): 67–82.

Kowert, Paul, and Jeffrey Legro. 1996. "Norms, Identity, and Their Limits: A Theoretical Reprise." In *The Culture of National Security: Norms and Identity in World Politics,* edited by Peter J. Katzenstein, 451–97. New York: Columbia University Press.

Krain, Matthew. 1997. "State-Sponsored Mass Murder: A Study of the Onset and Severity of Genocides and Politicides." *Journal of Conflict Resolution* 41 (3): 331–60.

Kratochwil, Friedrich V. 1989. *Rules, Norms, and Decisions on the Conditions of Practical and Legal Reasoning in International Relations and Domestic Affairs.* Cambridge, UK: Cambridge University Press.

Krause, Volker. 2004. "Hazardous Weapon? Effects of Arms Transfers and Defense Pact on Militarized Disputes, 1950–1995." *International Interactions* 30 (4): 349–71.

Kugler, Jacek. 1984. "Terror without Deterrence: Reassessing the Role of Nuclear Weapons." *Journal of Conflict Resolution* 28:470–506.

———. 1987. "Assessing Stable Deterrence." In *Exploring the Stability of Deterrence,* edited by Jacek Kugler and Frank C. Zagare. Boulder, CO: Lynne Rienner.

Kuhn, Thomas S. 1970. *The Structure of Scientific Revolutions.* 2nd ed. Chicago: University of Chicago Press.

Kupchan, Charles A. 2010. *How Enemies Become Friends: The Sources of Stable Peace.* Princeton, NJ: Princeton University Press.

Kydd, Andrew. 2000. "Arms Races and Arms Control: Modeling the Hawk Perspective." *American Journal of Political Science* 44:228–44.

Lakatos, Imre. 1978a. "Falsification and the Methodology of Scientific Research Programmes." In *The Methodology of Scientific Research Programmes,* Philosophical Papers, vol. 1, edited by John Worrall and Gregory Currie, 8–101. Cambridge: Cambridge University Press.

———. 1978b. "History of Science and Its Rational Reconstructions." In *The Methodology of Scientific Research Programmes,* Philosophical Papers, vol. 1, edited by John Worrall and Gregory Currie, 102–38. Cambridge: Cambridge University Press.

Lake, David A. 1992. "Powerful Pacifists: Democratic States and War." *American Political Science Review* 86 (1): 24–37.

Langlois, Jean-Pierre. 1991. "Rational Deterrence and Crisis Stability." *American Journal of Political Science* 35:801–32.

Latour, Bruno. 2007. *Reassembling the Social: An Introduction to Actor-Network-Theory.* Oxford: Oxford University Press.

Layne, Christopher. 1994. "Kant or Cant: The Myth of the Democratic Peace." *International Security* 19:5–49.

Leander, Anna. 2004. "War and Un-Making of States: Taking Tilly Seriously in the Contemporary World." In *Contemporary Security Analysis and Copenhagen Peace Research*, edited by Stefano Guzzini and Dietrich Jung, 69–80. London: Routledge.

Lebow, Richard N. 1981. *Between Peace and War: The Nature of International Crisis*. Baltimore, MD: Johns Hopkins University Press.

———. 1994. "The Search for Accommodation: Gorbachev in Comparative Perspective." In *International Relations Theory and the End of the Cold War*, edited by Richard Ned Lebow and Thomas Risse-Kappen, 167–86. New York: Columbia University Press.

———. 1997. "Transitions and Transformations: Building International Cooperation." *Security Studies* 6:154–79.

Leeds, Brett A. 2003. "Do Alliances Deter Aggression? The Influence of Military Alliances on the Initiation of Militarized Interstate Disputes." *American Journal of Political Science* 47 (3): 427–39.

———. 2005a. "Alliance Treaty Obligations and Provisions (ATOP) Codebook (version 3.0)." http://ruf.rice.edu/~leeds.

———. 2005b. "Alliances and the Expansion and Escalation of Militarized Interstate Disputes." In *New Directions for International Relations*, edited by Alex Mintz and Bruce Russett, 117–34. Lanham, MD: Lexington Books.

Leeds, Brett A., Andrew Long, and Sara McLaughlin Mitchell. 2000. "Reevaluating Alliance Reliability: Specific Threats, Specific Promises." *Journal of Conflict Resolution* 44 (5): 686–99.

Leeds, Brett A., Jeffrey M. Ritter, Sara McLaughlin Mitchell, and Andrew G. Long. 2002. "Alliance Treaty Obligations and Provisions, 1815–1944." *International Interactions* 28 (3): 237–60.

Leitner, Helga, Eric Sheppard, and Kristin M. Sziarto. 2008. "The Spatialities of Contentious Politics." *Transactions of the Institute of British Geographers* 33 (2): 157–72.

Lemke, Douglas. 2002. *Regions of War and Peace*. New York: Cambridge University Press.

Lemke, Douglas, and William Reed. 1996. "Regime Types and Status Quo Evaluations: Power Transition Theory and the Democratic Peace." *International Interactions* 22 (2): 143–64.

———. 2001. "The Relevance of Politically Relevant Dyads." *Journal of Conflict Resolution* 45 (1): 126–44.

Leng, Russell J. 1983. "When Will They Ever Learn? Coercive Bargaining in Recurrent Crisis." *Journal of Conflict Resolution* 27 (3): 379–419.

———. 2000. *Bargaining and Learning in Recurring Crises: The Soviet-American, Egyptian-Israeli, and Indo-Pakistan Rivalries*. Ann Arbor: University of Michigan Press.

Leng, Russell J., and Patrick M. Regan. 2003. "Social and Political Cultural Effects on the Outcomes of Mediation in Militarized Interstate Disputes." *International Studies Quarterly* 47 (3): 431–52.

Leonard, Eric K. 2005. *The Onset of Global Governance: International Relations Theory and the International Criminal Court*. Burlington, VT: Ashgate.

Levy, Jack S. 1981. "Alliance Formation and War Behavior: An Analysis of the Great Powers, 1495–1975." *Journal of Conflict Resolution* 25 (4): 581–613.

———. 1983. "Misperception and the Causes of War: Theoretical Linkages and Analytical Problems." *World Politics* 36 (1):76–99.

———. 1988. "Domestic Politics and War." *Journal of Interdisciplinary History* 18 (4): 653–73.

———. 1989. "The Causes of War: A Review of Theories and Evidence." In *Behavior, Society, and Nuclear War*, edited by Philip Tetlock, Jo L. Husbands, Robert Jervis, Paul C. Stern, and Charles Tilly, 1:209–333. New York: Oxford University Press.

———. 2008. "Counterfactuals and Case Studies." In *Oxford Handbook of Political Methodology*, edited by Janet Box-Steffensmeier, Henry Brady, and David Collier, 627–44. New York: Oxford University Press.

Levy, Jack S., and William R. Thompson. 2005. "Hegemonic Threats and Great Power Balancing in Europe, 1495–2000." *Security Studies* 14 (1): 1–33.

———. 2010a. "Balancing on Land and at Sea: Do States Ally against the Leading Global Power?" *International Security* 35 (1): 7–43.

———. 2010b. *Causes of War*. Chichester, UK: Wiley-Blackwell.

———. 2011. *The Arc of War: Origins, Escalation, and Transformation*. Chicago: University of Chicago Press.

———. Forthcoming. *Hegemonic Threats, Balancing, and War*.

Levy, Jack, and Lily I. Vakili. 1992. "Diversionary Action by Authoritarian Regimes: Argentina in the Falklands/Malvinas Case." In *The Internationalization of Communal Strife*, edited by Manus I. Midlarsky, 118–46. London: Routledge.

Lieberson, Stanley. 2001. Review Essay of *Fuzzy-Set Social Science*, by Charles Ragin. *Contemporary Sociology* 30:331–34.

Lipset, Seymour M. 1959. "Some Social Requisites of Democracy: Economic Development and Political Legitimacy." *The American Political Science Review* 53 (1): 69–105.

Lipson, Charles. 2003. *Reliable Partners: How Democracies Have Made a Separate Peace*. Princeton, NJ: Princeton University Press.

Lowi, Theodore J. 1967. "Making Democracy Safe for the World: National Politics and Foreign Policy." In *Domestic Sources of Foreign Policy*, edited by James N. Rosenau, 295–331. New York: Free Press.

Luard, Evan. 1986. *War in International Society*. London: I. B. Tauris.

Mackie, John L. 1965. "Causes and Conditions." *American Philosophical Quarterly* 2:45–64.

Mansbach, Richard W., and John A. Vasquez. 1981. *In Search of Theory: A New Paradigm for Global Politics*. New York: Columbia University Press.

Mansfield, Edward D., Helen V. Milner, and B. Peter Rosendorff. 2002. "Why Democracies Cooperate More: Electoral Control and International Trade Agreements." *International Organization* 56 (3): 477–513.

Mansfield, Edward D., and Jack Snyder. 1995. "Democratization and the Danger of War." *International Security* 30 (1): 5–38.

Maoz, Zeev. 1984. "Peace by Empire? Conflict Outcomes and International Stability, 1816–1976." *Journal of Peace Research* 21:227–41.

———. 1989. "Joining the Club of Nations: Political Development and International Conflict, 1816–1976." *International Studies Quarterly* 33 (2): 199–231.

———. 1996. *Domestic Sources of Global Change*. Ann Arbor: University of Michigan Press.

———. 2000. "Alliances: The Street Gangs of World Politics—Their Origins, Management, and Consequences, 1816–1986." In *What Do We Know about War?*, edited by John A. Vasquez, 111–44. Lanham, MD: Rowman & Littlefield.

———. 2004. "Pacifism and Fightaholism in International Politics: A Structural History of National and Dyadic Conflict, 1816–1992." *International Studies Review* 6 (4): 107–33.

———. 2005. "Dyadic MID Dataset (version 2.0)." http://psfaculty.ucdavis.edu/zmaoz/dyadmid.html.

———. 2006. "Democracy and Peace: Which Comes First?" In *Approaches, Levels, and Methods of Analysis in International Relations: Crossing Boundaries*, edited by H. Starr, 47–72. New York: Palgrave Macmillan.

———. 2009a. "The Effects of Strategic and Economic Interdependence on International Conflict across Levels of Analysis." *American Journal of Political Science* 53 (1): 223–40.

———. 2009b. "Primed to Fight: The Can/Must Syndrome and the Conflict Proneness of Nations." *Conflict Management and Peace Science* 26 (5): 1–26.

———. 2010. *The Networks of Nations: The Evolution and Structure of International Networks, 1815–2002*. Cambridge: Cambridge University Press.

———. 2011. *Networks of Nations: The Evolution, Structure, and Impact of International Networks, 1816–2001*. New York: Cambridge University Press.

———. 2012. "Network Science and International Relations." *Conflict Management and Peace Science* 29 (3): forthcoming.

Maoz, Zeev, and Nasrin Abdolali. 1989. "Regime Types and International Conflict, 1816–1976." *Journal of Conflict Resolution* 33:3–35.

Maoz, Zeev, and Ben Mor. 2002. *Bound by Struggle: The Strategic Evolution of Enduring International Rivalries*. Ann Arbor: University of Michigan Press.

Maoz, Zeev, and Bruce M. Russett. 1992. "Alliances, Wealth, Contiguity and Political Stability: Is the Lack of Conflict between Democracies a Statistical Artifact." *International Interactions* 17:245–67.

———. 1993. "Normative and Structural Causes of Democratic Peace." *American Political Science Review* 87 (3): 624–38.

Maoz, Zeev, and Randolph M. Siverson. 2008. "Bargaining, Domestic Politics, and International Context in the Management of War: A Review Essay." *Conflict Management and Peace Science* 25 (2): 171–89.

Maoz, Zeev, Lesley G. Terris, Ranan D. Kuperman, and Ilan Talmud. 2005. "International Networks and International Politics." In *Directions for International Relations*, edited by Alex Mintz and Bruce Russett, 35–64. Lanham, MD: Lexington Press.

Marshall, Monty G., and Keith Jaggers. 2003. *Polity IV Project: Political Regime Characteristics and Transitions, 1800–2002, Dataset Users' Manual*. College Park: University of Maryland, Center for International Development and Conflict Management.

———. 2004. *Polity IV Project*. College Park: University of Maryland, Center for International Development and Conflict Management. Available at http:/www .cidcm.umd.edu/inscr/polity.

Mattes, Michaela, and Greg Vonnahme. 2010. "Contracting for Peace: Do Nonaggression Pacts Reduce Conflict?" *Journal of Politics* 72 (4): 925–38.

Mayhew, David R. 2005. "Wars and American Politics." *Perspectives* 3:473–93.

McDonald, Patrick J. 2007. "The Purse Strings of Peace." *American Journal of Political Science* 51:569–82.

———. 2009. *The Invisible Hand of Peace, Capitalism, the War Machine, and International Relations Theory*. Cambridge: Cambridge University Press.

McGinnis, Michael, and John Williams. 2001. *Compound Dilemmas: Democracy, Collective Action, and Superpower Rivalry*. Ann Arbor: University of Michigan Press.

McLaughlin, Sara. 1997. "The Systemic Democratic Peace." PhD diss., Michigan State University.

Mearshemier, John J. 2001. *The Tragedy of Great Power Politics*. New York: Norton.

Midlarsky, Manus. 1989–2009. *Handbook of War Studies*. 3 vols. Vol. 1, Boston: Unwin Hyman; vols. 2–3, Ann Arbor: University of Michigan Press.

———. 1995. "Environmental Influences on Democracy: Aridity, Warfare and a Reversal of the Causal Arrow." *Journal of Conflict Resolution* 39:224–62.

Miller, Steven, and Douglas M. Gibler. 2011. "Democracies, Territory, and Negotiated Compromises." *Conflict Management and Peace Science* 28 (3): 261–79.

Mitchell, Sara McLaughlin. 2002. "A Kantian System? Democracy and Third Party Conflict Resolution." *American Journal of Political Science* 46 (4): 749–59.

———. 2010. "Norms Still Matter: What the Systemic Democratic Peace Can Teach Us about Conflict Processes." Paper presented at the "What Do We Know about War?" workshop, University of Illinois, Urbana-Champaign, October.

Mitchell, Sara McLaughlin, Scott Gates, and Håvard Hegre. 1999. "Evolution in Democracy-War Dynamics." *Journal of Conflict Resolution* 43 (6): 771–92.

Mitchell, Sara McLaughlin, and Paul R. Hensel. 2007. "International Institutions and Compliance with Agreements." *American Journal of Political Science* 51 (4): 721–37.

Mitchell, Sara McLaughlin, Kelly M. Kadera, and Mark J. C. Crescenzi. 2008. "Practicing Democratic Community Norms: Third Party Conflict Management and Successful Settlements." In *International Conflict Mediation: New Approaches and Findings*, edited by Jacob Bercovitch and Scott Sigmund Gartner, 243–64. New York: Routledge.

Mitchell, Sara McLaughlin, and Emilia Justyna Powell. 2011. *Domestic Law Goes Global: Legal Traditions and International Courts*. Cambridge: Cambridge University Press.

Mitchell, Sara McLaughlin, and Brandon C. Prins. 1999. "Beyond Territorial Contiguity: Issues at Stake in Democratic Militarized Interstate Disputes." *International Studies Quarterly* 43 (1): 169–83.

———. 2004. "Rivalry and Diversionary Uses of Force." *Journal of Conflict Resolution* 48:937–81.

Mitchell, Sara McLaughlin, and Cameron Thies. 2011. "Issue Rivalries." *Conflict Management and Peace Science* 28: forthcoming.

Moore, Barrington. 1966. *Social Origins of Dictatorship and Democracy: Lord and Peasant in the Making in the Modern World*. Boston: Beacon Press.

Mor, Ben. 1997. "Peace Initiatives and Public Opinion: The Domestic Context of Conflict Resolution." *Journal of Peace Research* 34 (2): 197–215.

Moravcsik, Andrew. 2000. "The Origins of Human Rights Regimes: Democratic Delegation in Postwar Europe." *International Organization* 54 (2): 217–52.

Morgan, T. Clifton, and Glenn Palmer. 2003. "To Protect and to Serve: Alliances and Foreign Policy Portfolios." *Journal of Conflict Resolution* 47 (2): 180–203.

Morgan, Patrick M. 1977. *Deterrence: A Conceptual Analysis*. Sage Library of Social Research, vol. 40. Beverly Hills, CA: Sage.

———. 2003. *Deterrence Now*. Cambridge: Cambridge University Press.

Morgenthau, Hans J. [1948] 1960. *Politics among Nations: The Struggle for Power and Peace*. 1st and 3rd eds. New York: Knopf.

Morrow, James D. 1991. "Alliances and Asymmetry: An Alternative to the Capability Aggregation Model of Alliances." *American Journal of Political Science* 35 (4): 904–33.

———. 1994. "Alliances, Credibility, and Peacetime Costs." *Journal of Conflict Resolution* 38 (2): 270–97.

Most, Benjamin A., and Harvey Starr. 1987. *Inquiry, Logic, and International Relations*. Columbia: University of South Carolina Press.

Moul, William B. 1988. "Great Power Nondefense Alliances and the Escalation to War of Conflicts between Unequals, 1815–1939." *International Interactions* 15 (1): 25–43.

Mousseau, Michael. 2000. "Market Prosperity, Democratic Consolidation, and Democratic Peace." *Journal of Conflict Resolution* 44 (4): 472–502.

———. 2002. "An Economic Limitation to the Zone of Democratic Peace and Cooperation." *International Interactions* 28:137–64.

———. 2002–2003. "Market Civilization and Its Clash with Terror." *International Security* 27:5–29.

———. 2003. "The Nexus of Market Society, Liberal Preferences, and Democratic Peace: Interdisciplinary Theory and Evidence." *International Studies Quarterly* 47:483–510.

———. 2009. "The Social Market Roots of Democratic Peace." *International Security* 33:52–86.

———. 2010. "Coming to Terms with the Capitalist Peace." *International Interactions* 36:185–92.

———. 2011. "Urban Poverty and Support for Islamist Terror: Survey Results from Muslims in Fourteen Countries." *Journal of Peace Research* 48:35–47.

———. 2012. "The Capitalist Civil Peace." *International Studies Quarterly* (forthcoming).

Mousseau, Michael, Håvard Hegre, and John R. Oneal. 2003. "How the Wealth of Nations Conditions the Liberal Peace." *European Journal of International Relations* 9:277–314.

Mousseau, Michael, and Demet Yalcin Mousseau. 2008. "The Contracting Roots of Human Rights." *Journal of Peace Research* 45:327–44.

Mousseau, Michael, and Yuhang Shi. 1999. "A Test for Reverse Causality in the Democratic Peace Relationship." *Journal of Peace Research* 36:639–63.

Mueller, John. 1988. "The Essential Irrelevance of Nuclear Weapons: Stability in the Postwar World." *International Security* 13:55–79.

———. 1989. *Retreat from Doomsday: The Obsolescence of Major War*. New York: Basic Books.

Murdoch, James C., and Todd Sandler. 2002. "Economic Growth, Civil War, and Spatial Spillovers." *Journal of Conflict Resolution* 46 (1): 91–110.

Murphy, Alexander. 1990. "Historical Justifications for Territory Claims." *Annals of the Association of American Geographers* 80 (4): 531–648.

Nadelmann, Ethan A. 1990. "Global Prohibition Regimes: The Evolution of Norms in International Society." *International Organization* 44 (4): 479–526.

Nalebuff, Barry. 1988. "Minimal Nuclear Deterrence." *Journal of Conflict Resolution* 32:411–25.

Newman, David. 1999. "Real Places, Symbolic Spaces: Interrelated Notions of Territory in the Arab-Israeli Conflict." In *A Road Map to War*, edited by Paul F. Diehl, 3–34. Nashville, TN: Vanderbilt University Press.

———. 2006. "The Resilience of Territorial Conflict in an Era of Globalization." In *Territoriality and Conflict in an Era of Globalization*, edited by M. Kahler and B. F. Walter, 85–110. Cambridge: Cambridge University Press.

Nielsen, Richard A., Michael G. Findley, Zachary S. Davis, Tara Candland, and Daniel L. Nielsen. 2011. "Foreign Aid Shocks as a Cause of Violent and Armed Conflict." *American Journal of Political Science* 55 (2): 219–32.

North, Douglass C., John Joseph Wallis, and Barry R. Weingast. 2009. *Violence and Social Orders: A Conceptual Framework for Interpreting Recorded Human History*. New York: Cambridge University Press.

North, Douglass C., and Barry R. Weingast. 1989. "Constitutions and Commitment: The Evolution of Institutional Governing Public Choice in Seventeenth-Century England." *Journal of Economic History* 49 (4): 803–32.

O'Loughlin, John. 2000. "Geography as Space and Geography as Place: The Divide between Political Science and Political Geography Continues." *Geopolitics* 5 (3): 126–37.

Olson, Mancur. 1993. "Dictatorship, Democracy, and Development." *American Political Science Review* 87 (3): 567–76.

Oneal, John R., Frances H. Oneal, Zeev Maoz, and Bruce Russett. 1996. "The Liberal Peace: Interdependence, Democracy, and International Conflict, 1950–85." *Journal of Peace Research* 33:11–28.

Oneal, John R., and Bruce Russett. 1997. "The Classical Liberals Were Right: Democracy, Interdependence, and Conflict, 1950–1985." *International Studies Quarterly* 41:267–94.

———. 2000. "Why 'An Identified Systemic Analysis of the Democracy-Peace Nexus' Does Not Persuade." *Defence and Peace Economics* 11:197–214.

———. 2005. "Rule of Three, Let It Be: When More Is Really Better." *Conflict Management and Peace Science* 22 (4): 293–310.

Onuf, Nicholas Greenwood. 1989. *World of Our Making: Rules and Rule in Social Theory and International Relations*. Columbia: University of South Carolina Press.

Organski, A. F. K. 1958. *World Politics*. New York: Knopf.

Organski, A. F. K., and Jacek Kugler. 1980. *The War Ledger*. Chicago: University of Chicago Press.

Osgood, Robert E., and Robert W. Tucker. 1967. *Force, Order, and Justice*. Baltimore, MD: Johns Hopkins University Press.

Owsiak, Andrew P. 2012. "Signing Up for Peace: International Boundary Agreements, Democracy, and Militarized Interstate Conflict." *International Studies Quarterly* (forthcoming).

Palmer, Glenn, and T. Clifton Morgan. 2006. *A Theory of Foreign Policy*. Princeton, NJ: Princeton University Press.

Parker, Geoffrey. 1988. *The Military Revolution: Military Innovation and the Rise of the West, 1500–1800*. Cambridge: Cambridge University Press.

Parrott, David. 2010. "From Military Enterprise to Standing Armies: War, State and Society in Western Europe, 1600–1700." In *European Warfare, 1350–1750*, edited by Frank Tallett and D. J. B. Trim. Cambridge: Cambridge University Press.

Paul, T. V. 1994. *Asymmetric Conflicts: War Initiation by Weaker Powers*. Cambridge: Cambridge University Press.

———. 1995. "Nuclear Taboo and War Initiation in Regional Conflicts." *Journal of Conflict Resolution* 39:696–717.

———. 2005. "Causes of the India-Pakistan Enduring Rivalry." In *The India-Pakistan Conflict: An Enduring Rivalry*, edited by T. V. Paul, 3–26. Cambridge: Cambridge University Press.

Peceny, Mark. 1997. "A Constructivist Interpretation of the Liberal Peace: The Ambiguous Case of the Spanish-American War." *Journal of Peace Research* 34 (4): 415–30.

Peceney, Mark, Caroline C. Beer, and Shannon Sanchez-Terry. 2002. "Dictatorial Peace?" *American Political Science Review* 96 (1): 15–26.

Petersen, Karen, John Vasquez, and Yijia Wang. 2004. "Multiparty Disputes and the Probability of War, 1816–1992." *Conflict Management and Peace Science* 21 (Summer): 1–16.

Pevehouse, Jon, Timothy Nordstrom, and Kevin Wranke. 2004. "The Correlates of War 2: International Governmental Organizations Data, Version 2." *Conflict Management and Peace Science* 21 (2): 101–19.

Pevehouse, Jon, and Bruce Russett. 2006. "Democratic International Governmental Organizations Promote Peace." *International Organization* 60 (4): 969–1000.

Poast, Paul. 2010. "(Mis)Using Dyadic Data to Analyze Multilateral Events." *Political Analysis* 18 (4): 403–25.

Poe, Steven C., and Neal Tate. 1994. "Repression of Human Rights to Personal Integrity in the 1980s: A Global Analysis." *American Political Science Review* 88 (4): 853–72.

Polanyi, Karl. [1944] 1957. *The Great Transformation: The Political and Economic Origins of Our Time*. Boston: Beacon Press.

Porter, Bruce D. 1994. *War and the Rise of the State: The Military Foundation of Modern Politics*. New York: Free Press.

Powell, Emilia Justyna, and Sara McLaughlin Mitchell. 2007. "The International Court of Justice and the World's Three Legal Systems." *Journal of Politics* 69 (2): 397–415.

Powell, Robert. 1987. "Crisis Bargaining, Escalation, and MAD." *American Political Science Review* 81:717–36.

———. 1988. "Nuclear Brinkmanship with Two-Sided Incomplete Information." *American Political Science Review* 82:155–78.

———. 1999. *In the Shadow of Power*. Princeton, NJ: Princeton University Press.

———. 2002. "Bargaining Theory and International Conflict." *Annual Review of Political Science* 5:1–30.

———. 2004. "Bargaining and Learning While Fighting." *American Journal of Political Science* 48 (2): 344–61.

———. 2006. "War as a Commitment Problem." *International Organization* 60 (1): 169–203.

Powers, Matthew A., and John A. Vasquez. 2011. "Do Alliances Really Deter?" Paper presented at the annual meeting of the Midwest Political Science Association, Chicago.

Pressman, Jeremy. 2008. *Warring Friends: Alliance Restraints in International Politics*. Ithaca, NY: Cornell University Press.

Price, Richard M. 1998. "Reversing the Gun Sights: Transnational Civil Society Targets Land Mines." *International Organization* 52 (3): 613–44.

———. 2007. *The Chemical Weapons Taboo*. Ithaca, NY: Cornell University Press.

Price, Richard M., and Nina Tannenwald. 1996. "Norms and Deterrence: The Nuclear and Chemical Weapons Taboos." In *The Culture of National Security: Norms and Identity in World Politics*, edited by Peter J. Katzenstein, 114–52. New York: Columbia University Press.

Prins, Brandon C., and Ursula Daxecker. 2008. "Committed to Peace: Liberal Institutions and the Termination of Rivalry." *British Journal of Political Science* 38:17–43.

Przeworski, Adam. 2000. *Democracy and Development: Political Institutions and Well-Being in the World, 1950–1990*. Cambridge: Cambridge University Press.

Przeworski, Adam, Michael Alvarez, Jose A. Cheibub, and Fernando Limongi. 1996. "What Makes Democracies Endure?" *Journal of Democracy* 7 (1): 39–55.

Przeworski, Adam, and Fernando Limongi. 1997. "Modernization: Theories and Facts." *World Politics* 49 (2): 155–83.

Putnam, Robert. 1988. "Diplomacy and Domestic Politics: The Logic of Two-Level Games." *International Organization* 42 (3): 427–60.

Quester, George H. 1986. *The Future of Nuclear Deterrence*. Lexington, MA: Lexington Books.

Ragin, Charles C. 1987. *The Comparative Method: Moving beyond Qualitative and Quantitative Strategies*. Berkeley: University of California Press.

———. 2000. *Fuzzy-Set Social Science*. Chicago: University of Chicago Press.

Raknerud, Arvid, and Håvard Hegre. 1997. "The Hazard of War: Reassessing the Evidence of the Democratic Peace." *Journal of Peace Research* 34 (4): 385–404.

Rasler, Karen A., and William R. Thompson. 1985a. "War and the Economic Growth of Major Powers." *American Journal of Political Science* 29:513–38.

———. 1985b. "War Making and State Making: Government Expenditures, Tax Revenues, and Global Wars." *American Political Science Review* 79:491–507.

———. 1989. *War and State Making: The Shaping of the Global Powers*. Boston: Unwin Hyman.

———. 1994. *The Great Powers and Global Struggle, 1490–1990*. Lexington: University Press of Kentucky.

———. 2001. "Rivalries and the Democratic Peace in the Major Power Subsystem." *Journal of Peace Research* 38:657–83.

———. 2004. "The Democratic Peace and the Sequential, Reciprocal, Causal Arrow Hypothesis." *Comparative Political Studies* 37:879–908.

———. 2005. *Puzzles of the Democratic Peace: Theory, Geopolitics, and the Transformation of World Politics*. New York: Palgrave Macmillan.

———. 2009. "Rivalry, War and State Making in Less Developed Contexts." Paper presented at the annual meeting of the International Studies Association, New York, February.

———. 2010. "Border, Rivalry, Democracy and Conflict in the Mideast Region, 1948–2001." Paper presented at the annual meeting of the Comparative Interdisciplinary Studies Section (CISS) [ISA section], Venice, Italy, July.

———. 2011. "Borders, Rivalry, Democracy and Conflict in the European Region, 1816–1999." *Conflict Management and Peace Science* 28 (3): 280–305.

Rauchhaus, Robert. 2009. "Evaluating the Nuclear Peace Hypothesis: A Quantitative Approach." *Journal of Conflict Resolution* 53 (2): 258–77.

Ray, James Lee. 1990. "Friends as Foes: International Conflict and Wars between Formal Allies." In *Prisoners of War?*, edited by Charles Gochman and Alan Sabrosky, 73–91. Lanham, MD: Lexington Books.

———. 1995. *Democracy and International Conflict: An Evaluation of the Democratic Peace Proposition*. Columbia: University of South Carolina Press.

———. 2000. "Democracy on the Level(s): Does Democracy Correlate with Peace?" In *What Do We Know about War?*, edited by John A. Vasquez. Lanham, MD: Rowman & Littlefield.

———. 2001. "Integrating Levels of Analysis in World Politics." *Journal of Theoretical Politics* 13 (4): 355–88.

———. 2005. "Constructing Multivariate Analyses (of Dangerous Dyads)." *Conflict Management and Peace Science* 22 (4): 277–92.

Raymond, Gregory A. 1994. "Democracies, Disputes, and Third-Party Intermediaries." *Journal of Conflict Resolution* 38 (1): 24–42.

———. 2000. "International Norms: Normative Orders and Peace." In *What Do We Know about War?*, edited by John A. Vasquez. Lanham, MD: Rowman & Littlefield.

Redlawsk, David P., and Richard R. Lau. Forthcoming. "Behavioral Decision Making." In *Handbook of Political Psychology*, 2nd ed., edited by Leonie Huddy, David O. Sears, and Jack S. Levy, chap. 3. Oxford: Oxford University Press.

Reed, William. 2000. "A Unified Statistical Model of Conflict Onset and Escalation." *American Journal of Political Science* 44 (1): 84–93.

Rees, Nigel. 2006. *Brewer's Famous Quotations: 5000 Quotations and the Stories behind Them*. London: Orion.

Reiter, Dan. 2001. "Does Peace Nurture Democracy?" *Journal of Politics* 63:935–48.

———. 2003. "Exploring the Bargaining Model of War." *Perspectives on Politics* 1 (1): 27–43.

Reiter, Dan, and Allan C. Stam. 2003. "Identifying the Culprit: Democracy, Dictatorship, and Dispute Initiation." *American Political Science Review* 97 (2): 333–37.

Reno, William. 2003. "The Changing Nature of Warfare and the Absence of State-Building in West Africa." In *Irregular Armed Forces and Their Role in Politics and State Formation*, edited by Diane E. Davis and Anthony W. Pereira, 322–45. Cambridge: Cambridge University Press.

Richardson, James L. 1994. *Crisis Diplomacy: The Great Powers since the Mid-Nineteenth Century*. Cambridge: Cambridge University Press.

Richardson, Lewis F. 1960. *Statistics of Deadly Quarrels*. Chicago: Quadrangle.

Rider, Toby, Michael Findley, and Paul F. Diehl. 2011. "Just Part of the Game? Arms Races, Rivalry, and War." *Journal of Peace Research* 48:85–100.

Risse-Kappen, Thomas. 1995. *Cooperation among Democracies: The European Influence on U.S. Foreign Policy*. Princeton, NJ: Princeton University Press.

———. 1996. "Collective Identity in a Democratic Community: The Case of NATO." In *The Culture of National Security: Norms and Identity in World Politics*, edited by Peter J. Katzenstein. New York: Columbia University Press.

Robinson, Gene E. 2006. "Genes and Social Behavior." In *Essays in Animal Behaviour: Celebrating 50 Years of Animal Behaviour*, edited by Jeffrey R. Lucas and Leigh W. Simmons, 101–13. Amsterdam: Elsevier.

Robst, John, Solomon Polachek, and Yuan-Ching Chang. 2007. "Geographic Proximity, Trade, and International Conflict/Cooperation." *Conflict Management and Peace Science* 24 (1) 1–24.

Rosato, Sebastian. 2003. "The Flawed Logic of Democratic Peace Theory." *American Political Science Review* 97 (4): 585–602.

Rosecrance, Richard N. 1986. *Rise of the Trading State: Commerce and Conquest in the Modern World*. New York: Basic Books.

———. 1999. *The Rise of the Virtual State: Wealth and Power in the Coming Century*. New York: Basic Books.

Rosen, Steven. 1972. "War Power and the Willingness to Suffer." In *Peace, War, and Numbers*, edited by Bruce Russett, 167–84. Beverly Hills, CA: Sage.

Rubin, D. B. 1979. "Using Multivariate Matched Sampling and Regression Adjustment to Control Bias in Observational Studies." Journal of the American Statistical Association 74:318–28.

Rueschemeyer, Dietrich, Evelyne H. Stephens, and John D. Stephens. 2000. "Capitalist Development and Democracy." In *Sociological Worlds: Comparative and Historical Readings on Society*, edited by Stephen K. Sanderson, 243–48. Los Angeles: Roxbury.

Rummel, Rudolph J. 1979. *War, Power, Peace. Vol. 4 of Understanding Conflict and War*. Beverly Hills, CA: Sage.

————. 1983. "Libertarianism and International Violence." *Journal of Conflict Resolution* 27 (1): 27–71.

Russett, Bruce. 1963. "The Calculus of Deterrence." *Journal of Conflict Resolution* 7:97–109.

————. 1988. "Extended Deterrence with Nuclear Weapons: How Necessary, How Acceptable?" *Review of Politics* 50:282–302.

————. 1993. *Grasping the Democratic Peace: Principles for a Post–Cold War World.* Princeton, NJ: Princeton University Press.

Russett, Bruce M., and John Oneal. 2001. *Triangulating Peace: Democracy, Interdependence, and International Organizations.* New York: Norton.

Russett, Bruce M., and Harvey Starr. 2000. "From the Democratic Peace to Kantian Peace: Democracy and Conflict in the International System." In *Handbook of War Studies*, edited by Manus I. Midlarsky, 2:93–128. Ann Arbor: University of Michigan Press.

Sabrosky, Alan Ned. 1980. "Interstate Alliances: Their Reliability and the Expansion of War." In *The Correlates of War*, vol. 2, ed. J. D. Singer, 161–98. New York: Free Press.

Sagan, Scott D., and Kenneth N. Waltz. 1995. *The Spread of Nuclear Weapons: A Debate.* New York: Norton.

————. 2003. *The Spread of Nuclear Weapons: A Debate Renewed.* New York: Norton.

Salehyan, Idean. 2009. *Rebels without Borders: Transnational Insurgencies in World Politics.* Ithaca, NY: Cornell University Press.

Sample, Susan G. 1997. "Arms Races and Dispute Escalation: Resolving the Debate." *Journal of Peace Research* 34:7–22.

————. 1998a. "Furthering the Investigation into the Effects of Arms Buildups." *Journal of Peace Research* 35 (1): 122–26.

————. 1998b. "Military Buildups, War, and Realpolitik: A Multivariate Model." *Journal of Conflict Resolution* 42 (2): 156–75.

————. 2000. "Military Buildups: Arming and War." In *What Do We Know about War?*, edited by John A. Vasquez, 165–95. New York: Rowman & Littlefield.

————. 2002. "The Outcomes of Military Buildups: Minor States vs. Major Powers." *Journal of Peace Research* 39:669–91.

————. 2011. "Arms Races: A Cause or a Symptom?" Paper presented to the "What Do We Know about War?" panel at the annual convention of the International Studies Association.

Sarkees, Meredith Reid, and Frank Wayman. 2010. *Resort to War 1816–2007.* Washington, DC: CQ Press.

Schabas, William A. 2011. *An Introduction to the International Criminal Court.* Cambridge: Cambridge University Press.

Schelling, Thomas C. 1960. *The Strategy of Conflict.* Oxford: Oxford University Press.

————. 1966. *Arms and Influence.* New Haven, CT: Yale University Press.

Schmitz, Hans Peter, and Kathryn Sikkink. 2002. "International Human Rights." In *Handbook of International Relations*, edited by Walter Carlsnaes, Thomas Risse, and Beth A. Simmons, 517–37. Thousand Oaks, CA: Sage.

Schroeder, Paul W. 1976. "Alliances, 1815–1945: Weapons of Power and Tools of Management." In *Historical Dimensions of National Security Problems*, edited by Klaus Knorr, 247–86. Lawrence: University of Kansas Press.

———. 1994. *The Transformation of European Politics, 1763-1848*. New York: Oxford University Press.

Schultz, Kenneth A. 1998. "Domestic Opposition and Signaling in International Crises." *American Political Science Review* 92:829–44.

———. 2001. *Democracy and Coercive Diplomacy*. Cambridge: Cambridge University Press.

Senese, Paul D. 1996. "Geographical Proximity and Issue Salience: Their Effects on the Escalation of Militarized Interstate Conflict." *Conflict Management and Peace Science* 15 (1): 133–61.

———. 2005. "Territory, Contiguity, and International Conflict: Assessing a New Joint Explanation." *American Journal of Political Science* 49 (4): 769–79.

Senese, Paul D., and John A. Vasquez. 2008. *The Steps-to-War: An Empirical Study*. Princeton, NJ: Princeton University Press.

Shannon, Megan. 2005. "The Democratic Community and the Expansion of International Organizations." PhD diss., University of Iowa.

———. 2009. "Preventing War and Providing the Peace? International Organizations and the Management of Territorial Disputes." *Conflict Management and Peace Science* 26 (2): 144–63.

Signorino, Curtis S. 1999. "Strategic Interaction and the Statistical Analysis of International Conflict." *American Political Science Review* 93 (2): 279–97.

Signorino, Curtis S., and Jeffrey M. Ritter. 1999. "Tau-b or Not Tau-b: Measuring the Similarity of Foreign Policy Positions." *International Studies Quarterly* 43 (1): 115–44.

Signorino, Curtis S., and Kuzey Yilmaz. 2003. "Strategic Misspecification in Regression Models." *American Journal of Political Science* 47 (3): 551–66.

Simmel, Georg. 1955. *Conflict and the Web of Group Affiliations*. Translated by K. H. Wolff and R. Bendix. New York: Free Press.

Simmons, Beth A. 1999. "See You in 'Court'? The Appeal to Quasi-Judicial Legal Processes in the Settlement of Territorial Disputes." In *A Road Map to War*, edited by Paul F. Diehl, 205–37. Nashville, TN: Vanderbilt University Press.

———. 2002. "Capacity, Commitment, and Compliance: International Institutions and Territorial Disputes." *Journal of Conflict Resolution* 46 (6): 829–56.

———. 2005. "Rules over Real Estate: Trade, Territorial Conflict, and International Borders as Institution." *Journal of Conflict Resolution* 49 (6): 823–48.

———. 2009. *Mobilizing for Human Rights: International Law in Domestics Politics*. Cambridge, UK: Cambridge University Press.

Simon, Herbert. 1955. "A Behavioral Model of Rational Choice." *The Quarterly Journal of Economics* 69:99–118.

Singer, J. David. 1963. "Inter-Nation Influence: A Formal Model." *American Political Science Review* 57:420–30.

———. 1972. *The Scientific Study of Politics: An Approach to Foreign Policy Analysis*. Morristown, NJ: General Learning Press.

———. 1979. *The Correlates of War*. Vol. 1. New York: Free Press.

———. 1980. *The Correlates of War*. Vol. 2. New York: Free Press.

———. 1987. "Reconstructing the Correlates of War Dataset on Material Capabilities of States, 1816–1985." *International Interactions* 14:115–32.

Singer, J. David, Stuart Bremer, and John Stuckey. 1972. "Capability Distribution, Uncertainty, and Major Power War, 1820–1965." In *Peace, War, and Numbers*, edited by Bruce Russett, 19–48. Beverly Hills, CA: Sage.

Singer, J. David, and Melvin Small. 1966. "Formal Alliances, 1815–1939: A Quantitative Description." *Journal of Peace Research* 3 (1): 1–32.

———. 1972. *The Wages of War, 1816–1965: A Statistical Handbook*. New York: Wiley.

Siverson, Randolph M., and Ross A. Miller. [1993] 1995. "The Escalation of Disputes to War." *International Interactions* 19:77–97. Reprinted in *The Process of War*, edited by Stuart A. Bremer and Thomas R. Cusack. Amsterdam: Gordon and Breach Science Publishers.

Siverson, Randolph M., and Harvey Starr. 1991. *The Diffusion of War: A Study of Opportunity and Willingness*. Ann Arbor: University of Michigan Press.

Siverson, Randolph M., and Michael R. Tennefoss. 1984. "Power, Alliance, and the Escalation of International Conflict, 1815–1965." *The American Political Science Review* 78 (4): 1057–69.

Skocpol, Theda. 1979. *States and Social Revolutions: A Comparative Analysis of France, Russia and China*. Cambridge: Cambridge University Press.

———. 1992. *Protecting Soldiers and Mothers: The Political Origins of Social Policy in the United States*. Cambridge, MA: Harvard University Press.

Slantchev, Branislav L. 2003. "The Principle of Convergence in Wartime Negotiations." *American Political Science Review* 97 (4): 621–32.

———. 2004. "How Initiators End Their War: The Duration of Warfare and the Terms of Peace." *American Journal of Political Science* 48 (4): 813–29.

Slaughter, Anne-Marie. 1995. "International Law in a World of Liberal States." *European Journal of International Law* 6 (4): 503–38.

Small, Melvin. 1980. *Was War Necessary?* Beverly Hills, CA: Sage.

Small, Melvin, and J. David Singer. 1969. "Formal Alliances, 1815–1965: An Extension of the Basic Data." *Journal of Peace Research* 6:257–82.

———. 1976. "The War-Proneness of Democratic Regimes, 1816–1965." *Jerusalem Journal of International Relations* 1 (4): 50–69.

———. 1982. *Resort to Arms. International and Civil Wars, 1816–1980*. Beverly Hills, CA: Sage.

Smith, Alastair. 1995. "Alliance Formation and War." *International Studies Quarterly* 39 (4): 405–25.

———. 1998. "Extended Deterrence and Alliance Formation." *International Interactions* 24 (4): 315–43.

———. 1999. "Testing Theories of Strategic Choice: The Example of Crisis Escalation." *American Journal of Political Science* 43 (4): 1254–83.

Smith, Alastair, and Allan Stam. 2004. "Bargaining and the Nature of War." *Journal of Conflict Resolution* 48 (6): 783–813.

Smith, Theresa C. 1980. "Arms Race Instability and War." *Journal of Conflict Resolution* 24:253–84.

Snyder, Glenn H. 1961. *Deterrence and Defense: Toward a Theory of National Security*. Princeton, NJ: Princeton University Press.

———. 1965. "The Balance of Power and the Balance of Terror." In *Balance of Power*, edited by Paul Seabury, 185–201. San Francisco: Chandler.

———. 1997. *Alliance Politics*. Ithaca, NY: Cornell University Press.

Snyder, Glenn H., and Paul Diesing. 1977. *Conflict among Nations: Bargaining, Decision Making, and System Structure in International Crises*. Princeton, NJ: Princeton University Press.

Sobek, David, and Cameron G. Thies. 2010. "War, Economic Development, and Political Development in the Contemporary International System." *International Studies Quarterly* 54 (1): 267–87.

Soja, Edward. 1980. "The Socio-Spatial Dialectic." *Annals of the Association of American Geographers* 70:207–25.

Sparrow, Bartholomew. 1996. *From Outside In: World War II and the American State*. Princeton, NJ: Princeton University Press.

Spiro, David E. 1994. "The Insignificance of the Liberal Peace." *International Security* 19 (2): 50–86.

Sprout, Harold H., and Margaret Sprout. 1965. *The Ecological Perspective on Human Affairs, with Special References to International Politics*. Princeton, NJ: Princeton University Press.

Spruyt, Hendrik. 1994. *The Sovereign State and Its Competitors: An Analysis of Systems Change*. Princeton, NJ: Princeton University Press.

Stanley, Elizabeth A., and John P. Sawyer. 2009. "Equifinality of War Termination: Multiple Paths to Ending War." *Journal of Conflict Resolution* 53:651–76.

Starr, Harvey. 1991. "Democratic Dominoes: Diffusion Approaches to the Spread of Democracy in the International System." *Journal of Conflict Resolution* 35 (2): 356–81.

———. 2002. "Opportunity, Willingness, and Geographic Information Systems (GIS): Reconceptualizing Borders in International Relations." *Political Geography* 21 (2): 243–61.

———. 2005. "Territory, Proximity, and Spatiality: The Geography of International Conflict." *International Studies Review* 7 (3): 387–406.

Starr, Harvey, and Christina Lindborg. 2003. "Democratic Dominoes Revisited—The Hazards of Governmental Transitions, 1974–1996." *Journal of Conflict Resolution* 47 (4): 490–519.

Starr, Harvey, and Benjamin Most. 1978. "A Return Journey: Richardson, Frontiers, and War in the 1945–1965 Era." *Journal of Conflict Resolution* 22 (3): 441–62.

Starr, Harvey, and G. Dale Thomas. 2005. "The Nature of Borders and International Conflict: Revisiting Hypotheses on Territory." *International Studies Quarterly* 49 (1): 123–40.

Stedman, Stephen John. 1997. "Spoiler Problems in Peace Processes." *International Security* 22:5–53.

Stinnett, Douglas, and Paul F. Diehl. 2001. "The Path(s) to Rivalry: Behavioral and Structural Explanations of Rivalry Development." *Journal of Politics* 63:717–40.

Stinnett, Douglas M., Jaroslav Tir, Philip Schafer, Paul F. Diehl, and Charles Gochman. 2002. "The Correlates of War Project Direct Contiguity Data, Version 3." *Conflict Management and Peace Science* 19 (2): 58–66.

Streich, Philip, and Jack S. Levy. 2007. "Time Horizons, Discounting, and Intertemporal Choice." *Journal of Conflict Resolution* 51 (2): 199–226.

Stubbs, Richard. 2005. *Rethinking Asia's Economic Miracle*. New York: Palgrave Macmillan.

Suganami, Hidemi. 1996. *On the Causes of War*. Oxford: Clarendon Press.

Tammen, Ronald L., Jack Kugler, Douglas Lemke, Allan Stam III, Carole Alsharabati, Mark A. Abdollahian, Brian Efird, and A. F. K. Organski. 2000. *Power Transitions: Strategies for the 21st Century*. New York: Chatham House.

Taylor, Brian D., and Rozana Botea. 2008. "Tilly Tally: War-Making and State-Making in the Contemporary Third World." *International Studies Review* 10:27–56.

Taylor, Peter J. 1981. "Geographical Scales within the World-Economy Approach." *Review* 5:3–11.

Terris, Leslie G., and Zeev Maoz. 2005 "Rational Mediation: A Theory and a Test." *Journal of Peace Research* 42 (5): 563–83.

Teschke, Benno. 2010. "Revisiting the 'War-Makes-States' Thesis: War, Taxation and Social Property Relations in Early Modern Europe." In *War, the State and International Law in Seventeenth Century Europe*, edited by Olaf Asbach and Peter Schroeder. Burlington, VT: Ashgate.

Thies, Cameron G. 2001. "A Social Psychological Approach to Enduring Rivalry." *Political Psychology* 22:693–725.

———. 2004. "State Building, Interstate and Intrastate Rivalry: A Study of Post-Colonial Developing Country Extractive Efforts, 1975–2000." *International Studies Quarterly* 48:53–72.

———. 2005. "War, Rivalry and State Building in Latin America." *American Journal of Political Science* 49:451–65.

———. 2007. "The Political Economy of State Building in Sub-Saharan Africa." *Journal of Politics* 60:716–31.

———. 2008. "The Construction of a Latin American Interstate Culture of Rivalry." *International Interactions* 34:231–57.

Thompson, William R. 1992. "Dehio, Long Cycles and the Geohistorical Context of Structural Transition." *World Politics* 45:127–52.

———. 1993. "The Consequences of War." *International Interactions* 19:125–47.

———. 1995. "Principal Rivalries." *Journal of Conflict Resolution* 39 (2): 195–223.

———. 1996. "Democracy and Peace: Putting the Cart before the Horse?" *International Organization* 50 (1): 141–74.

———. 2001. "Identifying Rivals and Rivalries in World Politics." *International Studies Quarterly* 45:557–86.

———. 2006. "A Test of a Theory of Co-Evolution in War: Lengthening the Western Eurasian Military Trajectory." *International History Review* 28:473–503.

———, ed. 2008. *Systemic Transitions: Past, Present, and Future*. New York: Palgrave Macmillan.

Thompson, William R., and Karen Rasler. 1999. "War, the Military Revolution(s) Controversy, and Army Expansion: A Test of Two Explanations of Historical Influences on European State Making." *Comparative Political Studies* 32:3–31.

Tilly, Charles. 1975. "Reflections on the History of European State-Making." In *Formation of National States in Western Europe*, edited by Charles Tilly, 3–83. Princeton, NJ: Princeton University Press.

———. 1985. "War Making and State Making as Organized Crime." In *Bringing the State Back In*, edited by Peter Evans, Dietrich Rueschemeyer, and Theda Skocpol, 171–86. Cambridge: Cambridge University Press.

———. 1992. *Coercion, Capital, and European States, AD 990–1992*. Cambridge: Blackwell.

———. 2003. "Armed Forces, Regimes and Contention in Europe since 1650." In *Irregular Armed Forces and Their Role in Politics and State Formation*, edited by Diane E. Davis and Anthony W. Pereira. Cambridge: Cambridge University Press.

Tir, Jaroslav. 2003. "Averting Armed International Conflicts through State-to-State Territorial Transfers." *Journal of Politics* 65:1235–57.

———. 2006. *Redrawing the Map to Promote Peace*. New York: Lexington Books.

Tir, Jaroslav, and John T. Ackerman. 2009. "Politics of Formalized River Cooperation." *Journal of Peace Research* 46 (5): 623–40.

Tir, Jaroslav, and Paul F. Diehl. 2002. "Geographic Dimensions of Enduring Rivalries." *Political Geography* 21 (2): 263–86.

Toft, Monica Duffy. 2003. *The Geography of Ethnic Violence: Identity, Interests, and the Indivisibility of Territory*. Princeton, NJ: Princeton University Press.

Tønnesson, Stein. 2011. "East Asia Peace since 1979: How Deep? How Can It Be Explained?" http://www.pcr.uu.se/about/news_archive/#eastpeace.

Tucker, Robert W. 1985. *The Nuclear Debate: Deterrence and the Lapse of Faith*. New York: Holmes & Meier.

UCDP Actor Dataset. 2010. http://www.pcr.uu.se/research/ucdp/datasets.

Valeriano, Brandon. 2003. "Steps to Rivalry: Power Politics and Rivalry Formation." PhD diss., Vanderbilt University.

———. 2009. "The Tragedy of Offensive Realism: Testing Aggressive Power Politics Models." *International Interactions* 35 (2): 179–206.

———. 2010. "Becoming Rivals: The Process of Rivalry Development." Paper presented at the "What Do We Know about War?" workshop, University of Illinois, Urbana-Champaign, October.

Valeriano, Brandon, and John A. Vasquez. 2010. "Identifying and Classifying Complex Interstate Wars." *International Studies Quarterly* 54:561–82.

Vasquez, John A. 1991. "The Deterrence Myth: Nuclear Weapons and the Prevention of Nuclear War." In *The Long Postwar Peace: Contending Explanations and Projections*, edited by Charles W. Kegley Jr., 205–23. New York: HarperCollins.

———. 1993. *The War Puzzle*. New York: Cambridge University Press.

———. 1995. "Why Do Neighbors Fight? Proximity, Interaction or Territoriality?" *Journal of Peace Research* 32 (3): 277–93.

———. 1996. "Distinguishing Rivals That Go to War from Those That Do Not: A Quantitative Comparative Case Study of the Two Paths to War." *International Studies Quarterly* 40 (December): 531–58.

——. 1998. *The Power of Power Politics*. Cambridge: Cambridge University Press.

——. 2000. "What Do We Know about War?" In *What Do We Know about War?*, edited by John A. Vasquez, 335–70. Lanham, MD: Rowman & Littlefield.

——. 2001. "Mapping the Probability of War and Analyzing the Possibility of Peace: The Role of Territorial Disputes. (Presidential Address to the Peace Science Society)." *Conflict Management and Peace Science* 18:145–74.

——. 2009. *The War Puzzle Revisited*. New York: Cambridge University Press.

——. 2011a. "Paths to War: The Territorial Origins of War." In *Territory, War, and Peace*, edited by John A. Vasquez and Marie T. Henehan, 148–76. New York: Routledge.

——. 2011b. "Territorial Paths to War: Their Probability of Escalation, 1816–2001." In *Territory, War, and Peace*, edited by John A. Vasquez and Marie T. Henehan, 133–47. New York: Routledge.

Vasquez, John A., Paul F. Diehl, Colin Flint, Jürgen Scheffran, Sang-hyun Chi, and Toby J. Rider. 2011. "The Conflict Space of Cataclysm: The International System and the Spread of War, 1914–1917." *Foreign Policy Analysis* 7 (2): 143–68.

Vasquez, John A., and Marie T. Henehan, eds. 1992. *The Scientific Study of Peace and War*. Lexington, MA: Lexington Books.

Vasquez, John A., and Marie T. Henehan. 2001. "Territorial Disputes and the Probability of War, 1816–1992." *Journal of Peace Research* 38 (2): 123–38.

Vasquez, John A., and Christopher S. Leskiw. 2001. "The Origins and War-Proneness of International Rivalries." *Annual Review of Political Science* 4:295–316.

Vasquez, John A., and Brandon Valeriano. 2009. "Territory as a Source of Conflict and a Road to Peace." In *Sage Handbook on Conflict Resolution*, edited by J. Bercovitch, V. Kremenyuk, and I. W. Zartman, 193–209. Thousand Oaks, CA: Sage.

——. 2010. "Classification of Interstate Wars." *Journal of Politics* 72:292–309.

Wagner, R. Harrison. 1991. "Nuclear Deterrence, Counterforce Strategies, and the Incentive to Strike First." *American Political Science Review* 85:727–49.

Wallace, Michael D. 1972. "State, Formal Organization, and Arms Levels as Factors Leading to the Onset of War, 1820–1964." In *Peace, War, and Numbers*, edited by Bruce M. Russett, 49–69. Beverly Hills: Sage.

——. 1979. "Arms Races and Escalation: Some New Evidence." *Journal of Conflict Resolution* 23:3–16.

——. 1980. "Some Persisting Findings." *Journal of Conflict Resolution* 24:289–92.

——. 1982. "Armaments and Escalation: Two Competing Hypotheses." *International Studies Quarterly* 26 (March): 37-56

Wallensteen, Peter. 1981. "Incompatibility, Confrontation and War: Four Models and Three Historical Systems, 1816–1976." *Journal of Peace Research* 18 (1): 57–90.

——. 1984. "Universalism vs. Particularism: On the Limits of Major Power Order." *Journal of Peace Research* 21 (3): 243–57.

——. 2002 [2007, 2011]. *Understanding Conflict Resolution: War, Peace and the Global System*. London: Sage.

——. 2006. "Trends in Major War: Too Early for Waning?" In *The Waning of Major War*, edited by Raimo Väyrynen, 80–93. London: Routledge.

——. 2011. *Peace Research: Theory and Practice*. New York: Routledge.

Wallensteen, Peter, and Karin Axell. 1993. "Armed Conflicts after the Cold War." *Journal of Peace Research* 30 (3): 331–46.

Walt, Stephen M. 1987. *The Origins of Alliances*. Ithaca, NY: Cornell University Press.

Walter, Barbara F. 2003. "Explaining the Intractability of Territorial Conflict." *International Studies Review* 5 (4): 137–53.

———. 2006. "Building Reputation: Why Governments Fight Some Separatists but Not Others." *American Journal of Political Science* 50 (2): 313–30.

Waltz, Kenneth N. 1967. "International Structure, National Force, and the Balance of World Power." *Journal of International Affairs* 21:215–31.

———. 1979. *Theory of International Politics*. Reading, MA: Addison-Wesley.

———. 1981. *The Spread of Nuclear Weapons: More May Be Better*. Adelphi Papers, No. 171. London: International Institute for Strategic Studies.

———. [1983] 2008. "Toward Nuclear Peace." In *Realism and International Politics*, edited by Kenneth N. Waltz. New York: Routledge.

———. 1990. "Nuclear Myths and Political Realities." *American Political Science Review* 84:731–45.

———. 2003. "For Better: Nuclear Weapons Preserve an Imperfect Peace." In *The Spread of Nuclear Weapons: A Debate Renewed*, edited by Scott D. Sagan and Kenneth N. Waltz. New York: Norton.

Wasserman, Stanley, and Katherine Faust. 1994. *Social Network Analysis: Methods and Applications*. Cambridge: Cambridge University Press.

Wayman, Frank Whelon. 1996. "Power Shifts and the Onset of War." In *Parity and War: Evaluations and Extensions of the War Ledger*, edited by Jacek Kugler and Douglas Lemke, 145–62. Ann Arbor: University of Michigan Press.

———. 2000. "Rivalries: Recurrent Disputes and Explaining War." In *What Do We Know about War?*, edited by John A. Vasquez, 219–43. Lanham, MD: Rowman & Littlefield.

Wayman, Frank Whelon, and Daniel M. Jones. 1991. "Evolution of Conflict in Enduring Rivalries." Paper presented at the annual meeting of the International Studies Association, Vancouver, British Columbia, March 20–23.

Wayman, Frank Whelon, J. David Singer, and Gary Goertz. 1983. "Capabilities, Allocations, and Success in Militarized Disputes and Wars, 1816–1976." *International Studies Quarterly* 27 (December): 497–515.

Weart, Spencer R. 1998. *Never at War: Why Democracies Will Not Fight One Another*. New Haven, CT: Yale University Press.

Weede, Erich. 1980. "Arms Races and Escalation: Some Persisting Doubts." *Journal of Conflict Resolution* 24:285–87.

———. 1981. "Preventing War by Nuclear Deterrence or by Détente." *Conflict Management and Peace Science* 6:1–8.

———. 1983. "Extended Deterrence by Superpower Alliance." *Journal of Conflict Resolution* 27:231–54.

———. 1996. *Economic Development, Social Order, and World Politics*. Boulder, CO: Lynne Rienner.

———. 2003. "Globalization: Creative Destruction and the Prospects of a Capitalist Peace." In *Globalization and Armed Conflict*, edited by Gerald Schneider,

Katherine Barbieri, and Nils Petter Gleditsch, 311–23. Lanham, MD: Rowman & Littlefield.

———. 2005. *Balance of Power, Globalization and the Capitalist Peace*. Berlin: Liberal Verlag (for the Friedrich Naumann Foundation).

Wendt, Alexander. 1992. "Anarchy Is What States Make of It: The Social Construction of Power Politics." *International Organization* 46 (2): 391–425.

———. 1999. *Social Theory of International Politics*. Cambridge: Cambridge University Press.

Werner, Suzanne, and Jacek Kugler. 1996. "Power Transitions and Military Buildups: Resolving the Relationship between Arms Buildups and War." In *Parity and War: Evaluations and Extensions of the War Ledger*, edited by Jacek Kugler and Douglas Lemke, 187–207. Ann Arbor: University of Michigan Press.

Widmaier, Wesley W. 2005. "The Democratic Peace Is What States Make of It: A Constructivist Analysis of the US-Indian 'Near-Miss' in the 1971 South Asian Crisis." *European Journal of International Relations* 11 (3): 431–55.

Wilson, Edward O. 1975. *Sociobiology: The Modern Synthesis*. Cambridge, MA: Harvard University Press.

Wolf, Aaron. 1998. "Conflict and Cooperation along International Waterways." *Water Policy* 1 (2): 251–65.

Wright, Quincy. 1962. *A Study of War*. Chicago: University of Chicago Press.

Wright, Sewall. 1920. "The Theory of Path Coefficients: A Reply to Niles's Criticism." *Genetics* 8:239–55.

Yamarik, Steven J., Noel D. Johnson, and Ryan A. Compton. 2010. "War! What Is It Good For? A Deep Determinants Analysis of the Cost of Interstate Conflict." *Peace Economics, Peace Science and Public Policy* 16 (1): 1–33.

Young, Patricia T., and Jack S. Levy. 2011. "Domestic Politics and Commercial Rivalry: Explaining the War of Jenkins' Ear, 1739–1748." *European Journal of International Relations* 17 (2): 209–32.

Zacher, Mark W. 2001. "The Territorial Integrity Norm: International Boundaries and the Use of Force." *International Organization* 55 (2): 215–50.

Zagare, Frank C. 2007. "Toward a Unified Theory of Interstate Conflict." *International Interactions* 33:305–27.

Zagare, Frank C., and D. Marc Kilgour. 2000. *Perfect Deterrence*. Cambridge: Cambridge University Press.

Zinnes, Dina A. 1976. *Contemporary Research in International Relations: A Perspective and a Critical Appraisal*. New York: Free Press.

Zizzo, D. J., and A. J. Oswald. 2001. "Are People Willing to Pay to Reduce Others' Incomes?" *Annales d'Economie et de Statistique* 63–64 (July–December 2001): 39–62.

Name Index

Subject Index

accommodation, and rivalry termination, 102

adjudication, 175, 184

Afghanistan, 243

alliances, 27–44, 307–11; categories of, 45–47, 49–55, 50*t*, 52–53, 53*t*; coding, 51; definition of, 45–46; and deterrence, 39, 45–62, 309–11; and dispute initiation, 33–40, 36*t*, 38*t*, 301, 309–11; empirical evidence on, 29–40, 36*t*, 38*t*, 310–11; purposes of, 43n1; and rivalry, 69–70, 75*t*, 77–78, 78*t*–79*t*; selection bias and, 55–60, 58*f*; targeted, 298; theory on, 28–29

Alliance Treaty Obligations and Provisions (ATOP) project data set, 27, 36, 45–62; and arms races, 121–22; criticisms of, 51–52; goal of, 45

allies, war between, 32–33

Arab states, and rivalry, 90–91, 96–97

arbitration, 175, 181, 184

Argentina, 86, 101, 155, 197–202

arms races, 111–38, 315–19; coding, 74; empirical and theoretical background, 113–20; methodology on, 120–25; and rivalry, 70–71, 77*t*, 79*t*; and war, 120–34, 126*t*–128*t*, 130*t*–131*t*, 133*t*–135*t*, 318

Asian peace, 270

asymmetry, nuclear, 154–56

ATOP. *See* Alliance Treaty Obligations and Provisions

Austria, 49, 267–68

balance of power theorists, 319–20; on alliances, 28

bargaining: demands in, and rivalry, 71–72; literature on, 272–73

basic rivalry level (BRL), 90

Beagle Channel islands, 86

bilateral negotiations, 184; and territorial issues, 19, 19*t*, 20

biological aspects, of territorial issues, 213–14

borders: need for research on, 22–23; and peace, 223–26, 225*t*, 306–7, 326–27; types of, 8. *See also* territorial issues

bounded rationality, 195

Brazil, 267

Britain, 49, 53, 111, 242, 267–68; and democracy, 175, 181; economic theories and, 197–202, 200*t*; and nuclear weapons, 155

Burma, 243

capability distributions, and war, 319–23

About the Contributors

Brett V. Benson is assistant professor of political science at Vanderbilt University and conducts research on topics related to international politics and East Asian political relations such as alliances, strategic interstate commitments, nuclear proliferation, and trade and interdependence. He has published articles in *Security Studies* and the *Journal of Politics*, among others.

Paul F. Diehl is Henning Larsen Professor of Political Science at the University of Illinois at Urbana-Champaign and director of the Correlates of War project. His most recent books include *The Dynamics of International Law* (2010) and *Evaluating Peace Operations* (2010). He has been president of the Peace Science Society (International).

Colin Flint is professor of geography at the University of Illinois at Urbana-Champaign and former director of the Program in Arms Control, Disarmament, and International Security (ACDIS). His main research interests are war, militarization, and just war theory. He is the author of *Political Geography: World-Economy, Nation-State and Locality* (with P. J. Taylor), 6th ed. (2011); *Introduction to Geopolitics*, 2nd ed. (2011); and coeditor (with S. Kirsch) of *Reconstructing Conflict: Integrating War and Post-War Geographies* (2011).

Daniel S. Geller is professor and chair of the Department of Political Science at Wayne State University. He has served as a consultant to the U.S. Department of State, Office of Technology and Assessments, and in 2009 he was a member of a senior advisory group to the U.S. Strategic Command on the Nuclear Posture Review. His most recent books are *Nations at War: A Scientific Study of International Conflict* (1998), with J. David Singer, and

The Construction and Cumulation of Knowledge in International Relations
(2004), coedited with John A. Vasquez.

Douglas M. Gibler is professor of political science at the University of Alabama. His most recent publications include *International Military Alliances,
1648–2008* (2008) and *The Territorial Peace: Borders, State Development,
and International Conflict* (2012)—and an assortment of articles in the
American Journal of Political Science, International Studies Quarterly, the
Journal of Conflict Resolution, and the *Journal of Politics* among others.

Gary Goertz is professor of political science at the University of Arizona.
His books include *Contexts of International Politics* (1994), *Social Science
Concepts: A User's Guide* (2006), and *International Norms and Decision
Making: A Punctuated Equilibrium Model* (2003), and with Paul Diehl, *Ter-
ritorial Changes and International Conflict* (1992) and *War and Peace in
International Rivalry* (2000).

Paul R. Hensel is professor of political science at the University of North Texas
and codirector of the Issue Correlates of War project. He has published articles
in the *American Journal of Political Science, International Organization, International Studies Quarterly*, the *Journal of Conflict Resolution*, the *Journal of
Peace Research*, and *Political Geography*, among others. His research focuses
on international conflict and conflict management, with a special emphasis on
the management of territorial claims and international rivers.

Choong-Nam Kang is assistant professor in the Department of Government,
Law and International Affairs at Murray State University. His main research
interests include alliances and war.

Jack S. Levy is Board of Governors' Professor of Political Science at Rut-
gers University and a senior associate at the Saltzman Institute of War and
Peace Studies at Columbia University. His most recent books are *The Arc
of War* (2011) and *Causes of War* (2010), each coauthored with William
R. Thompson, and *Explaining War and Peace: Case Studies and Necessary
Condition Counterfactuals* (2007), coedited with Gary Goertz. He has been
president of the Peace Science Society (International) and the International
Studies Association.

Zeev Maoz is Distinguished Professor of Political Science at the University
of California, Davis, as well as Distinguished Fellow at the Interdisciplinary Center, Herzliya, Israel. His most recent books are *Networks of Nations*

(2010), *Defending the Holy Land* (2006), and *Bound by Struggle: The Strategic Evolution of Enduring International Rivalries* (2002; with Ben D. Mor). He has been president of the Peace Science Society (International).

Sara McLaughlin Mitchell is professor of political science at the University of Iowa. She is codirector of the Issue Correlates of War project and an associate editor of *Foreign Policy Analysis*. She is coauthor of *Domestic Law Goes Global: Legal Traditions and International Courts* (2011), and she has published articles in the *American Journal of Political Science*, *International Studies Quarterly*, the *Journal of Conflict Resolution*, *Conflict Management and Peace Science*, and the *Journal of Politics*, among others.

Michael Mousseau is professor of international relations at Koç University, Istanbul, Turkey. He has articles on the democratic and the market-capitalist peace in *International Security*, *International Interactions*, the *Journal of Conflict Resolution*, the *Journal of Peace Research*, and *International Studies Quarterly*, among others. He is currently working on a book on capitalism, democracy, and war.

Karen Rasler is professor of political science at Indiana University and is currently a coeditor of *International Studies Quarterly*. Her main research interests involve international conflict, rivalry, war and state-building processes, and the democratic peace. She has recently coauthored *Puzzles of the Democratic Peace: Theory, Geopolitics, and the Transformation of World Politics* (2005) and *Strategic Rivalries in World Politics* (2007).

Susan G. Sample is associate professor of political science at the University of the Pacific. Her research interests include arms races and war. She has published articles in the *Journal of Conflict Resolution* and the *Journal of Peace Research*, among others.

William R. Thompson is Distinguished Professor and Donald A. Rogers Professor of Political Science at Indiana University. He is currently the managing editor of *International Studies Quarterly*. His coauthored or coedited recent books include *Limits to Globalization and North-South Divergence* (2010), *Causes of War* (2010), *Coping with Terrorism: Origins, Escalation, Counter Strategies and Responses* (2010), *Handbook of International Rivalries* (2011), *The Arc of War: Origins, Escalation and Transformations* (2011), and *Asian Rivalries: Conflict, Escalation, and Limitation on Two-Level Games* (2011). He has been president of the International Studies Association.

Brandon Valeriano is lecturer in the department of politics at the University of Glasgow. His ongoing research explores interstate rivalry, classification systems of war, complexity in international politics, territorial disputes, and Latino foreign policy issues. He has published articles in the *Journal of Politics*, *International Studies Quarterly*, *International Interactions*, and the *Policy Studies Journal*, among others.

John A. Vasquez is the Thomas B. Mackie Scholar in International Relations at the University of Illinois at Urbana-Champaign. His most recent books are *The Steps to War* (2008; with Paul D. Senese); *The War Puzzle Revisited* (2009); and *Territory, War, and Peace* (2011; with Marie T. Henehan). He has been president of the Peace Science Society (International) and the International Studies Association.

Peter Wallensteen is Dag Hammarskjöld Professor of Peace and Conflict Research, Uppsala University, and Richard G. Starmann Senior Research Professor of Peace Studies, University of Notre Dame. He is also the director of the Uppsala Conflict Data Program. His recent books include *Peace Research: Theory and Practice* (2011); *Understanding Conflict Resolution: War, Peace and the Global System*, 3rd ed. (2011); and *International Sanctions: Between Words and Wars in the Global System* (2005; with Carina Staibano).